Praise for
Raising a Sensory Smart Child

National Parenting Publications Gold Award Winner
iParenting Media Award Winner

"*Raising a Sensory Smart Child* is a comprehensive, informative, and practical book for parents. The authors explain sensory integration and sensory integration dysfunction in a way that parents can understand. They then provide very practical, hands-on examples for helping the child at home, in school, and in other settings. This is a must read for all parents who have children with sensory integration issues."
    —LARRY B. SILVERS, M.D., AUTHOR OF *The Misunderstood Child*

"Because most of us never experience anything quite like it, sensory integration disorder can be difficult to conceive, understand, or recognize. Lindsey Biel and Nancy Peske illuminate the mysteries of sensory integration disorder in clear, practical terms. Both parents and teachers will find a wealth of insight and advice on helping our wonderful—though sometimes challenging—kids."
    —PATTY ROMANOWSKI BASHE, M.S., ED., EXECUTIVE DIRECTOR, THE DAVID CENTER, AND COAUTHOR OF *The OASIS Guide to Asperger Syndrome*

"Lindsey Biel and Nancy Peske combine a professional and personal approach in creating a knowledgeable and supportive guide for parents. In a very readable manner they explain complex information and at the same time provide practical strategies that families can really use. I'll be recommending this book."
    —MARY SHEEDY KURCHINKA, AUTHOR OF *Raising Your Spirited Child* AND *Kids, Parents, and Power Struggles*

"As our world gets faster, louder, more crowded and stress-laden, it's not just kids with disabilities who experience sensory issues. It's all kids, to some extent or another. Yet many know little about sensory issues and how much they can compromise learning and functioning on a daily basis. Lindsey Biel and Nancy Peske have done a

bang-up job explaining the vast and far-reaching effects of sensory challenges. I've read many books about sensory integration. What makes this one stand out is the clear, conversational tone coupled with page after page of practical, helpful information. This is destined to become your 'bible' of sensory integration!"
—V. Zysk, *Autism Asperger's Digest Magazine*

"This book helps us understand that children with SI dysfunction do not experience the world as we do. They need help to learn how to self-regulate, adapt, and overcome. The authors are optimistic and encouraging about the potential of children to become happy, productive adults."
—L. Knight, *Advance Magazine for Physical Therapists*

"A wonderful resource for parents, teachers, counselors, and pediatricians who'd like to know more about sensory integration dysfunction."
—*Adoptive Families magazine*

"This is a valuable resource for all professionals working with sensory processing issues. It is a fabulous resource for parents as well."
—T. S. Bull, *Advance Magazine for Occupational Therapists*

"A 'must-have' reference for anyone involved with a child experiencing sensory integration issues. It is refreshingly pragmatic and highly useful, leaving the parent, educator, or service provider empowered and comfortable dealing with sensory issues."
—A. Shapiro, International Center for the Disabled

"This is the best book out there for explaining and treating symptoms of sensory processing/modulation disorders. It contains the most up-to-date information."
—Behavioral Clarity Consulting

Raising a Sensory Smart Child

The Definitive Handbook for
Helping Your Child with
Sensory Processing Issues

Lindsey Biel, M.A., OTR/L,
and Nancy Peske

PENGUIN BOOKS

PENGUIN BOOKS

Published by the Penguin Group

Penguin Group (USA) Inc., 375 Hudson Street, New York, New York 10014, U.S.A.

Penguin Group (Canada), 90 Eglinton Avenue East, Suite 700, Toronto, Ontario, Canada M4P 2Y3
    (a division of Pearson Penguin Canada Inc.)

Penguin Books Ltd, 80 Strand, London WC2R 0RL, England

Penguin Ireland, 25 St. Stephen's Green, Dublin 2, Ireland (a division of Penguin Books Ltd)

Penguin Group (Australia), 250 Camberwell Road, Camberwell, Victoria 3124, Australia (a divi-
    sion of Pearson Australia Group Pty Ltd)

Penguin Books India Pvt Ltd, 11 Community Centre, Panchsheel Park, New Delhi - 110 017, India

Penguin Group (NZ), 67 Apollo Drive, Rosedale, North Shore 0632, New Zealand (a division of Pearson
    New Zealand Ltd)

Penguin Books (South Africa) (Pty) Ltd, 24 Sturdee Avenue, Rosebank, Johannesburg 2196, South Africa

Penguin Books Ltd, Registered Offices:
80 Strand, London WC2R 0RL, England

First published in Penguin Books 2005
This updated and revised edition published 2009

10   9   8   7   6   5   4   3   2   1

PUBLISHER'S NOTE
Every effort has been made to ensure that the information contained in this book is complete and accurate. However, neither the publisher nor the authors are engaged in rendering professional advice or services to the individual reader. The ideas, procedures, and suggestions contained in this book are not
intended as a substitute for consulting with a professional who knows your child and is able to reliably
assess whether a program is resulting in meaningful changes. All matters regarding your child's health
require medical supervision from your child's pediatrician. Neither the authors nor the publisher shall be
liable or responsible for any loss or damage allegedly arising from any information or suggestion in this
book. The case studies in this book are based on actual stories of children, teenagers, and adults with
sensory integration difficulties; however, names and identifying characteristics have been changed.

Photographs courtesy of Southpaw Enterprises

LIBRARY OF CONGRESS CATALOGING IN PUBLICATION DATA
Biel, Lindsey.
    Raising a sensory smart child : the definitive handbook for helping your child with sensory processing
issues/Lindsey Biel and Nancy Peske.—Updated and rev. ed.
        p. cm.
    Includes bibliographical references and index.
    ISBN 978-0-14-311534-2
    1. Children with disabilities.   2. Sensorimotor integration.   3. Child rearing.   I. Peske, Nancy K.,
1962–   II. Title.
    HQ773.6.B53 2009
    649'.152—dc22   2009005368

Printed in the United States of America
Set in Minion with Goudy Sans and Helvetica
Designed by Sabrina Bowers

This book is dedicated to my parents, who taught me just about everything really important to know.

—LINDSEY BIEL

To D.G.D.

—NANCY PESKE

Contents

PART THREE:
Fostering Your Child's Development

PART FOUR:
Parenting with Sensory Smarts

PART FIVE:
Recommended Products and Resources

Foreword

by Temple Grandin

As a person with autism and sensory processing problems, I have always experienced the world differently. When I was in elementary school, the school bell ringing hurt my ears like a dentist's drill hitting a nerve. Loud noises such as balloons popping terrified me. Scratchy petticoats and wool clothes were like sandpaper against my skin. I still wear my underwear inside out so that the stitching does not rub against me. I wear old, well-washed, soft T-shirts under my new shirts to make them tolerable.

There are no cookbook recipes for what to do about your child's particular sensory issues, because sensory problems are highly variable in different children. That's why this book is so useful. It will help you to recognize your child's unique sensory issues, the impact of these issues on everyday experiences, and what you can do about them. One child may enjoy playing with running water and another may be terrified of it. One child may love to go up and down on an escalator, but another child avoids it because he cannot figure out how to get off it. The problem can range from very mild to severe. One child may just have mild sound sensitivity while another child may have a meltdown every time she goes into a large supermarket because of visual, auditory, and smell overload. When this child is in a store or other everyday environment, it may feel like she is inside both the speakers and the light show at a rock concert. When overload occurs, the nervous system shuts down. Some individuals with the most severe sensory problems are monochannel. They have to either look at something or listen to something. They cannot look and listen at the same time. Sensory issues are confusing. As a parent, you need information to figure out what's going on and practical solutions for what to do.

Sensory integration problems can also interfere with learning. When I was a child, I was not able to hear auditory details, and this made it hard to learn. I did not understand grown-ups when they talked fast. It sounded like a foreign language that consisted of vowels and no consonants. My auditory processing was terrible even though I passed a standard hearing test. I did not have visual sensitivity problems, but some children do. Children with visual processing problems often squint and appear to look out the corner of their eyes even though their eye exam is normal. They may complain that black print on white paper jiggles or vibrates. Tinted glasses, colored overlays, or printing their work on pastel or gray paper may reduce this problem. Fluorescent lights and TV-type computer monitors flash on and off like in a disco. This makes learning impossible. Using an incandescent desk lamp and replacing the computer monitor with one of the new flat-screen LCD monitors or a laptop computer with a full-size keyboard and mouse stops the flicker and may help save a student's academic career.

Sensory processing problems often occur in conjunction with many different diagnostic labels. Children and adults diagnosed with the following may also have sensory problems: developmental delays, autism, Asperger's syndrome, pervasive development disorder, ADHD (attention deficit hyperactivity disorder), learning problems, prematurity, fragile X, fetal alcohol syndrome, Tourette's syndrome, anxiety, and many others. A child can also just have sensory integration issues without any other diagnosis.

Working with an occupational therapist and other professionals on your child's sensory problems is very important. Therapy for sensory processing problems often makes other therapeutic programs such as speech-language therapy or applied behavioral analysis (ABA) more effective. Some children are like a TV with a broken cable that is getting static in the sound and "snow" in the picture. Calming sensory activities such as deep pressure under a heavy mat or slow swinging may reduce sensory scrambling and help information to get through to the brain. Other therapies may work better either during or immediately after the child has received the sensory input his body needs.

This book will help parents, teachers, and therapists understand and work with a child's malfunctioning sensory system. Unfortunately, some professionals have trouble recognizing the problems that sensory processing difficulties cause. It is hard for them to imagine that a child's sensory system functions differently from their own. Some people even think that treatment for sensory integration dysfunction is not very effective because other therapies such as applied behavioral analysis have more scientific studies backing them. One of the problems in doing scientific studies on sensory integration dysfunction is that the children's diagnoses may be for autism or ADHD instead of for specific sensory processing problems. Because the problems vary so much from child to child, a particular therapy may be useful for one child and not for another. In other words, it is extremely difficult to get a homogeneous sample to study because of the wide variation in sensory sensitivities as well as individual responses to sensory input.

This book will help you determine whether your child has sensory integration issues and provide you with immediate steps to take. You'll find a lot of practical information for addressing hyperactivity or low endurance, increasing a child's concentration and attention span, and improving behavior. You'll also find really useful tips and techniques for handling challenges you face each day with your child, such as washing, brushing, and cutting hair, dealing with clothing, going to big stores, picky eating, getting a good night's sleep, dealing with group situations such as school and parties, visiting the dentist, handling noise sensitivity, and much more. At last, here are the insights and answers parents have been searching for to help their children deal with and overcome sensory integration problems.

Dr. Temple Grandin is Associate Professor of Animal Science at Colorado State University and a person with autism. She is the author of Thinking in Pictures, Animals in Translation, *and other books.*

Preface to the New Edition

NANCY'S STORY

When I first decided to cowrite this book, my son had already made great progress with his developmental delays and sensory issues. By then, a sensory diet had become a part of our family's lifestyle, and I had educated myself about sensory processing to the point where I felt a strong need to help others in the position I'd been in when my son was first diagnosed—scared, overwhelmed, in need of guidance and reassurance, and utterly determined to find help. I was inspired by my son's occupational therapist, Lindsey Biel, and by the many parents who took time out from their busy and often stressful lives to offer me hope, advice, and "virtual hugs," as we would say when exchanging e-mails on a particularly challenging day.

After my son, Cole, left his full-time, year-round, special ed preschool, where he started as a preverbal child whose sensory issues caused him to actually hurt himself at times, he began his first year in a typical public school classroom as a kindergartener. When that year in general ed was over, and the reports were in from his private and school-based therapists, I finally felt confident that he could handle being in a regular classroom anywhere as long as he had a good speech language pathologist to help him with his receptive and expressive language difficulties. It gave my husband, George, and me the freedom to finally consider moving out of New York City, where the available services had been so wonderful, to an area of the country that was cheaper, quieter, closer to nature, and filled with opportunities for our growing son to stretch his wings. I will never forget that day a few weeks after I moved back to my hometown in the Midwest, when I watched my son with a new friend walking across a field in a park near our home. The boys grew smaller and smaller as Cole stayed in my sight but walked farther away from me than he ever had, not looking back for a moment. Tears swelled in my eyes as I realized we had closed a page on a chapter of our lives. Sensory issues were no longer holding him back. He was moving into a new independence, not so upset by a sensory onslaught that he would stare off into space, completely withdrawn from the world, or bang his head on the ground and scream, unable to cope with the sensations that were bombarding him and the unpredictability of a world I couldn't control for him.

Today, he is a happy, goofy, smart, funny, creative, sociable nine-year-old who loves the Cub Scouts, bowling, Gilda Radner, and discussing the powers of the Autobots vs. the Decepticons with his friends. If he has a problem, he no longer keeps it inside; he brings it up and talks it through with me or my husband. When he meets an adult, he looks that person in the eye, shakes hands, answers questions, and easily engages in conversation. When parents of other children or teachers at his school hear I've coauthored a book on sensory issues because of my child's experiences, they seem confused because unless you're a trained professional, you're unlikely to notice Cole's issues these days.

Not long ago, George, Cole, and I went to an afternoon outdoor concert featuring our family's favorite rock-and-roll artist. It was too hot, too sunny, and too loud, but Cole had really wanted to see her play. After Cole spent a few songs being hugged quite hard and chewing on his father's fingers—a regressive behavior Cole exhibits in a loud environment—he climbed up on the bench and began to watch. He insisted that I hold him tightly around the waist as he watched transfixed for the rest of the show, earplugs firmly in place. Afterward, in the car, he said, "That was awesome, Mom. I am so glad we went, because she *rocks!*" He has formed a band with his friends and plays drums like his dad does. He's developed the sensory smarts to handle whatever sensory challenges he faces along the way, whatever he chooses to do. For that, I'm deeply grateful.

—Nancy Peske
Shorewood, WI

LINDSEY'S STORY

The years since Nancy and I cowrote the first edition of *Raising a Sensory Smart Child* have been amazing. We simply had no idea how popular our book would be. We've received hundreds of letters from parents, therapists, and others across the United States and Canada, and as far away as England, Australia, the Philippines, and even from a priest running an orphanage in Ghana. We learned that in most parts of the world and even in parts of the U.S., there is absolutely *no* awareness of sensory processing problems, and if there is, there is often *no* help available locally. We've gotten letters thanking us for the book and our Web site and others asking specific questions about their personal situations, which we did our very best to answer. Who ever thought I'd be sitting at my desk in Manhattan helping a child on the other side of the planet? I've now lectured to *thousands* of parents, teachers, OTs, PTs, speech therapists, psychologists, and others across the nation. I've had the honor of speaking to children's librarians about how to make libraries friendly to kids with special needs. I've spoken to doctors about how to recognize sensory problems in their young patients and how they can help. I've spoken to therapists not just about how to work with children during their sessions but also about how to work with families and empower kids and parents to manage their issues. I have spoken to both large and small groups of parents—heard their concerns, felt their pain and confusion, helped to brainstorm solutions, and have learned so much from them. Most of all, I've cherished my time with my young clients, the funny, sweet boys and girls who teach me something new just about every day.

In 2008, I was delighted to be invited to speak at the University of Wisconsin at Whitewater, which would take me close to where Nancy had moved. After the conference, I went out to dinner with her family, which of course, included my former client, Cole. Aside from the delight in seeing how her charming little boy had turned into such a handsome, engaging young man, I had to just sit back and admire him. Here was this child, who used to bang his head so hard, sitting in a big, noisy, crowded Mexican restaurant charming me and handling the chaos so well—much better than I was dealing with it! It reminded me of why I love what I do and that while it's valuable for me to hand over my expertise and "tricks," when parents take that knowledge and add a few clever tricks of their own, and when we all work together to teach it to the child so that he *owns it*, we create a real synergy, an unstoppable force of change that far exceeds the sum of its parts. We can make such a profound and positive difference in how a young person experiences the world.

It was then and there that Nancy and I decided to expand *Raising a Sensory Smart Child* to include even more practical assistance to parents, caregivers, and professionals helping children with sensory issues. This updated and expanded edition has lots of changes—both small and large—including:

- *New solutions and techniques for handling everyday problems,* with entirely new sections dealing with:
    - Eating out
    - Going to the doctor
    - Handling holidays
    - Riding in the car
    - Going to amusement and theme parks
- *A new chapter on sensory issues and children on the autism spectrum.* While we can't emphasize strongly enough that just because a child has sensory issues, it does not mean he is autistic; most children and adults with autism do have very significant sensory problems. The first edition was crammed with information and advice that applied to children with autism, but we felt it essential to address the intense sensory sensitivities, processing problems, and related behavioral and social issues that are all too often part and parcel of having an autism spectrum disorder. If you are the parent of a child on the spectrum, you'll certainly want to read this chapter, but please also be sure to read the chapters on practical solutions for everyday problems, sensory diet, picky eating, and so on.
- *Sensory diet activities your entire family can enjoy.* Because most of us are already overbooked and overextended, we wanted to give parents some advice about how to incorporate sensory-rich experiences into activities you may already do—and how to get the whole family involved.
- *Sensory diet ideas specifically for teenagers and adults.* With appropriate intervention, the goal is to minimize or hopefully eliminate sensory sensitivities and processing problems by the time the child grows up. This does not always happen despite everyone's best efforts. And sometimes people do not "discover" sensory processing disorder until adulthood. Many people have requested information on sensory diet activities that are appropriate for teenagers,

young adults, and grown-ups. While you can adapt many of the sensory diet activities we have recommended in the earlier edition, we wanted to provide you with ideas that are specific to teens and adults.

- *Practical solutions for teens and adults.* Again, teens and adults can easily adapt most of the solutions we've provided for children. We've added new sections such as solutions for driving and working.
- *Essential information on weighted wearables* such as vests and blankets, including recommendations for use and important safety precautions.
- *Some of the latest scientific research* that underscores the neurological underpinnings of sensory issues.
- *Information about proposed new terminology.*
- *Additional resources for parents,* including more books, fabulous DVDs, Web sites, and more.

We'll continue to supplement the book with timely information on our Web site, including speaking engagements and seasonal tips. Please visit us often at www.sensorysmarts.com.

—Lindsey Biel, OTR/L
New York City

Acknowledgments

From both of us:
This book is the culmination of many minds, many perspectives, and many areas of expertise.

We had outstanding input from some of the very best professionals out there. We'd like to thank the wonderful occupational therapists who shared their expert knowledge and insights, especially Linda Calise, Tina Champagne, Prudence Heisler, Steven Kane, Lindsay Koss, Jerry Lindquist, Paula McCreedy, Claudia Meyer, Sari Ockner, Mary Petti-Weber, Anne Buckley-Reen, and Dr. Karen Roston. Thanks also to nutritionist Kelly Dorfman, M.S., L.N., N.D; developmental optometrist Dr. Fran Reinstein, O.D.; pediatricians Dr. Felicia Wilion and Dr. Jane Aronson; physical therapist Elizabeth Crawford; audiologist Louise Levy, M.S., CCC-A; speech-language pathologists Melissa Wexler Gurfein, Jodie Kertzner, and Risa Kirsh; dentist Dr. Allan Frankel; Dr. Linda Bambara, Ed.D.; Cindi Alfano, M.A., LMHC, NCC; Robin Angel, M.S. Special Ed.; Margaret Dunkle of George Washington University; and Shirley Schmidt, Ed.S. Special Ed.

We are so grateful to the parents, teenagers, and adults with SI dysfunction who shared their stories with us in hopes of encouraging and helping others, including Paul Balius, Heidi Buck, Missy Feldhaus, Barbara Hettle, Elaina Pagenkopf, Stacy-Ann Searle, Kassiane Sibley, and Kelly Wolbert. Thanks, too, to Rima Regas, who helps so many parents find support and information online.

A million and one thanks to computer genius Rick Frankel for his technical assistance and uncommonly good common sense, and for introducing us to flash drives. At least as many thanks to the incredibly talented Monty Stilson and Rebecca Alexander and to Tony, Kerry, Arlo. Thanks as well to Dario Mallerman of YAI/National Institute for People with Disabilities Network for his enthusiasm and support for this book and us.

We'd also like to thank our first editor, Janet Goldstein, whose remarkable vision, editorial guidance, and enthusiasm inspired us; Rakia Clark, who carefully shepherded the book as it gained steam; as well as Branda Maholtz, our marvelous editor for this expanded edition; Sabrina Bowers, our very talented book designer; and our agent, Neeti Madan, who believed in this project from the very beginning. Thanks, too, to Andrew M. Roussey, president of Southpaw Enterprises, Inc., for lending us photographs of products.

Finally, our deepest thanks to Temple Grandin for her inspiration, guidance, and support.

Lindsey also wishes to thank:

The parents and children who have welcomed me into their lives and taught me so much. It has been an honor and a pleasure! Special thanks to Amy Hochfelder, Joanne Sciortino, Elisabeth Radin, and Tamara Bernstein. Thanks also to The Town School and SteppingStone Day School of Manhattan for their professionalism and excellence, and the trust they have had in me over the years. And special thanks to Sally Poole, OT, CHT, clinical assistant professor at NYU, who taught me to love science.

My parents, William and Geraldine Biel, and brothers, Timothy and Michael, long a wellspring of love and support, helped me so much during the writing of this book. Minnie was always there to comfort me and spill my coffee, while Rick offered wisdom, encouragement, emotional and technical support, and meals worthy of the Iron Chef. He even did the dishes sometimes.

Nancy also wishes to thank:

The people who have offered support and advice to me and other parents over the years on various online support group boards and listservs.

Everyone at the YAI/NYL Gramercy School in New York City who provided my son with a loving, supportive, and enriching educational experience. I wish every parent of a child with sensory issues could have the blessing of these highly professional teachers, therapists, administrators, and social workers, such as principal Patricia Harmon, M.A.; Donna Mizrahi, C.S.W.; Wendy Kagan, C.S.W.; Mike Nandelli, M.S. Ed.; Kerry Weisinger, M.S. Ed.; Lauren Menkes, OTR/L; Jerilyn Fortsch, P.T.; Allison Haberman, M.A., CCC-SLP; and Elizabeth

Balzano, Jim Burns, and Bonnie O'Brien. I'd also like to thank speech-language pathologist Jodie Kertzner, who first clued me in to my son's dyspraxia, and Risory DeLeon, M.S.W., service coordinator at SteppingStone Day School, my EI provider.

My family members offered love and emotional support. A special thanks to those who provided practical support as well: my sister-in-law Carol Peske, who gave invaluable early feedback on early drafts as well as ideas about topics to cover, and my sister-in-law Virginia Darrow Menegaz, M.S., R.D., L.N., who helped us with nutritional information and encouragement, and who actually got my son to try tofu dogs and soy milk!

I especially thank my husband, George Darrow, who has a gift for working with children and boundless enthusiasm for carrying out our son's sensory diet and raising him with love and acceptance. And the hot meals and predeadline computer-virus-zapping were much appreciated! Most of all, to my little guy, whose kindness, curiosity, enthusiasm, and mischievousness bring me so much joy every day.

Introduction

NANCY'S STORY

On a lovely spring day, after a two-and-a-half-hour induced, epidural-eased labor that was so painless and spiritually uplifting that I was practically communing with my ancestors on the astral plane, I got the thumbs-up from the doctor: I'd given birth to my first child, a healthy little boy. My husband, George, and I had so many dreams for him already: he would be smart, verbal, polite, responsible, active—in short, perfect.

As the months passed, it was clear that we'd turned into those typically disgusting first-time parents, marveling over every minor milestone, cooing over personality quirks we were sure indicated a bright future, going through Costco-sized packs of film as we recorded every conceivable Kodak moment. What a delight he was, swinging for hours at a time, never fussing or getting bored in his suspended bouncy chair. What a brave boy he was, not even flinching when he got a vaccination. We laughed about what a character our little Cole was becoming, constantly shaking his head no until he burst into giggles, or smacking his toy drum harder than any of the other kids in his baby music class.

But for all our bright-eyed optimism, there were moments when we wondered, *What's up with this child?* At the playground, a siren would send him into a mini-trance: when an ambulance went by, he'd stop at the top of the slide, staring into space as the other kids piled up behind him. I would often shout his name and wave my hand in front of his face but got no response. *That's kind of weird,* I thought, but I shrugged it off. Maybe he was just a little more distractible than other kids were.

More distressing was the fact that for all his love of books, our constant verbal coaching, and his early speaking—he said "Mama" and "Dada" at six months and his first sentence at fourteen months— he seemed to lose every vocabulary word as soon as he gained it. A simple word like *water,* which he should have been using several times a day to ask for a drink, would pop out of his mouth unexpectedly, but then we wouldn't hear it again for months. Even though we insisted we didn't know what he meant when he held out his cup and grunted, he wouldn't say *water,* or even *wuh.* He would just grow increasingly frustrated.

At Cole's eighteen-month well-baby checkup, our pediatrician advised us to wait and see what happened, and we figured, well, he's the expert, so let's do our best not to worry. But by the time Cole was two, he was saying only seven words, so our pediatrician suggested we get him evaluated by a private speech-language pathologist. We were relieved our doctor was finally validating our concerns, but also wrestling with the awful feeling that something was, in fact, wrong with our child and we didn't know how bad it was. At the same time, we were confused and frustrated by lots of well-meaning advice from friends and family: "Don't worry, he'll talk when he's ready," "Stop anticipating his needs and he'll talk," "Boys always talk later than girls do," and "Einstein was a late talker, and he turned out to be brilliant."

When I learned that it would be four months until the speech-language pathologist could see my son, I didn't know what to do. Should I force myself to stop worrying and wait to see if Cole's language would take off in the next several months? In desperation, I posted a query on an online message board, figuring someone else might have been down this road before. I heard from a mom who urged me to have my son evaluated by my state's early intervention program. Under IDEA (the federal Individuals with Disabilities Education Act), every state provides a free evaluation and free or low-cost services for children under age three who may have developmental delays. It would take only a couple of hours to do the evaluation, which would include evaluating him for other skills besides speech, and to my son it would seem like he was just going to some big playroom to be fussed over and amused by a few interested strangers. I would walk out with peace of mind and reassurance that he was developing normally, or I would begin receiving free services in my home that would address my child's problems at an early stage in his development, when the brain and nervous system are so open to learning and remodeling. And the downside was . . . what, that I would seem foolish by admitting I was worried and wanted an answer?

George and I decided to go for the free evaluation, which was scheduled in a matter of weeks. We were a little nervous when the day came, even as Cole was clearly having a great time showing off his skills to three professionals: an occupational therapist, an educational evaluator, and a speech-language pathologist. We answered a barrage of questions about milestones and habits and began getting even more worried as they furiously scribbled in their notebooks. We started to feel a little defensive, frankly. Why were they interpreting every little behavior of Cole's as a problem, from flapping his hands excitedly in the shower to crying and insisting on a long, firm hug when he was toweled off? Wasn't he just a little . . . unusual?

Cole had an expressive speech delay for which they were recommending speech therapy twice a week; this is what we'd pretty much expected and prepared ourselves for emotionally. But we were then told that he had fine motor skill delays. We were shocked: Why should anyone care how he gripped a crayon at age two? And what were these "sensory issues" that called for occupational therapy twice a week?

We went back and forth between denial—it couldn't be as bad as they were saying, why, just look how smart he was!—and depression. Suddenly, all his charming little quirks brought tears to my eyes. What did all this mean for my son's future? Were they making too much of peculiarities that had no bearing on his speech delay, odd little habits that he'd probably inherited from my husband and me?

As time went by and I did more research, more talking to my son's new occupational therapist (OT), Lindsey, and to other parents in on-line support groups, my feelings and perceptions began to shift. I began to piece it all together and come to terms with the fact that there *was* something wrong with my son—a neurological glitch called sensory integration (SI) dysfunction. It helped that right away I noticed a big difference in Cole's ability to focus on playing and learning after one of Lindsey's OT sessions or an activity she'd suggested, such as pressing pillows on him to provide deep pressure against his skin, or having him compress his joints by jumping.

We began teaching Cole to recognize his own sensory needs and find acceptable ways to meet them so that he felt less overwhelmed by the unpredictable world around him. George played a big role, too, by adjusting his roughhousing sessions with Cole to make them even more effective for helping Cole get the sensory input he needed. Today, our attitude is, yes, he's wired a little differently from other kids, but so what? He's happy, well-adjusted, and well-behaved; he loves school and his various therapies; he's made great progress in many areas of development; and my husband and I no longer get scared when we learn he's fallen behind in some areas. (These sorts of setbacks are common in children with sensory processing disorder, as we'll explain in Chapter 8: Dealing with Developmental Delays.)

George and I have come to accept that having a child with sensory issues means every day is a little different. One day, he doesn't care what he wears, the next day, he is bothered by the remnant of a tag still attached to the collar of his shirt. Once George purchased round-trip nonrefundable ferry tickets for us for a long ride to an island and back, on an exceptionally windy day. "Well," I said, thinking of how Cole always has a strong reaction, negative or positive, to wind, rocking movements, and loud noises like ferry horns, "we're either in for a fantastic adventure or our own personal hell." We got lucky that day, but developing our sea legs and sensory smarts, and learning to work with Cole's oversensitivities and undersensitivities, is always an adventure.

LINDSEY'S STORY

When I decided to change careers from advertising to occupational therapy, I didn't know how I would pull it off. I was offered a full scholarship to graduate school from the New York City Department of Education in return for a two-year commitment to work in the city schools. While I had envisioned myself working with disabled adults, the school system scholarship seemed like the only way I could afford to earn a master's degree in occupational therapy. After all, I could always work with adults later on.

Talk about a change of life paths! I closed my advertising business and went from wearing tailored suits and heels to boring meetings to wearing fingerpaint and tuna-fish-smeared jeans and sneakers to treat children with everything from autism to learning disabilities to cerebral palsy. I fell in love with working with kids. I was thrilled that playing and being silly could help a child do really hard things really well. To help a struggling child, I had to make learning fun—whether it was a fourth grader learning at last how to correctly write the letter "D" in a bowl of chocolate pudding or a teenager in a wheelchair proudly learning to feed herself with a specially adapted spoon.

It was easier to help kids with obvious physical conditions. A child with spasticity benefits from well-known and widely taught techniques. Kids with learning disabilities benefit from other specific interventions. But there were a lot of children with nothing recognizably wrong with them who were suffering. Helping these smart but "lost" kids became my greatest challenge, just as writing an award-winning ad campaign had once been. Despite their obvious intelligence, these kids were unable to concentrate in class, prone to emotional outbursts, or painfully withdrawn and usually solitary in the playground. They couldn't write legibly, misplaced their homework, were physically clumsy, self-conscious, and usually sad and dispirited. All were labeled as having "behavior problems," and each child contained a mystery that would take patience, love, and hours of detective work to figure out. One girl in fifth grade was so oversensitive to noise that she blocked out all sounds, including her teacher's voice. One kindergartner was so fascinated by the way things smelled and felt that he'd wander around the classroom touching and sniffing things instead of learning. One teenage boy articulated feeling like a freak and wondered why everyone hated him.

By speaking with parents and teachers, observing these children in different school settings such as the classroom, gym, and cafeteria, and working with them one-to-one in a quiet, serene space, it became clear that all these wonderful children were having difficulties integrating sensory information. Without a well-functioning sensory system, these kids felt uncomfortable and unsafe in their bodies and in the world. They lacked the essential foundation of sensory well-being needed to learn, play, socialize, and live up to their full potential. I learned to take a two-prong approach: making changes in the physical environment to meet the unique needs of the child, and boosting the child's own ability to tolerate and integrate sensory stimuli coming from outside and inside their bodies.

Today I am in private practice, working in early intervention (birth to age three) and privately with older school-age children. I love what I do. Each time I meet a child, I wonder how we can have fun together and how I can help this child develop the skills needed to be more secure, independent, and successful in life. Most of the children are referred to me because of developmental delays such as lags in fine motor, visual perceptual skills, short attention span, or high activity level. Most also have some difficulty with communication. It usually becomes immediately apparent that poor sensory integration underlies their delays, and this comes as no surprise. Like constructing a building on sand, if you don't have a firm foundation of reliable sensory information, you lack a solid base on which to build all those developmental skills.

Nancy's son, Cole, had many developmental delays with underlying sensory issues. I worked with Cole and his parents twice a week for one year until he "aged out" of the early intervention system. He continues to get OT at school (he started off in a special preschool and now attends a regular public school). Cole's outstanding progress is the result of excellent communication between his therapists (OT and speech-language), teachers, and parents. Nancy and George wanted to know everything about sensory processing disorder, followed through on every recommendation, and developed a lot of great sensory and skill-enhancing activities on their own. Nancy and her husband are prime examples of how becoming sensory smart parents makes all the difference in the world for a child.

Until now, most of the available information about sensory issues has been confined to the professional community of occupational therapists or exchanged by parents who've learned on their own what works and doesn't work with their children. Nancy and I decided to write this book because we feel it's important to have a comprehensive, practical resource for information that will help parents as well as teachers, therapists, pediatricians, and other professionals working with kids who have sensory processing disorder, or even just mild sensory issues. We've talked to hundreds of parents and dozens of professionals, listened to their experiences, and researched many related topics in order to guide you in finding more information about everything from auditory processing to essential fatty acid supplementation. We hope this book will make it easier for you to be sensory smart—to increase your understanding of the child with sensory issues and empower you to help him to overcome his difficulties.

Our aim is not to transform you into a professional evaluator or occupational therapist. Your job is to be an informed parent, a huge challenge given the very best of circumstances. This book will give you the insights, advice, and information you need to fulfill your essential role as a knowledgeable team member. While the professionals have extensive training and experience, you know your child best and are the one who needs to deal with day-to-day parenting issues, follow through on therapy recommendations, deal with schools, agencies, and so on.

Within these pages, you'll learn how to . . .

- determine what are atypical behaviors, using a sensory checklist and a new way of looking at problems;
- differentiate between willful "bad behavior" and neurological over-stimulation (or understimulation)—and understand how helping your child's body enhances how he behaves;
- find and work effectively with an occupational therapist and other professionals;

- increase your child's ability to tolerate distressing sensations and situations at home, at school, and in the community;
- tune in to your child's unique sensory needs—and help her find acceptable ways to meet them;
- get the most out of your school system;
- implement strategies that nurture your child, reduce hard-to-handle behaviors, and empower him to tackle life's difficult challenges;
- address oral-motor issues such as delayed speech and eating problems;
- deal with developmental delays, learning problems, and disorganization;
- enhance your home to help your child, including having the right toys and equipment;
- use solutions and techniques to make parenting your child an enjoyable challenge instead of a frustrating ordeal.

You may also want to consult our Web site from time to time at www.sensorysmarts.com.

Sensory integration dysfunction is increasingly referred to as sensory processing disorder (SPD), and this will most likely become the official diagnostic label. You will also come across terms such as sensory modulation disorder (SMD) and older terms such as dysfunction of sensory integration (DSI) and sensory integrative disorder. We like the new classification, which you can read more about in Chapter 1, and believe it's important to start using the same labels as those outside the OT profession. Meanwhile, nothing has really changed when it comes to daily experiences. That's why we have always most often referred to "sensory problems" or "sensory issues."

PART ONE

Recognizing and Understanding Your Child's Sensory Issues

CHAPTER 1

Why Is My Child So . . . Unusual?

Katie is a happy, active four-year-old who loves dancing to the Wiggles with her sisters. After a few minutes, she is so wired that she runs in circles, throws herself on the couch, giggles, and sings "Fruit Salad" nonstop. She adores swimming at the beach and spends hours digging and rolling around in the sand, but try to put sunscreen on her and she cries inconsolably. And she'll walk on hot pavement or sharp gravel to get to the beach before she'll consent to wearing shoes, sandals, or flip-flops.

It might seem that Katie just has a few quirks, some more distressing to her parents than others. But when Katie began having problems in her classroom soon after starting preschool, her parents didn't yet have the sensory smarts to make the connection between Katie's odd little habits and her inability to fit in. They weren't surprised to hear that Katie couldn't calm down after the class's music and movement activity each day, but were stumped when the frustrated teacher asked how she was supposed to get Katie to sit for story time instead of rolling on the ground, running around, and smacking into other children. Katie would often lay her head down during art and refuse to cut and paste pictures, insisting she was tired even though she'd been at school for only an hour and got plenty of rest each night. They were also very surprised to hear that their outgoing little girl was spending free-play time far away from other children, vigorously shaking her head no when the teacher encouraged her to join in the fun.

Katie's problem was that her sensory issues weren't resulting in just a few tolerable quirks. They were interfering with daily life and her ability to learn and socialize. Katie has sensory processing disorder.

MAKING SENSE OF SENSORY PROBLEMS

Parents usually hear about sensory integration (SI) dysfunction or sensory processing disorder (SPD) in one of several ways. You may have been told your child has sensory issues after you had her evaluated through your state's early intervention (EI) program, which you called because you suspected language delays or observed unusual behaviors. Or perhaps your child was born prematurely or was adopted from another country, and you were told to contact early intervention if you noticed any developmental delays. You might even have been told to be on the lookout for sensory problems in your premature or adopted baby, and now you suspect she has them. Maybe your child is having difficulty in school and a perceptive school psychologist, teacher, or pediatrician mentioned SI dysfunction or SPD. Or, it could be you have a child with autism and you want to learn how to address her sensory issues. Then again, you may have heard about this book from someone familiar with sensory difficulties, or you may have surfed the Internet for help with your child's unusual behaviors and you came across the term.

Whether your child has extremely mild sensory sensitivities that concern you, or severe sensory issues that dramatically interfere with his—and your—life, there's a lot that can be done to help. If you have just begun the process of finding out what sensory issues are all about and what you need to do, you may want to turn right away to Part Two: Addressing Your Child's Sensory Needs to learn about getting an evaluation, occupational therapy, and practical solutions for everyday problems and activities you can start using right away.

What Is Sensory Processing?

Sensory processing refers to how people use the information provided by all the sensations coming from within the body and from the external environment. We usually think of the senses as separate channels of information, but they actually work together to give us a reliable picture of the world and our place in it. Your senses integrate to form a complete understanding of who you are, where you are, and what is happening around you. Because your brain uses information about sights, sounds, textures, smells, tastes, and movement in an organized way, you assign meaning to your sensory experiences, and you know how to respond and behave accordingly. Walking through a shopping mall, if you smell a powerful, sweet scent, you are able to identify it as a candle or essential oil and realize that you're walking past an aromatherapy store. You may linger a moment to enjoy it or hurry by to escape it.

Impairments in sensory processing have long been recognized as symptoms of stroke, multiple sclerosis, vertigo (an equilibrium disorder), and other medical conditions. However, in the 1970s, occupational therapist Dr. A. Jean Ayres laid the foundation for developmental SI dysfunction theory and practice. Ayres recognized that impaired sensory integration interfered with learning and development in the children she worked with. Since then, occupational therapists such as Lorna Jean King, Winnie Dunn, and Patricia Wilbarger, and other professionals have built on Ayres's work, drawing on clinical experience and research in neuropsychology, neurology, and child development. Firsthand, insider accounts by people with sensory challenges, such as Temple Grandin, helped further our understanding of sensory integration dysfunction, which is estimated to affect anywhere from 10 to 15 percent of children.[1] These professionals and researchers found that different sensory preferences and intolerances affect play, work, learning, social interactions, and everyday activities such as dressing and eating, and that there are specific techniques and strategies that can improve a person's ability to integrate and use sensory information.

New Terminology: SPD

New terminology has been introduced that includes patterns and subtypes under the umbrella of sensory processing disorder (SPD).[2] This proposed new classification system is diagnostically more precise, employs the same terms used by professionals in other fields, and was developed with the end goal of being included in a future edition of the American Psychiatric Association's *Diagnostic and Statistical Manual of Mental Disorders*. Here's how it works:

Sensory Processing Disorder (SPD)

Classification 1: Sensory Modulation Disorder (SMD)
Sensory Modulation refers to how the central nervous system organizes the way it responds to sensory stimuli. If a person has sensory modulation difficulty, his responses to sensory input may be out of proportion to the actual experience, and he may be overresponsive, underresponsive, or engage in sensory seeking behaviors. We discuss all of these behaviors at length throughout this book.

Classification 2: Sensory-Based Motor Disorder

If a person has a sensory-based motor disorder, he may be dyspraxic or have postural challenges. The dyspraxic person may appear awkward, clumsy, or accident-prone and struggle with motor skills. People with postural disorder may have poor balance, strength, and endurance. We discuss these challenges throughout this book.

Classification 3: Sensory Discrimination Disorder

A person with sensory discrimination disorder has trouble perceiving the salient qualities of sensory input and/or struggles to differentiate between the qualities of two sources of sensory stimuli. For example, a child might have trouble judging how much force to use on objects, breaking crayons when he colors. Again, we discuss these problems throughout this book.

What This Means in Real Life

For most of us, sensory processing occurs without conscious thought or effort. Let's say you're ironing and chatting with your child. You stay focused on your conversation and hear all the fascinating details of the latest episode of *Blue's Clues*. You may find that you've ironed an entire pile of shirts without even thinking. You certainly didn't have to consciously consider how to apply the correct pressure to the iron, or figure out what to do when you came across a wrinkle or finished a sleeve. You just ironed. That's how good you are at using your senses to function adaptively. Of course, if something unexpected happens, say, you notice a stain, your senses would sharpen and focus on this alerting information. Otherwise, no big deal—just another day, another pile of ironing.

For others, sensory integration happens inefficiently. People with sensory issues have great difficulty figuring out what is going on inside and outside their bodies, and there's no guarantee that the sensory information they're working with is accurate. In response, a child may avoid confusing or distressing sensations—or seek out more of the sensation to find out more about it. For example, a child who has difficulty integrating tactile (touch) input may avoid unpleasant touch experiences such as getting his hands messy with paint, sand, or glue, while another child may crave such touch input and actively seek it out.

If you had sensory issues, ironing would be extremely taxing, even dangerous, as you'd have to *think* so much about what you're doing. That same walk past the aromatherapy store might be so distressing that the smell might overwhelm you to the point where you become nauseated and upset and have to leave the mall immediately.

For most kids, sensory processing skills develop naturally. As children learn about new sensations, they become more confident about their skills, refine their ability to respond to sensory experiences, and are thus able to accomplish more and more. An infant startles and cries when a fire engine whizzes past blaring a siren, but years later when that baby is a teenager, the same noise might cause him to simply cover his ears as he watches the fire engine go down the street. As an adult, this person may merely stop talking with a friend until the fire engine passes. As sensory processing skills mature, vital pathways in the nervous system get refined and strengthened, and children get better at handling life's challenges.

For some children, sensory processing does not develop smoothly. Because they can't rely on their senses to give them an accurate picture of the world, they don't know how to behave in response, and they may have trouble learning and behaving appropriately. The essential first step toward helping your child with sensory issues is to develop empathy for how he experiences his world.

What Does SI Dysfunction/SPD Feel Like?

Imagine yourself making a spaghetti dinner. Using your eyes, you look around the kitchen and see your cooking equipment and all the ingredients for your meal. Your ears hear the whooshing sound as you open the refrigerator door and the crackle of the garlic peel as you unwrap it. Your skin senses the smooth, hard handle of the knife and the moist surface of the garlic clove as you chop. Your joints and muscles sense the weight of the cleaver and your body position as you move around. Your nose senses the aromas, and as you pop a sliver of bell pepper in your mouth, you enjoy its sharp flavor. And, though you are unaware of it, your body senses the earth's pull of gravity.

You might savor all these sensations or you might be oblivious to them because they're so, well, ordinary. Because your nervous system is functioning normally, you are processing all the sensory input well. Little pieces of sensory information are flowing into your brain in the form of nerve impulses. How do you derive meaning from all these tiny bits of sensory input? You bring all the parts together to make a whole. It's kind of magical, as if a multimillion-piece jigsaw puzzle scattered around your home suddenly transformed itself into a recognizable picture. Sensory processing allows you to focus on the "big picture" of what you are doing: in this case, preparing dinner.

Now imagine that your senses aren't working efficiently. The fluorescent light gives you a headache, and you can't find the tomato sauce in your crowded pantry. The lettuce in your hands feels slimy and repulsive. The smell of garlic makes you queasy. You don't hear the boiling water on the stove, and it bubbles over, flooding your pilot light so the stove won't relight. You bump your head on a cabinet, trip over the cat, and spill the salad. By the time dinner is on the table, you're a nervous wreck and you've yelled at everyone. All you want to do is crawl into bed and sleep.

What if you were to experience this disastrous dinner scenario every night, and no one seemed to understand? After all, everyone else is able to see the can on the shelf and the cat on the floor, so why can't you? Strong smells don't upset them and flickering, harsh lights don't give them headaches. In fact, they can prepare dinner under all these conditions without missing a beat, dropping a spoon, or feeling a moment's discomfort. And, when you try to describe why you are so stressed out doing such tasks, people think you're being ridiculous or difficult or lazy. If you can bring yourself to suffer through this unpleasant cooking experience again, the next time you decide to make the exact same meal because as difficult as it is to prepare it, at least you have some experience doing so. You definitely don't want to try something new and risk even more unpredictable annoyances.

This is what everyday experiences can be like for a child with sensory issues. For her, getting distracted and annoyed by her environment and her own body's response is the norm. To make matters worse, the sensory input she receives isn't consistent, and neither is her nervous system's response. The world seems like an unpredictable, frustrating, even dangerous place, and yet people expect her to happily go about the business of learning and focusing, and doing what Mom asks the first time she asks. No wonder kids with sensory problems are often highly distractible, anxious, or irritable. They may shut down and tune out or throw tantrums when yet another unpredictable stressor comes into their lives—a change in school routine, an unexpected cancellation of their plans for the morning, a favorite Elmo sippy cup unavailable for afternoon juice. They might become controlling and demanding: the Elmo cup *must* be found or else! Parenting these kids can be a real challenge.

How Well Do You Handle Sensory Input?

Most of us have sensory intolerances and preferences. It's really a matter of degree. How much do certain kinds of sensory input bother you? To what extent do you avoid them or try to compensate for them? You may well be the kind of person who never, ever goes on a roller coaster. Or you may be the nut sitting there in the first row, screaming with delight. To increase your understanding of your child's sensitivities, take a look at your own—and how you compensate without even thinking about it. What do *you* do about these common sensory annoyances?

You're in a monotonous lecture or meeting: Do you chew gum or drink coffee? Fidget or write silly notes to the person next to you? Zone out or doze off?

Street noise or noisy neighbors keep you awake: Do you sleep with earplugs, a fan, or the air conditioner on? Take Tylenol PM to knock yourself out? Put your pillow over your ears?

Touching mushy, wet substances bothers you: Do you wear dishwashing gloves to clean goop off dishes? Use a tool rather than your hands to touch gloppy stuff? Use spray-on suntan lotion and moisturizers?

Light touch irritates you: Do you wear long sleeves even on hot days if it's windy? Avoid loose jewelry? Prefer to wear hairstyles that keep your hair from touching your neck or forehead?

What's *Normal* and What Isn't

We're not big believers in the term *normal*. All it really means is that something falls within the norm, meaning it is average statistically. Of course, as a parent, you want all the things you find delightful about your child to be better than average or even extraordinary, which, of course, would fall under the definition of *abnormal*. So, you might want to toss out that *normal* label altogether.

While it's typical to have *some* sensory issues, kids with SI dysfunction have much more trouble with sensory processing. They usually show many of the following behavioral symptoms, which can interfere with daily activities and learning:

- oversensitivity or undersensitivity to touch, sights, sounds, movement, tastes, or smells
- high distractibility, with problems paying attention and staying focused on a task

- an unusually high or low activity level
- frequent tuning out or withdrawing
- intense, out-of-proportion reactions to challenging situations and unfamiliar environments
- impulsivity with little or no self-control
- difficulty transitioning from activity to activity or situation to situation
- rigidity and inflexibility at times
- clumsiness and carelessness
- discomfort in group situations
- social or emotional difficulties
- developmental and learning delays and acting silly or immature
- awkwardness, insecurity, or feeling "stupid" or "weird"
- trouble handling frustration, tendency to tantrum longer and more intensely than other children do, and more difficulty returning to a calm state
- problems transitioning from an alert, active state to a calm, rested state (for example, difficulty falling asleep or waking, or doing a quiet activity after being very active or vice versa)

Lots of kids show these signs for lots of reasons. Some of these behaviors are appropriate at certain ages. Most toddlers are pretty impulsive—that's the terrific but terrible twos. But a four-year-old who acts on every little impulse is a different story. A strong dislike of wool clothing, discomfort making eye contact with strangers, or fear of a goat that bleats loudly and unexpectedly at the petting zoo fall within the range of so-called typical sensory sensitivity for a child so long as these sensory experiences do not interfere with daily function. A child with sensory problems usually has maladaptive responses to everyday situations, consistently showing behaviors that are not age appropriate and that *can't* just be dismissed.

Hypersensitivity and Hyposensitivity

A hallmark of SPD/SI dysfunction is inconsistent responses to sensory information. Your child may very well be oversensitive (*hyper*sensitive) to certain types of sensory input and undersensitive (*hypo*sensitive) to other types of input. A child with auditory sensitivity may love sounds within a certain frequency range (such as a low-frequency lawn mower) and detest sounds at a different frequency range (such as a high-frequency ringing telephone). Another way to think of it is that a child who is hypersensitive may avoid that sensation, while a child who is hyposensitive may actually seek it out because it is calming and comforting. There are also children with mixed reactivity who may be *over*sensitive to a sensation one day, and *under*sensitive to it the next day. This can be really confusing and look like a behavioral issue more than anything else. Say, one day your son craves splashing around in a bubble bath, but the next day, he absolutely refuses to step foot in it. Rather than assuming he's just being difficult, it may be that yesterday his nervous system was "organized" enough to enjoy it, but today his "disorganized" nervous system just can't tolerate it. You can't always predict how a malfunctioning nervous system is going to react from day to day—or even hour to hour—or when a new sensory challenge is going to crop up.

Katie, whom we met at the beginning of this chapter, is *hyper*sensitive to the slimy feel of lotion or glue, but *hypo*sensitive to the gritty feel of sand or dirt on the floor at school. Feeling that roughness against her skin actually helps her to feel calmer and more relaxed, in the same way that twirling her hair or rubbing the satin on a blanket as she's falling asleep might soothe another child. But that slimy lotion or glue is so upsetting to Katie's sense of touch that for her, working with it is like touching a crawling tarantula covered in sticky goo.

Another dimension to sensitivity is the degree of control the child has over the input. A child who hates having a bright overhead light turned on unexpectedly may love turning that light on and off—over and over—if *she* does it. And the child who is frightened by loud noises may love them so long as *she's* the one making a racket.

To make matters more confusing, children may accustom themselves to a "repulsive" sensation and suddenly develop another sensitivity. A child who finally starts to tolerate having his hair brushed, washed, and cut might suddenly find it unbearable to have clothing tags or seams touch his skin. If you previously knew nothing at all about the nuances of sensory input, having a child with sensory problems will make you hyperaware of them!

The common denominator in these sensitivities and the resulting seeking and avoiding behaviors is that *these responses to sensory experiences are not completely voluntary*. They are unusual neurological responses that result in unusual behaviors.

So why doesn't your child just put mind over matter and tolerate the feel of the brush against his scalp and the foam of the toothpaste in his mouth? Well, many children do attain higher tolerance as they mature. And the older we get, the more we figure out ways to adapt to please other people, to be accepted, and to get along in the world while meeting our own needs. Those of us with typical sensory integration skills put up with scratchy clothing for a business meeting or eat calamari because we don't want to embarrass our hostess, but the younger a child is, the harder it is for him to fake it.

Also, the more outside stresses a child has in his life—the demands of school, illness, lack of sleep, tension at home, hormonal fluctuations of adolescence, changes in any medications—the harder it will be for him to "buck up" and tolerate his sensory issues as well.

Keeping Arousal Levels in Balance

One of the brain's most important jobs is to regulate reactions to sensory input so that the level of nervous system arousal, or alertness, is in proportion to the intensity of sensory stimulation the person experiences.

Your child's brain receives hundreds of millions of sensory messages throughout the day. The neurological process of *inhibition* lets him filter out or dampen unimportant sensory messages. For example, your child does not look at every object in your den when he is watching TV and does not feel his weight shift from foot to foot when he is walking. On the other hand, the process of *facilitation* draws his attention to important sensory messages, like the sensation of being pushed, and tells your child to adjust his body position or prepare to fall. Inhibition and facilitation of sensory messages normally balance out, resulting in a well-modulated, comfortable state of self-regulation. However, children with sensory problems are not well-modulated, and life rarely feels in balance.

SENSORY RESPONSIVENESS

	UNDERREACTIVE/ HYPOSENSITIVE	MODULATED	OVERREACTIVE/ DEFENSIVE/ HYPERSENSITIVE
What's happening in the nervous system	Nervous system *inhibits* sensory message, resulting in low or no arousal. Sensory input registers too little or not at all.	Nervous system registers and modulates incoming sensory messages well.	Nervous system *facilitates* sensory input message, resulting in inappropriately high arousal. Sensory input registers "too loud."
Outward behavior	Child tends to be passive, doesn't react quickly to stimuli. Child tends to have low muscle tone, a flat affect (not animated), and prefer sedentary activities.	Interacts age-appropriately with people and objects.	Child tends to be on guard to protect against noxious sensory stimuli. She may exhibit fight-or-flight behaviors (acting out) due to perceived threats to her safety.
How a child may compensate *(behavioral compensations can be really confusing; that's why you need to do your detective work with an OT to figure out what's really going on)*	Sometimes, an underaroused child may rev up his engine and be very active to keep his nervous system primed. So, paradoxically, a hyposensitive child can "look" like a hypersensitive child.	Child may occasionally be over- or understimulated, especially when tired or hungry, but is usually able to tolerate a wide variety of sensory experiences without unusual reactions.	Child may try to block out overwhelming sensory input by shutting down and tuning out. An overreactive child can look like a withdrawn, inactive child.

SENSORY PROBLEMS AFFECT EVERY ASPECT OF LIFE

How do sensory issues impact your child from day to day? Of course, life is a multisensory experience and most children with SPD/SI dysfunction have trouble with more than one sensory system. For the sake of simplicity, though, let's consider just one sense: touch.

Tactile Oversensitivity

A child who is tactile oversensitive will have difficulty in one or more of these areas:

- *Sensory exploration.* She might avoid making physical contact with other people and things in the environment, leading to impoverished sensory experiences and social isolation. A child uncomfortable with touch may not feel safe and comforted by a parent's hug. A child who avoids cold, wet textures won't discover the delight of making a snowman.

- *Emotional and social.* He may have trouble behaving according to social norms, may isolate himself from others, and become aggressive or depressed. A child who dislikes having other kids brush up against him or bump into him might avoid getting physically close and refuse to stand on line or hold another child's hand as requested. He may also refuse to participate during group activities by pushing other kids away or withdrawing into himself.

- *Motor.* She may be unwilling to try new fine and gross motor activities such as cutting with scissors or swimming, and have poor physical coordination. She may have trouble with motor planning, that is, doing physical things in sequence (such as holding both feet together while jumping, and landing with both feet together).

- *Cognitive.* Because he is distracted by his need to avoid tactile input, he may show attention and learning deficits. An infant may avoid learning to hold his bottle because he is distressed by how it feels in his hand. A teenager may be so distracted by the possibility that a rowdy classmate will bother him that he can't follow what the teacher is saying.

- *Speech-language.* If she avoids interaction with others, she may have poor communication skills. If she has tactile issues inside her mouth she may have trouble speaking and making her ideas, needs, and wants known.

- *Eating.* If he avoids certain food textures, he may become malnourished—often in subtle ways, as we shall see later on. If he hates the feel of eating with utensils, he may refuse to eat at all unless he can eat with his fingers. He may avoid social situations where he feels pressured to eat foods he finds repulsive, or even act out or have a meltdown when faced with this possibility.

- *Grooming and dressing.* She may refuse to brush her teeth or hair, use shampoo, or shower. She might insist on wearing clothing that is comfortable and familiar even if it is very dirty or inappropriate for the occasion or weather.

Tactile Undersensitivity

Children can also be *under*sensitive, needing more intense touch input to obtain the tactile information they need. A child who is undersensitive to touch may have these difficulties:

- *Sensory exploration.* He makes excessive physical contact with people and objects, perhaps even licking them, touching other children too forcefully or inappropriately (such as biting or hitting), fingering all the objects in a store, perhaps to the point of injuring others and breaking things.

- *Emotional and social.* She may crave touch to the extent that friends, family, and even strangers become annoyed and upset, scolding her and making her feel unwanted or weird. She might be the baby who constantly needs to be held, or the toddler who hangs on to her mother's leg, craving continual physical contact.

- *Motor.* The child who is undersensitive doesn't adequately register tactile input. To get more tactile sensory information, he may need to use more of his skin surface to feel he's made contact with an object. He may use his whole fist to really feel that marker in his hands, or sprawl on the floor to really know that it's beneath him. Because his ability to sense tactile input is impaired, he may have limited skills needed for precise motor tasks such as writing and catching a ball.

- *Cognitive.* Because she is distracted by her need to obtain tactile input, she may show attention and learning deficits. For example, if she is too absorbed in checking out how the pencil, paper, desk, and chair feel, she will be unable to concentrate on learning to form letters proficiently, or to put her thoughts together well on paper.

- *Speech-language.* If he doesn't process tactile sensations inside his mouth well, he may have trouble mastering the precise movements of the lip and tongue needed to produce articulate speech.

- *Eating.* If the skin in and around her mouth is undersensitive, she may drool, and food may pool inside her cheeks or remain in her mouth or on her lips. She might stuff her mouth with too much food to feel that there's something in there, to the point where it poses a choking hazard.

- *Grooming and dressing.* He may choose clothing that is, to you, unacceptably tight or loose. He may brush his teeth so hard that he injures his gums; a girl may wear braids so tight and keep them in for so long that it damages her hair. A child may insist on wearing her favorite sneakers even though they're way too small and cause blisters.

All of these examples may ring true for your tactile sensitive child—or not. Your child may not have tactile issues at all and may be struggling instead with her other senses. Whatever the case, if your child is having difficulties handling certain kinds of sensory input, you need to be aware that he may be experiencing problems in many areas of daily life that you may not have imagined.

NANCY'S STORY

It was easy for me to think of my son's sensory quirks as normal. After all, my mother and I have the habit of "zoning out" and staring off into space sometimes just like my son does, and my husband, George, says his strongest childhood memory is of lying on the floor and staring at the wheels of a toy car as he pushed it (one of Cole's favorite activities). If these are all "abnormal" behaviors, does that make my entire family abnormal? I was very resistant when the early intervention evaluators told me that "zoning out" and "perseverating" on the wheels of a toy car were not good things—that they could interfere with Cole's learning. Then again, my husband, mother, and I did not have developmental delays like Cole does. I realized that withdrawing allowed my son to cope with feeling overwhelmed by ambient sounds, and it's true, these behaviors were making him unavailable for learning or socializing.

Even Cole's idiosyncrasies that appeared to be assets could interfere with his ability to complete a task. For instance, he has always had excellent hearing—he will comment on the far-off sound of a train across the river—but he really didn't know how to prioritize the information coming in through his ears. He didn't have the skill to separate nuisance sounds from more important sounds like someone calling his name and asking him a question.

The same is true of his visual skills. I am amazed that Cole can locate his favorite book from across the room when just a tiny corner of it is sticking out on a crowded bookshelf; on the other hand, he had difficulty focusing on and completing a simple shape puzzle because he was usually too busy looking around and noticing all the unimportant details in a room, including assorted dust bunnies and a fallen cat whisker. When Lindsey taught me to simplify the visual field (place his other toys in bins, hide puzzle pieces and present them one at a time in sequence at first and then randomly), Cole's visual attention improved so much that he was able to complete the puzzle without getting distracted. Once I realized this, I opened my mind to the reality that Cole was experiencing the world very differently, and if I was going to help him catch up in the areas where he was delayed, I would have to develop a better understanding of how he perceives the world, integrates sensory information, and modulates his own nervous system.

Instead of assuming that Cole's quirks were normal, or even delightful and charming (What can I say? I'm prejudiced about how wonderful my son is, like any mother), I had to start listening to my instincts, which were alerting me to unusual behaviors and responses. Instead of getting hung up on the word *normal,* I threw that word out of my vocabulary because it was just making me anxious. Instead of feeling defensive because family members and I all seem to share some sensory behaviors with my son, I accepted that yes, some of his sensory behaviors are inherited, but since they were causing him problems, they needed to be understood and addressed.

LINDSEY'S STORY

Sensory processing disorder is a lot to take in. There are many new concepts, terminology, and things to do. We'll talk about getting an evaluation, therapy, and what you need to start doing in Part Two of this book. Meanwhile, please know that you're not in this alone. You're going to take this thing step-by-step, and you've got good help to start you off right here in this book.

When I met Cole for the first time, I felt my usual excitement about meeting a child I might see twice a week for a very long time. I instantly fell in love with this gorgeous, vivacious two-year-old with a mop of blond hair and huge brown eyes. His parents, Nancy and George, were obviously willing to do whatever it took to help their child. Both had been upset by the results of the early intervention evaluation. After all, they had taken him because they were worried about just his speech and were told he had several other problems. While Cole was very friendly and eager to play, he couldn't sit still long enough to fully engage in what he was doing. Instead, he'd bang on the couch with drumsticks, race to the corner where he'd spin around in circles, scratch his neck, refuse to touch the Play-Doh or vibrating ball I'd brought, get up and crash into a wall, and then suddenly shut down and space out.

It was easy for me to recognize the signs of sensory problems, but I knew I had a lot of explaining to do. After all, his parents weren't quite sure that his unusual behaviors were what they needed help with—wasn't the problem the developmental delays? As I explained sensory processing disorder and that Cole's sensory issues were interfering with his development, I waited for the dreaded what-planet-are-you-from look. Nancy nodded her head a lot. George *hmmmmmmed* a lot. Finally Nancy asked, "What can we do?" Bingo. We had taken our first step together toward helping Cole.

Over the course of several sessions, I explained how banging and crashing gave Cole "proprioceptive" input in his skin, joints, and muscles, increasing his body awareness; how spinning stimulated the sensory receptors in his inner ear; how certain types of textures and vibration and touch felt threatening; and how sensory overload forced him to withdraw and shut down to cope. Over time, Nancy and George began to develop the sensory smarts that allowed them to see

Cole's behaviors as part of a larger pattern of interpreting sensations differently, how their son was having trouble regulating his response to confusing sensory stimuli, and how this was all interfering with his ability to speak, eat, and learn.

Cole has progressed to the point where, with a few prompts, he can self-regulate and give his body what it needs to feel just right. He can tell his parents when he needs quiet time, or when he needs to jump on his portable trampoline or spin happily on his Dizzy Disc Jr. until you or I would throw up. He isn't "cured" because there isn't any disease. He is a child with mixed reactivity: someone who loves one thing one day and hates it the next. This has been hard for his parents, but over time, they have learned to help him know his body and what it needs to feel right.

Once you see that so many of your child's difficulties are due to underlying and often invisible sensory issues, it becomes crystal clear that there's a great deal you can do to improve how your child feels and functions. We'll explain the process of getting an occupational therapy (OT) evaluation in detail in Chapter 5: Finding and Working with an Occupational Therapist, but for now let's look more closely at your child's sensory system. The first step is to find out how your child's senses work—or sometimes trip him up.

CHAPTER 2

The Seven *Senses*

We all know there are five senses, right? Wrong. There are actually seven senses, and they're not as simple as they seemed when you learned about them in grade school. You're familiar with the external senses that pick up sensory information from the environment: touch, sight, sound, taste, and smell. Well, there are also two internal senses—the sense of movement and the sense of body awareness—that give you information about your body position and movement in relation to gravity.

The seven senses aren't really individual information channels. Everything you—and your child—experience actually affects more than just one sense, and all sensory input is processed together in the brain in many of the same neurological structures. For example, if you spin around in place with your eyes open, you will pick up sensory information about movement, body position, different sights, the feeling of your feet touching the ground and the air moving across your skin, and even the sound of your feet as they move. Life is a multisensory event.

TOUCH: OUR FIRST AND MOST PRIMAL SENSE

When you first held your baby in your arms, you felt the lovely weight of his body, inhaled that wonderful baby smell, rocked him ever so gently, listened to his breathing, and marveled at his soft, velvety skin.

The tactile system—the sense of touch—is the first sensory system to develop in the womb and is the largest sensory system in the body. There are tactile receptors not only on the outer skin but also lining the mouth, throat, and digestive system, inside the ear canals, covering the reproductive organs, and so on. Receptors pick up various touch sensations and transport them on specific nerve fibers at different speeds. The sensory signals travel along two separate pathways in the central nervous system and end up in the brain for processing. Any neurological miscommunication along this complex sensory network will result in confusing sensory experiences.

Types of Touch

When you think of touch, you may think of holding your child's chubby hands, a sensual caress, or the itchy sweater you got from Aunt Sophie last year. The tactile system encompasses many kinds of touch. Each child with tactile issues is different; some are oversensitive to one type of touch, undersensitive to another, or show a bewilderingly mixed response to touch that varies from day to day, from situation to situation. As you learn to understand your child's tactile problems, what may seem like erratic, confusing behavioral responses to tactile input start to look like predictable, understandable patterns.

Light touch, sensed by certain skin cells and the displacement of hairs on the skin, is often the most upsetting type of touch to a child with SI dysfunction. He may be mildly irritated or absolutely freaked out by certain clothing textures; by having someone softly touch him; by feeling grass, sand, or dirt on his skin; by having his face and hair washed, his hair or teeth brushed; and by feeling specific food textures in his mouth. For example, a gentle kiss on the cheek may feel like being rubbed by coarse sandpaper.

Deep pressure is often more tolerable than light touch for a child with tactile issues. Deep pressure sensations are created by activities such as bear hugs, massage, banging, crashing, rolling, and bouncing. These touch experiences also give important sensory information to the joints and muscles.

Vibration, such as from a battery massager, vibrating toy, or appliances such as a refrigerator or air conditioner, can be very alarming for some children with sensory processing issues. A tactile hypersensitive child may be extremely uncomfortable if she feels the vibrations of cars and trucks rumbling nearby. On the other hand, a hyposensitive child might think sitting on top of the washing machine is the best feeling in the world.

Temperature can be a highly subjective experience, depending on tactile sensitivity. Some children with sensory issues complain that their barely lukewarm bath or shower is too hot. Some children crave freezing cold ice cream while others want to gobble up pizza while the cheese is still bubbling. And some children refuse to eat any food that isn't exactly at their favorite temperature.

Pain sensations, from the sting of a paper cut to the excruciating torment of a ruptured appendix, are alarming to most of us. Some children with tactile problems are howlingly sensitive to a small scrape, while others are literally unaware of a broken bone.

There are actually two categories of tactile sensations: discriminative and protective. These two categories of touch travel along different tracts (nerve cell bundles) from tactile receptors to the brain. Touch carried along the *discriminative* tract lets your child feel differences in surfaces so that she can tell which toy is her fuzzy teddy bear and which is her smooth rubber ducky in her darkened bedroom. If all is going well, discriminative touch lets your child pull out a pencil rather than a marker from the bottom of his book bag.

Touch localization is how your child determines where she is being touched when her eyes are closed. Difficulty with tactile discrimination or localization skills results in poor recognition and exploration of objects since the child can't get adequate information about the object as she manipulates it. A child with poor localization skills knows she is being touched, but can't figure out if it's on her thumb or palm. A child who has difficulty locating the site of tactile input is likely to be on high alert whenever she's in an unpredictable environment like a playground full of active children.

Tactile input that travels on the *protective* tract moves quite rapidly to keep you and your child safe. He avoids touching things that hurt, reflexively pulling back his hand when he touches a hot stove.

Overall, smoothly operating discriminative and protective touch let children feel comfortable and confident interacting with objects and people.

Tactile Defensiveness and Other Problems

One of the most well-known sensory problems is tactile defensiveness, a condition in which all or some types of touch are perceived as noxious and dangerous. Like all sensory issues, tactile defensiveness can run from mild to severe. Consider Lia, a ten-month-old girl adopted from China whom Lindsey worked with. At the orphanage, she had been swaddled from head-to-toe in a blanket virtually twenty-four hours a day. While she was a cuddly baby who quickly attached to her adoring adoptive parents, Lia became extremely upset when anyone touched her hands and feet, avoided holding her bottle, protested when barefoot, would not play with textured toys, and touched things only with the index finger of one hand. As a result of her tactile oversensitivity, her fine motor and gross motor skills were significantly delayed. A more extreme—and less common—example of tactile defensiveness is a child who refuses to be held and is so unable to accept the sensation of food in his mouth and throat that he must be fed through a tube.

A child may also be tactile *under*sensitive. When Nancy's son, Cole, didn't flinch and even giggled when vaccinated, it was a sign of tactile undersensitivity. When he learned to walk, he often skinned his knees at the playground, got up, and kept moving, even as his knees were bleeding. He just didn't perceive the sensation as painful.

A tactile undersensitive child needs a lot of input to get the touch information he needs and often seeks it out on his own, often in unsafe ways. A tactile defensive child needs to be desensitized so he can more readily accept touch experiences. This can be tricky, because as a parent, you want to accommodate your child by helping him to avoid threatening experiences to make life easier and at the same time, build up his tolerance for inevitable unpleasant experiences as well.

Adapting to Touch

Another dimension of touch is how rapidly we adapt to tactile changes. Most of us quickly get used to the feeling of light touch or deep pressure, while we take longer to adapt to sensations of pain or change in temperature and so are more likely to be aware of them. For instance, you probably don't feel your socks soon after you put them on. A child with tactile issues may continue to be aware of his socks for hours afterward. His body perceives his socks as a new sensory event that is starting over and over again. When you get off an airplane in Florida, you may feel uncomfortable for several hours even if you're wearing warm-weather clothes because you're still used to colder weather. But your child may complain for your entire vacation that he is unbearably hot even though he's wearing shorts and a tank top.

It can be difficult to judge when you're pushing too hard to help your child with tactile issues. For instance, some parents, and some parenting experts, believe tickling a child is always wrong, hurtful, or overstimulating. Interestingly, tickling sensations travel mostly along the protective touch tract, which makes sense if you imagine that the tickling feeling could be a scorpion traveling up your leg! For the tactile defensive child, tickling can be intolerable. Yet many parents of kids with sensory processing disorder have noticed that their undersensitive and even oversensitive children adore tickling, ask for it, and even are calmed by it. You need to be the judge of whether tickling should be a part of your plan for tactile desensitization. You may need some guidance to figure out which techniques help your tactile sensitive child—and how to gauge the amount of tactile input your child can safely tolerate.

Common Signs of Tactile Sensitivity

While many children show these signs, consider whether your child shows them more often and more dramatically than other children do. Does your child . . .

- become upset—or not notice—when his hands, face, or clothing are messy with substances such as paint, glue, food, and sand?
- become anxious—or crave—walking barefoot on surfaces such as grass, sand, carpet, or linoleum (or even walk on his toes to minimize skin contact)?
- fuss excessively when it's time to get dressed, complaining that clothing is uncomfortable?
- avoid being touched, especially unexpectedly or by unfamiliar people—or constantly seek out physical contact?
- feel pain more or less intensely than others?
- strongly dislike grooming activities such as brushing teeth, having hair washed, or nails cut?

PROPRIOCEPTION: HOW THE BODY SENSES ITSELF

When you close your eyes, how do you know where your feet are? Your arms? Your hands? Proprioception is the internal sense that tells you where your body parts are without your having to look at them. This internal body awareness relies on receptors in your joints, muscles, ligaments, and connective tissue. They pick up information as muscles bend and stretch as well as when your body is still. The joints, muscles, and connective tissue in your buttocks, hips, and legs are compressed (pushed together) as you sit and read this. They are "distracted" (pulled apart) when you hang from a chin-up bar.

Information about body position travels through the spinal cord and into parts of the brain that are not conscious. Because of this, you are seldom aware of where your body parts are unless you actively think about them. As you read this book, your attention is focused on the concepts and information presented. You may be filtering out the sound of your children playing in the other room. Perhaps you're eating a snack. Whatever you are doing, you are probably not thinking about your body position. Yet you are not falling off your chair or the couch because sensory receptors are taking care of that for you.

Life for a child with impaired proprioception is not so easy. He's a "space cadet" because he doesn't know where his body is in space; there's no internal body map to ground him. He's not quite sure where any body part is at any given time unless he looks. Both moving and staying still take some conscious effort. Such kids may be physically clumsy or move slowly to compensate. Without proper proprioceptive input from his trunk and legs, your child might slide off a classroom chair, stumble on stairs, or fall when he runs.

Poor proprioception in the fingers makes it difficult to manage fine motor manipulations needed to write well, button clothing, and make a peanut butter and jelly sandwich without shredding the bread. Without being able to gauge the weight of things (think: compression of the joints), your child drops pencils or uses so much force to pick up things that he hits himself in the face.

Since proprioceptors detect the stretch and pull on muscles and joints, telling the brain just how much tension the muscles need, impaired proprioception robs the body of key information needed to maintain good muscle tone.

Laura, a preschooler Lindsey worked with, was an active, affectionate child at home, but her hugs were *way* too strong. At mealtimes, she spilled her juice, and her plate flew across the table onto the floor when she attempted to scoop up food with her spoon. She had a complete meltdown at her friend's birthday party when someone put a blindfold over her eyes to play Pin the Tail on the Donkey, and couldn't calm down until her mother hugged and rocked her for a very long time.

Laura wasn't being rough or destructive—it's just that without the knowledge of how to apply the correct amount of force on things, she couldn't fine-tune her movements because she was not getting reliable sensory information from inside her body. When blindfolded, Laura had no way to monitor her body and its position in space.

While Laura craved intense proprioceptive experiences, such as crashing into walls, banging toys, tumbling around in a pile of pillows, and general roughhousing to get stronger sensory messages, some children don't seek it out and may try to avoid such input as much as possible. They're the kids slumped over their desks like limp noodles while doing homework or who are usually "too tired" to play outside with the other children.

Common Signs of Body Awareness Problems

All children refine their body awareness as they mature. Compared to other children his age, does your child . . .

* seem to move awkwardly or stiffly?
* seem to be physically weaker than other children?
* use too little or excessive force on things (for example, has trouble attaching clothing snaps, pop beads, and Legos, writes way too light or too dark with a pencil, breaks toys often)?
* push, hit, bite, or bang into other children although he isn't an aggressive child?
* avoid—or crave—jumping, crashing, pushing, pulling, bouncing, and hanging?
* chew on clothing or objects more than other children do?
* always look at what he is doing (for example, he watches his feet when walking or running)?

THE VESTIBULAR SENSE: HOW THE BODY HANDLES MOVEMENT

Picture three preschoolers on the playground—we'll call them Lucia, Max, and Eduardo. Lucia runs to the swings and gets on, pumps her legs to get the swing moving, but, unsatisfied, she asks her mom to push her higher. After a few minutes, she runs over to the big slide, climbs up the ladder, waits her turn and goes down, giggling all the way. She then climbs the chain ladder and goes down the spiral slide, looking to make sure Mom is waiting for her at the bottom because that spiral slide is a bit scary. After a while, Lucia is ready for a snack and a break.

Max's mom is still coaxing him to sit on her lap on the swing. They've lost some time because he stumbled and fell yet again going over to the swings. Once she gets him up, he clings onto her for dear life, and she knows he'll tolerate it for just a few minutes before he starts squirming and looking pale. She hugs him, and they go play in the sandbox for a few minutes. When she asks if he'd like to go on the big slide he screams, "No!" He agrees to go on the baby slide which he finally—hurray!—does all by himself. Once on a quieter day at the playground, his mom was able to get him on the big slide by having him sit on her lap as they went down. Today, though, Max seems happy just playing in the sandbox or on the baby slide, although he looks sad when he sees what fun the other kids are having on the monkey bars.

Meanwhile, Eduardo is still having a blast on the swings. His mom simply can't get him off, even though it's already been a good twenty minutes of swinging. The other parents are starting to give her dirty looks because she's letting her son take such a long turn.

Three children, three different sensory processing profiles. Lucia is integrating vestibular sensations well. Max and Eduardo show signs of poor vestibular integration, with Max avoiding movement and Eduardo seeking it. Max is having a hard time with his balance, gets dizzy easily, and feels nauseated after swinging for just a few moments. He feels like he might fall any time his feet leave the ground, although it's much better when Mom is holding him tight. Eduardo simply can't get enough of it. He's a kid who's always on the go, and who rarely, if ever, sits still.

How the Vestibular System Works

Sensory receptors in the inner ear give your child crucial information about movement, gravity, and vibration. The vestibular system works twenty-four hours a day, since the pull of earth's gravity is constant and impacts everything we do. Every time your child's head moves, vestibular receptors receive extra stimulation, giving his body needed sensory information.

Structures within the inner ear have little hairs with tiny calcium carbonate crystals (like pebbles) resting on them. When your child tilts her head, moves it from side to side, or holds it upside down, the hairs and their crystals shift from their normal position, signaling a change in relationship to gravity. So when she bends over to drink from the water fountain, she can make postural adjustments and not lose her balance. And she can work on keeping her legs straight when she's doing a cartwheel.

The inner ear canals also detect acceleration and deceleration and ongoing rotary head movements such as spinning. Hair cells at the base of each canal are bathed with a fluid called endolymph. When you and your child take off in the car, the fluid bends the hairs backward. As you keep going at an even speed, the fluid stabilizes and the hairs return to a normal position so the movement is no longer actively felt. When you stop the car, the hairs bend forward. Quick start-and-stop movements give very intense vestibular stimulation. Some children are calmed by vestibular input such as being in a car or on a swing, while others are profoundly distressed by it.

Different types of movement provide different types of vestibular stimulation, all of which are important for normal vestibular function. When your child jumps up and down, such as when playing jump rope, the crystals jiggle up and down. Running and using swings make the crystals sway back and forth, and also make the fluids swish around. Spinning strongly activates receptors in the ear canals. When your child touches something that vibrates, her bones carry the vibration into the inner ear, activating receptors.

The vestibular system makes working against gravity and moving through space easy—such as bending over to pick up a backpack, riding the school bus, walking to the classroom, and playing sports. More subtle vestibular activities include maintaining seated posture during class, staying appropriately aroused and attentive, looking up at the board and back down to write notes, and using one's body in an organized, coordinated way.

Linking Up with Other Senses

When all is functioning well, the vestibular system is the primary organizer of sensory input. Children with sensory problems often have inconsistent or weak connections between the vestibular system and their other senses, which means they don't have reliable sensory information. Integrating vestibular input with the other senses is so essential because it:

- Helps your child interpret how her head and body are oriented so she can maintain her equilibrium. This provides a sense of physical and emotional security when moving in space. A child who is not confident about moving, particularly when her feet are not on the ground, may feel unsafe and insecure for good reasons.

- Reduces confusion about conflicting visual information. Without visual-vestibular integration, when a child hangs upside down it may seem that the *world* has literally turned upside down.
- Stabilizes the visual field by fixing the eyes as the head and neck move. For example, your child can keep his eyes on the basket as he runs and dribbles a basketball toward it. If vestibular input isn't integrating well with vision, a child may be able to read the board and his books well but may bump into desks and other children when he walks to the door.
- Strongly influences muscle tone and body posture, telling muscles how much they need to contract at any given time to stay upright and move against the constant downward pull of gravity.
- Helps regulate level of alertness and attention. Nervous system arousal is managed by a cluster of cells in the brain (the reticular activating system) that receives a lot of vestibular input. Slow, steady movement, such as rocking in a chair, usually lowers arousal, while fast, intense movement, like bouncing on a pogo stick, revs it up. Your child may need to walk to the water fountain to "wake up" during a long lecture. You may need to get up and move around for a while before you're really alert in the morning or take a break while you're reading because you haven't moved in so long.

Vestibular Sensitivities

The vestibular system has many different pathways and different jobs to accomplish. Remember, as with other sensory systems, some of these pathways may be working efficiently, while others are not working well at all. The difference between children who are oversensitive and undersensitive to movement can be dramatic. The brain normally processes vestibular and other sensations by facilitating protective responses if they are appropriate ("Watch out!") and inhibiting protective responses ("No need to worry—go for it!") or at least dampening them ("Proceed with caution") if there is no immediate threat. A child will typically assess the situation—*Am I in danger?*—and act accordingly. Not so for the child with a poorly functioning vestibular system.

Gravitational insecurity. A child with gravitational insecurity has an exaggerated emotional response to antigravity movements way out of proportion with the actual possibility of falling. The pull of gravity most of us trust and take for granted is perceived by this child as a primal threat to survival. Because there is no inner sense of gravity's reliability, just a bit of movement may feel like he's bungee jumping or being tossed into outer space. Research suggests that gravitational insecurity may be caused by poor modulation of input from the otoliths.[1] The gravitationally insecure child prefers to stay low to the ground—lying down or seated (often in W-sitting, see page 201 for an illustration)—rigidly fixing his body to prevent any possibility of movement, and avoiding most active physical tasks. This child becomes quite upset when movement is forced on him, especially if it is unexpected.

Max, the little boy afraid to get on the swings, is a classic example. He becomes fearful and anxious whenever his feet aren't firmly planted on the ground. He hates it when other people force him to move, but he pretty much trusts his mom. Other parents and babysitters in the playground are envious about how he never runs off like their children do. Instead, Max sticks right by his mom's side, looking for her to fend off all those kids who might bump into him or push him. He waits for her to recognize that he can't handle all the chaos and to safely guide him to the security of the sandbox where he can plop down in a corner, close to the earth.

Movement intolerance. Some children feel uncomfortable with fast movement or spinning. Children with vestibular sensitivity get dizzy or nauseated very quickly on merry-go-rounds or riding in a car. For children who also have visual sensitivity, just watching another child spin can make them sick because an eye reflex stimulates the vestibular system. A child may have both gravitational insecurity and movement intolerance.

Hyposensitivity to movement. When a child has a high threshold for sensory stimulation, she craves more, and more, and more of it to get the input she needs. A child who underresponds to vestibular stimulation may move a lot, but not necessarily in an organized, appropriate manner. She may have low muscle tone and difficulty moving against gravity. She may have difficulty transitioning from one position to another (such as getting up to walk), and problems starting and stopping movement. She may also move impulsively, without regard to safety.

Common Signs of Movement Problems

There's a wide variation in how much children like movement. Yes, some are happiest curled up for hours with a good book, while others go stir-crazy if they sit around too long. To determine if there's a problem, ask yourself whether your child . . .

- is constantly on the move (can't sit still, fidgets);
- dislikes—or craves—activities that require his feet to leave the ground or challenge his balance;
- seems to have a stiff head, neck, and shoulders—or always holds his head straight;
- hesitates or is afraid of climbing or descending stairs and playground equipment;
- seems overly fearful—or fearless—of movement, heights, or falling;
- gets dizzy very easily—or *never* gets dizzy;
- becomes easily carsick or falls asleep immediately in a car (or bus, boat, train, airplane).

AUDITORY: MAKING SENSE OF SOUNDS

Ralph is a quiet fourteen-year-old who loves reading, drawing superheroes, walking his dog, and, until recently, playing with his best friend, Sam. These days, Sam always wants to go to the mall, go in-line skating, or to parties. Ralph just wants to hang out with Sam at home, where he and Sam talk about almost everything. Get him in a group, and Ralph feels like everyone's jabbering at once, and it's too tiring and boring to listen. It's like at school. He can do the work just fine when the teacher writes down instructions, but if she just says them out loud, he gets all mixed up. The other kids are always so noisy. And his mom is always angry because he never listens to her. Sometimes he doesn't even hear her calling his name, especially when he's having fun playing a video or listening to music.

Gina's parents are worried. Their adorable toddler is so afraid of noise that she screams when her mom uses the vacuum cleaner. On the playground, Gina spends her time looking anxiously at the cars going past and stops what she's doing when she hears a bird chirp. She needs absolute silence to fall and stay asleep. Even the wind wakes her up! And what's most baffling is that Gina seems to hear things no one else hears.

Many children have difficulty handling auditory input, even if they have normal hearing and intelligence. Auditory processing refers to how the central nervous system and brain recognize and make sense of sounds. We "hear" when sound waves travel to the ear's cochlea and are able listen to this information once it is transformed into electrical impulses that can be processed and interpreted by the brain.

Having auditory processing problems is different from being deaf or having a hearing loss. Auditory processing disorder (also called central auditory processing disorder, central auditory dysfunction, and other terms) is a neurological problem caused by a mix-up with the signal of sound as it travels to the brain.

Reacting to Sound

Listening is an unbelievably complex process that involves both hearing and processing sounds. Sound has many dimensions: intensity (loudness, measured in decibels), frequency/pitch (number of sound waves per second), duration (how long the sounds continue), and localization (where sounds are coming from).

A child with sensory processing issues may have trouble putting all these qualities together. A child may have extremely sensitive hearing, picking up on things most people don't hear. While the normal volume threshold for hearing is zero to fifteen decibels, people with auditory hypersensitivity (hyperacusis) can actually hear sounds at zero or even at negative decibel levels (zero decibels does not equal the absence of sound). Understandably, with so much auditory input, a child with hypersensitive hearing has increased difficulty filtering out irrelevant sounds and attending only to salient sounds. And while most of us get uncomfortable when volume exceeds a certain level, an oversensitive child may become miserable at a much quieter volume.

Discomfort with sound isn't always due to high volume. Rather, it may be due to oversensitivity to particular frequencies.[2] Some children are oversensitive to higher frequency sounds (such as certain voices and specific speech sounds, and ringing telephones), which may be quite distressing. Other children may be oversensitive to low frequency sounds such as a lawn mower, air conditioner, or vacuum cleaner. On the other hand, some children underreact to sound. They need a lot of sound: animated voices or loud, vigorous music "wakes up" their ears.

In addition, a child may not be able to interpret where sound waves are coming from or how far they are traveling. He may, for example, perceive a truck rumbling outside as a nearby threat.

Auditory processing issues can also be a big problem even for children with a normal hearing threshold. Such children may not know *which* sounds are important to pay attention to and often have extreme difficulty filtering out background sounds—so the hum of the refrigerator has just as much auditory importance as your voice saying, "Wash your hands before dinner." A child may have to close her eyes or look away to reduce the sensory messages from one "channel" to turn up the volume for auditory processing.

Auditory Problems and Learning

Auditory sensory problems can significantly interfere with development and learning. In school, a child with auditory issues may use lots of mental energy to block out seemingly minor distractions such as the sound of another child writing, book pages being turned, or someone walking in the hall or even another classroom. The sound of a marker squeaking on a board or a ringing school bell may be excruciating. Obviously, if a child is preoccupied by the need to protect himself from potentially noxious sounds, he will be unavailable for learning. The child who needs more auditory input for it to register and stick is also at a loss when new information is presented orally. Sensory-based auditory problems are frequently found in children with developmental delays and learning disorders, as well as diagnoses such as autism and ADHD.

Children with auditory issues often have speech-language difficulties as well, such as trouble understanding what is being said, going off topic during conversation or written composition, problems with reading or spelling, or finding the right word to use. You'll learn more about speech-language problems on pages 236–240.

THE AUDITORY AND VESTIBULAR CONNECTION

The auditory sense is intimately associated with the vestibular sense, so much so that any time you hear a sound, it activates your gravity receptors, and any time you move, it activates your auditory receptors. Why? The vestibular system and cochlea (hearing portion of the inner ear) are anatomically and physiologically attached. They both are situated in the inner ear, their sensory receptors work the same way, they have common fluids, depend on the same nerve, and even share some of the same nerve fibers.

(continued)

So it makes sense that stimulating the gravity receptors by, say, swinging, also impacts hearing. And it also makes sense that a loud bang makes your child startle, rock 'n' roll might get him dancing like a madman, and gentle rhythms can lull his body into sleep. Research also shows that vestibular stimulation can increase spontaneous vocalizations,[3] which means that movement is quite important to cultivating speech for a child with speech delays.

Common Signs of Auditory Problems

Auditory issues can vary significantly, from a child who needs things repeated a few times to "get it" to a child who screams when a fire engine goes by a mile away. Does your child . . .

* have excessively strong reactions—or virtually none at all—to loud or unusual noises?
* not speak as well as other same-age children?
* seem to ignore you when you call his name although you know he can hear?
* have a significant history of ear infections?
* cover his ears frequently to block out sound—or for no apparent reason?
* seem uncomfortable or distracted in a group or busy room?
* react to sounds you don't hear—or react to them long before you hear them?
* have an unusually high or low voice volume?
* often ask others to repeat what they have said?
* have trouble with phonics and learning to read?

VISION: WHAT YOU SEE ISN'T NECESSARILY WHAT YOU GET

When most people think about vision, they think of a beautiful image like an awesome sunset or a child sleeping with her favorite stuffed animal. When they think of vision problems, they may imagine a Seeing Eye dog, the eye chart at the motor vehicles office, or eyeglasses. But vision involves more than the eyes' ability to pick up images accurately. Not only must you detect things in the environment, your brain must also process what this visual information means, remember it, be able to follow it as it moves or you move, know whether you need to respond to it, and if so, determine the best way to respond.

A baby learns to follow a moving object, like his mother, first with his eyes and later by moving his head. He learns to turn toward a sound. Later he learns more about interesting objects he sees by toddling over (finding out about the distance between himself and things), touching objects, gumming them, and learning how to push, pull, pick things up, and throw them. As your child matures, he becomes more able to use his vision to play and to learn. He is able to watch a ball and prepare to catch it. He watches the sequence of how letters are formed in order to write them. He develops his visual memory and uses his eyes in a smooth, orderly fashion to read a book.

How do images in the environment become information the brain can use? The answer is marvelously complex, but we'll keep it simple. Stimulation of sensory receptors in the eyes generates an impulse to the optic nerve, which sends the sensory messages to various sites in the brain where the information is perceived, sorted out, and linked up with all the other senses.

Ocular-Motor and Eye-Teaming Skills

Vision also depends on proper functioning of the eye muscles. Ocular muscles keep the eyes aligned and help them move smoothly and simultaneously. Visual acuity in each eye may be normal, but if the eyes don't work together as a team like a pair of binoculars, conflicting fields of visual input can result in confusing misperceptions about the world. Working in concert with vestibular and visual sensory information, the eye muscles must also be able to . . .

- follow moving objects such as a ball or children running in the playground;
- visually fixate on objects as you move to keep the visual field stable;
- control sequential scanning, such as when reading lines of print in a book;
- refixate from one point to another, such as from one word to the next when reading, or from near to far and back, such as when taking notes from the board.

A lot of children with sensory processing disorder have impaired ocular-motor and eye-teaming skills. This makes everyday tasks such as looking into someone else's eyes, climbing stairs, navigating obstacles like furniture and other people, playing sports, reading, and writing extraordinarily difficult.

The world is crowded with a constant barrage of visual images. As your child's brain matures, she learns to filter out what's not important and attend to what she actually needs to see. You could be standing next to the TV talking to her, but she will only see Dora the Explorer. You may have to raise your voice, tap her shoulder, or fully block Dora to get her attention. Another child might be sitting in a classroom looking at the teacher, following her every move. Or she might be looking all over the room, giving equal visual attention to the truck outside, her teacher's nice new boots, the half-erased chalkboard, and so on. It is hard for her to direct her visual attention because she is distracted by conflicting visual stimuli. She is looking at everything and learning, sometimes, nothing.

A child might compensate for faulty visual processing by hyperfocusing. Whereas the child engrossed in TV or video is following a story or game, the hyperfocused child doesn't *appear* to gain anything from this behavior. He is. He is taking a break from the demands of the world and tuning it out by focusing his vision, much like a yogi in meditation.

On one end of the spectrum, there are children who crave visual stimulation. They may actually be learning while staring at something and appearing to be tuned out. For example, Lindsey observed Marlon, who at age two loved nothing more than dumping out his bucket of letters, numbers, and shapes and looking at them for hours. Then, six months later, he spontaneously began to write and draw simple shapes with off-the-developmental-charts accuracy.

Like all sensory problems, visual sensitivity can run from mild to severe. During school recess, Nathan, a kindergartner Lindsey worked with, only wanted to play in the sandbox and would cry when no one else wanted to join him. Lindsey knew that Nathan, who has red hair, pale skin, and blue eyes, always closed the shades in his bedroom. Recognizing that blue-eyed people are more prone to photosensitivity, she asked his parents to send him to school the next day with sunglasses and a baseball cap for recess. Sure enough, when Lindsey coaxed Nathan to join little Josh on the teeter-totter, Nathan climbed on and howled with delight as she helped him go up and down. He also needed help to toss a basketball into the hoop but had lots of fun. The problem, Lindsey had realized, was that only the sandbox was in the shade. Nathan hadn't had a chance to join his friends and develop his skills on more challenging equipment because they were always in the full sun during recess.

Visual Hypersensitivity

Some people with autism, learning disorders, and developmental disorders suffer from scotopic sensitivity syndrome* (also called Irlen syndrome), a visual-perceptual problem caused by hypersensitivity to color, lights, glare, patterns, and contrast.[4] At its most severe, vision may be so problematic that a child may literally have a visual whiteout and temporarily lose the ability to see. Visual hypersensitivity can include:

Light sensitivity. Bright lights, sunlight, glare, and fluorescent light bombard the nervous system and result in fatigue, anxiety, dizziness, headaches, and other physical problems. Glare in the environment or on the printed page makes it hard to sustain visual focus. Fluorescent light, in particular, is problematic.[5] Fluorescent light flickers (turns on and off) at twice the frequency of the electrical supply. Some visually sensitive people can see this flicker while auditory-sensitive people can hear it as well. Such a visual and auditory distraction can seriously interfere with attention.

Contrast sensitivity. When most people read, they easily distinguish letters from the page. For others, the white background competes with the black letters, making letters lose their distinct edges. The white background may even dominate the entire page.

Impaired print resolution. Letters appear to be unstable, and shimmer, move, shift, or break apart. Difficulty with print resolution becomes more marked as a child grows and has to cope with smaller print, more letters and words per page, and the expectation to read for longer periods.

Restricted span of recognition. Because it is difficult to read groups of letters or words at a time, people with "tunnel reading" can't move from line to line or from one group of words to another easily, and so they have extreme difficulty reading, copying, and proofreading.

---

* The Irlen Institute estimates that this processing disorder affects more than 10 percent of the general population and nearly half of the autistic population.

Distortions in the environment. Like printed letters, objects may appear blurred, moving, or changing, or as if they are disappearing and reappearing. For example, stairs may wiggle or disappear, a parent's face may look "weird," the floor may move, and so on. In such a case, a child might, quite understandably, resist climbing stairs, avoid eye contact, and prefer to remain relatively still.

Keep in mind that vision skills are closely allied with motor skills. We use our eyes to guide our hands and feet for virtually any new skill. As your child learns to use the computer keyboard, he looks at his fingers. As your child learns to roller-skate, he looks at his feet. As new movement patterns become familiar, as mental maps for doing things get ingrained, your child relies less and less on vision. He can look at the computer screen as he types. He can check out the view as he skates. That's because the proprioceptive and vestibular senses have taken over.

Common Signs of Vision Problems

Because children don't realize when they see differently than anyone else does, you have to watch for sometimes subtle symptoms and behaviors. Does your child . . .

- complain of headaches or tiredness, rub his eyes often, or squint?
- have difficulty concentrating and paying attention?
- skip words or lines or frequently lose his place when reading unless he uses his finger as a guide?
- have poor handwriting and drawing skills?
- have trouble copying from the board?
- seem disinterested in, or overly distracted by, objects in the environment?

TASTE AND SMELL: THE YUM AND YUCK OF IT ALL

Smell is a primitive sense that has served humans well. We smell danger, sniffing out spoiled milk, rotten meat, toxic fumes, and other stinky stuff to ensure our survival. If your determination is "oh, gross," you pinch your nostrils and skedaddle. Odors are usually carried to the nose by free-flowing air currents. When we're unsure of what we're smelling or want to get a better whiff, we sniff to create stronger currents to pull more odor molecules up to the receptors in the nasal cavities. Once there, the molecules are absorbed by the nasal mucosa with its hairy sensory receptors that wave in the breeze. When enough odor is up there, an impulse travels up the olfactory (smell) tract.

Smell travels directly into the limbic system, which is the center of our emotions, memory, pleasure, and learning. No other sense taps into our feelings quite like smell. For Lindsey, who enters apartment buildings all over New York City to treat children, the odor of stewing brisket wafting through a hallway recalls all the sights, sounds, and warm, cuddly, kid feelings of her grandparents' Brooklyn apartment. For Nancy, the smell of new plastic conjures up childhood Christmases and Barbie and Skipper dolls.

The senses of taste and smell are intimately connected. Have you ever wondered why food loses its flavor when you have a head cold? Your stuffy nose is at fault, not your taste buds. While we can detect about ten thousand odors, we taste only five things: sweet, salty, bitter, sour, and umami (the recently discovered taste sensation triggered by monosodium glutamate). Everything else we think of as taste is actually smell. Food texture and temperature belong to the realm of touch. You taste sweet best on the tip of your tongue, salty on the sides and tip of tongue, sour on the midsection and sides of your tongue, and bitter mostly toward the back of your tongue. Before something can be "tasted," it needs a dissolving solution: saliva. That's why your mouth waters when anticipating food.

Working together, taste and smell give great pleasure and satisfaction to most of us. For some children with sensory processing issues, many tastes and smells can be repulsive. For kids who are affected, life really stinks—from that minty toothpaste and your coffee in the morning to the musty school bus, detergent on other kids' clothes, wood pencils, the school bathroom, and the typical smelly lunchroom.

Understanding Food Issues

Most of us automatically tune out most smells other than those that are particularly disgusting or wonderful. But some of us can't. Certain odors can be so noxious that they overwhelm a child and interfere with learning, playing, and, well . . . being a kid. The smell defensive child can be so offended by odors that she truly can't shift attention from her nose to anything else. Then there are other kids who want to smell everything. One kindergartener Lindsey worked with used to wander around the classroom sniffing everything, from blocks to clay to his teacher's hair.

A child who is undersensitive to taste often craves extra flavor, going for spicy potato chips, extra salt on his fries, lemon, and Tabasco sauce on his hamburger. (Eating strong-flavored foods can also be a symptom of zinc deficiency.) The taste defensive child may well be reacting to the smell of the food rather than the actual taste. Very often, however, a picky eater is really a child who avoids or seeks a particular texture. This is a tactile issue. A child may eat only foods that are smooth and creamy like yogurt or bananas. A child with weak jaw muscles may avoid chewy foods like meat or bagels. A child who craves crunchy, crispy things like pretzels and fried chicken may be seeking sensory input in the joints and muscles of his mouth. Another child may also be reacting to visual issues. A child might refuse to eat food that moves, such as Jell-O, or insist on only white foods: spaghetti with butter, cream cheese, saltines, chicken, egg whites, and vanilla ice cream.

Once kids find a food they know and like, they may want it the same way all the time. Say you're going out to dinner with another family in the next town. You think to yourself, well, the Chinese restaurant is a safe bet; chicken and broccoli is a favorite with your son. But then the food arrives and your child starts whining, "It's not right!" For a kid with strong sensitivities, it may *not* be right. The broccoli or chicken bits might be larger or smaller than he's used to. The oil for the wok at this restaurant might be canola instead of peanut oil. Or it's too hot or too cold. The variations are endless, and what's more, sensitivities can change from day to day or meal to meal. "Pickiness" often results in food battles. Not the fun ones like throwing your rice pudding across the lunchroom, but the kind where you and your child have an ongoing battle of wills. As with all the other senses, problems with taste and smell really aren't voluntary. When smell and taste go wrong, everyone suffers, including your child whose taste and smell sensitivities may result in nutritional deficiencies.

Don't forget the role of smell whenever you're considering *any* problematic situation. Remember Laura, the preschooler who hugged so hard it hurt? She loved riding in a car, train, or bus. Laura went through a long period of horrendous night terrors. The only way her parents could calm her was to take her for a drive. Every so often, though, seemingly out of nowhere, she would start screaming in the car. It finally occurred to her parents that this happened when they were at the gas station, had recently filled up the gas tank, or even passed by a gas station. The smell of gasoline, or sometimes simply the fear of smelling it, sent their daughter right over the edge.

Common Signs of Taste and Smell Sensitivity

It's a rare and blessed child who will eat everything and never say "oh, gross!" Does your child . . .

- avoid foods most children his age enjoy?
- have a limited repertoire of acceptable foods?
- crave or become upset by certain smells or tastes?
- hold her nostrils closed—even when nothing smells bad to you?
- gag, get nauseated, or vomit easily?

You just never know what's really going on with your sensitive child until you investigate each and every sense. Now that you know more about each sensory system and how they work, you can start tuning in to what's going on with *your* child.

Recommended Reading

Ackerman, Diane. *A Natural History of the Senses.* New York: Vintage Books, 1995.
Ratey, John J., M.D. *A User's Guide to the Brain.* New York: Vintage Books, 2001.

CHAPTER 3

Tuning In to Your Child

As a parent, you need to develop your sensory smarts as much as your child does. If the first step is to understand how the senses work and how a person can be oversensitive or undersensitive, the next step is to apply those "smarts" directly to your own child. Tuning in to his unique way of experiencing and responding to the world takes detective work, patience, and the willingness to look at him in a new way. Now you have a wonderful opportunity to stand back and really see what your child is struggling with. Fortunately, kids leave lots of clues. Just as they leave cookie crumbs all over the counter when they sneak a snack, they also put out subtle signals perceptive parents can pick up—especially if you know what you're looking for.

Remember, your child with sensory problems may have trouble with the most ordinary experiences. Much like a car, a well-tuned nervous system idles at just the right speed: neither too slow nor too fast. When that engine is running fast because he's anxious about unexpected changes in his routine, or because all the sights and sounds at your extended family's holiday gathering are overwhelming, it's very difficult for him to bring himself back to a moderate speed. Even an older child who is stressed out by having to keep it together all day at school, or who is miserable because of a heat wave, seasonal allergies, or raging hormones, can become oversensitive to sensations that he can normally tolerate. Alternately, he might seek out sensations that he instinctively knows will calm his system, whether or not the people around him appreciate him repeatedly smacking his body against walls or refusing to eat anything but pita bread cut in isosceles triangles with melted but definitely-not-browned Muenster cheese.

How do you sort out what's a sensory issue and what's just unusual behavior? *Can* you sort it out? Children are wonderfully complicated, changeable, and all too often, very confusing. The first step is to identify what the behavior is, and then look at all the possible contributing factors. A child who waves his hand in front of his face is telling you something about his visual processing. He may be using this odd behavior to get more visual information or using his visual skills to block out other kinds of sensory input, including you. The child who is always on the move is telling you something about how his body processes sensory information. He may be constantly on the run because his body just loves moving, or because his nervous system is so sluggish that he is forced to bounce around like Tigger to simply feel normal.

The inconsistency of your child's responses and the number of behavioral quirks and sensory sensitivities he has can be utterly exasperating, but as you develop sensory smarts, you'll find it easier to understand, work around, temper, and even predict how he'll act in a given situation—and what's going to work to help.

YOUR CHILD'S SENSORY PORTRAIT

The following checklist will help you to focus in on your child's unique sensory portrait. It is designed to help you deepen your understanding of his sensitivities and any triggers and patterns underlying worrisome behaviors. The checklist can be an important adjunct to a professional evaluation. It will help you, the occupational therapist, and any other professionals gain a holistic picture of your child and clarify which therapeutic approaches and practical solutions will be most helpful. Because school presents a whole different set of sensory experiences, you might ask your child's teacher to fill out this checklist too. This checklist and many of the practical tips you'll find later in this book are available in Spanish on our Web site, www.sensorysmarts.com.

While sensory sensitivities can vary from day to day, even from hour to hour, most parents can identify specific activities that are usually challenging in one way or another. Which sensory stimuli does your child typically avoid? Which does he actively seek out? Does he have mixed reactions, liking certain things sometimes but disliking them at other times? Or is he neutral, reacting neither more nor less dramatically than any other child his age?

TOUCH

	AVOIDS	SEEKS	MIXED	NEUTRAL
Being touched on some body parts, hugs and cuddles	☐	☐	☐	☒
Certain clothing fabrics, seams, tags, waistbands, cuffs, etc.	☒	☐	☐	☐
Clothing, shoes, or accessories that are very tight or very loose	☐	☒	☐	☐
Getting hands, face, or other body parts messy with paint, glue, sand, food, lotion, etc.	☐	☐	☒	☐
Grooming activities such as face and hair washing, brushing, cutting, nail trimming, tooth brushing	☐	☐	☒	☐
Taking a bath, shower, or swimming	☐	☒	☐	☐
Getting toweled dry	☐	☐	☐	☒
Trying new foods	☐	☐	☒	☐
Feeling particular food textures in the mouth (e.g., dry-crumbly, mushy, hard)	☐	☐	☒	☐
Standing close to other people	☐	☐	☐	☒
Walking barefoot	☐	☐	☒	☐

PROPRIOCEPTION (BODY SENSE)

	AVOIDS	SEEKS	MIXED	NEUTRAL
Activities such as roughhousing, jumping, banging, pushing, bouncing, climbing, hanging, and other active play	☐	☒	☐	☐
High-risk play (jumps from extreme heights, climbs tall trees, rides bicycle over gravel)	☐	☐	☐	☒
Fine motor tasks such as writing, drawing, closing buttons and snaps, attaching pop beads and snap-together building toys*	☐	☐	☒	☐
Activities requiring physical strength and force	☐	☐	☒	☐
Eating crunchy foods (pretzels, dry cereal) or chewy foods (meat, caramels)	☐	☐	☐	☒
Smooth, creamy foods (yogurt, cream cheese, pudding)	☐	☐	☐	☒
Having eyes closed or covered	☐	☐	☐	☒

---

* While there are several reasons why a child may avoid such tasks, many children with proprioceptive problems resist or do not excel at fine motor tasks requiring manual dexterity and coordination.

VESTIBULAR (MOVEMENT SENSE)

	AVOIDS	SEEKS	MIXED	NEUTRAL
Being moved passively by another person (rocked or twirled by adult, pushed in wagon)	☐	☒	☐	☐
Riding equipment that moves through space (swings, teeter-totter, escalators, and elevators)	☐	☒	☐	☐
Spinning activities (carousels, spinning toys, spinning around in circles)	☐	☒	☐	☐
Activities that require changes in head position (such as bending over sink) or having head upside down (such as somersaults, hanging from feet)	☐	☐	☐	☒
Challenges to balance such as skating, bicycle riding, skiing, and balance beams	☐	☒	☐	☐
Climbing and descending stairs, slides, and ladders	☐	☒	☐	☐
Being up high such as at top of slide or on mountain overlook	☐	☐	☐	☒
Less stable ground surfaces such as deep pile carpet, grass, sand, snow	☐	☒	☐	☐
Riding in a car or other form of transportation	☐	☐	☐	☒

AUDITORY

	AVOIDS	SEEKS	MIXED	NEUTRAL
Hearing loud sounds such as car horns, alarms, sirens, loud music, or TV	☐	☐	☐	☒
Being in noisy settings such as a crowded restaurant, party, or busy store	☐	☐	☐	☒
Watching TV or listening to music at very high or very low volume	☐	☐	☐	☒
Speaking or being spoken to amid other sounds or other voices	☐	☐	☐	☒
Background noise when concentrating on a task (other voices, music, dishwasher, fan, etc.)	☐	☐	☐	☒
Games with rapid verbal instructions such as Simon Says or Hokey Pokey	☐	☐	☐	☒
Back-and-forth, interactive conversations	☐	☐	☐	☒
Unfamiliar sounds, silly voices, foreign language	☐	☐	☐	☒
Singing alone or with others	☐	☐	☐	☒
Making noise for its own sake	☐	☒	☐	☐

VISION

	AVOIDS	SEEKS	MIXED	NEUTRAL
Learning to read or reading for more than a few minutes				☒
Looking at shiny, spinning, or moving objects				☒
Activities that require eye-hand coordination such as baseball, catch, stringing beads, writing, and tracing		☒		
Tasks requiring visual analysis such as puzzles, mazes, and hidden pictures		☒		
Activities that require discriminating between colors, shapes, and sizes		☒		
Visually busy places such as stores and playgrounds with a lot of children running		☒		
Finding objects such as socks in a drawer or a particular book on a shelf				☒
Very bright light or sunshine, or being photographed with a flash				☒
Dim lighting, shade, or the dark				☒
Action-packed, colorful television, movies, or computer/video games				☒
New visual experiences such as looking through a kaleidoscope or colored glass				☒

TASTE AND SMELL

	AVOIDS	SEEKS	MIXED	NEUTRAL
Smelling unfamiliar scents	☐	☐	☐	☒
Strong odors such as perfume, gasoline, cleaning products	☐	☐	☐	☒
Smelling objects that aren't food such as plastic items, Play-Doh, garbage	☐	☐	☐	☒
Eating new foods	☐	☐	☒	☐
Eating familiar foods	☐	☐	☐	☒
Eating strongly flavored foods (very spicy, salty, bitter, sour, or sweet)	☒	☐	☐	☐

WHERE TO GO FROM HERE

If you or your child's teacher checked off a lot of "avoids," "seeks," or "mixed," get an evaluation with an occupational therapist who is specially trained in assessing and treating sensory processing disorder. We'll discuss how to do this in Chapter 5: Finding and Working with an Occupational Therapist.

Rethinking Behavior as Symptoms

As you reflect on your answers, it will become easier to recognize what's beneath some of the confusing behavior you deal with each day. You may now realize that much of the behavior you've considered odd and inexplicable falls into certain patterns, with stronger avoiding or seeking behaviors in reference to a specific sense such as touch or movement. Rather than trying to change your child's symptomatic behavior, you're now better equipped to deal with the sensory issues themselves.

If your child hits or bites other children, instead of wondering how on earth you created such an aggressive child, you may realize that he's trying to defend himself from unbearable noise and unpredictable touch, or that he may not know how to be gentle when he does want physical contact. Instead of thinking that your child is some kind of neat freak because he insists on washing his hands in the middle of dinner, you may realize that his body is unable to tolerate slimy, sticky, or scratchy textures. Or that your teenager who blasts music so loud that your teeth rattle is trying to regulate his nervous system.

Sensory problems are certainly not an excuse for everything; after all, it's one thing to have insight into unacceptable behavior, and quite another to live with it. But only once you understand the *why* behind what your child is doing can you begin to really get a grip on what to do about it.

Keep a Behavior Journal

To further develop your sensory smarts, start keeping a journal of your child's unusual behaviors and reactions. Note the time of bothersome or puzzling behaviors, where they occurred, the events that preceded it, foods eaten, and any medications taken. You may need to ask your child's teacher to also keep a journal to help pinpoint out-of-bounds behavior patterns at school.

Many parents have found that keeping a behavior journal has helped them discover that their child has food intolerances, or is experiencing side effects from medication, or simply has too many activities without time for rest and regrouping.

In addition to interpreting behavior in terms of what caused it, look for patterns that occur over time. Consider the whole host of events that may factor in on a weekly, monthly, or other regular basis, such as housecleaning with chemical products like carpet fresheners, custodial visits with your ex-spouse, and time spent with other caregivers. For example, one parent found that her child always misbehaved Saturday night and Sunday. After recording behavior problems for a while, she realized that she used a babysitter on Saturday night who brought chocolate as a special treat.

A sample behavior journal page for a four-year-old:

DAY & TIME	BEHAVIOR OBSERVED	SITUATION	WHAT HAPPENED JUST PRIOR	WHAT HELPED?
Monday 12:30 P.M.	Temper tantrum. Throwing toys.	Getting ready to go to the park.	Had lunch— tuna sandwich, berries, and milk. (He eats this a lot with no problem, so it's probably not a reaction to the food.)	Gave him five minutes more to play before leaving. Next time, I won't just announce that we're going; I'll warn him about the transition.

In school, sensory problems may be more significant on a Monday when the child is transitioning from less structured time over the weekend, or on a Friday when the demands of a full week of school have accumulated. Also consider hormonal fluctuations. A teenage girl's sensory defensiveness may become significantly worse right before or during her menstrual period or at a different point in each monthly cycle. The point is, look for patterns that will help you anticipate and plan for—and hopefully avoid—triggers.

Question Everything

There really are only a few key things to ask yourself, or your child, to figure out what's up when he is fussing, behaving oddly, or being uncooperative. The older and more verbal he is, and the greater his own sensory smarts, the easier it will be to determine what is causing his distress. However, don't assume your older child will be aware that his senses work differently from anyone else's. If he is aware, he may be unable to articulate what he is experiencing and how it is affecting him. If you wear glasses, you may remember when you got your first pair. Had you been aware that your vision wasn't quite right, or did someone else discover it (a parent, teacher, or optometrist)? And if you were aware, could you have even described what the problem was: that faraway objects looked a little fuzzy, or that words on a page seemed to be bent? Chances are, you had nothing to compare your experience to, so your vision seemed normal to you.

To sharpen your sensory analysis skills, think of a particular situation in which your child has a hard time, and ask yourself some questions:

1. *Is there a strong auditory element to the experience? Tactile? Vestibular? Proprioceptive? Visual? Smell or taste?*

   Puzzling behavior: Your three-year-old has always fussed about taking a shower, but on vacation, you notice that she loves the outdoor shower.

   Unusual sensory elements: The shower is quieter because there is no sound reverberating against the tiles. The lighting is natural, which may be less irritating than the fluorescent light in your bathroom.

   Thinking more about it: You realize she protested less than usual when she took a shower at the in-laws' last month—and their bathroom seems to have softer lighting and less of an echo.

   What to do: Unless you can install an outdoor shower for use year-round, adapt the lighting and sound in your bathroom at home or switch to baths if she tolerates them better.

2. *When was the last time he engaged in this behavior? Has he behaved this way more than once? Was there a common element?*

   Puzzling behavior: Lately your son has been getting very wired and aggressive, even hitting his younger brother.

   The last time he engaged in this behavior: He's been doing it over the last several days, especially in the afternoons.

   What was the common element? Time of day.

   Thinking more about it: This week you've been letting him watch more TV, especially in the afternoons. And you've noticed that if he watches a nature program, which doesn't have a lot of fast-cut images, he doesn't get so hyped up.

   What to do: Cut down on TV, limit him to programs that don't overstimulate, and provide more opportunities for appropriate seeking of proprioceptive input (no to hitting brothers; yes to hitting drums, pillows, etc.).

3. *Is he experiencing a transition that might be too abrupt or jarring?*

Puzzling behavior: Your thirteen-year-old protests vehemently when you say that yes, we're going to the used comic book store, but first we have to stop at the post office before it closes.

The last time he engaged in this behavior: He fusses any time there is a sudden change in plans, but this is a major overreaction.

Thinking more about it: Aside from being disappointed, he had a long, hard day at school, and he finds sitting in the comic book store and reading very calming, while the post office is loud, bright, and crowded at this time of day and he knows it.

What to do: Reassure him that he will have plenty of time at the comic book store and that he can stay in the car while you go into the post office. Consider postponing the post office trip until tomorrow.

4. *Is there a lack of predictability?*

Puzzling behavior: Your six-year-old cries and says she doesn't want to go to Grandma's after school, which she does every day.

What has changed? Talking with Grandma, you learn that she served a different brand of yogurt last time: the premixed kind instead of the kind with fruit on the bottom and insisted that your daughter not waste good food.

What to do: Talk to Grandma about sensory issues! Ask her to buy the favored brand, or supply it yourself. Ask Grandma to warn your daughter when a food is different in texture, taste, or appearance from what she's used to and allow her to accept a more familiar snack as a substitute.

Roxanne's Story

Lindsey was called in to work with Roxanne, a slender first grader. While Roxanne was clearly quite bright, friendly, and good-natured, she preferred to be by herself or with an adult. At school, she frequently wandered off during fun group activities to sit in the coat closet. During

recess, she played alone by a brick wall. The teachers and school psychologist were worried about her "perseverative" acts (repetitive actions a
child gets stuck on), such as snipping at the air with scissors and wiping
the shiny paper-towel dispenser over and over. She jumped from toy to
toy during free choice time unless engrossed in a book. She complained
to her mother that she hated school because there were too many kids.

In one-to-one situations, such as at home with an adult, Roxanne
was happy, active, and sociable. She smiled often and showed surprisingly mature conversational skills, although she avoided eye contact.
She loved her little CD player and played the same song over and over
at high volume. As she lined up her books, she delighted in telling stories. She rocked while she was seated (her parents said she did that
a lot) and frequently stood up and moved around the room. She enjoyed bouncing while sitting on a therapy ball with her hips held for
stability, but she adamantly refused to roll on her tummy or back over
the ball. Roxanne enjoyed arts and crafts, such as gluing feathers onto
a picture of a bird, but she insisted on washing her hands frequently.
When she lightly scratched herself taking a Beanie Baby off her shelf,
she insisted on putting on a Band-Aid and rubbed the area repeatedly
over the next half hour. She drew a picture of herself with huge ears,
eyes with a line purposely drawn through them, a stick body, legs and
arms, and no hands or feet.

Her parents wanted to know why their articulate, sweet, intelligent
child was acting so strangely. Roxanne often seemed not to hear them
and insisted on playing music and television very loudly. She wanted
to sit in the back row at movies but could comfortably read a book up
close. An audiologist said she had normal hearing. The pediatrician
reassured the family that they shouldn't worry since Roxanne was doing well academically and had many friends outside of school. But her
parents knew something wasn't quite right.

What was going on. Because Roxanne was such a resourceful little
girl, she was able to mask her profound sensory problems most of the
time, and had figured out behavioral strategies to avoid sensory overload. Roxanne's "normal" audiology report showed normal hearing at
low frequencies and oversensitive hearing at higher frequencies. By
playing music and TV at high volumes, Roxanne was trying to desensitize her ears. At other times, she simply tuned out her auditory sense
in order to concentrate visually.

Roxanne also had tactile issues that caused her to withdraw from situations in which she might be touched, bumped, or pushed unexpect-

edly; get her hands messy; and have prolonged behavioral reactions to tactile input such as a very light scratch.

Roxanne had difficulty with vision on top of poor vestibular processing, so she avoided movements that required changes in head position. Roxanne was also struggling with convergence insufficiency, a problem with eye muscles that makes the eyeballs tend to move outward. Keeping them working together to maintain focus required great effort, so Roxanne experienced eyestrain and fatigue. Her poorly functioning eye muscles also prevented her from following moving objects, such as a ball in flight, other children walking or running, or figures on a movie screen. When she watched things from a distance, more sights fell within her central field of vision, and she had less need to move her eyes fully from side to side. No wonder she was uncomfortable in a noisy classroom and on a busy playground full of running, yelling children, and preferred quieter, more predictable grown-ups or just playing with one friend at home.

Besides working individually with Roxanne, Lindsey taught her parents and teachers to reframe their thinking about Roxanne's difficulties. Rather than label her as being oppositional or a behavior problem, they learned to analyze the sensory demands of each situation where Roxanne had trouble and to become, objectively, just as sensitive as she was. Recognizing that this child became easily overwhelmed by having a lot to see and hear, and had trouble processing touch and movement, it became clear why group situations—from the playground to the classroom to a birthday party to the amusement park—caused Roxanne enormous distress. Working together as a team, Lindsey, her parents, her teachers, and other important people in her life helped Roxanne to increase her tolerance for sensory challenges, learn positive ways to avoid overloading her system, and to defuse situations that proved to be too much for her. Roxanne and those who love her and teach her developed the sensory smarts needed to help her succeed.

Children like Roxanne struggle with sensory processing for a wide variety of reasons. And it's only natural for parents to want to know the root cause of sensory difficulties. We'll look at some of the possible causes next.

CHAPTER 4

Where Did the Wires Cross?

We wish there were a simple answer to give you as to why your child has sensory problems, but there are only theories and correlations, not clear causes. Before you get overwhelmed with what may underlie your child's sensory issues, remember that sensory processing disorder is just that: a disorder, not a disease. SPD frequently occurs on its own, without a coexisting diagnosis such as autism, and may be quite mild, moderate, or even severe. In its more severe forms, behaviors due to sensory problems can be very hard for parents and clinicians to distinguish from behaviors stemming from other potential diagnoses such as ADHD or anxiety disorder. Finally, keep in mind if your child does have another correct diagnosis such as autism or fragile X syndrome (which we'll discuss), by addressing the sensory issues that are symptomatic of the diagnosis, you can profoundly improve how he feels and functions in the world.

POSSIBLE CAUSES

A Difference in Wiring

Your baby is born with millions of nerve connections ready to chemically encode life experiences. Stimulating input such as your loving gaze, your caresses, and movements like rocking strengthen these connections. As your baby learns new things about the world, this neural network expands and increases its speed and efficiency.

As your baby developed in utero, cell division occurred at amazing speed. Nerve cells (neurons) differentiated and migrated to specific sites, and extended their branches to connect with other neurons to form little neighborhoods. During normal development, the brain overproduces connections that compete for nourishing chemicals needed to form lasting relationships. Losers that fail to connect or connect to the wrong neighbors typically die off. Winners flourish and form strong connections. During later stages of pregnancy, a wave of cell "pruning" wipes out the weak and faulty connections. It's like spring cleaning for the brain.

What happens if too many or too few neurons are pruned away? What happens when the wrong connections are strengthened and the right ones aren't? There are few definitive answers as yet. We do know that with so many connections in the brain, there's a huge variety of wiring configurations, and it's the way a child's brain is wired that accounts for how he experiences and responds to sensory input.

Problems with cell migration are now considered to be at least a contributing factor in autism, dyslexia, schizophrenia, epilepsy, and perhaps other disorders such as sensory processing disorder.[1] Scientists are also studying the correlation between impaired cell pruning, enlarged brain size in people with autism, and how this may impact sensory processing.[2]

Brain-stem structures play an important role in the initial processing and integration of sensory input. When it functions properly, the reticular formation acts as a gatekeeper for incoming sensory information, filtering out irrelevant stimuli and allowing only the most important sensory cues to pass through the brain to keep your child informed of what's going on in the world. This brain-stem structure plays an essential role in sleep and wakefulness, and helps your child to maintain an optimal level of arousal at which he can pay attention without becoming overstimulated. Studies have repeatedly shown abnormal arousal patterns in people with sensory processing disorder.[3]

Some sensory processing problems are related to an abnormal cerebellum, which studies suggest acts as a volume control for sensory input.[4] With faulty volume control, a person may perceive incoming sensory input as too "loud"—whether it's touch, movement, vision, taste, or another sensation.

The hypothalamus also plays a key role, affecting functions related to body temperature, hunger, thirst, circadian rhythms, and hormone regulation. Functioning like a relay station, the hypothalamus receives sensory information and shuttles it to specific areas in the brain. All sensory input, except smell, travels through the hypothalamus. Other limbic system structures also play a role, giving sensory experiences emotional tags and stamping them into memory.

Neurotransmitters also play an important role in sensory issues. Cells within the brain stem produce dopamine, norepinephrine, and serotonin that affect wide areas of the central nervous system and have a significant impact on arousal, as well as sleep, attention, and motivation. Researchers have also found abnormal serotonin synthesis in areas of the brain responsible for fine sensory discrimination.[5]

Recent studies show that children with sensory processing problems have nervous system disturbances.[6] The autonomic nervous system helps your body cope with changes in the environment. The sympathetic nervous system branch activates your body to fight or flee in response to high stress and emergencies, while the parasympathetic nervous system branch helps your body to calm down and self-regulate in the face of ever-changing stimuli. In scientific studies, researchers are finding that children who overreact to sensory experiences don't habituate to sensory input but instead feel it over and over as a brand-new experience that alerts the nervous system.

Genetics

While there's no definitive genetic data regarding sensory processing disorder, it is well known that conditions that frequently coexist with SPD, such as autism and ADHD, run in families. There is plenty of anecdotal evidence that SPD can be inherited. However, one family member's sensory issues might just be mild quirks, while another's sensory issues might severely disrupt learning, playing, working, and everyday living.

Looking back, you might realize your child's sensory issues began before he was even born. Some moms of children with SPD remember their child being an overly active baby in the womb and that once born, he could never settle in to a comfortable position, or he never seemed to move much at all. Others say their child was colicky from day one, or slept virtually every minute.

You might have more than one child with sensory issues, and one child might have sensory processing disorder and ADHD, while the other simply has sensory issues. It can be very informative to look at your child's biological family tree and discover eccentricities: relatives who never seemed to stop moving, who hand flapped, couldn't ride a bicycle, or were difficult toddlers whose tantrums lasted for hours.

Prematurity

Premature babies are at increased risk for sensory problems, especially those born the earliest and tiniest.[7] In the womb, a baby spends her time curled up, cozy and warm in the darkness, hearing your heartbeat and muted sounds from the outside world. If a baby is born prematurely, her immature, disorganized nervous system isn't ready to handle all the sensory messages bombarding her. Most neonatal intensive care units (NICUs) do their best to minimize overstimulation, but the inevitable beeping and buzzing equipment, 24/7 room lighting, and busy atmosphere can agitate sensitive preemies. The NICU primary care team, including neonatal nurses, occupational and physical therapists, and developmental specialists, work with parents to teach comforting, developmentally appropriate body positions and what types and intensity of sensory input (how much touching, murmuring, movement, etc.) work best to soothe a particular infant's distress and enhance her ability to self-regulate. Parents are usually sent home with warnings to look out for signs of sensory problems and developmental delays in their babies. Several moms say that after many months of dealing with their premature babies' various medical problems, getting the sensory processing disorder diagnosis wasn't particularly upsetting to them because it felt like just one more related medical condition or developmental problem that needed to be addressed.

Long-term effects of prematurity vary as much as children do, but preemies tend to . . .

- be highly sensitive to noise, light, touch, and movement—even beyond their second birthday;
- retain startle reflexes for longer than usual;
- have high muscle tone (stiffness), low muscle tone (floppiness), or a mix of both (while this can signal a serious neurological problem, abnormal muscle tone in preemies is often a temporary condition that resolves itself between twelve and eighteen months);
- be very distractible and highly active—or extremely quiet and sleep more than expected;
- have increased risk for vision problems such as nearsightedness and impaired binocularity;
- develop oral defensiveness because of negative oral experiences with feeding tubes, respirators, and suctioning. This can interfere with accepting touch around the mouth area and feeding. High or low muscle tone in the mouth can also make oral feeding difficult.

Birth Trauma and Hospitalization

Birth trauma such as oxygen deprivation, emergency cesareans, neonatal surgeries, and other medical procedures place a baby at increased risk for sensory issues. For example, noxious stimulation to fragile baby skin from IV lines, needles, pinpricks, and bandages may lead to tactile defensiveness.

Children who are quite sick, medically fragile, or have profound physical disabilities—whether they develop in the womb, at birth, or later on—are also at increased risk for sensory problems. For example, a child bedridden for extended periods misses out on vital opportunities for sensory exploration and adventure, from being hugged to being tossed up in the air, to hearing novel sounds, to moving around to explore and do interesting things. Hospitals are increasingly addressing low sensory stimulation with programs such as Therapeutic Touch, music therapy, and animal-assisted therapy.

If your child was born after a difficult labor and delivery, we hope you won't try to second-guess what you and the doctors might have done differently. Many, many moms say that they had perfectly uneventful pregnancies, labors, and deliveries and yet those babies turned out to have sensory processing disorder, while their other children, who were born after a difficult pregnancy and a complicated labor and delivery, ended up with no sensory issues whatsoever.

Adopted Children

Adopted children are at increased risk for sensory problems, with those adopted from overseas orphanages at higher risk.[8] The conditions in these orphanages vary greatly, but all too often facilities have limited resources, and malnutrition, lack of sensory stimulation, and minimal social interactions can lead to developmental delays, medical problems, emotional difficulties, and sensory processing disorder.[9]

Dr. Jane Aronson, adoption medicine specialist, notes that children placed in overseas orphanages—often born prematurely or with low birth weight—may be predisposed to problems that are compounded by the institutional environment. First, the biological mother may have had poor nutrition and limited or no access to prenatal care. The baby may have been exposed to toxins such as alcohol, drugs, and lead. In orphanages, there may be huge temperature swings and cheerless, uninviting surroundings. Children may sit with wet diapers for hours and may sleep on the floor because there are not enough beds. Lack of sufficient sensory stimulation—such as not being touched and rocked or having a chance to move around to explore the environment—can result in hyper- or hyposensitivity to sensory input. Lack of or minimal contact with caring people can lead to difficulties bonding with an adoptive family. Having an empty tummy or being overfed because of bottle propping can lead to nutritional deficiencies, oral defensiveness or hyposensitivity, and feeding difficulties. This is certainly not always the case, as conditions promoting sensory comfort in overseas orphanages range from setting to setting.

Domestically adopted children are at less risk due to factors including greater access to prenatal care and better living conditions in group homes and foster care families. Whether internationally or domestically adopted, the majority of these children adjust well to their new stimulating homes, especially with the help of an adoptive family that learns to read the child's behavior and uses sensory smarts to help.

Heavy Metals

Undetected heavy metal poisoning can cause sensory issues, along with a host of other quite severe neurological problems. Ingesting mercury at high levels during pregnancy can cause brain damage, lack of motor coordination, inability to speak, blindness, and other serious damage in the developing fetus. Lead poisoning can lead to learning disabilities, behavioral problems, and at very high levels, seizures, coma, and death. The Centers for Disease Control and Prevention Web site (www.cdc .gov) has invaluable information on heavy metal poisoning.

Because lead poisoning can occur without obvious symptoms, it may be more common than you think. The CDC currently recommends that children have no more than 10 micrograms of lead per deciliter of blood. Children who live in older housing are at greatest risk for lead poisoning, but lead poisoning doesn't just occur when children eat paint chips containing lead. Lead can also be present in the form of airborne dust from disintegrating paint, dirt that gets tracked into your home, toys and furniture (particularly items that are older or from overseas where lead hazard laws are lax), some china or ceramics, certain materials used in religious practices and ethnic folk remedies, vinyl mini-blinds made in Asia or Mexico, bathtub water (some manufacturers used poisonous lead in tub glaze until as recently as 1995), or water that comes through lead pipes. If someone in your home works with stained glass or repairs or replaces car batteries, or if you're renovating an older house, you may have a lead hazard.

It's tricky and sometimes quite expensive to remove lead hazards properly. If you suspect your child has lead poisoning, ask your doctor to have a simple blood test performed. You can get an inexpensive lead testing kit from your hardware store to test surfaces such as your bathtub. Your state or local health department can test for lead in your water or home. In any case, you should always use cold tap water, not warm, to cook with or drink because warm water can loosen lead in pipes, causing contamination.

Mercury poisoning is most common in people who eat large quantities of contaminated fish or in people exposed to mercury from fish as vulnerable fetuses. The FDA warns that nearly all fish and shellfish contain traces of mercury, and currently states that shark, swordfish, king mackerel, and tilefish all contain high mercury levels and should be avoided. Shrimp, canned light tuna, catfish, pollock, and wild Alaskan salmon are generally lower in mercury but you should be aware of any local advisories issued about fish in your area and keep abreast of any changes in the recommendations. You may want to check out the FDA's Web site (www.fda.gov) for more information on mercury poisoning.

There has been much debate over the years about the safety of amalgam fillings. However, the FDA's own Web site states that "dental amalgams contain mercury, which may have neurotoxic effects on the nervous systems of children and developing fetuses. When amalgam fillings are placed in teeth or removed from teeth, they release mercury vapor. Mercury vapor is also released during chewing." Many dentists continue to support the safety of dental amalgams—or at least consider it safer to replace amalgams one at a time rather than yanking them all out at once. Talk to your dentist about safe amalgam removal and the safety of mercury amalgam vs. resin composite, porcelain, gold, and other filling materials. Composite fillings (a mix of glass and plastic chemicals) are relatively durable, inexpensive, and very common, but the safety of plastics used, such as Bisphenol A, is highly controversial.

Where else might your child pick up excess mercury? Following the standard schedule of vaccinations before 1999, children received mercury as part of a preservative called thimerosal—cumulatively more than some experts consider safe.[10] Since 1999, manufacturers for the U.S. market either eliminated thimerosal from most bulk vaccines or reformulated them, leaving "trace amounts" the CDC considers equivalent to thimerosal-free products. As of early 2009, with the exception of most flu vaccines and one brand of DTap vaccine, the vaccinations regularly recommended by American physicians do not contain even a trace of thimerosal according to the CDC. Significant amounts may also be in older vaccine inventory and in vaccines used overseas. Then, too, some parents and professionals question the accuracy of CDC statistics about thimerosal. See the CDC Web site at http://www.fda.gov/cber/vaccine/thimerosal.htm#t1 for a list of vaccines that still contain some thimerosal.

Preservatives such as thimerosal, phenol, and 2-phenoxyethanol are used in vaccines to kill bacteria and fungi that may grow after a vaccine bottle leaves the manufacturer. Multidose vaccines without preservatives have resulted in deaths in the past, so the U.S. Code of Federal Regulators has required preservatives in most multidose vaccines since 1968 (a notable exception is the live polio virus vaccine). Some have called for greater availability of single-dose vaccines to further reduce any potential risk from preservatives. You might ask your physician about ordering single-dose vials. Consider, too, reading the product insert that comes with the vaccine before agreeing to have it administered to your child if you're concerned about the ingredients.

Some parents claim their child developed autism almost immediately after multiple vaccinations on one day or a combination vaccine, particularly the MMR (measles, mumps, rubella). The majority of studies show no link between vaccines and autism, and the CDC says their current recommended vaccine schedule is safe. However, there is controversy about many of the studies that have been done and some new research that suggests that vaccines containing thimerosal may have, in the past, played a role in the autism epidemic. Our suggestion is to avoid the few vaccines that contain thimerosal and use the versions that are completely mercury free, which is not difficult to do. Don't vaccinate your child when he's sick or recovering from an illness, even a mild cold; let him fully recover even if it means delaying a vaccination by a few days. Don't give your child more vaccinations in one office visit than the standard schedule suggests just because it may be convenient to do so. Some pediatricians have suggested altering the standard, CDC-recommended schedule slightly, administering all the vaccinations but avoiding multiple vaccines on the same day and spacing them out over a greater period of time. The downside to this is twofold: a greater risk of contracting a disease because the vaccination has been delayed and the inconvenience of many trips to the doctor's office. If you want to use one of these alternative vaccine schedules, we urge you to be realistic about the commitment this requires and decide accordingly. Some parents have chosen to have titers drawn to determine whether a child has immunity from a previous vaccine before administering a booster shot (boosters are designed to provide immunity to the small percentage of people who received a vaccine and didn't develop immunity). While school systems and physicians often don't recognize titers as being "proof" of immunity, it may ease your worries if you use them to determine whether it's safe to slightly delay a booster shot in order to avoid having your child get more than one vaccination on one day.

We suggest that if you're concerned about the safety of vaccines, read the CDC Web site as well as other sources of information about how immunity works in individuals and populations in order to help you weigh your individual child's risks against the risks to your child as well as the greater community created when you delay vaccinations or don't vaccinate at all for particular diseases. The theory of herd immunity says that the more members of a group who are unvaccinated against a specific disease, the more likely the group is to experience an epidemic of that disease. We've seen that the elimination of polio vaccine programs in Africa led to polio outbreaks in ten African countries and the paralysis of 200 children. In a world where travel is becoming easier than ever, we all have to be aware of the potential for outbreaks of disease. Whatever your specific concerns about vaccinations, discuss them with your pediatrician and do your research before making the decision not to administer a recommended vaccine or altering the standard, recommended vaccine schedule.

COEXISTING CONDITIONS

While sensory processing disorder can appear on its own, it often occurs alongside other diagnoses, which can, confusingly, overlap with one another. Sometimes it's virtually impossible to tell the difference between sensory processing disorder and the symptoms of other diagnoses we'll be discussing. Remember that many childhood diagnoses such as ADHD and oppositional defiant disorder are based on subjective assessment of symptomatic behaviors rather than a biological test (such as a blood test).

If you suspect your child has sensory issues, and especially if professionals have diagnosed your child with SPD, address the sensory problems *first* and then see what symptoms remain. Your child's anxiety may dissipate when he starts to feel more secure amid a daily barrage of sensory information. His impulsive, dangerous behavior may cease once he gets enough "heavy work" (proprioception) and movement and learns to self-regulate his system so he isn't so wired and hyped up. However, if you relieve your child's discomfort due to sensory issues and he is still anxious, depressed, rigid, and so on, you may want to consult a neuropsychologist or psychiatrist who specializes in pediatrics. This clinician will draw on DSM criteria (from the American Psychiatric Association's *Diagnostic and Statistical Manual of Mental Disorders*) to make a formal diagnosis, and may prescribe medication and recommend therapy for your child and possibly family therapy.

When thinking about various diagnoses, remember that all disorders fall on a continuum, and that people rarely fit into tidy diagnostic categories. Sometimes it's impossible to discriminate between innate temperament and a diagnosable disorder.[11] We'll look briefly at these conditions and the related sensory issues. You'll find Web sites and organizations that provide more information and support on these disorders in the back of this book.

Food Intolerances

Children with SPD who also have food intolerances often find their sensory issues are improved greatly when offending foods are removed from their diet. It's possible that the foods themselves contribute to sensory issues, but the problem may be that the extra work the body must do to digest that food leaves the child with less energy for controlling sensory sensitivities. For more about food intolerances and how eliminating certain foods or providing certain supplements such as digestive enzymes might help your child with sensory issues, see Chapter 13: Complementary Therapies and Approaches.

Autistic Spectrum Disorders

There is a great deal of confusion about the connection between autistic spectrum disorders and sensory processing disorder. We cannot emphasize strongly enough that just because a child has sensory problems, it does *not* necessarily mean he is autistic. Given this, it is also clear that many of the behavioral, medical, and nutritional interventions often used to help the autistic child may not necessarily be appropriate for the child with sensory problems who is *not* autistic—with the exception of those that target the sensory issues they have in common.

Autistic disorder. Research shows that the vast majority of people with autism have sensory problems, with hearing, touch, and vision typically the most seriously affected. Autism is one of five pervasive developmental disorders (PDDs), and may range from quite mild to very severe. To be diagnosed as autistic, a child must show a strong degree of impairment in social interactions and responsiveness, communication, and behaviors, interests, and activities. Symptoms, with onset before age three, include:

Social Interactions and Responsiveness
- extreme impairment in using and reading nonverbal social behaviors such as eye contact, facial expressions, body postures, and gestures
- failure to develop age-appropriate peer relationships
- lack of spontaneous sharing of enjoyment, interests, or achievements with other people
- lack of emotional and social reciprocity

Communication
- delay or complete lack of spoken language, without using gestures or mimicry to compensate
- if speech is present, it is minimal, immature, and unspontaneous with inability to start or continue conversations; may be highly repetitive or have an unusual tone, volume, or pitch; may be quite concrete, without ability to understand or use abstractions or metaphors
- lack of spontaneous make-believe or social imitation play

Behaviors, Interests, and Activities
- intense, unwavering interest in one or just a few topics
- rigid adherence to nonfunctional routines or rituals
- repetitive physical mannerisms, such as hand flapping or rocking
- preoccupation with *parts* of objects, such as the wheels on a toy truck

A person with autism may also have unusual responses to sensory stimuli; cognitive impairment or scattered skill development; poor coordination; abnormal eating, drinking, and sleeping patterns; problems with mood swings and anxiety; and self-injurious behaviors.

Bear in mind that many people, especially younger children, show many of these symptoms to varying degrees, and it *is* a matter of degree that you must consider. Your child may go through a period of being obsessed with cars or geography, and it may take some patience and creativity to get him to think and talk about something else, but that's often to be expected for a child who's learning about something he finds new and thrilling. Your child may insist on the exact same breakfast cereal morning after morning, or avoid making eye contact, or love to line up his toys; but these behaviors, which may all be based in sensory problems, do not necessarily signal autism. Be sure to express any concerns you have about autism to your pediatrician and get a comprehensive evaluation from qualified professionals.

Asperger's syndrome. Like the child with autism, the child with Asperger's syndrome has major impairments in social interaction, along with repetitive, restricted, and stereotyped patterns of behavior, interests, and activities—and more often than not, significant sensory problems. Here, though, there is no significant delay in language or cognitive or self-help skill development. The child with Asperger's syndrome frequently has gross and fine motor delays, is physically clumsy, and may have special skills, such as extraordinary mathematical abilities.

Pervasive developmental disorder-NOS. Pervasive developmental disorder not otherwise specified (PDD-NOS) is a catchall diagnosis used when there's severe and pervasive impairment in social interaction, verbal or nonverbal communication, or when stereotyped behavior, interests, and activities are present, but the criteria are not fully met for other diagnoses, or if impairments began *after* age three. Many children with PDD-NOS have significant sensory issues.

In the next chapter, we'll take an in-depth look at sensory issues and autistic spectrum disorders.

Attention Deficit Disorders

ADHD (attention deficit hyperactivity disorder) and ADD (attention deficit disorder) are now household words.* In a way, that's good because parents, teachers, and family members can look at a child having trouble with focus, attention, impulsivity, and hyperactivity and consider interventions to help him function better. However, a child might *appear* to have symptoms of ADHD and yet actually have something different going on—such as sensory processing disorder. This can lead to confusion, misdiagnosis, and possibly, unnecessary medication.

---

* ADD is no longer included in the *DSM*. The *DSM-IV* differentiates between three types of ADHD: ADHD with inattention, ADHD with hyperactivity-impulsivity, and ADHD combined type.

The bottom line is this: attentional disorders describe behaviors, and these behaviors may be due to assorted reasons. Child and adolescent psychiatrist Dr. Larry Silver, author of *The Misunderstood Child*, states that ADHD is actually the *least common* reason for hyperactivity, inattention, distractibility, and impulsivity. He lists the leading reasons as anxiety, followed by depression, learning disability, and sensory processing disorder.[12]

ADHD is a neurological condition resulting from chemical imbalances in the brain. Medications such as Ritalin, Concerta, and Adderall work to correct this imbalance. It should be noted that any person who takes a stimulant medication will show changes in their behavior. Therefore, a positive response to medication (such as increased focus) is not in itself a validation of the diagnosis.

Diagnosing Attention Deficits

Attention problems usually become increasingly evident once a child goes to school as demands to concentrate and focus for long periods increase each academic year. Dr. Judith Rapoport and Deborah Ismond note that learning disabilities, mental retardation, or even a poor match between a student's abilities and academic demands can cause restless behavior in school that looks a lot like ADHD.[13] Likewise, sensory issues can result in the very same, hallmark symptoms of ADHD, which include:

Inattention
- doesn't pay attention to details and makes careless errors
- may avoid or dislike tasks that require sustained attention
- does not appear to be listening
- doesn't follow through on instructions or finish schoolwork, chores, or duties—not because he refuses or doesn't understand
- has problems organizing activities and tasks and is often forgetful
- frequently loses and misplaces belongings such as toys and school supplies
- is easily distracted by conflicting stimuli

Hyperactivity and impulsivity
- always "on the go"
- fidgets, squirms, or gets up when expected to remain seated
- talks excessively
- has difficulty taking turns, interrupts, or intrudes on what others are doing
- has trouble participating quietly in leisure activities

- blurts out answers midquestion
- a younger child may run around or climb things inappropriately, while an adolescent may be extremely restless

To meet the official diagnostic criteria for ADHD, the symptoms must appear before age seven, occur for at least six months, interfere with function, and occur in two or more settings (such as at school *and* at home). Thus, if your child is inattentive and restless *only* at school, the cause is probably not ADHD.

It can be extremely difficult to tell the difference between ADHD and sensory processing disorder since many of the symptoms are identical, and a child may have both. It's awfully hard for a child to focus on a teacher's lecture when he has auditory processing problems, is distracted by visual clutter in a classroom, or can't stop thinking about how much his clothes are bothering him. When a child is running in circles, bumping and crashing into his classmates, it could be that he's a kid with SPD seeking proprioceptive and vestibular input to calm his system.

Keep your perspective—and your temper—if your child's teacher (or your in-laws or your neighbor) presents you with an unsolicited ADHD diagnosis and recommends medicating your child.* Only a qualified clinician can diagnose and prescribe medication. However, all of these people giving you advice may be noticing very real, very problematic behaviors that need to be addressed. Your child's teacher plays a crucial role in *helping* to make a diagnosis in terms of reporting behaviors at school (remember, symptoms must occur in two or more settings). If someone recommends medication for ADHD, think twice. Has this physician or other person considered whether your child has sensory processing issues, is anxious or depressed, or has a learning disorder, and whether his behavior is simply on the far edge of normal for his age? The medication might have serious side effects, may be untested on children, and may be unnecessary and ineffective. Remember, though, that some children who *do* have ADHD greatly benefit from a combination of medication and behavioral changes (medication alone does not solve problems).

---

* Some teachers and school administrators recommend and even *require* children with certain behavioral problems to take medication. More than a dozen states have already outlawed this practice, and the trend may go nationwide. A bill called The Child Medication Safety Act has been bouncing back and forth between the House and Senate since 2003. This act would prohibit public elementary and secondary school personnel from requiring that a child take any controlled substance as a condition of attending school or receiving services.

Oppositional Defiant Disorder

Like ADHD, oppositional defiant disorder (ODD) is a diagnosis based on behavior observed in several settings over the course of at least six months. Unlike ADHD behaviors, which are considered involuntary, ODD behaviors are considered voluntary. ODD consists of defiant, hostile, and negative behaviors that interfere with a child socially and at school and includes temper tantrums, arguing, defying the rules, blaming others for one's mistakes or misbehavior, deliberately irritating others, being testy, spiteful, and vindictive. The amount and intensity of these behaviors are extreme for the child's age and development level.

Like ADHD, ODD focuses on behavior, and its symptoms can overlap with behaviors caused by sensory issues. After all, some children respond to sensory overload by becoming argumentative, controlling, or easily annoyed.

One mom, Erika, said, "At one point my son had an ODD diagnosis but once we got his sensory issues under control he no longer fit the criteria for that. In addition, his focus improved with therapy for the sensory integration, so his ADHD has gone from severe to mild."

Keep in mind that it's extremely unusual for a child to have just an ODD diagnosis; 40 percent of children diagnosed with ADHD also get an ODD diagnosis, 15–20 percent of kids with ODD also have a diagnosis of anxiety/depression.[14]

Depression and Anxiety

Many children with sensory issues are moody. They may always be tense and on high alert, or withdrawn, lethargic, or just plain sad. Living with sensory issues is no cakewalk. If your child is sick and tired of being different from all his friends, not being able to enjoy a carefree day at the playground or hanging out after school like everyone else, is he clinically depressed or just understandably fed up? If your child is constantly preoccupied with concerns about being touched unexpectedly or losing her balance, how can you tell whether she has an anxiety disorder or if it's yet another symptom of sensory processing disorder? If he insists on doing things a specific way (his), is he trying to gain just a bit of control over his world, or does he have obsessive-compulsive disorder? Ultimately, it doesn't matter; your child needs help.

Clinical diagnoses such as anxiety and depression often go hand in hand, and there is plenty of evidence of genetic and biological underpinnings. Both involve biochemical and cognitive changes that strongly influence how a child experiences the world. Coping skills needed to tolerate a highly stimulating environment or to remain on an even keel amid academic and social pressures can wobble and fall apart when a child's biochemistry and thought process are significantly disrupted. Here are some things to look for:

Depression
- depressed or irritable mood nearly every day
- diminished interest or pleasure in most activities
- significant weight loss or gain (or your child does not gain weight as expected)
- insomnia or oversleeping almost every day
- observably "slowed down"
- loss of energy
- feelings of worthlessness, hopelessness, or inappropriate guilt
- poor concentration or indecision
- recurrent thoughts of death or suicide

Anxiety
- restlessness or feeling on edge
- easily fatigued
- poor concentration or blanking out
- irritability
- muscle tension
- sleep disturbances (it's hard to fall asleep, stay asleep, or sleep is unsatisfying)

As with all diagnoses, if these behaviors persist after you've addressed the sensory issues, be sure to consult your pediatrician.

Bipolar Disorder

Bipolar disorder, formerly called manic depression, is another mental illness now recognized in children. According to the Academy of Child and Adolescent Psychiatry, up to one-third of the 3.4 million American children and adolescents diagnosed with depression may actually have bipolar disorder. These children cycle between depressed and manic states. The manic state may include extreme irritability, silliness or elation, overinflated self-esteem, decreased sleep, increased talking, distractibility, hypersexuality, and disregard for risk. The manic state may mimic ADHD, ODD, or even conduct disorder (which includes aggression to people and animals, property destruction, deceitfulness, and serious rule violations). Here's some help to clarify the confusion between bipolar disorder and ADHD:[15]

Destructiveness
ADHD: breaks things carelessly
Bipolar: breaks things out of anger

Duration of angry outbursts
ADHD: calms down in less than thirty minutes
Bipolar: feels and acts angry for up to four hours

Tantrum triggers
ADHD: reacts to sensory and emotional overstimulation
Bipolar: reacts to limit setting such as "no"

Arousal and alertness
ADHD: tends to wake up quickly and be alert within minutes
Bipolar: may be irritable and fuzzy headed for hours after waking up

Learning disabilities
ADHD: often has coexisting learning disabilities
Bipolar: learning problems more likely due to poor motivation

Obsessive-Compulsive Disorder

People with obsessive-compulsive disorder (OCD) have obsessive, persistent thoughts, impulses, or images that may lead to compulsive, repetitive behaviors or mental acts such as excessive hand washing, counting, following rigid rules of order, or constant checking (Is the door locked? Is my favorite pen where I left it?). These obsessions and compulsions consume much of the person's day, and when resisted or blocked cause extreme anxiety and upset. The child with "just" Sensory Processing Disorder who struggles to keep overwhelming sensory input under control may develop her own rituals and rigid behavior patterns in an attempt to cope and manage the onslaught but does not experience the severe, disabling anxiety of OCD. Of course, it is possible to have both OCD *and* sensory problems.

Tourette's Syndrome

People with Tourette's syndrome (TS) have involuntary motor and vocal tics, ranging from involuntary blinking to blurting out words or sounds (contrary to the stereotype, fewer than 30 percent of people with TS involuntarily blurt out obscenities or socially unacceptable words). The tics occur almost every day or even several times a day, and over the course of a year, there is not a three-month period that is tic free. People with TS can learn to control their tics to a certain degree, but the tics may become worse once unsuppressed. A child might "hold it together" at school only to have the tics go wild when he gets home. Children with TS are often oversensitive or undersensitive to touch, and have auditory processing problems, floppy limbs when they move, poor balance and coordination, and perceptual-motor problems that can all be addressed with occupational and/or physical therapy. There are medications that can decrease tics if they significantly interfere with daily living and learning.

Fragile X Syndrome

Fragile X syndrome is a genetic disorder that affects both boys and girls (although in girls, the symptoms tend to be milder and more subtle). Symptoms include mild learning disabilities to mental retardation; sensory issues such as overreactivity to stimuli; hyperactivity; anxiety and mood instability; short attention span; low muscle tone and lax joints; large ears, long face, and large testicles in males; and one horizontal crease on the palm of the hand instead of two. If you are concerned about undiagnosed fragile X, discuss it with your pediatrician, who can diagnose it through a blood test. While there is no cure for this rare condition, occupational therapy can be extremely helpful with many of the behavioral symptoms.

Fetal Alcohol Syndrome and Related Disorders

Babies exposed to alcohol in utero may develop physical, mental, and neurobehavioral birth defects known collectively as fetal alcohol syndrome (FAS). Often the result of exposure is not full-fledged FAS but alcohol-related neurodevelopmental disorder or alcohol-related birth defects, which occur at triple the rate of FAS. Children with FAS have growth deficiencies, mental retardation, cognitive problems, brain and facial structure differences, and central nervous system problems. They are often hypo- or hypersensitive to sensory input; have difficulty with visual-perceptual skills, speech and language, auditory processing, and information storage and retrieval skills; and tend to engage in repetitive behaviors. If your child displays symptoms and it's possible that he was exposed to alcohol in the womb, consult a developmental pediatrician.

Cerebral Palsy, Down Syndrome, and Other Disabilities

Children with conditions such as cerebral palsy, Down syndrome, and torticollis caused by damage to or abnormality in nervous system structures may well have sensory difficulties, but their impairments may be directly related to the altered physical structures. For example, children with Down syndrome typically have structural cerebellar abnormalities that result in problems such as low muscle tone and impaired balance. You can't change the structure of the cerebellum, but you can address the neuromuscular and sensory issues.

All too often, children with disabling conditions have limited access to the sensory stimuli that naturally occurs in the environment. A child with cerebral palsy may have difficulty initiating, grading, or coordinating movement and may develop abnormal postures that make it hard to explore the sensory environment through tactile, visual, or vestibular routes. A child with torticollis, sometimes called wryneck, has limited side-bending and rotation of the neck and head (his head tilts to one side), resulting in limited visual access and opportunities for tactile input in the affected area—unless an active stretching and strengthening program is put into place.

If your child has a disabling condition, you'll want to work closely with occupational and physical therapists to minimize any excess disability caused by sensory problems.

Medication for some of the disorders we've discussed above can make a huge difference; in some cases, they may reduce some sensory sensitivity as well. Please note, however, that we do not advocate medication unless absolutely necessary.

Whatever your child's diagnosis—whether he has "just" sensory processing disorder or another diagnosis such as autism with its symptomatic sensory problems—there is much you can do to address your child's sensory needs and foster his development.

Recommended Reading

Armstrong, Thomas. *The Myth of the A.D.D. Child.* New York: Plume, 1997.

Bashe, P. R., and B. Kirby. *The OASIS Guide to Asperger Syndrome.* New York: Crown, 2001.

Koegel, Lynn K., and Claire LaZebnik. *Overcoming Autism.* New York: Viking, 2004.

Koplewicz, Harold S. *It's Nobody's Fault.* New York: Three Rivers Press, 1996.

Madden, Susan L. *The Preemie Parents' Companion.* Boston: The Harvard Common Press, 2000.

Ratey, John. *Shadow Syndromes.* New York: Bantam Books, 1998.

Sears, Robert. *The Vaccine Book: Making the Right Decision for Your Child.* Boston: Little Brown & Co., 2007.

Waltz, Mitzi. *Pervasive Developmental Disorders.* Sebastopol, CA: O'Reilly, 1999.

PART TWO

Addressing Your Child's Sensory Needs

CHAPTER 5

Finding and Working with an Occupational Therapist

Regardless of where you are in the process of dealing with sensory processing disorder—whether you're just coming to terms with the concept or have been working with an occupational therapist for some time—like many parents, you may feel relieved to know that your child's difficult behaviors are rooted in a physical problem you can do something about. One mom, Allison, said, "As a kid, I was always labeled a brat, and finding out that my daughter had sensory issues made me realize, hey, this is me too! It was nice to get an answer as to why my child and I act the way we do. When someone would say that my daughter, Emily, wasn't putting on her socks because she was playing games or being manipulative, I'd defend her because I remember that when I had to wear socks as a kid that it physically bothered me, and I *wasn't* being manipulative."

Parents whose children have other diagnoses, such as autism or ADHD, may be frustrated to learn that their child has yet another diagnosis, or they may be relieved to hear that at least some of their child's problems can be addressed directly with a form of therapy that they've been unaware of until now.

Some parents feel guilty they didn't see a problem before or do something sooner. The truth is, when you live with your child, you lose some perspective. You may have thought: *Don't all kids act like this? Isn't this normal for this age? Maybe she's just a little unusual, and that's not such a bad thing.* Many parents don't understand why their pediatrician said there's nothing wrong with their child, not realizing that SPD isn't something a pediatrician can easily diagnose in a brief office visit, even if he is familiar with sensory issues. Other parents have been falsely told that their child will just grow out of his unusual, sensory behaviors. Yes, sometimes kids do, but more often, the wait-and-see approach results in children unnecessarily continuing to struggle and feel uncomfortable in their bodies and the world.

GETTING HELP

Assuming you haven't already done so, the first step is to get your child properly evaluated by professionals who can help you sort out the problems and develop a therapeutic action plan. If you've been working with an OT and perhaps other therapists on your child's sensory issues for a while, it may be helpful to quickly review this chapter before moving on to another.

Evaluation and Therapy for Children Age Birth to Three

If your child is under age three, you can get a free evaluation through your state's early intervention (EI) program. These programs are federally funded and go by many different names, such as "Birth to Three" or "Child Find." You'll find a full listing of contact numbers for EI programs by state on our Web site at www.sensory smarts.com.

One of the greatest benefits of getting your child evaluated through early intervention is that the evaluation may be multidisciplinary. An occupational therapist (OT) is usually the primary professional for treating sensory issues. However, even if you're concerned only about sensory issues, your child may also be evaluated by a speech-language pathologist, special educator, and often, a physical therapist, in addition to an OT. This is because it is very common for children to have developmental delays in addition to sensory issues.

If your child qualifies for services, EI will provide them for free or for low cost, depending on your state's program. Usually, the therapy sessions will take place in your home, or less often, in an early intervention center-based program. While she is in EI, your child's therapy will focus on everyday life activities, such as playing, doing puzzles, running and jumping, holding a crayon and coloring, dressing, and eating. The document outlining therapy goals and services (which you will be a part of creating) is called an IFSP, or Individualized Family Service Plan. When your child "ages out" of EI around her third birthday, your service coordinator will help you transition to services supplied by your local school system or in your community. Sometimes these transitions are virtually seamless, particularly if the child has been getting services

TYPICAL MEMBERS OF THE EVALUATING TEAM

In addition to playing the lead role in working with sensory issues, an *occupational therapist* also addresses fine motor skills, gross motor skills, visual-perceptual skills, self-help skills, and other important skill areas we'll describe in detail in Chapter 8: Dealing with Developmental Delays. In a nutshell, though, occupational therapy addresses all the skills needed for the "job of living"—all those tasks that occupy one's time such as playing, going to school, eating meals, and so on.

A *physical therapist* (PT) looks at difficulty with neurological, musculoskeletal, sensory, or other issues that impair mobility, balance, coordination, strength, range of motion, and endurance. A PT works on developing a child's gross motor skills—to crawl, sit, stand, walk, hop, jump, and run. In treatment, a PT addresses postural control, stability, joint alignment, muscle tone, and motor planning skills. In the EI evaluation, the OT may assume the role of both OT and PT in assessing motor skills.

A *speech-language pathologist* (SLP) looks at both receptive and expressive language problems, auditory processing, and oral-motor difficulties such as low tone and feeding problems. SLPs often work closely with OTs on oral-motor issues and with audiologists on receptive language and auditory processing problems.

A *special education teacher* considers cognitive development and learning issues as well as behavioral issues and social skills.

A *case coordinator* will also be present during the EI evaluation, taking the lead in learning about your family's history and your child's developmental background, and coordinating the entire process.

at a preschool that is not only an EI provider but has a contract with the school system to serve children ages three to five.

If your child is about to "age out" of early intervention and you're being told he doesn't need to transition to a three-to-five program, but you feel he still needs therapy, you can contest this decision. Ask to see the testing they have done that led them to this conclusion. If the testing hasn't been done, request it in writing, and keep a paper trail. You may want to get private testing done.

At any point in your child's development, if you feel he is being denied services he needs, don't be intimidated. Work with your EI program or school district, gather more information, and don't be afraid to push for continued or increased services if you truly believe your child requires them.

Evaluation and Therapy for Children Over Age Three

Once your child reaches age three, he is no longer eligible for EI, but can get an OT evaluation through the school system. Whether your child is three years old and still not in preschool or age thirteen and attending junior high, your local school district is required to evaluate your child for developmental delays. You can call the special education director at your local school district and ask to set up an evaluation (follow up with a written request). If your child is found to be eligible for services, he will get an IEP, or individualized education plan.

Because schools sometimes don't recognize the importance of sensory problems, it will help to notify them of any diagnoses your child has (such as ADHD) or developmental delays you are concerned about (such as if he seems uncoordinated or has difficulties with physical activities such as buttoning, writing and drawing, and catching a ball, or if he has trouble following verbal instructions). See Chapter 8: Dealing with Developmental Delays for more information on common delays that often coexist with SPD. Should "related services" such as OT be recommended after evaluation, the school district is mandated by law to provide therapy.

While there are many wonderful OTs with strong backgrounds in treating sensory issues working in the schools, there are many others who are more expert at evaluating and treating difficulties with fine motor, gross motor, and visual-perceptual skills. Therefore, you will have to politely insist that the OT evaluator (and the treating therapist, should OT be recommended) be very knowledgeable about sensory processing issues.

Other Options for Finding Help

In a perfect world, all school districts would be well aware of the problem of SPD and all school-based occupational therapists would be well versed in working with kids who have sensory issues. Unfortunately, this is not always the case.

If you have trouble getting OT through your school district because they don't recognize sensory issues and your child doesn't have enough of a delay in a related area to qualify for services, you can always hire an OT privately. You may be able to easily get insurance coverage for the OT of your choice, or you may have to first ask the insurance provider if they have a pediatric OT on their list of plan-approved providers. If they do, call the OT to find out her specialty, because it may well be that she specializes in something like orthopedics or geriatrics, which is not what you're looking for; you need an OT who works with kids who have sensory issues.

Finding a private OT who can work with your child's sensory needs isn't always easy. You might ask your pediatrician, any other therapists your child sees, or a local parent advocacy center for a referral. You might join an SI support group through Yahoo Groups (go to www.yahoogroups.com and search for "sensory integration" to find appropriate groups) and ask members for recommendations for OTs in your area. The KID Foundation's SPD Network has an extensive online listing of OTs and other professionals who are trained and experienced in helping kids with sensory issues (see www.foundation .net).

Another possibility is to contact the OT department at a university or college in your area. Ask to speak with a faculty member who teaches pediatrics to see if she can recommend a university-based evaluation program or refer you to an OT specializing in sensory processing problems. The American Occupational Therapy Association Web site, www.aota.org, lists accredited university programs and provides links to state OT associations. The state contact person may be able to put you in touch with an OT as well. You can also try the AOTA's specialist directory on their Web site to see if a pediatric OT with training in sensory issues has listed herself. To find an OT in Canada, try www.otworks.ca. Another option is to check the Web site of Western Psychological Services at http:// www.wpspublish.com/Inetpub4/w090308.htm, which lists occupational therapists who are certified to perform the Sensory Integration Praxis Test (SIPT).

Another option for finding an OT is to contact a charitable organization, such as Easter Seals, and ask whether they can help fund an OT evaluation and services. Some parents with low incomes have even been able to get these types of organizations to pay for therapy equipment.

Even if you find the perfect OT, it can be a good idea to request a multidisciplinary evaluation from a university-affiliated center or private group practice. One mom, Michelle, says, "The best thing we ever did for Jackson was to get a multidisciplinary team evaluation at a university center for evaluating children, which is part of their department of pediatrics. He saw the OT, a speech therapist, a physical therapist, a geneticist, a developmental pediatrician, and a psychologist all at one time, all in one place. If I could change anything, I would've done that sooner. He got the Asperger's syndrome diagnosis there, and we were able to rule out some other things and get a sense of how his symptoms fit together. Before that, Jackson had all these evaluations separately and didn't neatly fit into a category, so the OT would say, 'Oh yeah, this treatment isn't quite working. Let's see what the neurologist says.' And then the neurologist would say, 'I don't know. What does the OT say?' By getting this multidisciplinary evaluation, we eliminated the 'go see another person' stuff, because the professionals had to work together to come up with some sort of assessment."

THE SENSORY INTEGRATION AND PRAXIS TESTS

Some therapists (OTs and, less often, PTs) have a special qualification called SIPT certification. SIPT stands for Sensory Integration and Praxis Tests, an extremely detailed, lengthy, and costly assessment of sensory processing skills appropriate for children ages four through eight. An SIPT-certified therapist has successfully completed the extensive training needed to administer and interpret the SIPT. While it is great to work with an SIPT-certified therapist (provided she has sensory smarts, hands-on experience, and a personality that meshes with you and your child), it is not necessary, and the qualification itself does not mean the therapist is definitely the right one for you and your child.

OT AND YOUR CHILD

While you may be a little bit anxious about how your child will handle therapy, rest assured: most kids adore OT. Even older kids who don't want to do anything their friends aren't doing usually enjoy the sessions and the way they make them feel.

Many parents are a little intimidated by their child's OT or other therapists at first. After all, she's supposed to be the expert on what's troubling your child, right? Actually, you, the parent, are the one true expert on *your* child: what makes him tick; his likes, loves, and hates; the experiences that really turn him on; and the situations and tasks that he just can't handle. No one knows him better than you, even if some of the things he does are really confusing. So think of your OT as a resource for invaluable information and someone who is your *partner*.

What an OT Will Do

OT is fun—lots of fun, even though it may be challenging and sometimes even a little scary for your child. Remember, children learn through play. In the beginning, the OT (and any other therapist) starts by establishing a positive rapport with your child to develop comfort and trust and to discover your child's likes and dislikes, strengths and weaknesses. You can be a big help at this early stage. If the OT comes to your home, help your child welcome the OT and show off his favorite toys. Tell the OT about any household items that distress your child (such as if your child screams when you use the vacuum cleaner).

As the therapeutic relationship deepens, your OT will start presenting activities and tasks that are just slightly beyond easy for your child, that is, that present enough familiarity not to be overwhelming, but enough novelty and challenge to be exciting. Delia, mother to one-year-old Ivy, said that in her daughter's OT sessions through early intervention, "The OT basically never let up. If Ivy refused to do something, the OT would immediately redirect her into doing something else. In the beginning, if Ivy didn't want to play with an object the OT had brought, she would throw it. The OT taught her she may put it aside for a few minutes and go on to something else but eventually she would come back to it in the same session."

The "Just Right" Challenge

Finding a challenge that is "just right" is the true art of therapy. Not too much challenge, and not too little either (although the therapist may sometimes let your child engage in familiar tasks she is good at to bolster her comfort and self-confidence). Your child should never be bored during therapy, although an older child may claim he's bored to avoid tasks that are hard for him.

At the core of occupational therapy is a goal of active participation in "functional activity." For example, spinning the wheels on a toy car is not functional because it does not serve a purpose (other than, perhaps, to relax a child or help him tune out). The OT will show you how to build bridges into more productive actions, such as counting the four wheels or making a highway out of blocks for the car to travel on.

A typical OT session will start with sensory modulating activities because a hyped-up child needs to calm down, while a sluggish child needs to become more alert. It is very important that you, the parent, learn how to implement these sensory modulation activities, which might include brushing with a soft surgical scrub brush, rolling over a therapy ball, swinging, massage, blowing bubbles, dancing to music— what works will depend on your child, and may change over time. Taking into account your child's individual sensory and developmental needs, the OT may engage your child in the following activities:

- swinging on suspended equipment
- sensorimotor work such as climbing through tunnels and over a mountain of cushions
- messy projects such as fingerpainting, sculpting with clay or Play-Doh, doing arts and crafts
- tactile exploration such as finding small toys buried in a bin of dry rice or beans or Styrofoam peanuts
- fine motor work such as writing with a finger in shaving cream, using tongs to pick up toys, and fun hand-strengthening exercises
- oral motor desensitization and strengthening using items such as oral vibrators, food, feathers, and bubbles
- auditory stimulation with musical instruments or specially engineered CDs of music

Tell your OT about the favorite activities that you do with your child. She may show you how to build on those activities to make them even more beneficial. For example, you may love to cook together. Your OT may recommend that you have your child mix cookie batter with her hands instead of with a spoon, or suggest that you give your child cookie cutters to make French toast really special while working on grading arm pressure. The OT can recommend lots of new activities you and your child will both enjoy that provide a "just right" challenge.

The Sensory Gym Experience

A sensory gym may be recommended for your child. Located in therapy clinics and in some schools, sensory gyms have a variety of interesting equipment and toys. This might include lots of suspended equipment—such as platform swings, bolster swings, net swings (see photos on pages 391–392)—as well as scooter boards, climbing equipment, spinning equipment, trampolines, and other very exciting, enticing items, all surrounded by thick mats and padding. A child gets to do things here that may surprise her—and you. You may find that in this setting your child is now willing to climb a ladder, go on a swing, and do activities you both never thought possible. Unlike a playground or even a regular gym, a sensory gym provides a safe, supportive environment for pushing past perceived limitations—all graded with the "just right" challenge your child needs to move forward. A sensory gym can be a godsend for a child who is so active that he bounces off the walls and needs very intense movement and deep pressure, as well as for a child unwilling to try new sensory experiences such as using a swing in a high-stimulation setting like a busy playground.

Being in a special environment also has its disadvantages. What your child learns to do here may not carry over into everyday life settings: a noisy classroom, the playground, or at home. Ideally, children who attend a sensory gym should also receive OT at home, school, and in a playground to ensure that skills being developed in the sensory gym are "generalized" and carried over into daily life.

Also, a sensory gym can be quite stimulating and distracting. Children love active play in this setting and it may be hard to settle down afterward and attend to quieter tasks such as tabletop work (handwriting, drawing, and so on). For children in early intervention especially, therapy in natural environments where the child usually interacts with everyday objects and people is essential. After all, you need your child to be comfortable in all kinds of environments doing everyday things like dressing, eating, going to school, and whatever else she finds she must accomplish each day.

NANCY'S STORY

When Cole first began occupational therapy, Lindsey suggested that we buy some items that would really help him get the sensory input he needs to calm and organize his system: a therapy ball, a hopping ball (the kind with a handle, where you sit on it and bounce across the room), a mini-trampoline, a bin of beans or birdseed for tactile exploration, some kid-friendly musical instruments, and a Dizzy Disc Jr. spinning toy. My first thought wasn't the expense so much as, where was I going to fit all this in our tiny New York City apartment?

With a little creativity, George and I found places for everything: the plastic bin of "dinosaur sand" (birdseed and toy dinosaurs) fits under our bed, for example, and the balls rest on a shelf George put up in the bedroom. Lindsey also suggested ways we could use our bed as a miniature sensory gym: Cole will crawl under the fitted sheet or the blankets, fall over from a standing position onto pillows, lie on his back and kick the therapy ball as we toss it toward him, and beg us to pile pillows, stuffed animals, and even ourselves onto him as he lay there. So, even when we can't get to the playground, we always have our miniature sensory gym in our home.

WHAT OTs DO FROM THE INSURANCE PROVIDER'S POINT OF VIEW

If your insurance carrier covers OT services, your child should be eligible if OT interventions result in improved performance in areas such as fine motor skills, gross motor skills, motor planning and coordination, self-care, or visual-perceptual skills. Remember, the OT is not, for example, brushing your child because your child enjoys it, but to help your child be able to tolerate getting dressed (a "functional activity"). Thus it makes total sense for an OT to use procedure codes in her documentation that reflect functional interventions and outcomes rather than simply billing the insurance company for using sensory integration techniques. If you have any questions about how this all works, talk to your OT.

What to Look for in a Therapist

The therapist you want working with your child . . .

- treats you like a member of the treatment team, and works with you to develop and prioritize goals for your child;

- smiles when she greets you and your child;
- laughs with your child (and you) when things are amusing;
- thinks your child is interesting and appreciates what is delightful about your child;
- shares techniques, tips, and activities with you, teaching you how to follow through on interventions;
- individualizes sessions to your child's interests—if your child is crazy about trains, she incorporates trains into play;
- never forces your child to do something or pushes your child too far past his comfort zone;
- is flexible and respects your family's needs and values;
- returns your phone calls promptly;
- does not make you or your child feel stupid, lazy, or bad.

Your Responsibilities

- Work with therapists to develop clear, consistent goals for your child. Is it important to you that he be able to dress himself? Do you want him to take a bath with less fussing? Think about your own goals for your child and be willing to carry through on recommendations to meet those goals.
- Respect your therapist's time and personal needs. Do not call her every other day with minor questions that can wait until the next session. Do not call her at home late at night, very early in the morning, or on weekends unless absolutely necessary.
- Reschedule your session if your child is ill or has a contagious condition such as conjunctivitis, even if you think your child might enjoy the session. No therapist wants to get sick or pass your child's germs to other children.
- Follow through on recommendations. A therapist can't work magic in just a few hours a week. If you don't agree with or understand a recommendation, or don't feel you can follow through for any reason, discuss it with her.
- Remember that your therapist has in-depth training and expertise. What she does may seem like child's play, but it is artfully structured play with a therapeutic purpose. If you are curious, ask her to explain how the toys and techniques she is using help meet goals, and how you can support her work with your child. You can do this in a way that's not nosy—and learn a lot.
- Don't engage in tangential conversation while she is working with your child; it might distract either the OT or your child.

- If you need to speak with the therapist at length, let her know before the session starts. A therapist plans sessions carefully and often has to move quickly from session to session. If you need more time to talk than usual, she must schedule it in.
- Let your therapist know what you find works and what doesn't. You may have a special way you help your child calm down that your therapist could use too.
- Give your therapist feedback—both positive and constructive. Let her know when you are pleased with how things are going and when you aren't. Let her know about special situations that are hard for your child, such as that every time your child goes to church or synagogue, she gets rambunctious and uncontrollable. Therapists aren't mind readers, and they are all committed to doing the very best for you and your child. Thank her when she deserves a thank-you!
- Provide a clean, safe environment for your therapist to work in. Reschedule the session if that's the only time the exterminator can come (avoid subjecting your child, too, to these toxic chemicals!). Make sure there's soap available for the therapist to wash her hands with at the end of the session.

THE THERAPIST-PARENT COLLABORATION

Don't make the mistake of thinking that your child will be "cured" because she receives OT once a week—or even if her issues are severe and she gets OT three times a week with speech-language therapy three times a week, PT twice a week, and special education every single day. Changing a person's neurological wiring takes time, patience, and consistency, even when that child is very young and her nervous system is most malleable.

To achieve the best results, even the most talented teachers and therapists need active involvement and follow-through from you—as well as other family members, teachers, and those who interact with your child regularly. You're the one who lives with your child and deals with him twenty-four hours a day, seven days a week. If your child has trouble sleeping, or refuses to take a bath, or has a meltdown at a birthday party, you're the one who will handle it—not one of your child's therapists.

If your child receives more than one kind of therapy, make sure the therapists all collaborate and communicate with one another. If your child's OT has him practicing biting skills using licorice strings, for example, and the speech therapist is teaching licking skills *without* biting down on the licorice, and you don't want your child eating licorice at all, your child is going to be totally confused and neither therapist will get anywhere. So you all have to collaborate. *You* are the common thread here, so make sure you and everyone who works with your child are all on the same page. In fact, you may want to bring a notebook to your child's sessions so that the various therapists can leave short notes for one another.

Be an Active Participant

When your child first begins therapy, try to be there consistently to watch and learn and ask questions. We cannot emphasize enough how important it is for you to observe and participate in these sessions, unless your presence is too distracting for your child, as determined by you and the therapist. This is easiest to do when your child is in early intervention when therapy occurs at home or in a clinic setting where you bring your child. Once you understand what the therapist is doing and why, and are clear on what you are supposed to be doing to carry over techniques and strategies into everyday life, you should still attend therapy every so often, especially when therapy goals and techniques used are changing. For example, once your child has achieved the goal of being able to sit at the dinner table for fifteen minutes, you and the therapist will jointly need to set a new goal: perhaps to expand upon the types of foods he will eat. At the end of each session, speak with the therapist to find out what was accomplished, and how you can help. Let the therapist know your concerns and your observations of your child, and ask questions, while being respectful of time limitations.

You can help to coordinate therapy between therapists and make sure you are doing your part to help your child. You are, in effect, the team leader. One mom, Michelle, says, "The OT really needs to hear what is working or not working after the kid goes home. One OT we worked with was doing a lot of movement activities like spinning and my son can only take so much of it, and it has to be followed by tons of deep pressure input, or he gets really wired. By communicating with her we were able to resolve the problem." (You and your OT should always be on the lookout for signs of sensory overload, as described on page 110.)

Remember to include your primary child-care provider (such as your nanny, au pair, or babysitter) in this process, because she also needs to learn how to help your child and discuss her observations and concerns with the therapists.

If your child receives therapy in an OT clinic, sensory gym, or privately in your home, you will need to encourage the OT to communicate with your child's teachers (and any school-based therapists if your child also receives OT in school). Set up a meeting at the start of every school year to establish joint goals and strategies, and encourage ongoing communication between therapists and the school. Some parents find it extremely useful to have their nonschool therapists consult with teachers, make frequent classroom observations, or even treat their child at school from time to time. Not only does this help your child carry over what he's learning at home or in the clinic and gain new skills within the context of school, it also helps to identify discrepancies between behavior at school and at home. For example, a teacher told Lindsey that a child Lindsey works with, Melissa, refused to join the other kindergarteners during dress-up time. Lindsey knew that at home, Melissa adored dress-ups, especially putting on her Little Mermaid costume. Lindsey was then able to advise the teacher to have Melissa put on her costume before or after the other kindergarteners did, since it was the chaos of twelve children fumbling around in the costume bin that made Melissa withdraw from this fun activity.

School-based occupational therapy uses an educational model in which therapy goals must be related to accessing the school curriculum. We'll talk more about this in Chapter 15: Advocating for Your Child at School. For now, though, bear in mind that if your child sees an OT at school, this therapist will also want to know what's happening outside of school and your perspective on what's going on with your child. For example, a school-based OT would probably never know that your child throws a tantrum every time you brush her hair in the morning unless you tell her. This may be a key factor in why your daughter arrives at school upset and wired each day. Because it impacts your daughter's school experience, the OT can work on this issue with you.

Finally, the older a child is, the more he is able to be part of the team. As your child matures, he can take more responsibility for his sensory needs, and may require less frequent direct, one-to-one therapy. You may find, for example, that your preteen or teenager needs to see the OT only once a week, or once a month, or just every so often—especially once she gets the hang of what she needs to do to make herself feel and function better. This places more responsibility for following through on therapy interventions on your child's shoulders—and yours. Most older kids incorporate sensory smart techniques quite quickly, and enjoy feeling in control.

If You're Unhappy with a Therapist

If you feel uncomfortable or angry with your OT or other therapist, talk with her, not at her or around her. Don't, for instance, bring up concerns with the person who coordinates your child's therapy first before speaking with the therapist herself. The best way to speak with a therapist whose behavior makes you uncomfortable is to start with the assumption that there's something you're not "getting" or that she's not communicating, rather than assuming that the therapist is doing a bad job or doesn't like you or your child. Accusations will put her on the defensive and can lead to unproductive conversations. Give the therapist the benefit of the doubt and say, "When you (*state the therapist's behavior*), I felt (*how you felt or how you think your child felt*). Is it possible to (*how you would like the therapist to work in the future*)?" Some great questions that will not put her on the defensive but encourage her to come up with productive solutions are: Does this make sense to you? What do you think? What should we do? What are your ideas?

Carl Jung wrote, "Psychotherapy has taught us that in the final reckoning it is not knowledge, not technical skill, that has a curative effect, but the personality of the doctor."[1] The same holds true for the therapist who works with your child. Good technique and good intentions are crucial, but they are inadequate in and of themselves. Find someone who is very skilled and who will also love your child and create a safe, warm environment in which your child can express himself and flourish. Because only a therapist—or any caregiver for that matter—with an open, loving heart and a good eye and ear for spoken and unspoken needs will really be able to help.

The truth is, some people in the helping professions lack people skills. This does not necessarily make them bad therapists—just bad for you and your child. A negative relationship yields negative results. If you are unable to work through communication blockages or just feel "creeped out" by this person, move on.

The Magic Ingredients

As a parent, or a therapist, or a teacher, we all sometimes feel that if only we knew more tricks or had more inside information, we could fix a child's problems. It's true that you need tools and techniques to become sensory smart, and that's why you're reading this book. Yet, ultimately, the real gift that you offer your child—*you*—is infinitely more important than what you *do* for your child.

You can have an arsenal of techniques and thousands of dollars' worth of sensory-based toys and equipment and yet, if you do not observe his behavior for subtle clues as to what's up, listen to your child to learn what really makes him "go off," and let him know he is loved and supported no matter what, all your sensory recipes and techniques will not have their full effect. Compassion, patience, and unconditional love are the real magic ingredients for working with any child, especially one with sensory issues.

CHAPTER 6

The Sensory Diet of Daily Activities

Getting OT for your child is wonderful and will make a huge difference for your child. But these few hours a week of therapy alone won't do the job. It's crucial for your child to get needed sensory input at regular intervals throughout the day, every day. This input calms and helps organize his nervous system. Think of how great you feel after a good workout and a shower: focused, centered, and yet energized too.

OTs use the term *sensory diet* (coined by OT Patricia Wilbarger) to describe a personalized schedule of sensory activities that give your child the sensory fuel his body needs to get into this organized state and stay there. By providing beneficial sensory input throughout the day, you can create profound, long-lasting changes in your child's nervous system, which in time will become permanent.

GIVING YOUR CHILD'S BODY WHAT IT NEEDS

Just as you wouldn't wait until dinnertime to give your child all the nutrition she needs for the day, you also can't wait until evening to feed your child's sensory needs. You've got to keep her "full" all day long so she can feel her best. Otherwise, she'll act out because she's starved for sensory input, or withdraw because she's feeling bombarded by sensations that she hasn't been primed to handle. Tactile input before she puts clothes against her skin, or predictable and enjoyable movement activities that prepare her for the day ahead will help regulate her system. Sensory input just prior to, or during, other interventions such as speech therapy or applied behavior analysis (an intensive behavioral instruction program often used for autistic children) can boost their effectiveness. Simply hoping your child will keep it together until she is done with daycare or school and can get the sensory input she needs during OT or at home with you puts enormous stress on her, so a sensory diet throughout the day is absolutely essential for her well-being.

An OT will help you by using her advanced training and clinical skills to develop a sensory diet for your child that easily fits into your family routines. Use your own sensory smarts to work with the OT, and be sure to involve all the people who spend a major portion of the day with your child: teachers, daycare workers, full-time babysitters, your spouse, grandparents, etc. Explain to these key people why it is so important for them to carry through on sensory-based activities, and demonstrate how to help your child get what her body needs.

The guiding principle is to give your child the right kind of sensory input in controlled doses so she won't resort to maladaptive ways of getting what she needs. For example, if you give your child with vestibular issues safe opportunities for movement, she won't be bouncing off the walls when the teacher needs her to sit down and do a math worksheet. The child who tunes out when she goes on sensory overload may be able to stay tuned in if given regular opportunities to take a breather in a quiet space with soft lights. If your child stays over at Grandma's house and takes a soothing bath and gets firmly rubbed down with a soft towel, she may not give Grandma such a hard time about going to sleep. If your listless child engages in alerting activities, she may be able to sit up and attend to the movie she's been whining for you to take her to see.

Infants, young children, teens, and grown-ups alike can all benefit from a sensory diet. As an adult, you may be unaware that you, too, have a sensory diet you give yourself without even thinking. You may sip coffee and take a hot shower to fully wake up, or you may wind down at the end of the day with a glass of wine or cup of soothing herbal tea. Your child doesn't necessarily know how to do this—or, as is often the case, she isn't *allowed* to follow her natural drive to do this for herself when she needs to. A child who simply has to get up and stretch a moment, or take a one-minute walk to keep her body available for learning, may be chastised to "sit still" and "stop fidgeting" for longer periods than her nervous system can handle. That's why it's especially important that teachers are willing to help carry through your child's sensory diet.

Most children with sensory issues have both up times and down times, but usually tend to be *generally* either more hyped up or more sluggish. Some of the same activities can meet both sets of needs. "Heavy work" (proprioceptive input) in particular helps kids calm down. There are countless ways to incorporate heavy work into everyday routines: carrying heavy objects, playing tug of war, moving furniture, wheelbarrow walking, doing push-ups, molding clay, chewing gum, or eating crunchy pretzels are just a few of the possibilities.

Of course, proprioception is only one ingredient in the diet. Your child may also need visual, auditory, tactile, vestibular, and even smell input. How the ingredients are all blended together depends on your child's unique makeup and needs.

SENSORY DIET INGREDIENTS

Here are some sensory-rich activities to get you started. You can modify them depending on the age, arousal level (does he need stimulation or relaxation?), whether he is in school, at home, or away, and whether you have special equipment available or not. If your child currently receives OT, discuss with his occupational therapist which activities would be most appropriate for him. If you're waiting to start services, try out some of these activities to see what works best.

Just as you would never force-feed your child, never coerce your child into a sensory diet activity. However, if your child rejects an activity—for instance, a massage before bedtime—because his body doesn't want it, that's different from him saying no to a massage because he would prefer to stay up an extra half hour watching a Harry Potter movie. If you don't mind him watching the movie, and he is relaxing nicely, you could massage his legs while he's watching. Or, if your child is feeling under the weather, don't demand that he jump on a trampoline just because it's on the agenda. Sensory needs are inconsistent, after all, and change from day to day. There's a time and place for everything, and you need to be flexible about giving your child what he needs when he needs it.

If your child tends to avoid sensory activities, you will have to be especially careful about presenting them in a form that she can tolerate. A child who completely balks at touching sticky stuff might be open to playing with stickers featuring her favorite characters. If you can make the activity fun, and keep the challenge level "just right," you'll be more likely to motivate her to get the sensory input she needs.

There's no cookbook for a sensory diet, but you and your OT will want to add in a bit of each type of ingredient, adjust accordingly to taste—and convenience—and make changes to your recipe over time. Then too, just as when you're cooking, you may need to improvise if you are missing a piece of equipment: when you're stuck in a doctor's office, or on a boat, and your child needs comforting and organizing input, you can't exactly pull out a mini-trampoline! However, you can hold his hands as he hops in place, or play a clapping game, or give him some wonderful bear hugs.

Please note that many of the items mentioned in this chapter are available from therapy catalogs, some of which are listed in Part Five's Sources for Useful Toys, Equipment, and Products.

Proprioceptive Input

Heavy work activities provide joint compression and traction and help us feel grounded in our bodies. Of course, the type of activity you will use depends on your child's age, physical ability, and interests.

- Have your child jump on a mini-trampoline or from a stable chair or sofa onto a crash pad of pillows, cushions, or beanbag chairs. For safety, you might want to try a mini-trampoline that comes with a handle (available from www.integrationscatalog.com and other sources).
- Encourage her to do push-ups (on the floor or against a wall) or, if she's older, supervised weight training (ask your OT or PT if this is appropriate for your child). For younger kids, try wheelbarrow walking: hold your child by the ankles or thighs and have her walk on her hands across a room or even up a flight of stairs, with her legs straight if possible. Have her do donkey kicks, crab walking, frog jumps, and heavy marching. Babies also benefit from weight-bearing activities, such as propping up on their forearms to look at an interesting mobile or using a little muscle power to push a stuffed toy off the changing table.
- A toddler can push his own stroller, and a stronger child can push a stroller or cart filled with weighted objects such as groceries. A much older child can push a lawn mower or wheelbarrow full of dirt.
- Your child can wear a backpack or fanny pack filled with toys or books (remember, not *too* heavy!).
- A young child can hammer wooden pegs into a peg bench while an older child can do real construction projects. An older child can put ice cubes in a plastic bag and smash them with a mallet or hammer for iced lemonade.
- Throwing gives the joints a lot of traction (pulling apart) input. A child who throws toys around the room or at other children can get

Hold your child's ankles (or thighs or hips if she needs more support) as she "wheelbarrow walks."

the same traction by throwing blocks or beanbags into a bucket, rocks into a pond, or a basketball into a hoop. Hanging from monkey bars also provides excellent traction input.

· Your child can bounce while sitting on a therapy ball or use a hopping ball with a handle to bounce around the room. Older children can bounce on pogo sticks.

· Games like hopscotch and tug-of-war, play wrestling, and sports like swimming, biking, skating, martial arts, and skiing also provide heavy work.

· Cymbals and drums are great, but oh so noisy! An older child can use a drum pad with headphones so only he hears it (keep the volume low to protect his ears).

· Housework is great: a child can help wash windows and tabletops, vacuum, load or unload the dishwasher or washing machine full of wet and heavy clothes, or take out the trash.

· Play catch with water-filled balloons, weighted balls, and even a large therapy ball, and play hot potato or beanbag catch.

- Your OT may recommend using a weighted blanket, vest, or lap pad, which you can make or buy from a therapy catalog.

Vestibular Input

Vestibular input can be the most intense, long-lasting type of sensory input. It can be obtained by spinning and swinging, and to a lesser extent, any type of movement.

Swinging that is slow and rhythmic is usually calming, while fast, erratic swinging is alerting. Try various types of swings: standard playground type, tire swing, hammock swing, and ropes. Try different movements, such as forward and back, side to side, and untwisting after you've wound up the swing chains. Have your child try lying over the swing on his belly. Stop the swing every so often to allow your child to integrate sensations from her inner ear. Face your child and assess her reaction to swinging and stopping. Does she make eye contact? Laugh? Get angry? Is she dizzy? Overstimulated? Ready for more? A child who is underreactive to vestibular system input and begs you to push him harder and faster may unexpectedly switch into sensory overload and have a very hard time calming down. Learn to recognize when he needs to stop swinging *before* he reaches this point.

Try different types of swings to provide various vestibular sensations, but be aware that your child may need a lot of patience and encouragement to get on an unfamiliar swing. A hard, flat bench-type swing may be unnerving at first to a child used to flexible, leather strap seats; or she might take a long time graduating from enclosed baby swings to open swings.

Never force your child onto a swing. Let him stop when he wants to. If your child has a highly reactive vestibular system (is very uncomfortable with movement), modify the activity. If he can't tolerate regular playground swings, he may be able to deal with a platform or tire swing, or swinging gently in your lap with a lot of body support. Keep in mind too that the distractions of the playground—the sights, the light, the noise, the movement around him—can make a child skittish about getting on a swing, so he may be more tolerant of swinging in a less hectic environment: home, a sensory gym, or the playground during off-peak hours. Sensory gyms have many alternative kinds of swings, including large platform, bolster, net, and cocoon swings, and you can buy such swings for your home and hang them from a ceiling beam or swing stand; see photos on pages 390–391.

Spinning is also a great source of vestibular input. While swinging provides linear input, spinning gives rotary (around and around) input, which an oversensitive child may need given to him in graded doses. Your child can get excellent spinning input by using a chair hammock, a swiveling office chair, a Sit 'n Spin (also great for motor planning and strengthening), or a lazy Susan–like spinning disk toy such as Dizzy Disc Jr. (which is generally easier for children to propel by themselves than the Sit 'n Spin; see photos on page 392). As with swinging, it's important that you stop and restart any spinning movement every so often. With sustained movement (like riding in a car or airplane), the inner ear fluids and sensory receptors stabilize and habituate so that movement is no longer actively felt. It's movement that starts and stops and starts and stops within a relatively short time frame that gives the most information to vestibular receptors.

Other ways to have fun while giving vestibular input:

- Have your child run in circles, do cartwheels, ride a carousel or even a roller coaster, hang upside down on the monkey bars, roll down a grassy or snowy hill, go sledding, ride a bike, or skate.
- Hold your young child's arms and legs and spin him around or have him do a "monkey" flip: hold his hands as he faces you and have him walk up your thighs and flip over.
- Drag or swing your child around in a sturdy sheet or blanket or heavy-duty laundry basket, or push him around in a wheelbarrow.
- Use a four-wheeled scooter board to go down an appropriately angled ramp (you can have him crash into some mats at the end for excellent proprioceptive input). Older kids can use a two-wheeled scooter or skateboard, which are great for motor planning.
- A therapy ball can be a useful vestibular tool for younger children and even babies. Stabilizing the ball with your own body, you can have your child roll on her tummy or back with gentle back-and-forth and side-to-side movements. Bouncing your child while she is seated on the ball may be enough vestibular stimulation for her (be sure to stabilize the ball and hold her at the hips). Doing an "airplane" on a therapy ball can help a child with low muscle tone (hypotonia): stabilize the ball and your child as she lies with her tummy on it and stretches out her limbs and raises her head (see photo on page 393).
- A rocking chair can be soothing to infants, kids, and adults alike.

WATCH OUT FOR SIGNS OF SENSORY OVERLOAD

As a sensory smart parent, you know that your child with sensory issues has a very quirky nervous system and may react strongly to sensory input. Give a child with an underreactive vestibular system a lot of movement input, and she may overreact. Give a child who withdraws from touch lots of tactile stimulation that she accepts because she trusts you and has an intrinsic desire to explore these sensations, and she may have a rebound reaction. Be on the lookout for undesired nervous system responses such as . . .

- higher level of activity or sensitivity than is typical;
- increased distractibility, disorientation, or confusion;
- nausea or vomiting;
- sudden paleness or flushing—or sweaty or clammy skin;
- rapid breathing or slower, shallow breaths;
- undesired decrease or increase in muscle tone;
- unexpected drowsiness;
- tremors, glazed look in the eyes, or other signs of a possible seizure.

Such nervous system responses are rare, but they underscore why it's so important to work with a knowledgeable OT who can help you design a sensory diet and teach you how to counteract any negative effects. If you see any of the above signs, stop what your child is doing right away and provide deep pressure input to normalize the arousal centers in the brain. If your child unexpectedly falls asleep and you are not able to arouse her, get medical attention immediately.

Tactile Input

Tactile input affects the sense of touch and includes texture, temperature, pressure, and more. Don't forget that the tactile system includes not only the skin covering your child's body but also skin linings, such as inside the mouth. In general, a child who is hypersensitive to touch will be more able to tolerate firm touch than light touch. However, your child may love tickling and gentle caresses from you even if she dislikes unexpected touch of any type from other people.

- Make a "sandwich" by firmly pressing on your child's arms, legs, and back with pillows or sofa cushions.
- Create a "burrito" by rolling her up snugly in a blanket, or let her crawl inside a Body Sox, made of Lycra (see photo on page 395).
- "Roll out cookie dough" by evenly rolling a big ball firmly over each limb and back.
- Let your child use the playground sandbox or create your own at home, filling a large bin with dry beans and rice or Styrofoam peanuts. Encourage your child to explore it with his hands and feet. Set up a construction site for trucks. Bury small toys and ask him to find them with his eyes closed.
- Have your child play with inexpensive, interlocking foam alphabet mats—a toy that can be stepped on, thrown, and thrashed around on, providing tactile input safely.
- Encourage water play. You can add food coloring, bubbles, and Silly String to increase interest. Use cups, strainers, ladles, plastic fish, and other toys your child enjoys. Taking a bath is an excellent opportunity for a child to get tactile input from the water as well as from items used in the bath, from squishy water squirters to boats, funnels, cups, foam letters that stick to the wall and tub, shaving cream or foamy soap, soap crayons, and both smooth and nubby washcloths.
- Play with foamy soap or shaving cream on a table, adding sand for extra texture. Use fingerpaint, play with glitter glue, mix cookie dough and cake batter, and so on. Practice writing or drawing with a finger in various textures—shaving cream, chocolate pudding, fingerpaint, wet and dry sand, and on carpet squares. If your child is repulsed by a substance, don't force her to touch it. Let her use a paintbrush, stick, or a toy for cautious exploration before gently prodding her to try touching with her hands.
- Use modeling clay such as Play-Doh. The classic Play-Doh Fun Factory, a lever contraption that you press down on to squeeze out "snakes" of Play-Doh, provides excellent proprioceptive input as well.
- Encourage your child to feel various textures with her hands and help her label them—velvet is soft, Velcro is scratchy, marble is smooth and hard, and so on.

- Dress up in fun costumes to get used to the feel of unfamiliar clothing. Play with makeup and face paint.
- Garden and repot indoor plants.
- Use vibration: a vibrating teether (such as the one available from The First Years), vibrating toothbrush, a vibrating pen (like the Squiggle Wiggle Writer), foot massagers, vibrating pillows, vibrating hairbrushes, and toy massagers like the Vibrating Bug, a vibrating ball like the Bumble Ball, or any handheld vibrator. Vibration often works like a massage on your child's skin.
- Older children can sculpt, sew, weave, crochet, or knit; create a scrapbook (lots of pasting and working with different textures); use sandpaper to smooth a woodworking project; or take a very cool or very warm shower or bath.
- Don't forget the skin inside the mouth! Let your child eat Pop Rocks candy or drink plain seltzer to experience bubbles in her mouth (you can flavor it with lemon, cranberry juice, etc.). Encourage your child to eat a wide variety of textures and consistencies. Eating very cold and even frozen foods like Popsicles and frozen juice cubes really wakes up the mouth.
- Give your child deep pressure input through massages and firm, full-body bear hugs, squeezing your child as tolerated under a pillow, cushion, beanbag chair, or ball. Give your child firm pressure in the palms of her hands and soles of her feet.
- Squeezing an object can give soothing tactile input. "Fidgets" such as squishy balls or Koosh balls are available practically everywhere these days and can be used for self-calming when your child needs a way to redirect his hands. You can also give your child a "worry stone" to hold and rub if he finds this soothing, or even a swatch of fabric, such as velvet, satin, or corduroy, which you can sew right into a pocket if need be.
- Ask your OT whether a "brushing program" is right for your child. If so, have the OT teach you and other caregivers how to do it— not just demonstrating it for you, but having the OT brush *you* and observing you brushing your child. The pressure to be used is much firmer than you might expect from just watching the procedure.
- You can also use a soft scrub brush or soapy washcloth, nylon bath scrubby, or loofah to desensitize your child's skin and increase body awareness. While long, firm, downward strokes (such as shoulder to hand) are usually recommended, your child may sometimes prefer gentle strokes and circular movements. Allowing your child to exert

some control over these touches can be very empowering and a pleasant break from touch experiences he can't control.

Weighted and Pressure Materials

Many children and adults respond positively to feeling heaviness on their bodies such as from blankets, a heavy winter coat, or a loaded backpack. Others prefer tightness such as snug-fitting bike shorts, neoprene wet suits, or tights with a control top. You can find many pressure garments such as neoprene pressure vests and tank tops in therapy catalogs. Weighted products that you can buy from therapy catalogs (or make yourself) include weighted vests, weighted belts, lap pads, dress-up costumes, ankle weights, shoulder wraps, and plush toys.

Weighted vests are a very popular type of weighted wearable, especially for school. Studies have been conducted to assess the best body weight percentage for children and adults, but like so much else, each person has her own preferences and sensory threshold. You should consult with a trained therapist, who is likely to recommend that the weight be about 5 percent to 10 percent of the child's body weight[1] (so a child who weighs 50 pounds should wear a weighted vest of between 2 and 5 pounds of weight). Weighted vests, like backpacks, should certainly never exceed 15 percent of body weight to avoid fatigue, breathing problems, and stress on the neck, shoulder, and back. Weighted vests should be put on and taken off at regular intervals so the body and brain do not habituate to and thus ignore the added sensory input. While most therapists recommend a wearing schedule of twenty minutes on, twenty minutes off, some studies show that wearing a weighted vest for up to two hours may work best for enhancing behavior and attention. Again, please be sure to consult with a trained OT or PT about the right amount of weight (most vests have weights you can add or remove) and the right wearing schedule for your child, likely to be somewhere between twenty minutes (twenty minutes on, twenty minutes off) to two hours (two hours on, two hours off).

While your child may initially be distracted by the new input into his sensory receptors, in a short time, he may well find that he enjoys wearing his "cozy vest." You will need to take off the vest every so often, but make sure you don't simply end up disrupting him because this defeats the whole purpose. For example, if a child is seated in floor time for thirty minutes and is actively engaged in building with blocks along with some classmates, don't interrupt him and break his concentration just because the twenty minutes are up and you want to remove the weighted vest. Instead, plan on having him wear it for a specific activity. You might decide that since your child is so squirmy when you read books together, this is the perfect time for him to wear his weighted vest, or it might be very helpful during circle time at school. Remember, it may take a bit of trial and error to find the correct weight and wearing time.

Neoprene pressure garments can be worn for longer periods because they move along with the child. Lap pads and shoulder wraps that are easily removed by the child can also be used more freely. However, it's again best to save these for specific situations that are hard for your child to handle. For example, if your child has trouble sitting still at the dinner table, you might have her use her "lap buddy." It might give her the calming input she needs plus a sensory cue that she needs to stay seated (we're not suggesting that you weigh down your child so that she *can't* get up—just adding a few pounds of soothing input that might make it easier for her to remain at the table). For some kids, sitting on an inflatable seat cushion like a Swiss Disc or Movin' Sit *plus* using a weighted lap pad might be a winning combination.

There are now many adorable weighted toys kids can carry around or wear on their shoulders. There are even weighted costumes kids can use for dress-ups and Halloween, available in catalogs such as www.funandfunction.com and www.integrationscatalog.com. Weighted belts like the Miracle Belt (www.miraclebelt.com) can give important sensory input that not only grounds the child, but can also be worn in a way that helps with gait and even toe walking when used under the supervision of a PT or OT.

Weighted blankets are very powerful sensory tools that can be quite calming and relaxing. Some children (and adults) like to wrap themselves in a weighted blanket while they're reading, watching television, and so on. For some people, the deep pressure input is so soothing that it can be miraculous in helping them to fall asleep. Many adults with sensory issues find that they sleep better using a weighted blanket all night, or even simply a heavy blanket.

Please be aware that as great as they are, weighted blankets can be dangerous if misused. We *strongly* urge you to follow these guidelines with a child:

- Keep the weight of the blanket appropriate to the child's weight, size, respiratory status, and physical/cognitive ability to take it off. It should be extremely easy for the person to remove the blanket!

- Never, under any circumstance, cover a child's head and neck with a weighted blanket. You must always be able to observe that the child is breathing and comfortable.
- If you want to roll up the child in a blanket, his head and neck must be completely out of the blanket and you (or the therapist or other trained person) should remain by his side, watching out for any negative reactions such as increased anxiety, restlessness, or paling or reddening skin.
- The child must *want* to use the weighted blanket (despite some initial hesitation) and should use verbal or nonverbal communication to indicate her consent to using it.
- A weighted blanket or other weighted item should never, ever be used as a restraint or punishment for a child.
- If your child has breathing, cardiac, or circulatory problems, epilepsy, extreme low muscle tone, fragile skin, or other medical issue, discuss this with your OT or PT when considering a weighted wearable.

You can make weighted items yourself (see www.ot-innovations.com and other Web sites for instructions on making blankets and toys) or purchase weighted blankets from makers such as Weighted Wearables (www.weightedwearables.com, 715-505-3651), Dream Catcher (www.weightedblanket.net, 406-777-2267), and Stitches By Anne (www.stitchesbyanne.info, 478-719-3149).

*Brushing: the Wilbarger Protocol.** While "brushing" a child with a surgical scrub brush every so often is a common sensory diet activity, there's a special method used for severe sensory defensiveness. Julia and Patricia Wilbarger define *sensory defensiveness* as "a constellation of symptoms that involve avoidance reactions to sensations from any sensory modality." The Wilbarger brushing protocol consists of giving deep pressure with a particular soft bristled brush applied in a specific method followed by joint compressions. The entire procedure is repeated every ninety minutes to two hours, depending on the child's tolerance and scheduling practicality. This is a very intense approach designed to help a deeply sensory defensive person, and requires the OT to have specialized training and very good clinical skills. If this protocol is called for, your OT will give you (or help you

---

*Now officially called the Deep Pressure and Proprioceptive Technique (DPPT).

buy) the right brush, teach you how to do it, observe you to make sure you use the correct procedure, and monitor how your child is doing. While there has been little scientific research on the effectiveness of this technique, many OTs report positive results. As with any sensory diet activity, be wary of pushing your child past her limits of tolerating the activity. And always work with an OT to be sure you're brushing correctly.

THE SQUEEZE MACHINE

"As far back as I can remember, I always hated to be hugged. I wanted to experience the good feeling of being hugged, but it was just too overwhelming. It was like a great, all-engulfing tidal wave of stimulation, and I reacted like a wild animal."

—TEMPLE GRANDIN, *Thinking in Pictures*[2]

Temple Grandin has written and lectured extensively on what it is like to be an autistic person with sensory problems. As a child, she craved physical pressure, getting it at first by wrapping herself in blankets and then under sofa cushions. Visiting her aunt's ranch in Arizona, she observed how cattle led into a squeeze chute for vaccinations relaxed when pressed between the panels. She persuaded her aunt to let her try the squeeze chute herself. After a few moments of "sheer panic," she experienced a "wave of relaxation" and felt "very calm and serene" afterward. "This was the first time I ever felt really comfortable in my own skin," she writes. She then built a squeeze machine for people and has improved on the design over the years.

Grandin and others have conducted research to confirm her initially intuitive findings about the squeeze machine.[3] Grandin's Squeeze Machine can be obtained commercially for about two thousand dollars from the Therafin Corporation (www.therafin .com; 800-843-7234). The Steamroller, which provides deep pressure to the front and back of the body rather than the sides as in the Squeeze Machine, is available from www.southpaw enterprises.com. (See the photo of the Steamroller Deluxe on page 394.)

Oral-Motor Activities

From infancy to adulthood, we all gain comfort and self-regulate through oral activities such as sucking on a nipple, pacifier, thumb, or hard candy. So don't forget your child's mouth when thinking about a sensory diet that feeds all of her needs. There are many ways to integrate oral sensory input into your daily routine. For **sucking**, use a variety of straws—regular straws, crazy straws, coffee stirrers, and even sports bottles—to suck liquids of varying thickness from water to milkshakes. Resistive **biting** and **chewing** give the mouth lots of tactile and proprioceptive input. As your child's mouth skills develop, you can add items such as fruit leather and pretzels, and nonfood items such as Chewlery (chewable jewelry), Chewy Tubes, Theratubing cut and placed on the end of a pen, and ChewEase Pencil Toppers can be used discreetly by older children (all available from therapy catalogs in the back of this book; see photos on page 395).

If your child has oral defensiveness, your SLP or OT can show you how to desensitize her mouth. Likewise, if your child is *under*responsive to mouth sensations, you can learn ways to increase her sensitivity.

Don't Forget Breathing! Children with low muscle tone need opportunities to work on their respiration skills. Low muscle tone can affect breathing muscles too, resulting in shallow breaths. Learning to breathe deeply helps your child stay calm, and controlling respiration lets him speak clearly and in longer sentences.

Blowing is also an important mouth skill, and can often transform a bad mood into a pleasant one. Have your child blow on his food to cool it down, use whistles and pinwheels, blow feathers off your hand, have a race blowing cotton balls across a tabletop, or blow through a straw into a bowl of soapy water to create a mountain of bubbles. A young child will love blowing out birthday candles over and over on a cupcake or make-believe Play-Doh cake. BLOpen markers are lots of fun too. They can get very messy—the ink gets on little hands and saliva gets all over—but are a great way to practice blowing and also motor planning as the child needs to blow and move the pen at the same time. Practice alternating blowing with inhaling to encourage breath control. Toys like Whistle Sippers can be blown like whistles and used as a sucking straw too.

Yoga is a wonderful way to learn to regulate the breath and use it to relax, and there are DVDs and classes especially designed for children.

Auditory Input

Auditory input is what we hear and is connected with our sense of movement. In addition to listening to various types of music, both recorded and live, here are some ways to get calming and organizing auditory input.

- Encourage your child to listen to nature. Go to the beach. Listen to a thunderstorm or the wind.
- Have him listen to recordings of natural sounds such as a rainstorm, waves crashing against the beach, or animals in the forest. Sometimes natural sound recordings also feature light instrumentation with flutes, keyboards, etc.
- Play a listening game: you and your child sit very quietly and try to identify the sounds you hear (a car in the distance, a bird singing) and identify where the sounds are coming from.
- Have her listen to recordings of sounds and music specially engineered to promote calm, focus, energy, or creativity. Check into Hemi-Sync recordings (from www.hemi-sync.com) and CDs such as *Mozart for Modulation*.
- Experiment with different types of music, live and recorded. A child who can't tolerate symphony music might love reggae or Celtic harp music. A child who can't abide the sound of a piano might enjoy playing or listening to a toy piano or a xylophone.
- Encourage your child to learn to play a musical instrument.
- For a child with auditory sensitivity, controlling the sounds she hears can be especially helpful. If your child is fearful of loud noises, let him control the volume on the stereo, exploring soft versus loud music.
- Get a white-noise machine, tabletop rocks-and-water fountain, or aquarium.
- Your OT or SLP may recommend a therapeutic listening program that uses specially engineered music and headphones. See Chapter 13: Complementary Therapies and Approaches for more information on therapeutic listening.

Visual Input

Visual input includes various sights, colors, contrasts, and movement. If your child is visually distractible, simplify the visual field in his home or school environment for a calming effect. Alternately, if your child seems visually tuned out, add brightly colored objects to attract visual attention. For example, a child who has trouble getting jazzed up to play energetically may be attracted by a brightly painted toy chest filled with colorful toys. Watch out at all times for visual overload.

- Use dim lighting for calming and relaxation. Experiment with colored lightbulbs to see if there's one that's right for your child's visual needs. Consider various types of lightbulbs (incandescent, full spectrum, halogen).
- Give your child visual novelty that's within her range of tolerance. A child who lives in a city will be amazed by the sights and sounds of the country and vice versa.
- Have your child bring a hat with a wide brim or visor and/or sunglasses outdoors on a sunny day or if you'll be outside when the sun is low in the sky and creating a lot of glare.
- Respect your child's color preferences. If she's happy wearing purple, let her wear it every day. Avoid toys, clothes, and towels in colors that your child finds stress inducing such as bright orange, yellow, and red (or whatever colors bother her).
- Play games that help develop visual skills: flashlight tag, pushing dry spaghetti or pick-up sticks through a straw, and catch (use a balloon, which moves more slowly than a ball does, or a Nerf, SloMo, or Gertie Ball, which won't hurt if it hits your child). Prewriting activities such as mazes, dot-to-dot books, and tracing all encourage hands to work with eyes. See www.activitypad.com for free downloads of mazes and connect-the-dots pictures.
- If your child has difficulty with visual skills such as convergence and tracking, your optometrist and OT will teach you specific vision exercises to do with your child at home (which may supplement in-office vision therapy). See Chapter 13: Complementary Therapies and Approaches.

Smell (Olfactory) Input

- Certain odors can stimulate, calm, or send a smell sensitive person into sensory overload. Explore scents with your child to find the ones that work best to meet your goal: whether it's to calm down or to wake up. While everyone has their preferences, vanilla and rose are generally calming.* Peppermint and lemon are usually invigorating. Let's say your child needs help staying calm and loves vanilla. You can use vanilla soap, bath oil, and lotion at bath time, vanilla candles or oil in an aromatherapy machine, or a scented eye pillow at bedtime.

- If your child is overtired at the mall and you know scents help, carry along her favorite scent or stop into a store that sells scented candles and soaps.
- Play a smelling game with your child. Have her close her eyes or wear a blindfold and try to identify smells such as maple syrup, apple, peanut butter, hyacinths.
- You might try using very pure vanilla oil in your nursery with your child to see if it helps him sleep, especially if he's a preemie or has frequent sleep awakenings. A study in a French neonatal ICU found that pleasant odors, particularly vanilla, led to improved breathing during sleep for premature infants and reduced awakenings due to sleep apnea.[4]
- Life stinks sometimes. Accept your child's opinion about something he thinks smells gross. Then help him find something that smells nice.

Taste Input

Taste input is strongly influenced by smell (as an experiment, chew some gum until the flavor is gone, then hold a lemon under your nose; the gum will taste like lemon).

- Strong tastes can stimulate your child's mouth and make him more willing to try new foods. Before presenting new foods, let your child have one peppermint, sour gummy bear, or other strong-flavored food.
- If your child doesn't become hyper or get very sleepy after consuming refined sugar, get an assortment of flavored jelly beans. Eat one at a time, and have her guess which flavor it is.
- A child will be more likely to taste something if he helps prepare or select it. Give him a choice between chicken or fish, string beans or peas. Let him help you cook and serve.

---

* Recent studies indicate that shampoos, soaps, and body lotions containing lavender and tea tree oil may cause hormonal imbalances in young boys. (No effect has been reported in young girls.) Avoid these ingredients and find scents your son will enjoy.

Provide a Safe Space or Quiet Spot

We all need to "get away from it all" from time to time. Your child may need this even more if she is overwhelmed by a lot of sensory stimuli. After a long day at school, she may need to go to her room to be alone for a few minutes or even a few hours to recover. If socializing is hard, she may need to take a short break to regroup before she can continue to play without acting out. This is not the same as a time-out that you impose, although it may serve the same function of temporary disengagement and defusing. Ideally, your child will learn to recognize when she is about to hit overload, excuse herself from the room, and take a few minutes to compose herself before rejoining other people.

A safe space is comfortable and private. It can be a special corner of a bedroom with a beanbag chair, a swivel chair with high arms, or a pile of pillows, soft lighting, and a few items that soothe your child, such as stuffed toys and picture books, puzzles, and hand fidget toys like Koosh balls (whatever items provide a sense of safety and security). Your child may want to wrap herself in a blanket, climb into a tent, or use a certain piece of therapy equipment such as rolling on her belly over a therapy ball or using an indoor swing. What makes a space feel safe is rather subjective, and you and your child will need to figure out what works best.

You and your OT should consult with your school for how to create a safe space there as well if your child needs it to stay focused and available for learning. This can be tricky to pull off because you don't want to *excuse* your child from participating in classroom activities. However, a teacher who recognizes that your child tunes out or acts out because of sensory overload may be open to allowing your child to "take five" and regroup in a quiet, safe space so he can soon rejoin the class and be an active learner. Many more progressive classrooms already have a cozy reading nook that can easily be used for this purpose. Older students may be able to take a short break in a designated safe spot outside of the classroom if he is responsibly self-reliant and the school approves.

For an easily overstimulated infant, you have to do some guesswork to find the set-up and toys that help your baby to calm and reorganize. You, too, probably already benefit from a special part of your house where you can retreat when you need to. Sometimes just going to the bathroom or preparing dinner alone in the kitchen fills this purpose.

It's not always practical for your child to retreat to her safe space. You may want to develop a portable self-calming kit—a shoebox filled with self-calming items you can take along when traveling in the car, waiting in the doctor's office, or on sleepovers.

A Workable Plan

As you can see, the sky's the limit when it comes to selecting sensory diet ingredients. You may need to come up with new ideas to keep it interesting, but you may well find that your child wants the same exact input over and over. If the thought of doing so many different activities makes you feel, "Oh brother, not more things I have to do to deal with this sensory integration stuff!" remember that you can use your sensory smarts to transform simple games and everyday tasks into beneficial sensory input. It's really not that hard when you take into account that everything in life already has, or can have, a powerful sensory component. You just need to bone up on how to take advantage of it. And you need to be willing to make meeting sensory needs a priority in your home.

While, of course, the world can't stop just because your child is taking time to explore the yucky sensation of cookie dough on her fingers, recognize and reward the importance of her new sensation experiences by not allowing *yourself* to get distracted. Get other children engaged elsewhere or have them actively join you, don't talk on the telephone (turn the ringer off), and don't schedule unnecessary visits that will disrupt your routine. Just be there with your child physically and emotionally.

As a sensory smart parent, you're well on your path toward satisfying your child's sensory needs at home. But fulfilling your child's sensory needs at school is a bit trickier since you're not there to do it.

Family Sensory Diet Activities

Many families resist incorporating a sensory diet into their child's life because they feel they're already too busy and it seems impossible to schedule in yet another thing to do. Once you get clear on what kinds of sensory input and sensory diet activities benefit your child, it gets easier to integrate this into activities your child already does. What's more, many sensory diet activities can be done as a family, strengthening bonds and building sibling relationships.

Because everyone has different preferences, you'll need to put some thought into how to make the activities pleasurable for each person. Consider it an opportunity for everyone to learn how to respect each other's needs as well as their own, and encourage everyone to be adventurous, patient, and positive. You might be surprised at how one sibling can coax another into trying a challenging activity. Remember to keep a close eye on your child with sensory issues to determine if an activity is too much, and talk about it with him before and after to see if you need to adjust it to make it more comfortable. Be sure to check the next chapter for easy tips on how to modify sensory experiences such as a family outing.

Dancing. Teach your child some moves and have her teach you some. Consider taking a family folk-dancing class or going to a class yourself and then teaching the moves to your kids. Learn fun, old-fashioned dances like the Jitterbug, Charleston, Twist, Swim, Pony, Pogo, Stroll, Electric Slide, etc., and do them with your children. Family dances are becoming more common in various communities, but check them out before committing—often, the music is very loud and they're crowded. Let the kids take turns choosing the music. You might even buy an inexpensive disco light to give your "dance hall" some added ambience. Take turns choosing the music so everyone can dance to his or her favorite tunes.

Water parks. Indoor and outdoor water parks offer a wide variety of opportunities for sensory input, and most have a "lazy river," Jacuzzi, and quieter area with gentle sprinklers, as well as lounge chairs where you can take a break from the more intense activities. The sound level in an indoor water park can be more intense than at an outdoor one. Remember to bring goggles and plenty of towels as well as waterproof sunblock if you'll be outdoors. (Reapply sunblock often because the intense activities often wash it away fairly quickly, and consider wearing swimsuits with greater coverage, such as short wet suits.) If your child has special dietary needs, bring a small cooler bag for his food. Try to go on a weekday and, if it's an outdoor park, go earlier in the summer before there are many crowds (indoor parks are most crowded in winter).

Fitness video games. Video games like Wii Fit, as well as Dance Dance Revolution (DDR), which is available for several game systems including Wii, require some physical activity and can be used by children and adults (although you may want to preview DDR as the graphics and lyrics on some versions are rated T for Teen and may seem too risqué for your family). You might want to try these games at a friend's house, arcade, or a recreation department program (your child's school or the local library may even own them), or buy them from a dealer who specializes in used video games and will take trade-ins, instead of committing immediately to an expensive game.

Some libraries are now sponsoring Wii and DDR activities for families, and sometimes assisted living centers for seniors have Wii Fit games like bowling and encourage their residents to invite the grandchildren to play along.

Gardening. Although gardens can take a lot of time and effort to yield the results you want, you can keep it simple with container gardening and flowers and vegetables that grow easily in your area. Ask your neighbors what works for them or get advice from a local gardening store to find low-maintenance plants, such as geraniums, that provide a satisfying result. Get the whole family involved digging up dirt, planning, planting, weeding, watering, and composting. Sunflowers can be especially fun because they grow so tall, and you can eat the seeds.

Backyard fun. Set up your yard with rubber horseshoes, a basketball net and balls, hopping balls, and other toys conducive to physical play. Provide sidewalk chalk and a quiet, shady area as a retreat.

Snow fun. Make sure everyone has waterproof clothing he or she can tolerate. Fleece may be an alternative to nylon, repelling water somewhat. If you can, bring extra clothing and plan for a place to change—maybe your sensory child has to wear fleece mittens and change them each time they start to get wet. Find a good sledding hill; but if your child is afraid to go down it, start near the bottom or on a gentler hill nearby. Keep hot chocolate or herbal tea in a Thermos in the car and let your kids take breaks to warm up. If your child can't handle being outdoors for long, bring snow inside the house to continue the fun. Place it in a large plastic bin on top of a vinyl mat or tablecloth. Have plenty of rags available to clean up the puddles.

Outdoor water play. Sprinklers, hoses, water guns (use spray bottles if you're uncomfortable with guns), Slip 'n' Slides, and water balloons can be great fun. If your child gets overstimulated by outdoor water play, take breaks. You might wrap her up in a big, fluffy towel and hug and hold her tightly. Carrying a watering can to water plants or playing in mud can also be calming. Wash the car while you're at it, and have your child rub the exterior with wax and chamois, or dry the car with old towels and rags.

Shop work. Carrying heavy items such as boards or toolboxes can provide calming input. Encourage your adolescent to put on noise-reducing headphones and safety goggles (with soft padding under the elastic if that's an issue) to use a saw or screw gun. Using various tools to create objects (such as a birdhouse) or fix things can give a young person, male or female, a sense of power and control. Set up younger boys and girls with age-appropriate building tools, like the Quercetti Tecno Toolbox or a Bob the Builder set. Even toddlers can "work" using a classic wooden hammer and peg set.

Food preparation. Preparing foods together gives picky eaters a greater sense of control and encourages more adventurous eating—children are more likely to want to try the tomatoes they grew in the garden than ones you brought home from the grocer. Working with food is a very sensory-based experience your child may find either enjoyable or repulsive. He may be willing to try breaking eggs as long as he can wash his hands immediately afterward. He can also work on proprioceptive processing skills by learning to snap off the tips of string beans or break off the tough part of asparagus spears. An extra benefit of preparing meals together is a healthier diet with fewer processed foods.

Bicycling. Have your child measured and fitted with a bike and helmet at a good bicycle shop; a too-big bike can cause a child to feel anxious and uncomfortable riding. Allow your child to use training wheels as long as she needs to and encourage her to develop her skills, even if she does so very slowly. Drive your family to a bike trail, and ask at a bike shop where families tend to ride so you can avoid aggressive riders and racers. Biking is not only good exercise, it also prepares young people for navigation and driving skills, and gets everyone into nature and in tune with their bodies.

Hiking and walking. Explore the side streets of your neighborhood, stroll through the woods, around a lake, or along a bike path. Bring a water bottle for everyone (preferably one you have to squeeze and suck, for your sensory kids). Be respectful of your children's discomfort with smells and bugs and find ways to modify the walk to make it more pleasurable. The proprioceptive input from walking, especially uphill or on uneven surfaces, can be very calming.

Beach or lake outing. Oceans and beaches can be very challenging for a sensory child, but they can also turn out to be marvelous for children if you respect their sensory issues and accommodate them. Choose a time to go when the beach or lake is not overcrowded. Bring or rent an umbrella or tent for shade. Throwing or skipping rocks (away from people, of course) can be very calming. Bring a small ball to toss back and forth in the water. Bring plenty of towels, hats, and beach food. Bring water to drink and to rinse hands with before eating. Walk in wet sand and in the surf, build a sandcastle, and bury someone in the sand. Teach your kids to *never* throw sand or rely on a floating device to keep them safe in deep water.

SENSORY DIET AT SCHOOL

Incorporating your child's sensory diet into the school day can take quite a bit of creativity on your part, and require open-mindedness from teachers and school administrators. Meeting your child's needs at school may call for adding both sensory input on a regular basis and making some minor environmental modifications. Once the school staff understands that these simple accommodations do not cost anything and will enable your child to be a more productive member of the classroom, they will probably be willing to give it a try. Many educators already recognize that simple activities like a one-minute stretch break help *all* children learn better, although they may not consciously recognize the sensory connection. (If you run into any resistance from the teacher, check out Chapter 15: Advocating for Your Child at School.)

Here are some simple ways to incorporate a sensory diet at school. The guiding principle is to troubleshoot *before* sensory-based problems crop up. Before going to sit at a desk or at circle time or participate in any task that requires attention and focus, your child needs to satisfy her body's needs. Many children find that it is extremely helpful to have a moment to stretch, twist, jump, push, pull, or do some kind of heavy work prior to a "sit still and be quiet" activity. A few push-ups against a wall, jumping jacks, or even a walk to the water fountain can often do the trick. Sometimes a few sips from a water bottle, giving herself a hug, chewing on something, or doing a few finger exercises (such as making a fist and releasing or gently stretching fingers against a tabletop) can help your child stay alert and on task. When listening to the teacher read at circle time, subtly bouncing on an inflated seat cushion while using a fidget toy can give just enough controlled movement that a child can sit and listen through to the end of the story.

Some other suggestions:

- Prior to writing tasks, have your child do some fine motor "olympics" to prime his arms and hands. This can include reaching for the sky and then the ground, pressing his palms together, pulling on each finger, using a hand gripper or squeeze toy, manipulating therapy putty or modeling clay, or twirling a pencil from point to eraser a few times.
- To enhance active listening, have your child gently grasp his earlobes and pull them downward and outward.
- To maintain attention while sitting in a chair, have her do chair push-ups with hands flat on the seat pushing her body up, squeeze the chair legs with her feet, do pocket push-ups pushing her fists deeper into her pockets, wear a weighted vest or lap pad (talk to an OT about these items), or have her hold a heavy book in her lap. She can also use her feet to push up against a Thera-Band or Thera-tubing (a wide elastic band, available from therapy catalogs) stretched around a chair's legs or in her hands while she's sitting on the floor.
- If she needs it, your child can sit with her back against a wall or bookcase for additional tactile and proprioceptive input.
- If your child sucks or chews on his clothing, have him chew gum, or gnaw on Chewy Tubes, Chewlery, and Ark's Grabber (available from therapy catalogs; see photo on page 395). Chewing these items meets oral needs and helps some kids focus.
- Have her wear sound-protecting earmuffs or headphones to dampen auditory distractions in the classroom or earplugs on the playground or in gym. Have her listen to soft music while doing classwork.
- Have the teacher assign active tasks to your child, such as carrying notes to the main office; erasing the board; moving A/V equipment or chairs, desks, and books; and helping distribute worksheets, pencils, and art supplies.

Environmental Modifications

Simple changes in the classroom environment can make a big difference in your child's ability to focus and learn. You may need to have them added to your child's IEP (more on this in Chapter 15: Advocating for Your Child at School) as official accommodations. Your OT can help figure out how to modify the classroom environment, but here are a few ideas to get you going.

- The sensory defensive child who needs to avoid an unexpected, light touch may benefit from structured, separated spaces like assigned carpet squares on the floor for circle time, and accommodations such as having a blotter on her desk, having a soft mat or sheepskin on her chair, rubber tips on chairs and desk legs, and reduced environmental stimulation (natural lighting, having the door shut, curtains or blinds on windows, and perfume-free teachers and classmates).

- Have your child sit on a beanbag chair, floor cushions, or a pillow from home instead of in a chair. If he does use a desk chair, make sure it is at the right height: feet should be flat on the floor; ankles, knees, and hips at ninety-degree angles; and a table height that's comfortable for arms and elbows. If your child's feet do not reach the floor, use a low stool or make footrests that attach to his chair (use wood or rigid foam). You can do this at school, at the dinner table, and at your child's home desk.

- To add a little motion to sitting, use an inflatable, bumpy cushion like a Disc'O'Sit (see photo on page 395). Some kids do really well sitting on a therapy ball on which they can gently bounce. There are ones with built-in feet as well as ring seats specifically designed to hold a ball in place. A child can also sit on a T-stool (available from Southpaw Enterprises or you can build one;* see photo on page 396), a rocking chair, or a regular chair with one or two shortened legs for gentle rocking.

- Tape a piece of carpet under your child's desk so that he can rub his feet on it for extra tactile input.

- A tilt-top desk or tabletop slant board (available in therapy catalogs) will improve your child's arm position and pencil grasp, and help him avoid slumping over his desk or craning his neck. When the child is supposed to copy from the board, he can sit close to it and write on a slanted surface such as a three-inch-thick three-ring binder with the thick end facing the board and the thinner end facing him. Make sure your child's desk faces the front of the room.

- Have her place Dycem or inexpensive no-skid rubber matting from the hardware store under items on her desk (or lunch tray) to keep them from rolling off. Use masking tape to stabilize paper as she writes.

- Use masking tape or even a marker (if it's a desk at home) to outline where paper should be placed on the desk.

---

* Instructions for building a T-stool can be found in *The Out-of-Sync Child Has Fun* by Carol Kranowitz.

- To help your child time her movements and develop a steady rhythm, try using a metronome, which keeps a steady, audible beat (available from music stores and therapy catalogs).
- Have the teacher allow your child extra time for note taking, and provide him with special papers that are helpful for kids with fine motor and hand-eye coordination difficulties, such as graph paper, paper with high contrast lines, or paper with raised lines (available from www.guide-write.com and some therapy catalogs).
- Have your child use a vibrating pen, gel roller pens instead of ballpoint pens, or a keyboard.
- For art projects, provide glue sticks rather than liquid glue, and a paintbrush rather than fingerpaint.
- If vibration calms your child significantly, consider a Vibramat: a quiet, vibrating mat you can put under your child's chair or have her sit on during circle time (available from the *Integrations* catalog). You can also use it at home under her mattress to enhance sleep.
- If you've ever worked in an office with a big open space, you know how distracting it can be to see all your workmates around you. Build up the sides of a desk with cardboard to block out distracting stimuli, or use a study carrel. *Integrations* has a portable one.
- Keep in mind that there are many choices for common classroom products. For example, a child who is uncomfortable using standard scissors with two round loops may be happy using one with rubberized loops, or the more ergonomically correct ones by Crayola or Fiskars that have one small loop for the thumb and a bigger one for a few fingers to fit in. A child who hates the smell of Elmer's glue may be fine with a different brand of squeeze glue or even mucilage. It's hard to imagine any teacher objecting to your supplying these items, although you probably have a right to ask the school to provide them.

The key to finding the right ingredients for a sensory diet and environmental modifications for school is to identify your child's sensory needs and to figure out how to meet them in a way that is appropriate in terms of required school behavior. You can be less concerned with age-appropriate behavior at home, where you may let your child roll around on the floor for ten minutes before dinnertime.

Getting OT services at school can really bolster your child's sensory diet. If OT is provided outside the classroom, your child can get a much needed chance to do the rolling he needs, or to crash into a pile of mats, or jump on a trampoline. The school-based OT should help you integrate sensory diet ideas into the classroom, and help the teacher understand how sensory-based activities make everyone feel and function better.

When you or your OT speak with the school, request that your child not be singled out whenever possible. For example, if your child will be sitting on a cushion from home during circle time, all children should be allowed to bring one to school. When presented with these ideas, teachers are often concerned that such items will disrupt their classroom. They may envision children having pillow fights or flinging fidget toys or weighted lap pads across the room. However, given clear rules, most children use such items appropriately once the initial novelty wears off. See Chapter 15: Advocating for Your Child at School for more help in getting the school to incorporate sensory diet activities and modifications into the classroom.

SENSORY DIET ACTIVITIES FOR TEENS AND ADULTS

Movement and Proprioceptive Input

Physical activity can work miracles in helping you keep it together in an overstimulating world. Here are a few ideas:

- Work out on a treadmill, cross trainer, stationary bicycle, or other piece of gym equipment. Using a punching bag and lifting weights can help too.
- Try sports activities such as swimming and diving, jogging, bicycling, skiing, skating, and martial arts. If you've avoided sports because you fear sensory discomfort, or having other people judge your performance, the good news is that as an adult, you have options you didn't have back in physical education class as a child. You can take a private class, bring a supportive friend, hire a personal trainer, avoid the aspects of the sport that you dislike, and begin learning the basic skills slowly.
- Buy some light weights and keep them on your desk, and do a few biceps curls every so often while you're working. Or try "lifting" some cans from your kitchen pantry. Create your own "punching bag" out of cushions.
- Use a mini-trampoline made for adults, often called a rebounder. Before purchasing any trampoline, be sure to investigate its safety

and check your homeowner's insurance policy to make sure you're covered if someone else is hurt while jumping on it.

- Turn on some music and dance.
- Set up an old futon, mattress, or couch cushions on the floor to dive into. Roll yourself up tightly in a blanket or large towel.
- Chores such as housecleaning, washing and waxing a car, and chopping wood all provide excellent input.

Tactile Input

- Taking a hot, warm, or cool shower or bath often works very well as a "state changer," shifting you from high gear to low gear or vice versa. Try an Epsom salt bath for relaxation.
- Have an OT teach you how to self-administer therapeutic "brushing" (see page 115).
- Massage lotion into your hands and feet, using lots of pressure.
- If you like the feeling of pressure on your skin, wrap yourself in a heavy cotton blanket or put on tight clothing. Away from home, try wearing a Lycra leotard or biking gear under your regular clothing and carry a fidget or worry stone in your pocket (a smooth stone you can stroke—you might also carry a piece of fabric that feels good when you stroke it).
- Arts and crafts materials are good sensory tools and can be very relaxing to use. Using clay, paint, or collage materials or knitting, crocheting, or sewing are all worth exploring.
- Use a hand fidget, which you can find in just about any drug store or dime store these days. Squeezing and manipulating items such as Koosh balls, Tangles, Silly Putty, and so on, can all help. Rubik's cube puzzles can be fun or frustrating, depending on your perspective, but simply rotating them can feel great. Consider keeping a bowl of assorted fidgets on your desk or anywhere that you spend a lot of time.
- Cooking and baking are great for all the senses. Knead and work with dough, whether you bake cookies, pies, or pizza crusts. Working with gingerbread, which is full of thick molasses, provides a lot of tactile as well as proprioceptive input to the hands.
- Whether you're male or female, get massages and facials if you find them relaxing. Beauty schools will often offer low-cost massages and facials (although you may not like the novice student's touch), or you can sign up for e-mail notifications of discounts at your local spa. If you enjoy a great massage, you and your partner may want

to take a class on how to give a massage and invest in a portable massage table.

Auditory Input

- Music is a powerful way to self-modulate. Some people relax best to highly structured types of classical music such as Baroque chamber music while others prefer a "wall of sound" like the music of Nirvana. It's a good idea to explore different kinds of music to discover what helps you rev up and what helps you calm down. Internet radio can be a great way to discover new music.
- Listen to relaxation or meditation CDs, or white noise CDs that feature nature sounds.
- If you feel best when it is quiet, try noise-canceling headphones or earplugs.
- Water sounds can be soothing. Go to the ocean or a river and just listen. Consider installing a garden fountain, or even an indoor fountain that can easily be installed on the floor or the wall, or even a smaller, tabletop fountain.
- While the even tick-tick-tick of a clock may annoy some people, others find it reassuring. You might also try a metronome, either an old-fashioned mechanical kind or one of the modern digital types you can find online.
- Speak to an OT about doing a listening program such as Therapeutic Listening (www.vitallinks.net), REI (www.reiinstitute.com), or The Listening Program (www.thelisteningprogram.com).

Visual Input

- If you're feeling overwhelmed, look at something that makes you feel good: flowers, a plant, your cat, a fish tank, a lava lamp, or a picture of a place, person, or thing that you find especially comforting.
- Try visualization: Close your eyes, and mentally transport yourself to a place where you tend to be most relaxed and happy. Conjure up the entire sensory experience: not just what it looks like, but also what it smells like, what sounds you would hear, what touch sensations you would feel, and so on. For example, if you are happiest walking through a forest, picture the trees, the wildflowers, and woodland creatures you'd see; smell the lovely pine odor; hear

the birds singing and the wind rustling through the leaves, and so
on. It takes some practice, but after a while, you may find that you
can escape to your special place in your mind when you need a
quick break.

- If you work at a computer or are doing a lot of reading and you
start to feel overloaded, stop and refocus your eyes on something at
least a few feet away, or better yet, out the window. Stand up and
take a stretch break every so often.

- Experiment with sunglasses of various colors, from amber to gray
to rose, if you're bothered by bright lights or glare. If you wear prescription lenses, you can ask the optician to add a light tint to your
regular indoor glasses. Transitional lenses automatically darken
when there is more glare.

Taste/Smell/Oral Input

- Tune in to your taste buds. Some tastes are more alerting, while
others are more soothing. Food responses are highly individualized
so you'll need to find what works best for you.

- Chewing gum, eating crunchy or chewy foods, or sucking thick liquids through a straw can all be powerful state changers.

- Discover what smells you find calming versus arousing. Check out
various scented lotions, candles, essential oils, aftershave, perfume,
shampoos, and so on, to find what smells work best for you. Place a
strong-smelling bar of soap on your desk or sprinkle some drops of
essential oil into a bath. Sometimes just the smell of coffee is all you
need to perk up when you're feeling sluggish.

- Smell things in nature: fresh-cut grass, flowers, freshly chopped
wood, your child, fresh fruit, and so on.

Retreating to a Quiet Spot and Managing Anxiety

- Learn to become aware of your triggers, paying attention to when
you're feeling yourself becoming anxious, tense, or fearful. At school
or work, designate a place to escape to if sensory input becomes too
intense. Taking a few minutes to close your office door and shut the
lights off, or sit in a bathroom with the lights off, or relax in your car,
or step outside to a quiet area can help you get through a full day of
sensory onslaught. If you're attending college, ask your professor if
you can sit in the darkened classroom afterward for a few minutes,

listening to music on your iPod, to regroup. Consider making a room or corner in your home into a retreat area, with comfortable lighting and a beanbag chair or other chair that you can sink into, and perhaps a weighted blanket to drape over yourself.

- Meditation and breathing practices that involve slow and deliberate deep breathing, such as those taught in yoga classes, can help you relieve stress, slowing down your body's primitive panic reactions and reducing your anxiety in the moment as well as overall. Regular mindfulness meditation practice can be especially effective at helping you become aware of stress triggers before you go into sensory overload.

- Regular exercise has been shown to reduce anxiety and stress and help even out moods. Make it a part of your sensory diet. If you don't like "exercising," get creative and introspective to discover a form of movement you enjoy, whether it's bouncing on a mini-trampoline, using a home exercise machine, or doing stretches while watching your favorite TV show; taking a yoga class; or walking with a friend while socializing. Remember what you enjoyed as a child and do it, whether it's sledding or playing soccer. Make sure you plan different exercise activities for nasty weather so that when it rains several days in a row or the cold weather sets in, you don't find your sensory issues worsening, because you're still physically active.

Recommended Reading and Resources

See Sources for Useful Toys, Equipment, and Products for guidance on where to get some of the products mentioned in this chapter.

Kranowitz, Carol S. *The Out-of-Sync Child Has Fun.* New York: Perigee, 2003. An excellent source for sensory diet ideas, especially for younger children.

Zysk, Veronica, and Ellen, Notbohm. *1001 Great Ideas for Teaching and Raising Children with Autism Spectrum Disorders.* Arlington, TX: Future Horizons, Inc., 2004. Wonderful sensory diet activities for children with *or* without autism spectrum disorders, plus great communication, teaching, and behavior management strategies.

Cut and Paste Sensory Diet, by Your Therapy Source, www.yourtherapysource .com. Downloadable eBook that helps you create personalized visual sensory diet books for home and school, including 150 sensory activity picture/word cards.

DVD Series: *OT in the Home* and *OT in School,* Agoura Hills, CA: TRP Wellness, 2008. Excellent demonstrations and information about sensory processing and sensory diet activities. Britt Collins, OTR/L, instructor; Rachel Hunter, host; Lindsey Biel, OT consultant.

CHAPTER 7

Practical Solutions for Everyday Sensory Problems

As the parent of a child with sensory issues, you've probably learned to avoid unnecessary situations that upset or overwhelm your child. Needless to say, life presents all too many situations you and your child simply can't avoid or don't want to avoid: from going to school to washing hair to dealing with periods of frequent transitions to taking a vacation. His unique sensory sensitivities and intolerances will determine which situations your child has trouble dealing with and what you can do about them, whether your child is struggling with self-care issues, difficult environments, group situations, or changes in routine.

When you stop to analyze a situation or task that your child has trouble with, there's almost always something you can alter. Think about the noise, the sounds, the smells, the tastes, the sights, the movements your child must make. Is there anything you can modify in the environment to improve things? What can be done in a different way? How can you help your child cope with situations that can't be controlled? This kind of analysis may take extra time and understanding just when you're in a rush or feeling impatient. But the effort can really pay off.

Also, consider your own role in creating what's uncomfortable about the situation. Is your tone of voice or how you are physically handling your child setting her off? Are you communicating your own anxiety, dread, or anger? We don't mean to make you feel guilty or to place blame on you. But figuring out what *can* be changed when your child is having a meltdown each morning will make you both feel better!

Ask yourself whether you are providing an adequate sensory diet. For example, are you giving him enough tactile and deep pressure input before an activity such as bathing? Do you need to speak with your OT about modifying the sensory diet—or about how to handle a persistently challenging task such as putting on hats and mittens? Your OT can also give you her perspective on why your child freaks out every time you take her to the supermarket.

It also helps to give your child some sense of control and pre- dictability. Let him know you understand that things are hard for him and that you're working on discovering solutions *together*. It may take some trial and effort, but you're not going to give up . . . and you can't do it without his help. Before doing something differently, *tell* your child if he is capable of understanding. For example, rather than plop on a shower visor unexpectedly, explain that you know he hates get- ting soap in his eyes and that the visor may feel unfamiliar, but it's going to keep his eyes soap free.

You'll need to have a load of tricks up both your sleeves. In this chapter we provide some tips and techniques OTs and parents have used successfully at home and at school, but you will find even more practical solutions specifically for the school environment in Chapter 15: Advocating for Your Child at School, along with advice on how to get the school to provide accommodations and carry through with a sensory diet.

SELF-CARE CHALLENGES: GROOMING, DRESSING, AND TOILETING

Grooming

Bathing

- Before a shower or bath, provide tactile and deep pressure input (see Chapter 6: The Sensory Diet of Daily Activities).
- If your toddler hates the bath, start small: Place your naked child in a dry bathtub along with a dishpan or plastic bin filled with warm water (have another one filled with warm water nearby, for rinsing). Let her use bath toys, a washcloth, and soap to play. If she likes dolls, have her wash the doll, then herself. Wash her using the water in the container, and rinse with the nonsoapy water from the other con- tainer. You can also bathe a small child in a plastic tub-within-a-tub. Never leave a young child unattended in a tub.
- Install an unbreakable, steam-free mirror on the wall of the shower, or even on the ceiling. Sometimes, seeing herself as she washes her face or shampoos or rinses her hair will make a child feel more se- cure.

- Sometimes it's the sound of the water filling the tub that bothers the child. Try filling the tub with the door closed and call him in when the bath is ready.
- Use a bath mitt to wash your child's hair. Press down to give extra proprioceptive input.
- For a small child, try placing removable vinyl pictures on the shower ceiling for him to look up at while having his hair rinsed; talk about the pictures while rinsing to distract him. Alternately, have him lean forward so that his face is downward while rinsing. Or, hide a toy under the bath bubbles while he closes his eyes and you rinse the shampoo; anticipating the fun of searching for the toy might help him tolerate rinsing.
- Have your child take a bath or shower after others do so that the room is already warm. Heat up the towel in the dryer for a few minutes, if necessary.
- Use a handheld sprayer connected to the faucet, so your child can control the spray when he rinses himself. Also, the spray is often gentler than a showerhead.
- Let your child stand in the tub watching the shower for a few minutes before venturing into the spray.
- If your child doesn't like soap or shampoo, buy or make foamy soap (which is also good for tactile play, and unlike shaving cream, it doesn't have to have a strong smell). Economical soap makers that turn liquid soap to foam can be found in kitchen supply stores, online, and, often, on eBay.
- Let your child regulate bath or shower temperature, within reason (be careful with small children who are tempted to adjust the faucet by themselves). Kids with sensory processing issues can have a very different sense of "cold" and "hot." For safety's sake, and to prevent a nasty shock of too-hot water, make sure the temperature on your water heater is set on a safe maximum level.
- Consider using Hot Stop's anti-scald shower head, hand shower, and tub spout, which reduce water flow to a trickle when hot water reaches an unsafe temperature, and starts reflow when the water cools down. Available from www.h2otstop.com.
- Some children with sensory problems react badly to artificial colorings not only in foods but in bath soaps and shampoos as well. If you suspect this is a problem, look for products without these colorings. Be forewarned, however, that "natural" baby and kid-care products sold in health food stores are often not tear free.

- Let your child pick out a shampoo and soap she thinks smells pleasant. This is good for encouraging hand washing too.
- Play music while your child is in the shower or bath to soothe her (keep radios and CD or tape players far from the tub).
- For some kids, an "army shower" works best: turn off the shower while lathering with soap and shampoo, rinse, and get out.
- If your small child gets overly excited in the shower and starts jumping around, be sure you have an extra-long bathmat to keep him from slipping. You might even want to bring one with you on vacation or overnight visits.
- Experiment with bubble baths. Your child might enjoy a bath filled with bubbles or he may want just enough so that he can play with the bubbles but see the bottom of the tub or his body underneath the water.
- Provide plenty of bath toys to make it user-friendly. In fact, allowing kids to fingerpaint with washable paints in the bathtub, and rinsing them off later, is a great way to get them used to both the tub and paint.
- Don't let your child drink bathtub water or mouth bath toys unless you are absolutely certain your tub is not leaching lead, as many porcelain bathtubs do. (You can use a simple lead test available in any hardware store to test your tub.)

CAUTION:

Avoid using products (detergents, hand soaps, dish soaps, laundry soaps, toothpaste, cosmetics, and others) that contain triclosan, a powerful antibacterial/antimicrobial chemical, which is classified as a pesticide. Triclosan is a chlorophenol, similar in molecular structure to some of the most toxic chemicals on earth including dioxins and PCBs. Doctors recommend washing well with regular soap and water.

Diaper changes

If your baby resists diaper changes, take heart. He may potty train early because he finds diapers so uncomfortable. In the meantime, here are some solutions for resisting diaper changes.

- Have him stand instead of lie down as you change him.
- Use Pull-Ups or GoodNites-type diapers as soon as you can in order to make changes go faster.
- Use a diaper wipe warmer.
- Sing a distracting song while she's being changed. Change the volume as you sing, use different voices, and make exaggerated facial expressions if she finds this fascinating and not frightening. Or, chew bubblegum and blow bubbles to distract her. Give her something to hold to keep her busy.
- Change the baby on the floor, over a pad, instead of on a changing table.

Hair washing

- Use a large container of water for rinsing; the extra weight of the water might feel better on his head than sprinkling from a shower or a cup. Alternately, sprinkle water from a sprinkling can (often available in kids' beach toy collections) or cup to rinse. If your child hates rinsing, you might build up to it: start by rinsing his legs, then rinsing from his shoulders, and then pouring rinse water over his head. Or count off the transition together: one, two, three, rinse.
- A hat, braids (regular, French, or cornrow), or ponytail can provide constant pressure to the scalp, which is calming for some children (and adults) with sensory issues.
- Before, during, or after hairbrushing, use a soft surgical scrub brush or vegetable brush to stimulate the scalp.
- Wash just the ends of the hair—not the scalp—and over the course of several sessions, work up to washing all the hair.
- Try No-Rinse shampoo and bathing products (www.southpaw enterprises.com or www.drugstore.com)—no water necessary.
- Use a foam visor (available from www.onestepahead.com, drugstores, and some therapy catalogs) or a washcloth held over his face when rinsing. You might also dry his face immediately after washing it even if he's still in the shower or bath.
- If you take a bath with your small child, let her pour water over your head and face before doing it to her.
- Massage the scalp before getting it wet. Some parents swear by using a vibrating hairbrush (available from *Integrations* and other therapy catalogs) just before hair washing, or as part of the sensory diet.
- Use earplugs to prevent water from getting in your child's ears.

- Have your child wash her doll's hair, or yours, before she has hers washed.
- Sometimes children with sensory issues resist closing their eyes when having shampoo rinsed off because they're afraid of falling and are unsure of where their body is in space. Use a tear-free shampoo so she can keep her eyes open. Or have her hold onto you or use your hands to press down on her shoulders to help her know where her body is when her eyes are closed.

Hair brushing

- Prepare the scalp beforehand by pressing down on the head or giving a nice head massage.
- Use a tangle-free conditioner.
- Use a brush with a lot of give to the bristles so you don't yank hair—or use a special detangling comb or the Goody Ouchless brush.
- Sometimes if children can see themselves in the mirror while their hair is being brushed, they have a greater sense of control and can tolerate the brushing more easily.
- If your child can brush her hair by herself, let her: she might have an easier time anticipating and controlling the pain of hitting a snarl.
- Try having your child sit in a beanbag chair for deep pressure—or wear a weighted vest or use a weighted lap pad—while you're brushing.
- Always brush from the bottom up to avoid creating snarls. If the hair is long, hold the shank with one hand while brushing the ends with the other to minimize tugging at the scalp.
- Fun hair accessories and "doing each other's hair" with another friend or with Mom might inspire her as well.
- Consider the virtues of a short cut! Remind your daughter that Dora the Explorer has a short bob.

Haircutting

- As with hair brushing, decrease tactile sensitivity on your child's head before a haircut by giving a deep pressure massage to the head and scalp.
- If your child is auditory sensitive, avoid using a buzz-cut razor or having his hair cut when someone in the barbershop is using one.

You can also try to desensitize him to the sound of a barber's clippers by having the barber "play" it for him sometime when you stop by, and are not getting your child's hair cut that day. Or have your child hold a vibrator or electric toothbrush to his hairline and temples and near his ears. You could also let him wear earplugs or listen to music.

- Go to a kid-friendly haircutting place, or create your own at home with snacks and an absorbing video.
- Have the barber or stylist give your child a big, soft brush, a dry washrag with baby powder, or a hairdryer set on cool to brush or blow off stray hair as it is cut. Use baby powder on irritated skin afterward. Avoid letting clipped hair fall on your child's arms. You might want to use a handheld vacuum to suck up hair as it falls if the sound won't upset your child.
- Use a towel and a clip rather than a plastic cape: the plastic or Velcro fastener can be even more irritating than stray hair falling on the neck. You can also wrap your child snugly in a towel or in clothes that cover him completely.
- Bring an extra shirt along so your child can change afterward. Or cut hair at home so he can take a shower immediately to rinse off any stray hairs.
- Consider cutting your child's hair at home or at a barbershop where there are no overwhelming smells like perm chemicals. Or ask for a salon appointment at a time when there will not be any coloring, straightening, or permanents going on.
- If your child's tolerance for haircutting is very low, you might want to trim his hair over the course of a few days. Yes, he'll look a little goofy for three days, but keeping him still for the entire cut in one sitting might be more trouble than it's worth.
- Strange as it may sound, you might be able to get away with cutting your child's hair while she is sleeping (especially if she is sleeping upright in a car seat) or while she is in the bathtub, distracted by bath toys.
- With very small children, use the word *trim* not *cut* to make the process seem less frightening.
- Try holding a small child on your lap or have him sit on a low chair as the high chairs in barbershops can be scary for a child with SI dysfunction.
- If possible, schedule your appointment so your child can see someone else getting his hair cut first.
- Let your child use a weighted lap pad for calming, or play with a toy.

Toothbrushing

- Let your child pick out her own soft, child-size toothbrush (Barbie or Elmo? Yellow or hot pink?). Let her make the decision about whether to brush her teeth before or after her bedtime story and stick to that order from then on.
- Develop a predictable routine for when and how to brush. For example, she could decide to always start with the top teeth and to brush from left to right, front to back. A consistent brushing pattern will help your child motor plan this complex activity and learn to predict when and where she will feel various sensations.
- Model proper toothbrushing, and as you brush, make it fun. Brush teeth together and have a race: whoever brushes longer, wins. Use a two-minute timer. Read books on toothbrushing such as *Does a Lion Brush?* by Dr. Fred Ehrlich.
- Kids with sensory issues may react negatively to foam in their mouth. Try Orajel Toddler Training Toothpaste, which doesn't foam, or a flavored fluoride rinse poured on the toothbrush. If your child hasn't yet learned to spit, use a nonfluoride toothpaste such as Nature's Gate or Tom's of Maine Silly Strawberry to minimize fluoride intake. Check with your dentist to determine whether you need to use fluoridated toothpaste or have your child drink fluoridated water.
- To desensitize gums, provide tactile input: Try using a vibrator, vibrating toothbrush, or vibrating toy on the outside of the mouth near the jaw. Or, wear a rubber finger cot or use a Nuk massager or Infa-Dent (see photo on page 397), or swipe with a washcloth or Dentips or Toothettes (available from many therapy catalogs).
- Let your child chew on a damp washcloth before and after meals if she resists tooth brushing.
- Try using a lot of water: wet the toothbrush between every few strokes.
- Let your child adjust the water temperature if that makes him more comfortable.
- Lots of kids react very positively to vibrating toothbrushes, finding them calming, easy to use, and fun. Be sure to look for the versions with smaller heads for smaller kids. Sonicare has an especially quiet motor, which is great for auditory sensitive kids.
- When flossing teeth or teaching your child to do it, try ribbon floss, such as Glide, and gently work it into the space between the teeth rather than snapping it in. Children who crave strong flavors might prefer flavored flosses, such as cinnamon or mint.

- Distract young children from discomfort by making a game out of brushing. For instance, as you brush, describe a book or TV character that you "see" in her mouth and have the child guess who you're describing.
- Your child may resist toothbrushing because she hates to do it in the bathroom. If your bathroom can't be made user-friendly (see page 171 for tips on how to do this), have her brush over the kitchen sink, or even over the sink in the laundry room if that's more comfortable. If your dentist says that swallowing the toothpaste she's using is okay, you might even try having her lie flat on her back as you brush. Some little children feel more comfortable lying down as you press against their chest with your forearm and brush their teeth with your other hand.
- Tape paper over the mirror if it's distracting for your child to look into as he brushes, or have him brush his teeth at the kitchen sink.
- Be certain to gently brush your child's tongue and between the gums and teeth. Children with poor oral-motor skills often end up with food stuck in this area.

Tooth grinding (bruxism)

Some children grind their teeth while awake or even sleeping due to anxiety, an abnormal bite, or high muscle tone. Others do it purely for the sensory input it gives them through the teeth and jaw. Many kids outgrow this when they get their adult teeth. However, if tooth grinding persists, it can wear down teeth and lead to headaches and a sore jaw.

- Your dentist may recommend a mouth guard. Don't assume your child will hate it. It may allow him to get the proprioceptive input he needs while he's sleeping while it protects his teeth. Be sure to specifically ask your dentist whether your child's bite may need correction.
- Address any underlying anxiety or sleep issues.
- Make sure he drinks plenty of water since some research shows that dehydration may be linked to teeth grinding. Note that if his urine is dark in color, it's a sign that he may be dehydrated.
- If tooth grinding is due to high oral muscle tone, avoid having your child chew on nonfood items such as pencils, pens, and ice cubes as well as chewing gum as this increases jaw muscle clenching which makes your child even more likely to grind her teeth.

- If it is purely a sensory seeking behavior, give your child lots of opportunities to get intense proprioceptive input in the mouth, providing snacks such as pretzels, carrot sticks, and fruit leather, and using "chewies" as needed.
- Playfully encourage your child to yawn. Play "lion" with her, opening up your jaws as wide as possible to roar, which stretches and relaxes the muscles.
- Get jaw muscles to relax by holding a warm washcloth against your child's jaw joint (the cheek area in front of the earlobes).
- Make sure your child goes to bed as relaxed as possible, using a warm bath and massage. See the information on sleep and stress on pages 289–98.

Trimming nails

- Massage your child's hands, and compress his fingertips gently before trimming his nails.
- Trim nails when they are wet and soft, after a bath or shower.
- Trim them while your child is asleep.
- Make a game out of it. Pretend the nails are people getting their hair trimmed, or monsters that need to be cut down to size.
- When you clip, be sure to leave a little white edge rather than cutting them right up to the skin.
- Put a weighted blanket over your child while you're clipping.
- Let him hold a lollipop in one hand to distract him from what you are doing with the other. A spin lollipop is especially distracting.

Grooming products

- When your child begins to use deodorant, try the spray-on or dry roll-on kind; it's less wet and sticky than liquid roll-on.
- Look for perfume-free, allergen-free makeup, such as products made by Almay, if your daughter wants to use makeup but can't tolerate the smell. Water down or add light moisturizer to makeup if she dislikes the thick feeling of foundation. Encourage her to take good care of her skin—drinking lots of water and using a mild cleanser.

Clothing, Eyeglasses, and More

Everyday clothing and underwear

Sensitivity to fabrics is often one of the first sensory issues that a parent notices. A baby may hate having his diaper changed because he's uncomfortable with changes in body position, powders, or lotions, or the way he's handled, but sometimes it's the diaper itself that he finds irritating. Later, there may be particular fabrics that the child just can't tolerate. The child who is ultrasensitive to tactile input may be feeling his sock seams or his shirt cuffs all day long.

It's okay to send kids to school in comfy clothing. Lots of kids come home, tear off their school clothing, and put on their cozy sweatshirts with the hood up and sleeves pulled down to their fingertips. It's not all that unusual for a child to wear only one or two particular shirts and soft sweatpants. That's fine for younger kids but it becomes a real problem if she insists on wearing sweatpants and UGG boots even in summer. Clothing issues can cause embarrassment and discomfort for the teenager who wants to fit in but can't tolerate the feeling of the latest fashions, like tight blue jeans or super baggy pants.

- Consult with an occupational therapist about tactile desensitization techniques such as deep pressure massage, therapeutic "brushing," and using a sensory bin.
- Some kids are more comfortable in loose clothing or if they wear tight clothing beneath their other clothes. Try bicycle shorts (such as the all-cotton ones from www.sensorycomfort.com), tights, "too small" T-shirts, and so on. A hooded sweatshirt provides great input when the child pulls the hood up, sticks his fists in the pockets, and pushes downward, tightening the fabric.
- Use tightly fitting pajamas instead of chemically treated flame-retardant pjs if the chemicals irritate your child's skin.
- Buy softer fabrics: cotton, fleece, and flannel. Many parents swear by the soft cotton used in Lands' End and Hanna Andersson clothing. Avoid items made of polyester blends, which can pill, causing them to become uncomfortably rough.
- If your child can only tolerate really well-laundered clothes, wash new clothes multiple times or buy them "preconditioned" from a consignment or thrift shop.
- Consider using laundry products without added perfume or dye. Fabric softener (liquid or sheets) may or may not be helpful; it does make clothing softer but the strong scent may bother some children.
- Before your child gets dressed after a bath or shower, rub in a high-quality moisturizer with glycerin or lanolin while his skin is still damp. This is especially important in winter, when skin tends to get dry and itchy, and in dry climates.

- Experiment with different weights of clothing, as well as different fabrics. One child might prefer loose heavy clothing while another might prefer lightweight, stretchy clothing.
- If you're buying more than one of the same item in different colors, check to make sure the fabric feels the same. Sometimes the fabric will be scratchier or heavier in one color than in another.
- Remove bothersome tags using a seam ripper or very sharp scissors, cutting as close to the seam as possible (you may make small holes in the fabric, so be careful). Check out Hanes's tagless underwear and T-shirts for children and adults. Calvin Klein sells seamless underwear for girls and women.
- Look out for typical clothing irritants: elastic at the wrist or ankles, scratchy backings on appliqués or patches that rub against the skin, tight collars, or waistbands that don't have cloth covering the elastic. Underwear with cotton-covered elastic waistbands are available from www.sensorycomfort.com.
- Turtleneck tops can be very distressing. Even if they're not too tight around the neck (you can stretch them out so they're baggier), your child may not be able to tolerate the feeling of getting it stuck over her face as it goes on and off. You may want to look for shorter mock turtlenecks or skip them altogether.
- Buy seamless socks made by Stride Rite or from www.sensorycomfort .com or www.smartknitkids.com, or just cut the loose threads off of sock seams. Stride Rite also makes seamless tights. You can always put socks on inside-out to minimize annoying seam lumps and snip off any excess.
- Consider cotton panties in a larger size if your daughter hates tight panties, or buy her cotton boxer shorts (the Gap and Joe Boxer brands feature unisex prints).
- If seams in pants or other clothing bother your child, sew moleskin over them.
- If your child has trouble manipulating buttons and zip flies on pants, look for Velcro closures and pull-up waistbands, such as the kind in sweatpants. If you need stretch waistband pants that are dressier, try khaki or cargo pants from Lands' End, L.L. Bean, or Old Navy.
- Try lined wind pants as an alternative to sweatpants.
- If snow pants are a problem, layer fleece pants or nylon wind pants over tight, long underwear for short exposures to the cold.
- If your daughter needs a bra but finds it uncomfortable, have her fitted by a trained clerk at a lingerie or department store if your

daughter is open to it. A properly fitted bra is much more comfortable than an ill-fitting one.

- Buy all-cotton bras with soft cotton bands, and without extra lace or underwire (sources include www.sensorycomfort.com and the Hanes Pure Bliss line, www.purebliss.com).
- Try a sports bra or camisole top with a built-in bra. Remember that sports bras are tighter than traditional styles, so your daughter might find them more or less comfortable depending on her sensitivities.
- If your son must wear a jock strap, look into sports briefs and soft cups such as those found at www.internationaljock.com.

Eyeglasses

- If your child resists wearing glasses, point out fictional characters like Harry Potter or celebrities who wear them (depending on your child's age). Sparkly diva sunglasses might entice one child, whereas bright red frames might entice another child who loves anything red.
- Try ultralight, flexible glasses; brands include Flexon, Easytwist, and Como Baby by Solo Bambini. These weigh far less than regular glasses and can be twisted and bent without breaking.
- Try an elasticized strap to hold glasses on. The extra pressure against the head might be comforting to the child as well.
- Be sure your child can tolerate the visual field of small lenses before committing to them; looking down to see her homework paper or plate of food may require a visual adjustment.
- Some kids will pull glasses off when the frames get a little bent, so if she's doing this, check to see if you need to have them adjusted back into shape.

Hats, gloves, and mittens

- Massage your child's head and hands before she puts on a hat or mittens.
- A tighter or looser hat, gloves, or mittens might be more tolerable for your child. Try snug glove liners beneath mittens.
- Look for fleece hats, gloves, and mittens, which are less scratchy than acrylic and wool.
- A child might be more open to wearing clothing that at least looks familiar or friendly. Choose clothes in his favorite colors, with his

favorite characters on them, or that resemble clothing he's found comfortable in the past.

- Place your baby's bell socks on his hands instead of mittens; the sound of the bells chiming within the material might be so fascinating that he forgets his discomfort with having something on his hands.
- Remember that a tactile sensitive child might need a hood or hat to protect him from the uncomfortable feeling of even a small amount of rain or snow falling on his head.
- Consider letting your child learn by doing. Maybe he would rather come in early from playing in the snow or even suffer frostnip (red, tingly, or numb skin) than tolerate winter clothing. Getting chilled does not directly cause colds, and you can warm her skin by soaking it in warm (not hot) water. Exposed skin will develop frostbite (pale or mottled, numb or painful skin), however, so be very cautious about exposure.
- Some children can tolerate a hood better than they can tolerate a hat.
- A muff doesn't leave hands free but may be more tolerable for a child who can't stand gloves or mittens. Try fingerless gloves with a flap that folds over and transforms the gloves into mittens (available from stores such as The Gap and Lands' End).

Helmets

Safety helmets are a must for skating, skateboarding, or riding a bicycle and are recommended for sledding too. If your child has a great appreciation for rules, you may be able to talk him into wearing a helmet because it's "the rule" (and the law!). Otherwise, here are some ideas for getting that helmet on.

- Massage his scalp several times a day for a few days before having him put on the helmet, and immediately before he actually puts it on.
- Let him explore various helmets. If need be, let him touch them without trying them on at first, and build up to actually putting one on.
- Have your child try on dress-up hats to increase tolerance for hats and helmets. You can often find these for very little money at party stores, thrift stores, and garage sales.

Shoes, shoelaces, and boots

Feet are one of the most sensitive parts of the body, especially the soles, so it's no surprise that a lot of kids are very particular about socks and footwear. Some are uncomfortable being barefoot, and some insist on having something on their feet at all times. Others have trouble adjusting to a new pair of shoes, which can be a real problem as feet grow and seasons change. Also, tying shoelaces is a complex task that requires more advanced, fine motor, visual-perceptual skills, and proprioceptive processing skills. Fortunately, there are many accommodations for kids with sensory issues and motor planning issues.

- Desensitize your child's feet before trying on shoes. When you go to the shoe store, bring along seamless socks she tolerates well.
- If he can't tolerate leather shoes, try slippers or moccasins, or canvas shoes, which are breathable. Many sneaker styles are dressy enough for special occasions.
- Investigate whether very tight, thin socks or really thick socks or seamless socks make shoes more comfortable.
- Many older kids prefer high-top sneakers that provide some ankle support.
- Shearling-lined boots may be tolerable for your child during the cold-weather months.
- Try old-fashioned galoshes over favorite shoes or sneakers if your child insists on his everyday shoes despite the awful weather.
- If your child is struggling to learn how to tie shoelaces, teach her how to tie laces with the shoe or sneaker *off* her body first to eliminate the challenge of bending over or being in an awkward position with her foot up. Provide different color laces to help tell them apart. Try both the one-loop and two-loop (bunny ears) methods to see which is easier for her to learn.
- Break down shoe tying into small steps. Start with having her make an X with the laces, then pulling the one on top under and through. Then teach her how to hold on to the laces while forming a loop, and so on. Don't press her to move forward to the next step if she's becoming frustrated.
- While your child is learning to tie shoes, empower him to be independent instead of having to ask an adult for help. Trying to find styles with Velcro closures can be hard as your child ages and fashion changes. To get around this, your child can use ordinary elastic shoelaces that you tie just once, knot, and then stretch open to put the shoe on, or curly elastic laces that don't need to be tied at all (available from www.theraproducts.com, Amazon, and elsewhere). Other elastic shoelace systems that don't require tying include ones

from www.locklaces.com, www.tyless.com, www.lifesolutionsplus.com, **and** www.bunjeez.com.

Toileting

Potty training

Entire books have been written about how to potty train your child, and the usual techniques might work for you. However, kids with sensory processing disorder often train later than other children because of their sensory issues. After all, if a child isn't bothered by the sensation of dirty diapers or underwear, he's not going to be as motivated as if he were. The upside is that some children with sensory issues toilet train early because these sensations bother them so much.

- If your child can't tell when he is wet, try training him by letting him walk around the house bottomless, or put him in clothes rather than diapers. You can also use briefs-type diapers such as Pull-Ups, which are convenient when you're not home; unfortunately, they can also make toilet training far more difficult because your child can get used to peeing or pooping in an underpants-like garment.
- Some children are disturbed by the size and feel of a large toilet seat. Bring your child to the store and help her to pick out a potty chair, or a small, cushioned vinyl ring that fits into an adult toilet seat.
- Try keeping the door to the bathroom open to reduce sounds bouncing against tile walls.
- If your child is bothered by the sound of urine splashing against the water in the toilet, mask the sound by talking or singing together. Or, place a layer of toilet paper on the water in the toilet to muffle the sound.
- The height of the toilet causes small children to have trouble balancing on it, with their legs dangling. If your child doesn't like a potty chair, which is lower to the ground, try having him use the toilet with his feet on a stool.
- Some children are frightened by the sound of flushing. A sense of control might help: together, count off to the flush: "One, two, three, *flush!*" Make lots of noise as the toilet is flushing, shouting "yay!" or "flush!"
- If your child is frightened by the sound of the toilet flushing, you can desensitize him to the sound by recording the flush and listening to it

together when it's not potty time. Allow your child to raise and lower the volume as he wishes to give him some control. Or play the "Toilet Flush" track from the Sound-Eaze CD (from www.route2greatness .com) that combines sounds many children are afraid of with calming, rhythmic music to increase familiarity and comfort with unavoidable sounds.

- To help a child make the connection between wetting his diaper, training pants, or underpants and needing to use the potty, you can use a special musical sensor that plays when it gets wet (www.tinkle toonz.com/special_needs.html). Tinkletoonz also makes a musical potty that provides additional incentive for kids to "go" in the potty.
- To help your boy develop aim and enjoy using the toilet, try Toilet Targets (www.toilettimetargets.com/), flushable colorful animal cutouts he can try to hit with his urine stream.
- Sometimes, tight clothes provide tactile pressure input that distracts the child from the sensation of needing to use the potty. Loose clothing such as cotton elastic-waist pants or boxer shorts might help him realize he has the urge to go.
- For some kids, intestinal gas, mild diarrhea, or constipation can complicate matters. If this is the case, it might be due to a nutritional problem, such as intolerance to dairy products, or fecal impaction. Consult a pediatrician or even a nutritionist if you think this might be the case.
- A child who is hyposensitive may require his bowels or bladder to be *very* full in order to feel the urge. You will need to bring such a child to the potty on a regular basis rather than ask him if he needs to go.
- If your child has trouble wiping, try having her use flushable baby wipes instead of toilet paper.

Bed-wetting

- If your child is too big for regular diapers, try overnight diapers in larger sizes such as GoodNites. You can also try using diaper doublers—pads to place in the diaper to soak up extra liquid.
- Double-make the bed—a rubber mattress pad or rubber sheet on the bottom, a sheet, a rubber sheet, and another sheet—so that you or your child can strip off a layer of bedding in the middle of the night without having to make the bed again. Have extra bedding and pajamas easily available.

- Never scold, punish, or ridicule a child who wets the bed. Remember, he isn't doing it on purpose!
- Most children spontaneously stop wetting the bed. If your child continues to do so beyond age seven (or is distressed by it after age five), speak with your pediatrician about behavioral treatment. This usually consists of a device called a bell and pad. The pad, usually placed under the sheets, senses wetness which then triggers a bell that wakes up the child.

Meal Time

Group meals are a unifying, bonding ritual and an invaluable opportunity for children to socialize and learn good manners. With parents who are overworked and children who are overbooked with after-school activities, many families find they have to give up on family meals. If at all possible, try to have family members eat together at a regular time each day. Ideally, this is a social time when everyone can catch up with one another. If your child has food-related issues, try to avoid food battles at the family meal, and focus instead on sharing the pleasure of one another's company. And remember, when your young child sees parents and any older siblings using utensils and drinking from grown-up cups and enjoying a variety of foods, it's an added incentive to master eating skills and try new things.

- If your child is tactile hypersensitive, she may object to the sensation of a metal spoon in her fingers or inside her mouth. Try a plastic or rubber handle (and spoon bowl). Some kids love to eat with chopsticks, or even Zoo Sticks (tongs available from www.pfot .com—also available under different names such as Fish Sticks in other therapy catalogs; see photo on page 396).
- If your child has trouble stabilizing the bowl while eating, place it on a nonskid placemat, or consider one with a suction-cup bottom. Provide a small piece of bread as a pusher to help get food onto the spoon and get the helping hand more involved. Also think about the shape of the bowl or plate itself. Does a too-high or too-curved rim make it overly difficult to scoop food out?
- To encourage utensil use, serve foods such as yogurt and soup that can't be picked up with fingers.
- Think about the dining environment. Is it hectic? Is it conducive to relaxing and enjoying food? Are the food smells coming from the kitchen too strong for your child? You might want to play quiet

background music and use soft, soothing lighting. Do dishes and utensils make a lot of noise? How about using a tablecloth and plastic dishes and serving bowls that don't clatter against the table? Eating at a breakfast nook looking out the window might be lower pressure for a child with eating issues than sitting at a formal dining room table. Try a family picnic in the living room on occasion, complete with ground mat.

- If your child has trouble using utensils and regular cups, speak with your OT about the wide variety of adapted utensils and special cups and dishes, which can be purchased from therapy catalogs.

Eating Out

When it comes to eating out, there are many things to consider aside from food. Your child may be just fine in one or two familiar restaurants, where he can get his favorite foods and they always look and taste the same. But while you probably stick to a few restaurants that are known winners in your family, there's going to be a time when you're going to eat somewhere *different*. Chicken and broccoli doesn't taste the same at a different Chinese restaurant. Even your child's favorite fast-food chain restaurant's cuisine may vary by location.

If your child has food issues, simply tolerating being in an unfamiliar restaurant may be enough of a challenge. If you know that asking your child to eat his food *and* behave appropriately is going to push him over the edge, feed him beforehand or bring along food he can tolerate. While you may feel self-conscious about appearing to cater to your child's whims, it can be even more uncomfortable to have a child throw a tantrum in a restaurant. If anyone asks, you might simply say that you're working on expanding your child's diet at home and that dining out is a special event you all want to savor.

- Don't expect a child who can't sit still in school or at home to remain seated in a restaurant. Bring an inflatable seat cushion or pillow from home and plan to take breaks in a hallway, entry area, or outside. Develop a secret hand signal your child can use when he needs a break, and learn to observe the warning signs if he can't tell you before he goes into overload.
- Bring a "busy bag" full of small table toys such as crayons, a drawing pad, Silly Putty, and hand fidgets. Ask the waitress to bring something for your child to eat to keep him busy right away, such as breadsticks or crackers.

- Many restaurant managers think it enhances the atmosphere to play loud background music and to not use drapes or other sound-absorbing materials. If the restaurant is noisy, don't hesitate to politely ask a waiter or hostess to turn down the music. Most adults in the room will appreciate it too! You can also have your child wear earplugs, and, of course, ask to sit in the quietest part of the room.
- While it may seem antisocial for a child to wear headphones, it's more social to have him sitting at the table relatively happy listening to his favorite music than having a meltdown because he can't handle the ambient noise of a restaurant.
- If the restaurant allows smoking, ask the hostess to seat you as far away from the smoking section as possible. A cigarette a few tables away may not be noticeable to you but the smell may be overwhelming to your child. Try to find nonsmoking restaurants.
- Take a quick look around the restaurant upon entering and request a table that is not only in the nonsmoking section, but in an area away from a jukebox, the kitchen door with all its noise spilling into the room, noisy heaters, and so on. A quick assessment of the best location for your sensory child to eat may make your dining experience, and everyone else's, far more pleasant. Outdoor tables, which often have less noxious acoustics, are usually a good choice.
- Carry a Theraband or piece of Lycra to stretch across and tie around the front legs of your child's chair so that he can push against that with his feet or use it as a footrest if his feet can't touch the floor.
- When eating out, your child may be distressed by the aroma of unfamiliar foods, the scent of other people (especially perfumes and deodorants), and unfamiliar cleaning products. Use a scented hand lotion or essential oil you know your child likes, such as sweet orange, to mask intolerable smells. You can sprinkle a few drops on a cotton ball, spare handkerchief, or piece of fabric—or mix some up with cosmetic-quality almond or jojoba oil and apply sparingly on the skin just under her nose. Either way, she'll be smelling something she enjoys rather than something "gross."

Swallowing and Taking Capsules

Much of the time, vitamin supplements and medications need to be taken at mealtime, but swallowing capsules, tablets, and "horse pills" can be almost impossible for a child with sensory issues. If your child has trouble swallowing pills, investigate alternatives, such as a liquid formulation or a smaller-sized pill. The following solutions may help but if the pill is a medication, be sure to talk to the doctor to make sure that it's okay to break open a capsule or serve it with juice (avoid grapefruit, apple, and orange, as they can affect how the medication is used by the body).

- If it's okay with the doctor, break open capsules and sprinkle the contents into foods such as oatmeal, pudding, applesauce, ice cream, ketchup, or mashed potatoes, or mix them in with peanut butter or jelly on a cracker, muffin, or bread.
- If you mix a supplement or medication into food, taste it first to be sure you've disguised any unpleasant flavor. You don't want your child to balk at food because she doesn't trust you anymore now that you've been caught doctoring it!
- Use an infant medicine syringe to get liquid supplements or medications into a child's mouth quickly.
- If you supplement with fish oil and your child won't accept it in his food, rub it into the soles of his feet—perhaps while he's sleeping. Follow up with a sweet-smelling lotion to get rid of the fishy smell.
- If your child is at least three years old, try putting the capsule or pill at the back of his tongue and have him tilt his head back as he's drinking water to wash it down. You may want to coat the pill in butter, jelly, or honey to make it go down more smoothly.
- Try the Oralflo Pill Swallowing Cup. The pill sits in a grille right above the water and when you take a drink through the angled mouthpiece, you swallow the pill and liquid together (available from www.oralflo.com or 1-888-843-1631).
- Find out if there is a pharmacy in your area that does special medicine formulations like custom flavoring, lollipops, transdermal gels, and custom doses.

For more on eating, be sure to read Chapter 10: Improving Speech Skills and Picky Eating.

SPECIAL TIMES, AT HOME AND AWAY

Amusement Parks, Water Parks

- If your child is unable to wait in line, many amusement and theme parks will let you use their handicapped entrance that allow you to bypass a long wait in line. You must have a doctor's note to use this option at most parks. Disneyland and Walt Disney World have special passes for guests with special needs that require no note. Of course, you should use this option only if your child really needs it.

- If your child tends to be a vestibular sensory seeker, she's likely to adore rides with intense movement—but watch out for overload in which she has suddenly had enough and needs to stop. If your child tends to avoid vestibular input, don't force him onto any ride. Just watching the ride going around and around may provide all the input he can handle, at least at first. Consult with your OT to find out which rides may be most tolerable. Remember that amusement parks are not fun for everybody, kids and adults alike!

- If your child is hesitant about going on a ride, coax her gently but also ask the attendant if he'd be willing to stop the ride on your cue and let her get off. The ride operators at smaller amusement parks, and kiddie sections within larger parks, often are very willing to do this and to guide you on how to limit the movement of the ride. On a hot day, bring a lightweight jacket to place over a hot vinyl or metal seat.

- Before getting on any ride, observe it carefully. Your eager child may not realize that after it spins around a few times it rises into the air or reverses direction. Don't be shy; ask people getting off what it's like inside the Haunted House (loud surprises, jerky motions, and maybe even a musty smell) or other ride with hidden elements.

- If your child gets dizzy or nauseated, teach her to look away from the rides while she's waiting in line so that she's not queasy by the time she gets to the front. Teach her that on spinning, swinging, or dipping rides, she should fix her eyes on a stationary spot, such as her hands or the person seated in front of her, if she begins to get nauseated.

- Water parks can be an excellent choice for a sensory seeking child, with opportunities to fly down water chutes followed by a calming float in a "lazy river." If the park is large and connected to a theme park, look at the map and locations for food, parking, and lockers to ensure smoother transitions between wet bathing suit play, eating, long walks in flip-flops, and changing into dry clothes. If it's an indoor water park, you may want to take breaks in a quieter area away from the smell of chlorine and the echoes.

- As eager as your child is to jump on the next ride, pay attention to your instincts about whether he's becoming overstimulated and take a break for a calming activity, such as a long walk at the edge of the park to get to the rides on the other side, or a few minutes in a quiet, shady corner where he can jump off a small retaining wall, do wall push-ups, perform deep breathing on a park bench, and so on.

- Bring some healthy snacks or even a meal in a cooler bag if you can. Many amusement parks offer nothing but sugary and fried foods that may make your child more hyper and overstimulated.
- Avoid the worst crowds: if you can, go to the park first thing in the morning, on a weekday, and not during the most heavily trafficked times of the year.

Bike Riding

Riding a bike is a great way to get sensory input and exercise, but don't forget how complex this activity is. Your child needs to have adequate strength and motor planning ability plus use visual information to navigate obstacles. It's a lot to sequence and organize! For young children with visual issues, you might consider one of the new styles of first bikes that have a long handle for you to guide your child—or for you to push when he's tired.

- If your child is having trouble learning to ride a bike, use a smaller bike or lower the seat so he can easily stick his foot out and stop himself from falling over (when a bike is adjusted "properly" for riding, the child should be able to touch the balls of his feet to the ground while seated, but not able to place his feet flat on the ground; your child may be more comfortable with the seat at a different height).
- Have him wear protective gear (wrist guards, knee pads) in addition to a helmet, and practice on a mat or rubberized surface, if possible.
- If your child has trouble reaching the pedals, securely fasten blocks to the pedals to shorten the distance.
- If your child (or you) is having a very hard time getting the hang of bike riding, consult with your OT or physical therapist. You can also check www.losethetrainingwheels.org to see if they're offering a workshop near you.

Birthday Parties and Other Parties, Indoor and Outdoor

- Many families today throw big, lavish birthday parties for their children that can be overstimulating. While it may seem old-fashioned, what seems to work best is to limit the number of children to the age of the child: three children on his third birthday, four on his fourth, etc.

- Seriously consider how important it is that your child wear that poufy little dress or adorable clip-on tie. The important thing is that your child be as comfortable as possible. Of course, before you give up on dressing up, try removing all of the clothing tags and snip out all of the itchy stray threads. Allow your daughter to wear her favorite top and leggings with a pretty party skirt. Or let your son wear the Wiggles T-shirt and bathing suit bottom he insists on wearing at home beneath his button down shirt and dress pants.

- Find out what activities will take place at the birthday party your child has been invited to. Many party games are overwhelming for kids with sensory issues—imagine a child who can't bear unexpected touch playing Duck-Duck-Goose. If there is a messy party project, allow the child to use a paintbrush or rubber gloves (you'll probably need to take these along if the party is not at your house). If there's an activity planned that you know will be too hard for your child, have an alternative ready beforehand. For example, if the kids are going to play tag, you can give your child a graceful out by asking her to help you prepare the cupcakes or to help you set the table. However, peer pressure is powerful. The child you *never* imagined to be able to play in a room full of kids chattering loudly as they pull out every toy imaginable may have a wonderful time in all the chaos (and may run away from you, laughing, afterward because she's so overstimulated).

- Create some structure if that will help your child. Smaller kids' birthday parties tend to only be a couple of hours long, with a specific sequence of activities that you can discuss beforehand with your child so he knows what to expect. If it's a less structured party, you can preplan activities so he knows what to do with himself. For example, if the party is at a local gymnastics center and you learn that it's one hour of free play, then food, then cake, your child can preplan that he will first play on the trampoline, then in the ball pit, and then on the teeter-totter before eating.

- If your child has trouble with unfamiliar places and you have the opportunity to visit where the party will take place, it's a good idea to do so to increase your child's comfort level when it's time for the actual party.

- Parties, especially little kids' birthday parties, tend to get really noisy. Quiet kids down by dimming the lights rather than shushing or raising your voice. If the party is not at your house, prearrange this with the host. Simply explain that you noticed how great dimming the lights worked at the last party you attended and ask the hostess to try it.

- Watch out for entrances and exits. Teach your child to stick out his hand for a handshake, which should be an acceptable substitute for a hug if he has trouble tolerating hugs. If you know you have a particularly touchy-feely relative or guest who always grabs your child for a big bear hug, you may need to speak with this person beforehand, and explain that your child is more comfortable with a handshake as a greeting. Tough luck if they don't like it! It's not their need for affection that you should be concerned with.

- Help the child find a spot in the room where he feels he can control unwanted touches. He may be happiest at the end of a table or on a chair along the side of the room where he can monitor who is nearby without risking a surprise "attack" from behind.

- Party decorations are usually vibrant and patterned. If your child tends to visually overload, find a special spot for him to go to that has soft lighting and fewer colors and patterns. You may even need to bring a soothing storybook you can look at together to help your child reorganize during a break. A break outside, sitting quietly for a few minutes, may help him regroup.

- A party may not be the time and the place to insist on eye contact. It may be too much to insist that a child look at the hostess when saying "thank you." Work on eye contact when there is less sensory stimuli for the child to deal with.

- Party time is also not the time to insist on having your child try food items he detests. Bring along a well-tolerated food (and even a dessert) so your child can eat along with everyone else, especially if she has food allergies. You may want to discreetly exit the party before she begins to eat so that the other children don't begin protesting because she has the "better" snack.

- If your child's birthday is coming up and he has trouble with being sung to and then blowing out the candles, practice beforehand. Put birthday candles in a pretend cake made out of Play-Doh or a cupcake, sing "Happy Birthday" to his Elmo toy (that can sit on the chair opposite), and blow out the candles. Then do it for Big Bird, then for Cookie Monster, and so on. If your child blows through his teeth instead of his lips, ask your OT or SLP how to facilitate blowing. For example, you can help your child to relax his jaw and move his lips forward by placing your index finger and thumb on either cheek between his mouth and his jaw and gently pressing inward and forward. Raise the cake and candles so it's easier for him to aim for the flames when he blows.

- If the party is at your home, have your child put away special toys she won't want to share. Holding it together during a raucous birthday party is enough pressure without having to share favorite possessions too.
- Small children might enjoy a craft session as part of the festivities, and it might provide calming tactile input. Older children might enjoy a more sophisticated version, such as a party at a do-it-yourself bead shop.
- Make sure there's a quiet, low-stimulation place your child can retreat to if overwhelmed: a bedroom, a bathroom, a yard, a car (obviously, never leave a small child alone in a car). Some small children find it calming to play in water, so a kiddie pool or even splashing around in a sink can help them regroup.
- Many children with auditory processing problems find it easier to handle a loud party when it's outdoors because the sounds don't reverberate like they do in a confined space. Also, outdoors they often have more freedom to run and jump, getting lots of sensory input. Consider your child's sensitivities when you're planning where to hold a party.
- If your child can't handle birthday parties at all but is invited to one, consider having her tell her friend she can't make the party but would love to have her come over for a special playdate featuring cupcakes with birthday candles, a present, and one-on-one play the week of the child's birthday.

Dentist Appointments

Children with sensory issues—especially those with oral sensitivities—can have a very difficult time at the dentist. It's worth taking time to shop around for a practice with a child-friendly waiting room and offices. A good pediatric dentist will already incorporate many of the following tips into her practice, but you can use them with any cooperative dentist. Remember that all kids, and many adults, have issues with going to the dentist, so don't expect perfect behavior even if you do your best to accommodate your child's sensory issues. Acknowledge his feelings, but at the same time let him know that going to the dentist is a part of life. It may take time before your child gains enough comfort that he doesn't resist the trip.

- For dental checkups, start early (when the first tooth appears) and go often (every six months). Look for a dentist with a child-friendly waiting room and offices, a good rapport with kids, and a flexible attitude toward time, which is essential for kids who need a lot of coaxing and reassurance. Consider checking out the dentist's office before bringing your child there for the first time, and explaining what your child's sensitivities are.
- Schedule the appointment so there's plenty of time for alleviating apprehension, explaining procedures, and letting the child check out the tools that will be used.
- If you have another child who is comfortable at the dentist, make a separate appointment for her and take plenty of photographs of her in the waiting room, in the dentist's chair, having her teeth cleaned, etc. Use the photos to make a little storybook for your child with sensory issues before his appointment. Or, have him come along for an appointment for another child who can handle the situation well: a peer showing that the dentist's procedures aren't so horrible may ease your child's fears.
- Read a comforting book about dental checkups, such as *The Berenstain Bears Visit the Dentist,* to help prepare your child for the experience.
- Depending on your child's age, write a personalized story (using his name) about going to the dentist.
- Call ahead to see if the office is running on schedule or late, to shorten time spent in the waiting room.
- Give your child earplugs or headphones with music or an audio book to listen to while his teeth are being worked on. Some pediatric dentists offer headphones as well as cartoons on a television for their patients.
- Give your child sunglasses to protect her eyes from the bright light that shines down onto the examination chair.
- Even if X-rays aren't being taken, place the weighted lead bib on your child's chest to provide calming, proprioceptive, and deep pressure input.
- Bring comfort toys, fidget toys, or Silly Putty or Play-Doh for him to squeeze.
- If your child is orally hypersensitive, do oral desensitization work such as using a vibrating teether or toothbrush or another oral vibrator such as Ellie the Elephant Jiggler; massaging gums with a finger cot; or using a Z-Vibe with textured tips. You can also use "chewies" such as the Ark Grabber, Chewy Tube, or Chewlery.

- Practice playing dentist at home with a reclining chair, a dental mirror (available from www.drugstore.com), and a bowl to spit in. Take turns playing patient so your child can feel in control.

- For kids who are uncomfortable with changes in head position and movement, being put passively into a reclining position and feeling the dentist chair being raised and lowered can be very distressing. If your child is small, he can sit on your lap as you sit on the dentist's chair. Give him opportunities to experience "riding" a chair (an adjustable office chair or car seat) when he's not already upset about the dentist.

- Have your child wiggle her fingers while getting a novocaine shot to distract her from the sensation. Tell the dentist up front if your child needs extra novocaine and insist on testing how numbed the area is before starting a procedure.

- Before you try to describe a procedure to your child, talk to your dentist. The procedure may have changed since you had it. Also, the dentist may have suggestions for describing the procedure that will make it sound less frightening. For instance, a novocaine shot may not feel like getting a shot depending on your dentist's technique for administering it, so you don't need to say "You'll get a shot."

- Dentistry and materials change often. Talk to your dentist about all the options and their pros and cons before committing to one type of filling versus another, or to coating your child's teeth to prevent cavities. Proper use of fluoridated water, toothpaste, or rinses on the surface of the teeth (you don't have to actually drink fluoridated water to get its benefits); good dental hygiene; and avoiding snacks that stick to the teeth (refined-flour crackers and pretzels, gummy candies, etc.) are all tools for preventing dental caries that you can consider.

- A reward is almost always appropriate, even if your child had a hard time with the visit to the dentist. He deserves something special!

Doctor's Appointments

Between the fluorescent lights, crinkly paper on the examining table, dressing gown, the tongue depressor, having bright lights in your eyes, and getting a shot, the doctor's office can be terrifying for a child. Here are some ways to make it more bearable.

- Bring some fun activities—stickers, paper or small coloring books and crayons, Post-it notes, a doll or action figure or car, etc.—if you're going to be stuck in a waiting room. An older child can carry her own book, hand-held computer game, or other toy. While you're waiting, have your child do wall push-ups or chair push-ups (holding the chair while seated and lifting her bottom); or squeeze her limbs tightly, working your way up from fingers to shoulders; or simply hug her or hold her tightly if that will calm her.

- If your child is asked to change into a gown, ask the doctor if your child can wear a loose oversized supersoft man's shirt from home so it looks, feels, and smells familiar.
- Allow your child to listen to his favorite music. Let him wear a cap or visor to shield sensitive eyes from the fluorescent lights. Bring along that inflatable cushion so he can sit more comfortably on the examining table. A weighted blanket or shoulder wrap may be calming for when he is lying down.
- If your child is unusually sensitive to shots and getting blood drawn (all kids hate them, but some don't recover for hours, days, or weeks), try using EMLA cream to numb your child's skin beforehand. It's a mix of lidocaine and prilocaine and does not require a prescription. Ask your doctor about it.
- Reduce the fear factor by playing doctor at home, taking turns being the patient, and reading reassuring books such as *Froggy Goes to the Doctor*.

Holidays

You may recall childhood holidays as a joyful time when everyone sat around and ate and talked for hours. But for a child with sensory issues, holidays can be a real challenge.

- Get your child involved in the preparations. You can often find craft activities in holiday season magazines, or enter the name of the holiday into your web browser (such as Google). Young children will love adding colored feathers and wiggly eyes to a pine cone to make a turkey. Kids can glue large sequins or buttons onto a Christmas tree cut out from green construction paper or felt. Glue three Styrofoam balls together and decorate it to make a snowman. Make a Kwanzaa kinara or a menorah out of clay. Use tactile desensitization techniques your OT shows you to help your child feel more comfortable touching "yucky" materials.
- Cooking is a wonderful sensory experience. Let your child help you pour, mix, blend, and decorate holiday food. Even if you're going to

someone else's home to celebrate, help your child to cook a special side dish or dessert to bring along.

- Reduce the element of surprise. As much as possible, tell your child in advance what will happen on the holiday. Let her know who is going to be there and what activities will take place.

- Have a place your child can retreat to. Work with your child to fig-ure out, in advance, where she can go and what she can do if she begins to feel overwhelmed at a holiday gathering. It's much better for your child to take a break than to feel trapped in a situation she can't handle. If you're home, let her know she can politely excuse herself to go to her room if she needs some time to compose her-self. But if you're at your in-laws or other relatives, you will need to work out a place where your child can take a break. Ask whether she can retreat to a bedroom, a den, or elsewhere.

- Keep your child happy, even if your guests/relatives don't under-stand why you are doing what you're doing. Bring along your child's favorite activities, such as crayons and paper. Also bring any especially calming items: a lucky rock, a favorite stuffed toy, Play-Doh, bubbles, and so on. An older child may feel less trapped if he can listen to his favorite music over headphones or bring a book or hand-held video game. Give your child the sensory input she needs. If she has to jump and crash twenty times before sitting down to eat, let her do it. A hearty walk is a great idea after a big meal, and helps with digestion too. Walk through a pile of leaves, stomp in the snow, or roll down a hill.

- Just because you dress up for the holidays doesn't mean it's worth forcing your child into clothing that will make her miserable. Scratchy petticoats, lace, and bows on girls' dresses may be too irritating. Your son may be unable to tolerate a tie and dress shoes. But you never know, your child might love his special holiday outfit! Give it a test-drive several times before the event, and have a back-up plan (bring a change of clothing just in case). As always, the key is to be flexible.

- Bring along your child's own pillow and/or bedding if you plan to stay overnight. Bring a night-light or any other bedtime necessity.

- Don't force your child to eat something "gross" just because it's the mandated holiday food. If you know your child won't eat turkey, bring along something nutritious that he will eat. Certainly offer him some turkey; this may be the time he'll finally try it, especially if there are beloved relatives who seem to like it.

- If your child reacts badly to sweets, be prepared. Holiday gather-ings often include candies, cakes, and sodas. This may be a great opportunity for you to introduce healthier desserts to others as you bring along acceptable desserts you know your child enjoys. If you have a limited-sweets policy for your child, recognize that it's going to be quite hard to maintain it when all the relatives are having "just another sliver" of pie or munching on holiday cookies. If your child doesn't have allergies, you might want to let him indulge in a special treat—just be prepared for any behavioral reactions (increased physical activity, mood swings, or whatever) that crop up. For example, if you know your child gets hyper after eating sugary foods, plan to do some physical activity after she consumes them.

- Read Chapter 17: Empowering Your Child in the World if you're concerned about the reactions of friends and relatives to your accommodating and respecting your child's sensory needs.

Outdoor Events

Much as we all want our children to appreciate the great outdoors, to a kid with sensory issues it can be very upsetting. Bright sunshine, irritating winds, scratchy grass, and buzzing insects in front of the face are just a few of the things that can make a child hate being outdoors.

- Just as you protect your child's skin from harmful UV rays, protect his eyes too by having your child wear high-quality sunglasses in bright sunlight. Consult your local optician, or look online at Web sites such as www.sunprotectionzone.com, which features sunglasses with a neoprene headband for three- to seven-year olds—as well as other sun protection products.
- If your child won't wear sunglasses and she can't confine herself to the shade without spoiling her fun, have her wear a baseball cap or a hat with a wide brim. Use a beach umbrella or a tent/beach cabana to create shade and shelter her from insects and wind.
- Bug repellent and sunblock now come in lotion and spray forms. Neutrogena makes a spray-on sunblock that contains no perfumes. Banana Boat makes a stick sunblock that you rub on the skin to apply; a child who hates light touch might prefer this type of applicator. Note that there are now products that contain both sunblock *and* insect repellent.
- Bring a beach mat that's easy to brush off (instead of a towel) to a beach or to a picnic in the park so that your child doesn't have to sit on sand, dirt, or grass.

Public Bathrooms

Public bathrooms can be excruciatingly nasty places for children with auditory, visual, and smell sensitivities. Flickering fluorescent lights, industrial toilets flushing suddenly, hand dryers blowing loudly, and people coming in and out of a small, echo-filled room can overwhelm a child. Earplugs can help the child with auditory sensitivity. The younger your child is, the more likely it is that a nice store owner will allow your child to use her small, private facilities. If you can, plan to be near bathroom facilities you know your child can tolerate.

- Since soaps in public places are often slimy and stinky, carry diaper wipes or an alcohol-based hand soap that doesn't contain tri-closan.
- Place Post-it sticky notes over automatic toilet sensors to avoid un-pleasant, sudden flushing, which can be loud and frightening for a small child. Carry purse-size packages of soft tissues to use in lieu of the scratchy toilet paper provided.
- For toddlers and preschoolers, you can bring a portable potty on road trips: if you can find a discreet place to use it, your child can avoid going into a public bathroom. These include Inflate-a-Potty and On-the-Go Portable Potty by Potette, from www.onestepahead .com. You can also buy a potty cushion, such as the one from One Step Ahead, that you can take with you to make large, cold toilet seats more acceptable.

Shopping Trips and Chores

- Whenever possible, leave your child with your spouse, sitter, friend, or relative while you do your shopping; have someone else shop for you; or shop online. Nowadays, you can even buy groceries and drugstore items online.
- Some children may find it comforting to get into an elevator or on an escalator and ride it for a few minutes, as it's relatively quiet and calm.
- If you must take your child, pick a time when the stores are less hectic: grocery shop in the evening, or do your back-to-school shopping on a weekday.
- Give your child some control and a sense of predictability. Young children can help you find groceries on the shelf, match groceries

to a picture list, or follow a picture list of chores you will be doing that day. Older kids can help you write lists, find items, pull out coupons, or check items off your to-do list.

- Let your child push the grocery cart for proprioceptive input. Many supermarkets have junior-size carts for smaller children. Also, pushing her own stroller can help a toddler or preschooler get calming proprioceptive input. Add packages for extra weight.
- Have your child wear a backpack; as it fills up with purchases she'll get proprioceptive input.
- For a calm time-out, stop into a pet store and watch the fish in the aquariums (often located in the back of the store, where it's quieter). Or, stop by a florist's shop to smell the flowers (also, the oxygen given off by the plants can help soothe and energize your child). Be aware, however, that for a child who is agitated by strong scents, a florist, candle, or pet store can be aggravating.

Summer Camp

Summer camp can be heaven or just the opposite for a child with sensory problems. Whether and when she's ready depends on her level of maturity and independence, and definitely on the camp itself. There are several day and overnight camps that have been specially created by OTs and others for children with sensory issues. Here's a sampling:

- Camp Dove-Avanti East in Carmel, NY. Contact Dove Rehabilitation at 516-935-3683. Web site: www.doverehab.com.
- Sensory Adventure Camp in Pittsburgh, PA. Call Center for Creative Play at 412-371-1668. Web site: www.cfcp.org.
- Over the Rainbow in Maryland. Call Kids Therapy Works at 301-384-5081.
- Summer Adventure Camp in Washington, DC. Call 202-244-8089.
- Sense-Ational Play Time in Maryland. Call 301-942-6006.
- Camp Little Tree, ages 8 to 12, and Camp Big Tree, ages 12 to 16, at the Breckenridge Outdoor Education Center, Breckenridge, CO. Call 720-777-6590. Web site: www.thechildrenshospital.org/conditions/rehab/camps/index.aspx.
- Camp Littlefoot, ages 5 to 7, Rockville, MD. Call 301-424-5200. Web site: www.ttlc.org/camp_littlefoot.htm#campLittlefoot.
- GMS Institute in Manassas, VA. Call 703-392-5055. Web site: www.gmskids.com.

If your child receives school-based services twelve months a year, it's possible that the school district may pay for camp. So check into these camps and ask your OT, teacher, or others if they know of any camps that incorporate sensory integration principles. Some OTs and PTs working in the schools pick up summer work at camps, as do some teachers well versed in sensory issues.

If you send your child to a traditional camp, you will need to make sure the camp counselors will be sensitive to your child's needs and willing to accommodate her and follow through on her sensory diet. Ask your OT to communicate and consult with the camp director and counselors, and, if possible, make a few visits to check whether any environmental accommodations will need to be made.

Swimming

- Chlorinated pools smell bad, and the water can sting children's eyes. Consider swimming in clear-water lakes (rock and sand bottoms instead of mud bottoms are best), home pools (which usually have less chlorine than public pools), or pools that are kept clean without the use of chlorine. Swimmer's earplugs may reduce the discomfort of hearing all the echoes in an indoor pool.

- Swimming goggles and masks provide deep pressure input while protecting eyes from chlorine and the feel of water against the eyeballs. They also let children easily see underwater, which can help them feel more at ease. Some kids prefer to swim with nose plugs and/or earplugs to prevent the discomfort of water getting into ears and noses. You can get earplugs as well as a neoprene stretch headband to cover them from www.earplugstore.com. You can also have your child hold his nose with his fingers when he jumps in. Teach your child how to clear his mouth and nose if water gets in, and to tip his head to drain excess water from his ears.

- Entering a cold body of water can be a challenge for anyone but especially so for a child with sensory issues. Some kids prefer to jump or dive in and start moving quickly to warm up. Other kids need to adjust more slowly. Try having your child wet his feet, then his legs, then splash his shoulders and chest, then wet his head a little before going in completely. Consider having him shower beforehand.

- Have your child try on his swimsuit and get it wet and even sandy before a trip to a beach or lake. A child who can tolerate knee-length dry swim trunks at home may be miserable once they are wet and sandy; better to find this out at home.

- Apply sunscreen fifteen minutes before heading to the beach. This gives it ample time to soak into skin for proper sun protection and ensures it will be dry by the time you hit the sand.
- Consider swimwear that doesn't "flap"—nylon, Speedo-type bikini racers for boys, the newer one-piece racing suits or short wet-suit styles, and girls' styles without skirts or ruffles. Have your child try on several types of suits. One girl may find a two-piece suit, which exposes her belly to the light touch of breezes, unbearable while another may not be able to tolerate a one-piece because of the movement of material against her belly.

Waiting in Line

- If your child is uncomfortable standing in line at school because she doesn't want to get bumped, have her stand at the front or the end of the line where she'll have more personal space.
- If your child is getting antsy in a line with you, let her stand a few feet away, or ask the person in front of you if he would mind whether you step out of line to join your child a few feet away for a couple of minutes. Let her push up against a nearby wall, do a shuffle walk, or jump in place or off a small retaining wall for sensory input.
- Give your child an opportunity to move even as she waits in line. She can roll on her feet from heel to toe and back, count how long she can stand on her tiptoes, on one leg, and so on.

Waiting Rooms

- Bring some fun activities if you're going to be stuck in a waiting room with a small child: stickers, paper, Post-it sticky notes, crayons, small coloring books, a doll or action figure or car. An older child can carry her own book, Game Boy, or other activity. While you are waiting, have your child do wall push-ups or chair push-ups (holding the chair while seated and lifting her bottom), squeeze her limbs tightly working your way up from fingers to shoulders, or simply hug her or hold her tightly if that will calm her.

HOME ENVIRONMENT

Bathroom

* Consider the surface your child is standing on (bench, rug, chair, etc.) when grooming at the sink or in front of the mirror. Make sure the step stool is sturdy and has a surface that isn't slippery.
* Consider the sound of the bathroom. Think about installing low-noise toilets, running the tub with the door closed while your child is not in the bathroom, and/or replacing some of the tile with a more absorbent material (Sheetrock, for example). The more objects—especially sound-absorbing towels and bathrobes—you have in the bathroom, the less noise.
* Reconsider bathroom lighting (see below).

Bedding

* Use well-laundered, soft sheets such as high-thread-count cotton or jersey. New sheets, particularly polyester ones, can be scratchy and stiff. Your child might like flannel sheets, but some pill after a few washings and can be very uncomfortable against the skin.
* Consider the mattress: Should it be firm or soft? A child who is sensitive to movement might prefer a futon mattress on a platform or having a wooden board between the mattress and box spring.
* Some children are comforted by sleeping under something heavy. You can use several blankets or a weighted blanket (talk to your OT about this), or attach some weighted items to a regular blanket.
* Your child might prefer to sleep in a sleeping bag as if she were being swaddled.
* If your child is anxious about heights, forget the box spring, and place the mattress on the floor.
* If your child frequently falls out of bed, you can add safety rails to a standard bed (available from www.onestepahead.com).

Lighting

* Many lights are simply too bright. Install dimmer switches so you can control the amount of light in a room.
* Replace fluorescent bulbs with incandescent or full-spectrum bulbs, which provide a more natural type of light. You can find these at good hardware stores or at www.fullspectrumsolutions.com. If it's the

flicker that your child can't stand, try Cozy Shades (available from *Integrations* catalog), which fit over standard fluorescent fixtures and soften harsh lighting. You can also turn off overheads altogether and use a floor lamp.

- If you can, avoid compact fluorescent bulbs, which contain mercury. Although there is some cost savings, if a bulb breaks, you will need to follow the EPA's nine-step decontamination procedure. See www.epa.gov/mercury/spills/#fluorescent for information on cleaning up spills and special recycling required for compact fluorescents.
- Some children are calmed by colored lights.
- Hang heavy curtains (corduroy or canvas work well) to dampen outdoor noise, drafts, and light. Vinyl miniblinds made from thick vinyl and S-shaped slats are extra effective at blocking light (but be sure to cut blind cords if you have small children because of the strangulation hazard, and test them for lead if they were manufactured outside the U.S.).
- Provide ample lighting for your child's work and play areas. If your child has attention issues, create a warm spotlighting effect on his desk and lower lighting elsewhere in the room to encourage visual focus on work.

Noise and Smell Reduction

- Move the child's bed or desk away from noisy radiators or walls with water pipes that make noise every time someone uses water. Noisy radiators can often be quieted by having the radiator system flushed.
- Install soundproofing on the walls of your child's bedroom.
- If you have a choice, situate your child's room as far as possible from areas that will remain noisy after bedtime (e.g., an older child's room), and as far as possible from the kitchen and garbage areas.
- When installing any new features in your child's room or areas where she plays or spends a lot of time, be aware that new carpets, curtains, and blinds, as well as paint, can emit very strong odors for some time. You might have to make other arrangements for your child to sleep, study, and play while these new items are airing out, or put the items outside in the yard for a few days.

Room Décor

- Avoid visually cluttered décor. Store items behind doors or in bins that you can't see through. Cover a shelving unit with doors or a curtain. Avoid busy rugs, patterned wallpaper, and decorating in colors that your child might find overstimulating (commonly, the fiery colors red and orange), particularly in the child's bedroom or play area.
- If your child is old enough, involve him in decisions about how to decorate his room.
- Don't use scatter rugs that can result in slips and falls. Tack them down with doublestick tape or place no-skid rubber mats under them if you must have them.

MISCELLANEOUS CHALLENGES

Car Rides

- Provide your child with a weighted lap pad, hand fidgets, juice boxes (sucking through the thin straw provides calming input), and crunchy, healthy snacks that don't stick to teeth, such as carrot or celery sticks.
- If your child is bothered by the seat belt or safety belt on a car seat, use a "seat belt buddy" made of shearling or other soft material you can wrap and secure around the strap to keep it from digging in. You can buy one commercially or simply place some soft thick material between his body and the strap or buckle. At the same time, consider adjusting what your child wears underneath the seat belt. Too many layers, such as a jacket and a shirt, may feel confining or provide too much confusing sensory input. Simply taking his jacket off may help him tolerate the seat belt. Be sure the straps are properly adjusted and not too tight.
- If your child feels physically insecure, try wedging a footstool in front of your child's seat so his legs aren't dangling. (Be sure the footstool is secure so it won't become a projectile in an accident.)
- Play music your child finds soothing, which will also help block out disturbing sounds.
- Bring small toys and books with lots of pictures to look at. Discourage reading in the car if your child gets carsick easily. Consider using trivia toys such as Brain Quest cards instead of books with a lot of text.

- If your child is prone to motion sickness, try Psi Bands (see www .drugstore.com), bracelets that use acupressure to prevent nausea.
- Talk to your child about whether air-conditioning or open windows are more comfortable. Fresh air, even if windows are open just a crack, can often reduce carsickness, but in some cars, opening just one or two windows a crack may cause unpleasant vibratory noises.
- Never allow anyone to smoke in your car when children are present. And if your child is sensitive to smell, you may want to ban smoking in your car altogether.
- A child who just came out of a car that was traveling on hilly roads may need a good, long stretch of lying on the ground or sitting quietly to regain her equilibrium after all that vestibular stimulation.
- Have older kids play the alphabet game, trying to find each letter, in order, as they look at signs and license plates. Challenge them to add up the numbers on license plates. Play 20 Questions or other word games. Bring along good car toys like travel-sized Connect Four, Magnadoodles, and hand-held electronic games. Laptops or other DVD players can calm some children, but they can also cause motion sickness and backseat arguments so use them judiciously.
- Make frequent stops and allow your kids to get physical activity to work off their pent-up energy.

Elevators, Escalators, and Sliding Glass Doors

Elevators and escalators can really dumbfound even kids who don't have sensory issues. Elevators provide lots of movement input, especially when it starts and stops on several floors, providing confusing "invisible" vestibular stimulation to the inner ear, because the child feels she is moving up or down but everything she *sees* tells her she's standing still. An auditory sensitive child may find the mechanical vibration and noise distressing. Escalators propel your child upward or downward while she stands still, again providing unusual vestibular input. What's more, she must time her steps to get on and off safely. Sliding glass doors seem to work like magic and can startle a child who already feels visual information is unpredictable.

- Explain to your child how elevators work, using toys you may already have, such as the Fisher Price Garage, or set up a bucket on a pulley to show him. Explain what those hidden sounds are. Let him wear earplugs or cover his ears if the noise upsets him. Teach him to watch the numbers for each floor, or, if it's an ADA-compliant building, to count the beeps as the elevator reaches each floor. Let him move if there's room—he can do wall push-ups, for example. If it won't disturb anyone, have him jump up and down while the elevator is in motion.

- Teach your child how escalators work. Show him a real tractor or a toy tractor (the belt on an escalator works like the tractor treads). Help him learn to time step-on, step-off movement by counting "one, two, three, step." If he's nervous going down, let him stand behind you. Look for an elevator or staircase if he cannot use the escalator safely.
- Children often don't recognize that sliding glass doors work on a cause-and-effect basis. Have your child observe and take note of the area other people step on to activate the doors, and count how long it takes them to pass through until the doors close again. Show him that no one ever gets squished between the doors!

Hand Flapping and Head Banging

(See pages 216–17 in Chapter 8: Dealing with Developmental Delays for information about these behaviors.)

Hand flapping

- Try to train her to clap her hands or hug herself instead.
- Provide deep pressure and proprioceptive input into the shoulders, arms, and hands via sensory diet activities such as wheelbarrow walking, brushing, and joint compressions.
- Distract your child with a favorite toy or activity that requires her to use her hands.

Head banging

- Check for an ear infection, vision problems, and teething. Some kids will head bang to distract them from headaches, and this behavior could, in rare cases, be the only noticeable sign of a seizure. If head banging is persistent, talk to your pediatrician who may refer you to a pediatric neurologist.
- Regularly massage her head and face with hands or a vibrator.
- If head banging is intense, your pediatrician and/or OT may suggest that you have your child wear a helmet to prevent injury (these can be found in *Abilitations* and other catalogs).

- Pull your child's crib or bed away from the wall and place it on a thick rug. Use a padded crib bumper, securely attached, that goes all the way around the crib.
- Use the behavior as a guide to the sensory input you will provide in a sensory diet, and provide tactile, proprioceptive, and vestibular input.
- Speak with your OT about using a weighted hat (see *Abilitations* or other therapy catalogs), or add weight to a cap you have to give your child more sensory input on his head.
- Encourage your child to push her head into a pillow or beanbag chair.
- Massage her face with your hands or a vibrator. Let her sit on your lap, facing you, and grind her face into yours. Try pressing your chin against her forehead and moving your jaw back and forth as you hum.
- Let her push items with her forehead: a pillow-filled box or a dust mop across the floor.
- Playfully push your child over with your hand against his forehead as he sits on a soft surface such as a bed, cushion, or large pillow.

Temperature Sensitivity

Many kids will stay in a pool or lake until their lips turn blue because they're having so much fun. But tuning in to extremes in temperature can be much more difficult for a child with SPD who is hyposensitive to temperatures. In rare cases in which the nerve tract that processes temperature is truly impaired, your child may be unable to register temperature. In such a case, you will need to compensate by turning down the water heater, putting covers on the radiators, and taking dials off the stove. You will have to be especially vigilant, and of course, teach your child which things are too hot for him to be close to.

- Teach your child about variations in temperature. Put out several bowls of water at varying temperatures. Have her touch each one and help her label the temperature: hot, warm, cool, freezing. Set up science experiments. What happens when you put an ice cube in warm water? What happens when you put warm water in the freezer?
- If your child craves warmth, use a well-insulated hot water bottle or microwavable heat pack, and warm up clothing and bedding in the dryer. Do not use heating pads, which can cause burns. If your

child craves coolness, let her hold an insulated ice pack or give her an ice pop. You can cool down her clothing by putting it in the refrigerator or freezer.

General Noise Sensitivity

- Respect your child's auditory sensitivity. It really hurts! Avoid noisy places whenever you can, walk down another street if there are jackhammers, and duck into a store if there are sirens.
- Let your child use noise-blocking headphones, earmuffs (available at hardware stores or www.sensorycomfort.com), or earplugs. If she uses earplugs, make certain that they are clean and fit safely. The Ear Plug Super Store (www.earplugstore.com) has an excellent selection of premolded and moldable silicone earplugs designed to fit kids' ears. They offer an assortment pack for you to figure out which kind your child will find most comfortable.
- Let her wear a stretchy headband and pull it over her ears if she becomes uncomfortable with sound levels.
- If your child can tolerate it, have her flush or vacuum up Cheerios or Goldfish crackers by herself. Having control over the sound very often helps kids tolerate it. Similarly, some kids can better tolerate the sound of a loud noise, such as a coffee grinder, if they count down to it because they can brace themselves for the sound.
- Use a white noise machine, or an aquarium, fan, or a radio set on static. A CD called *For Crying Out Loud,* which consists of background noises, restaurant chatter and clatter, windshield wipers, and other noises some babies find comforting, can be found at www.amazon.com, www.store.babycenter.com, www.colichelp.com, and other places. You might want to play this or another soothing CD on repeat.

A NOTE ON EARPLUGS

Several times we've recommended earplugs for various noisy situations. However, your child should not wear earplugs all the time—only when she really needs them. Otherwise, her ears and brain will become used to them and the earplugs will no longer be effective.

Fear of Specific Noises

Lots of children are distressed by sounds such as the vacuum cleaner, barking dogs, hair dryers, and thunder. Many simply get over this fear with time and exposure. Others, especially those with auditory hypersensitivity, do not. In this case, you'll need to take a multipronged approach to help your child feel more comfortable with the inevitable sounds out there.

1. Protect your child's ears from painful sounds.
2. Ask your OT about participating in a therapeutic listening program to reduce general noise sensitivity.
3. Progressively desensitize your child to the sound. If your child is absolutely terrified by something, you may need to start with just a picture of the object. Then you can slowly start to add the sound—very quietly, very gently, in a safe, secure environment. For example, he can listen to a lawnmower sound as he snuggles up in your arms holding his teddy bear and sucking on a lollipop.

You can record the sound yourself, or use the Sound-Eaze CD from www.route2greatness.com. This CD combines sounds that are frequently scary to kids with soothing, rhythmic songs, lulling kids into a calm state with a song that explains the sound and then introduces the sound itself. Allow your child to lower the volume if the sound is unbearable and then slowly raise the volume. He can stop and start it himself too. The idea is to let your child develop a sense of predictability and control over what feels chaotic.

The School-Eaze version of the CD includes the sounds of a school bell, changing classes, cafeteria, fire drills, and field trips. Again, allow your child to turn it on and off and to lower and raise the volume to give him a sense of control.

Personal Space Issues

- Teach your child to stay an arm's length away from other people to grant them personal space. Have him imagine a bubble around his body that extends out as far as his arm can stretch.
- Let your child sit at one end of a rectangular table to give him ample elbow room.

Picking Up Toys

- Use designated places for toys. Keep all the toy cars in one drawer or bin, Barbie dolls in a clear shoe holder hanging from the back of a door, etc. If the system is too complex—for instance, if you designated separate drawers for trucks, cars, and airplanes even though your child plays with all of them pretty much in the same way at the same time—your child will be less motivated to put toys away. If the system is too simple—everything gets dumped into one huge bin—the child may put things away readily but will have to dump everything out to find what he wants.

- Keep toy areas from getting too cluttered. For kids who easily get visually overstimulated, don't store toys in see-through containers. Instead, put a picture of what's inside on a drawer you can't see through.

- Break down a huge cleanup into smaller tasks. Tell your child to put the train set in the train drawer, and then tell him to put the dump truck on its special shelf. If there are a lot of toys out, you may need to help him, or let him start by cleaning up just two toys before saying, "Now you'll need to pick up those puzzle pieces and put them in the bag inside the puzzle box," and so on.

- Try to train your child to play with one toy at a time instead of spreading them all out at once. It's easiest to start this when he is very young and you are supervising play.

- Older kids' possessions can go in a twenty-four-hour time-out box: they must do without or somehow earn them back.

- Make it fun. Sing a cleanup song together as you go, or set a timer and see if your child can "beat the clock." Maybe she can put all her toys away before you finish singing a particular song, or listen to a fast-paced Wiggles tune that will motivate her to move quickly.

Toe Walking

If your child tends to walk on the balls of her feet or on tiptoes, consider the following, discussing them first with your OT or physical therapist. Also see page 200 in Chapter 8: Dealing with Developmental Delays.

- Desensitize feet by massaging them (with or without lotion or oil), brushing with a soft scrub brush, or rubbing with a washcloth. Have your child explore different materials with her feet (stand in a bin of dry rice or beans, sand, or Styrofoam peanuts).

- Teach your child to be aware of body parts. Cue him to walk or run with his heels down, but avoid nagging.
- Look for patterns: When does she walk on her toes? When she is barefoot, or when she's wearing shoes? On carpet, hardwood flooring, grass, or at the beach? If you can discover what triggers it, give her playful opportunities to explore the texture.
- Consider more cushioned shoes (sneakers) or less cushioned shoes (leather soles), and try different types of socks (thick versus thin, or seamless socks). A therapist may recommend high top sneakers or a special orthotic shoe insert.
- Have your child hop on a mini-trampoline, holding your hands or a safety bar if necessary. Make sure she lands with her heels down.
- Attach ankle weights with Velcro straps to increase sensory input to the ankles and feet. Have your child sit in a chair while she plays

Stretching tight calf muscles by standing on a wedge

or eats with her knees at a ninety-degree angle and her feet flat on a towel or other item with an interesting texture laid on the floor.

- Have your child hold onto a table or chair, keep her heels on the floor, and tap her toes to music, using both feet together, then create rhythmic patterns by alternating the feet.
- Stretch the calf muscles and Achilles' tendon. Have your child stand on a wedge (available in many therapy catalogs) with her toes facing up along the thicker part of the wedge, and her heels downward along the thinner part of the wedge. Gravity will do the work, slowly pulling her heels downward. Start with less than a minute if she's too uncomfortable, and slowly increase standing time. She can stand on the wedge while playing on a tabletop, drawing on an easel, etc.
- If toe walking persists, you may need to consult an orthotist or pediatric podiatrist about inserts that will help support proper alignment and hold the heel down.

Quick Tips for Calming an Overwhelmed Child

- Dim the lights.
- Lower your voice.
- Have the child breathe deeply ten times.
- Be sure the child isn't overheated—remove his sweater or bring him near an air conditioner or fan.
- Change where the child is sitting (for example, have her move closer to the teacher).
- Offer the child a bear hug or cuddle, or rhythmically and firmly rub her back or press downward on her shoulders.
- Give the child water or something to suck on such as a lollipop or hard candy. Crunchy food such as crackers or pretzels can also be soothing.
- Bring the child to a less busy part of the room for a few minutes—not as punishment, but to enable the child to self-regulate.
- Let the child listen to calming music, using headphones if appropriate.
- Take the child to a "cozy corner" to relax. This space may have a beanbag chair, soft lighting, and a book or a soft toy to enjoy until he regroups.
- Have the child sit in a rocking chair or bounce on a ball chair.
- Help the child do wall push-ups or chair push-ups.
- Provide a hand fidget like a Koosh ball, provided the child does not throw it.

- Take the child outdoors for a few minutes to get the wiggles out, or have him climb up and down stairs.
- Repeat a soothing phrase such as "It will be okay" or "Everything is all right."

PRACTICAL TIPS FOR TEENS AND ADULTS

Many teenagers and adults have sensory issues intense enough to significantly interfere with work, socializing, schooling, and parenting. Fortunately, the older we are, the more independence and control over our lives we have and the better we're able to observe and communicate our needs, accommodating our sensory issues before we become too stressed by them. Never forget that the latest research shows you can retrain the nervous system to function more typically no matter whether you're three years old or seventy[1]; it will just take longer to "reprogram" your system to better tolerate and process sensory information.

Most of our tips for children can be used by teens and adults, some with no modification whatsoever. As you come to accept your sensory differences, you'll start finding the confidence to leave your Orajel Toddler Toothpaste on the bathroom sink (because you make no apologies for needing foamless toothpaste!) or insisting on sensory breaks, retreating to a quiet room during loud family gatherings.

There are OTs who can work with adults and teens on a regular or consulting basis, and you may find that the complementary therapies we've suggested are helpful for you as well.

Environmental Issues

As an adult, you can exert a lot more control over your environment in order to adapt it to your sensitivities and intolerances. However, in situations such as working in an office or staying in a hotel, your sensory solutions may need to be more creative. Thumb through the solutions for kids and adapt them to your own needs. Also consider the following:

- If you find fluorescent lights intolerable, keep in mind that changing a fluorescent fixture is costly—and if you work in an office, stay at a hotel, or even live in a school dorm, it may be impossible. You may find that replacing the tube with a full-spectrum fluorescent does the trick, providing a more natural type of light. You can find these at good hardware stores or at www.fullspectrumsolutions.com. You may need to check with your company's human resources department before you go ahead and alter the lighting. If you can't turn off the overhead light, as is often the case in a work setting, try adding an incandescent or full-spectrum light at eye level. Cozy Shades (available from *Integrations* catalog) attach right to existing ceiling fixtures to filter out some of the harsh lighting. You can also try wearing glasses with a light tint (10 to 20 percent) indoors.

- If you use a computer, avoid straining your eyes. Eyestrain symptoms include headaches; tired, itchy, dry eyes; blurred vision; increased light sensitivity; and visual after-images. Here are a few solutions:
  - Look away every so often, refocusing on something far away.
  - Use indirect light, making sure that the monitor doesn't reflect any overhead light or lamps. Position your screen so that it is perpendicular (at a right angle) to any windows to reduce outside glare. Close blinds or shades if necessary. Use a glare screen or monitor shield to reduce glare if needed.
  - You may need a special eyeglass prescription specifically for computer use.
  - Use ergonomic principles: The monitor should be eighteen to thirty inches away, with the first line of type just below eye level. If your monitor is very large, position it farther away and use a larger font if you need to. Place your keyboard directly in front of the monitor to avoid looking at the screen at an angle, causing each eye to focus at a different distance. Enter "Computer Workstation Ergonomics" on the CDC Web site (www.cdc.gov) for complete computer-use recommendations.
- Rather than simply closing your office door at work, communicate to your boss and coworkers why you need to do this (to block out visual and auditory distractions). Explain that it doesn't mean you are unavailable and that they can knock on your door at any time.
- Use a white noise machine, fan, or even a radio set to static to block out background noise. Use earplugs while working or studying if that helps you to focus.
- If you are smell sensitive, try chewing mint or cinnamon gum. Experiment with air fresheners, aromatherapy sprays, or an essential oil diffuser.
- If you find vibration soothing, use a vibrating massage chair, massage cushion you can add to your regular chair, or a Vibramat you can place on the floor under your chair. Try a vibrating pen such as

the Tran-Quille or the pen tip for the z-Vibe massager (available in therapy catalogs).

- Try an inflatable seat cushion like the Move n' Fit (larger size) or Swiss Disk (available in therapy catalogs).
- Use soundproofing in your home or office. Keep in mind that the more soft objects in a room (pillows, couches, curtains, etc.), the fewer the echoes. If you've got the financial resources, look into companies that install easily removable double windows, such as CitiQuiet (http://www.citiquiet.com), that seal out street noise.
- Experiment with different earplugs and noise-canceling headphones. Use a personal listening device, such as an iPod, to block uncomfortable sounds.
- If you have taste and texture sensitivities and are invited to someone's home for dinner, keep in mind that most people are used to dietary restrictions. Ask what's being served and offer to bring a dish you know you can eat, or eat a light snack beforehand.
- If you're traveling and staying at hotels, bring along your own pillow or pillowcase (remember to take it with you!). Bring some air freshener or Febreze fabric refresher.
- If you can't tolerate live music indoors, attend outdoor concerts where the acoustics are different and you have more control over the volume because you can walk farther away from the sound.

Learning to Drive and Driving

- Driver rehab has become a specialty for some occupational therapists, who are trained in building daily life skills. To find an OT who can help you learn to drive or improve your driving skills, go to http://www.drivered.org/custom/directory/.
- Take driving lessons from an instructor who is willing to work slowly, starting you out in a big empty parking lot and letting you slowly work up to driving almost-deserted streets. Ask to have your instructor break down tasks into their smallest steps; for example, instead of saying "Pull out and make a left turn here," have her tell you the sequential movements.
- Don't feel you must drive in heavy traffic or on highways. Work your way up to more challenging roads and more maneuvers.
- Music can help you drown out background noise but be careful not to make it so loud that you can't hear what's going on around you (such as an approaching emergency vehicle's siren).
- Use a weighted lap pad while driving if it helps you to remain calm.

- Chew gum if it helps you to focus.
- Try a "seat belt buddy" made of shearling or plush fabric that you can attach to your seat belt.

Doctor and Dentist Visits

- Consider seeing a pediatric dentist or asking your doctor or dentist to talk to you about ways to make your visit less stressful. Ask what procedures will be involved and talk about modifications. For example, instead of using the modesty gown, maybe you can bring in your own bathrobe. At the dentist's, you may want to have them drape the lead bib over you just for a teeth cleaning. Schedule visits for first thing in the morning so that you don't become anxious waiting around for the doctor to see you should he or she be running late. Don't be afraid to speak up for yourself and your needs.
- Build in a reward for yourself for undergoing an unpleasant procedure, whether it's a massage or an ice cream sundae.
- See pages 161–164 for a comprehensive list of solutions.

As you continue to develop your sensory smarts, you'll probably find that you come up with some pretty ingenious fixes for everyday problems. In addition to trying the practical solutions we've given you here, speak with your OT and any other therapists as well as other parents, or adults with sensory issues themselves, who may have come up with other great ideas.

PART THREE

Fostering Your Child's Development

CHAPTER 8

Dealing with Developmental Delays

Perhaps your child isn't speaking as well as other children are, or is behaving badly, or just isn't coping well with everyday life. We hope you will get your child evaluated through early intervention, or the school system, or through some of the other sources we talked about on pages 88–92. In fact, you may have skipped ahead to this chapter to learn more about developmental delays your child is already getting therapy for, wondering what they have to do with his sensory issues.

If you have just learned that your child has several developmental delays, take a deep breath; it's not so bad. It's very common for kids with SI dysfunction to have developmental delays, and vice versa, and both can be addressed at the same time. In fact, you may well find that addressing your child's sensory issues will help with his developmental delays. For instance, some moms have noted that brushing their children using the Wilbarger brushing protocol (or DPPT: see pages 115–16) not only decreased tactile sensitivity but improved auditory processing, or that their child started really making progress in speech therapy after beginning occupational therapy for her sensory issues.

Nancy's Story

While I really do accept Cole as he is and I don't feel I should compare him with anyone else, I still have moments when I feel deeply jealous of how easy other children and parents seem to have it. Recently, I was on a playground next to another mom at the swing set. Her daughter, who couldn't have been three years old, jumped onto the swing and began happily pumping her legs to propel herself higher and higher. Meanwhile, even though my husband and I have repeatedly explained to our five-year-old how to pump, and demonstrated it over and over, he just doesn't "get it" yet and has to be pushed. At times like these, my personal pity party starts without any conscious decision on my part. I try to quickly snap out of it and remind myself how ridiculous it is to compare. I always forgive myself for those fleeting feelings of anger, disappointment, and envy, because I truly feel that even if other kids have it worse than my kid does, it's only natural for a parent to struggle with those darker emotions when her child has *any* sort of delay or disability.

Why So Many Children with Sensory Issues Have Developmental Delays

Remember, children learn through their senses. If a child has difficulty interpreting, integrating, and using sensory information from inside and outside of her body, her development may lag a bit or even a lot. In fact, most parents don't seek help for their child because they are worried about sensory integration skills but because she doesn't seem to be keeping up with her peers. Often, it's a fine motor delay, clumsiness, or a speech-language delay that parents and teachers notice. Or the child has behavioral issues, such as out-of-control temper tantrums that aren't age appropriate, that motivate the parents to get help.

Developmental delays can occur for a variety of reasons, and SI dysfunction is just one of them. The majority of children with sensory problems do experience some measure of developmental delays, but some do not. But before we go into what these delays are about, it's very important to keep in mind that children develop at different rates. The child who is "supposed to" be able to catch a large ball between twenty-four and twenty-six months may master this skill at twenty-two months or twenty-eight months. Does this mean your child is physically gifted or delayed? That age range of twenty-four to twenty-six months is an average for typically developing children. But *average* is a mathematical concept, and human beings have a wide variation in what they can and cannot do—and *when*.

What's more, there are a multitude of developmental scales that sometimes contradict each other. For example, the *HELP Strands Curriculum-Based Developmental Assessment* states that a child should be able to build a six-block tower by twenty-two to twenty-four months of age. Meanwhile, the *Brigance Diagnostic Inventory of Early Development* does not expect a child to build a six-block tower until twenty-four to thirty months. So much depends on the developmental scale used. Moreover, a child who never plays with blocks doesn't have the opportunity to practice this task. This child will be an inexperienced tower builder and during an evaluation would probably appear to be delayed at this task.

The child with sensory issues may do very poorly at building a block tower. He may exert too much force when placing one block on top of the other, knocking it down on the third block. Another child who is uncomfortable with how the block feels in her hand may release it before carefully positioning it on top. Another child may so enjoy feeling the block in his hand that he won't let go of it at all. And the child with visual issues may have trouble aligning the blocks. So does this mean he is delayed? Well . . . yes. Is it a crisis that your child can't build a six-block tower by a certain age? Not really. A child may get bored by the fourth block. Some of us are simply not tower-building people—and we're fairly certain block-tower building is not on the SATs. But not meeting developmental milestones is a good indicator that *something is up* that needs to be explored, understood, and addressed—especially when there are several age-appropriate tasks that your child hasn't mastered.

Because there are so many developmental scales to choose from, and because scoring is often based on subjective observation (How is the child performing the task? Is the skill emerging? What is interfering with task completion? Is she comfortable in the evaluation setting? Is she tired or hungry?), it's essential that you have your child assessed professionally rather than rely on developmental milestones you may come across in a magazine or parenting book. Even so, remember that an evaluation is just a snapshot of how your child performs at a single point in time, not a complete picture of who your child really is in terms of day-to-day function. That's why you, as a parent, must be part of the team, giving vital background information that helps complete your child's portrait.

Should your child be found to have developmental delays, try not to panic. A developmental delay is just that: a delay. It does not mean that your child is not intelligent or that he lacks the capacity to catch up.

COMMON DEVELOPMENTAL DELAYS

Developmental delays range from very mild to severe. Say your two-year-old isn't making circular scribbles when all the other children in day care are, yet she has developed her other fine motor skills. She may be scribbling circles soon enough with time and opportunity to observe and practice. On the other hand, a child who still cannot stand on one foot for a few seconds by age four is more significantly delayed. So in some cases, delays are minor and may be overcome naturally over time with the process of normal maturation and with a little extra help, while others are severe and require intensive intervention.

How can you tell the difference between a simple delay that will resolve itself and one that won't? You can't know for certain, so the best thing you can do is to get an evaluation. Even then, the evaluator may be unable to predict whether your child will "grow out of it" if your child has subtle delays and is quite young. In such a case, the evaluator will probably recommend therapy to address mild delays or to monitor development.

Another aspect to consider is how many age-appropriate tasks are too hard for your child within a particular skill area. If your five-year-old can string beads, assemble a jigsaw puzzle, build a fort out of Legos, and button her shirt, but can't use scissors, does she truly have a fine motor delay? Also, a child who is delayed in one area is quite likely to have other delays as well. At the same time it's quite common for a child who is delayed in one area to be ahead of the game in another area. It can all be very confusing, and for a parent, upsetting. With so many variables, it's essential to get professional help to identify and sort out your child's strengths and weaknesses, and to provide appropriate interventions.

We'll give you a few developmental benchmarks here (based loosely on a combination of developmental scales), but keep in mind that age expectations vary between scales, evaluation is subjective, and most developmental delays are not an irreversible, major catastrophe.

Self-Regulation Skills

Self-regulation skills are a person's ability to master her moods, self-soothe, delay gratification, and tolerate transitions. To self-regulate, a child needs to be neurologically "organized"—that is, able to moderate internal highs and lows. It's a key skill many children with SI dysfunction have great trouble with. A child with poor self-regulation skills might have trouble falling asleep and staying asleep, being woken up, or sleeping at inappropriate times. She may become hungry at irregular intervals or at unexpected hours in the middle of the night. She might be unable to focus when she needs to (like when her speech therapist is trying to get her to blow bubbles) and unable to draw herself away from a task she's focused on when it's time to move on (such as chasing bubbles around the room). The smallest shift in routine, an unexpected stressor, or just a bad day overall can result in an extreme overreaction. One mom inadvertently set off a two-hour-long tantrum when she gave her four-year-old with sensory processing issues the choice between sleeping with her bedroom door closed or slightly open. Another mom noticed that whenever she dressed her toddler in red, he became so visually overstimulated that he had tantrums all day long.

Your child's ability to self-regulate forms the foundation for developing other skills. A child with sensory problems, whose difficulty handling sensory input results in disorganized levels of arousal and activity level, strong behavioral responses, and inability to sustain attention for long periods of time, may have profound problems mastering developmental skills that require organized, focused behavior and concentration.

Regulation of arousal, attention, affect, and activity. As they mature, most children develop regular cycles of alertness, attentiveness, emotional states, and activity level. Some children are simply born easy. Most babies quickly learn to self-calm by sucking on their hands or fingers, rocking, looking at a favorite object like a mobile, and so on. They establish predictable sleep and hunger cycles and are most attentive and active at certain times of day. They tolerate changes and transitions well and are usually in a good mood. Other babies are more difficult. You can never predict when they're going to be awake and alert or when they'll be hungry and cranky, and they always seem fussy or temperamental. They never settle into a predictable routine.

"Dysregulated" babies and children have difficulty learning to console themselves, delay gratification, and handle the unexpected. Parents may spend hours and hours each day consoling their unhappy child. As a parent, you might find yourself dragging a stroller everywhere, never knowing whether your little one is going to want to ride in it from the moment he sets foot outside or whether he's going to want to push it, running, for ten blocks as you speed walk to keep up. Older children may rant and rave, throwing frequent, age-inappropriate temper tantrums.

Some self-regulation milestones . . .
By about six months:
  * tolerates and enjoys being touched and moved
  * maintains active interest in objects and people for more than one minute

- no longer cries for no apparent reason, and can usually self-console

By about nine months:
- plays attentively with one toy for two to three minutes
- maintains attention to pictures and to a speaking person

By about twelve months:
- moves in response to musical rhythms (bounces, moves from side to side)
- sleeps twelve to fourteen hours at night, naps once or twice daily for one to four hours (may outgrow morning nap)

By about eighteen months:
- enjoys messy play (such as playing with food, or water and soap)
- sleeps ten to twelve hours at night, naps once for one to three hours
- prefers some toys over others

By about twenty-four months:
- plays purposefully, actively attending, by himself for a few minutes
- freely plays with paint, Play-Doh, and other substances
- enjoys roughhousing

By third year:
- wants to do things independently
- may give up naps
- participates in interactive and circle games

By fifth year:
- attends to an activity without adult supervision for ten minutes

Fine Motor Skills

Fine motor skills refer to the development of control over movement in the arms and the hands, most notably in the wrists and small joints and muscles of the fingers. Fine motor skills are involved in grasping a Cheerio and releasing it, activating toys, holding a marker, stringing beads, and the like.

Development of fine motor skills follows a general pattern:

Stability. To use her hands proficiently, your child needs to have a stable base. She needs postural stability to be able to reach for objects without falling over. She needs shoulder stability to get her arms and hands in a good position to use her fingers, in the same way your shoulders maintain a stable position while you brush your hair. She needs hand stability to anchor part of her hand as she uses another part to do harder fine motor tasks, such as stabilizing the pinky side of her hand against the table as she writes. Once she has a stable foundation, she can increase her fine motor strength and mastery.

Bilateral coordination. If you observe your own hands as you go about your daily routines, you will notice that you usually use both of them: one hand stabilizes objects as the other hand manipulates them. For example, as you sew on a button, your "helping hand" holds the material as your more skilled, dominant hand pushes the needle through. In the first year, a baby typically learns to use both hands together to transfer a toy from one hand to the other. In the second year, typically by eighteen months, he brings his hands together in midline (the center of the body). He then learns to cross the midline of his body to reach for an object, such as reaching with his right hand for the stuffed toy to the left of his body's center. Over time, usually when the child is a toddler or preschooler, he begins showing hand preference and later, hand dominance.

Children with sensory issues often show delays in bilateral integration and crossing midline, and may develop hand dominance very late or very early. Two-year-old Mickey was referred to early intervention due to "behavioral outbursts" as well as speech delays. A major problem was that Mickey would often tantrum during play: screaming, throwing toys, and biting his parents. Mickey tried to do everything with just one hand. He'd pull on one pop bead to detach it, but of course, since his helping hand wasn't on the adjacent bead, the entire strand of beads would simply move. He'd scribble on paper, and the paper would fly off the table because his other hand was in his lap. He was understandably frustrated! In therapy, Mickey learned to use his helping hand to stabilize objects while he was working. As it became clear that he had greater skill in his right hand, he was encouraged to reach across midline to his left side using his right hand. Mickey also needed to learn to ask for help when he needed it, and about concepts such as *almost* and *try again*. Only then did he become more willing to persist at and master more difficult, age-appropriate tasks.

PEDIATRICIANS AND
DEVELOPMENTAL SCREENINGS

Developmental pediatricians have special training and expertise in children's atypical development and behavior. As a result, they are often more adept than traditional pediatricians at recognizing the often subtle signs of sensory processing disorder, as well as developmental delays, autistic spectrum disorders, and other conditions. Of course, many traditional pediatricians are also fabulous at recognizing developmental difficulties and conditions such as SPD.

Which type of pediatrician should you go to? Any pediatrician should regularly do a first-level developmental screening, says Margaret Dunkle, Senior Fellow in the Department of Health Policy of George Washington University. She quotes a 2002 American Academy of Pediatrics study finding that only 15 percent of pediatricians always use a developmental screening tool.[1] The study found that "7 out of 10 pediatricians rely on clinical judgments—even though this method identifies less than 30 percent of children with mental retardation, learning disabilities, language impairments, and other developmental disabilities, and less than 50 percent of children with serious emotional and behavioral disturbances."

So, make sure your pediatrician does a proper developmental screening. You might ask your pediatrician whether she uses one of the screening tools the American Academy of Pediatrics rates as "excellent" (the *PEDS [Parents' Evaluation of Developmental Status]*, the *Child Development Inventories*, or the *Ages and Stages Questionnaires*) because simple checklists, informal assessments, and tests such as the *Denver II* aren't nearly as accurate. If problems are identified through a screening tool, immediately see a developmental pediatrician or other appropriate professional to get help. Every month counts, especially in children ages birth to five, when their brains and development are the most "plastic."

Coordination and dexterity. As a child touches things, manipulates items, and gains fine motor experience, he learns how things feel on his skin and inside his joints and muscles. He learns the best way to position his fingers, wrist, and arms to get the job done. He learns to "grade" his fine motor movements, applying just enough force to make nice crayon marks but not so much that he breaks the crayons. He can discern a buttonhole from a button and manipulate it just so that it slips through without him looking. Later on, he develops precise movements that allow him to sew his own buttons back on.

Fine motor coordination and dexterity depend on virtually all the senses. For instance, to string beads onto a lace, a child must be able to discriminate between tactile sensations ("this is the lace and this is the bead"), localize tactile sensations ("the lace is between my thumb and index finger"), use vision to guide movements ("here is the hole where the lace goes"), use proprioception to adjust movements ("I need to bend and straighten my fingers just a bit to push the lace through the hole"), and process vestibular input ("I have to stay upright against gravity and bend over to pick up any fallen beads"). He needs to be able to filter out extraneous sounds, sights, and smells to maintain his concentration.

Some fine motor benchmarks . . .

By about seven months:
- bangs two objects together
- pokes objects with index finger
- has good grasp and voluntary release

By about thirteen months:
- marks paper with crayon
- puts three or more objects into small container

By about sixteen months:
- points with index finger
- builds tower using two cubes

By about eighteen months:
- one hand holds object, while the other manipulates
- scribbles spontaneously

By about twenty-four months:
- snips with scissors
- strings one one-inch bead
- imitates vertical stroke and circular scribble

During fifth year:
- prints first name
- writes numbers 1–5

BRAIN PLASTICITY

The brain is constantly evolving, with neurons continuously competing for connections and room. Let's say you're learning to play guitar. When you first play a chord, a neural connection is made. Each time you play the chord, the connection is facilitated until, eventually, your fingers know how to play it without conscious thought. You have, in effect, remodeled your brain.

Any time you challenge your brain by learning something new, you alter the quantity and strength of neural connections. While it was once believed that children's brains had plasticity—that is, were capable of structural change—only until about age seven, studies now show that people retain the ability to remodel their brains until they die.

Brain plasticity is why *intervention for sensory problems can make such a huge difference at any age.* By providing carefully designed sensory experiences, positive neural connections are enhanced while negative connections are, hopefully, weakened and pruned away.

Gross Motor Skills

The gross motor skills parents are most aware of are those that inspire grabbing the camera and calling Grandma: when their child first sits alone, walks, climbs stairs, and runs. However, several gross motor skills must be "hardwired" first to reach these milestones. The typical baby first lifts her head while on her tummy at about two months old, then supports herself on her hands, sits up, crawls, stands, and shifts her weight from one leg to the other, all the while learning to use both sides of her body cooperatively. Finally she takes a step, and before you know it, she walks and runs. All the while, her senses have been integrating to work against the pull of gravity, to influence her muscle tone, to get her interested in exploring the environment.

Like all developmental skills, gross motor development requires sensory systems to work together well. For instance, to ride a bicycle, a child needs muscular strength, the ability to coordinate both sides of his body, to feel comfortable balancing and moving through space on wheels, to visually perceive how far he is from obstacles, and to be able to change direction or speed as needed.

Poor sensory processing, problems with muscle tone, persistent neurological reflexes, and many other factors can cause delayed gross motor skill development. If a child has limited strength and endurance, or difficulty with motor planning, or trouble with sensory processing, she might run in the high-guard position with her elbows up for stability, avoid walking up or down stairs, or insist on using a railing or holding your hand even for just a few shallow steps. She may be sedentary, preferring to hang out and watch TV or read.

Yet gross motor skills may be an area of strength for children with sensory issues. Your child may love the intense sensory experiences of running, jumping, and climbing, and may use gross motor tasks to keep her body revved up and in tune.

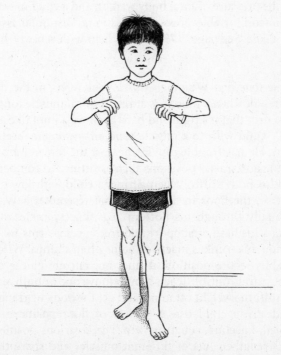

A child in high-guard position

If your child has gross motor delays, she will probably work with a physical therapist (PT) (see page 89 for a description of what a PT does).

Toe walking. Does your child tend to walk and run on her toes, and rarely place her heels down? Do her calf muscles seem overly strong and hard? Does she seem to get ahead of herself when walking or running? Does she stumble often? Toe walking—which looks like walking on tippy toes or on the balls of the feet—is fairly common in children age three and younger. However, if your child is still walking on tiptoes beyond age three, or begins to do so at a later age, it can be a neurological "soft sign" that might indicate an underlying medical condition. For children with SI dysfunction, you can almost bet it's a sensory-related behavior, but check with your pediatrician and OT or PT to be sure.

The child with tactile sensitivity may be attempting to avoid the feeling of a shoe or sock or the feeling of grass or sand or carpet on bare feet, so she walks on as little of her foot as possible. The feet bear the pressure of total body weight, and a child may toe walk to avoid uncomfortable pressure sensations. Vestibular issues may also play a role. See pages 179–181 for help with sensory-based toe walking.

Low muscle tone and W-sitting. *Muscle tone* refers to the degree of tension present when a muscle is at rest. Typical muscle tone is firm, but not so firm that it's rigid and hard to move a joint like an elbow or knee. A child with low muscle tone, or *hypotonia,* seems loose and floppy. He has trouble moving against the force of gravity and maintaining antigravity positions such as sitting. To compensate, he may hold his body stiffly. When sitting, a child with low tone may always sit on the floor in a position that resembles a W, bearing weight equally through his bottom, legs, knees, ankles, and feet. This widens his base of support and frees up his arms for play. In this position, his trunk is inactive and he often slumps. While this is a very stable, secure position, it does not encourage the development of postural control. Teach him to move one or both legs out of the W to shift the weight off joints and get the body working against gravity. Ideally, a child uses a variety of floor positions—sitting cross-legged, kneeling, squatting, etc. These various positions activate and strengthen lots of different muscles and spare the joints undue stress.

A child may W-sit to increase stability.

Some gross motor benchmarks . . .

By about six months:
* supports most of weight on hands while on tummy
* brings feet to mouth
* sits for a few seconds

By about one year:
* stands alone for a few seconds
* walks with hands held

By about sixteen months:
* walks independently
* bends and straightens knees to squat down and stand back up
* throws a ball underhand while sitting

By about twenty-six months:
* walks up a few steps
* catches a large ball while standing
* generally runs well without arms up in high-guard position

By third year:
- stands on one foot for several seconds
- walks down several stairs
- pedals a tricycle a few feet forward

Motor Planning Problems

Motor planning, also called *praxis,* is the ability to conceptualize, plan, and perform an unfamiliar motor action. At a playground he's never been to before, a child might spot a fun-looking climbing structure, and use his motor planning skills to figure out where to place his feet and hands to climb it and get to the top.

Apraxia and *dyspraxia* are conditions in which a person's ability to conceptualize, plan, and carry out a motor action is impaired. The term *apraxia* is used for adults who have motor planning problems due to brain injury or disease, while *dyspraxia* is used for children when their motor planning problems are developmental.

If a child is dyspraxic, he has trouble figuring out how to do non-habitual actions. The problem may occur at any point in the process: a child may have trouble coming up with an idea of what to do, how to plan and organize what his body needs to do, and/or how to sequence and execute movements. At home, when a dyspraxic child tries to dress himself, he might get frustrated because he puts both feet into one pant leg, pulls, and gets stuck. He may be clumsy and move awkwardly, often tripping when he tries to run. His handwriting may be illegible. Even moving from one body position to another, such as from sitting to standing, can be hard. Imitation games like Simon Says and the Hokey Pokey can be painfully difficult, especially if he's expected to do them rapidly. To the dyspraxic child, life is like a chorus line and he's the one who shows up late, doesn't know the steps, and can't follow the dizzying, quick movements of everyone around him.

Dyspraxia of the mouth can make eating and forming speech sounds difficult as well, as you'll read about in Chapter 10: Improving Speech Skills and Picky Eating. Is it any wonder that dyspraxic children often crave predictability, sticking to familiar activities and routines, given how difficult it is for them to be in step with the rest of the world?

Children with dyspraxia benefit from hand-over-hand help to learn new tasks, having multistep activities taught step-by-step, having instructions slowed down (for example, singing "Head, Shoulders, Knees and Toes" at a much slower speed), and having extra opportunities to practice. They may need to be cued again and again, until the brain "gets" it and they can start to generalize and apply what they've learned in one situation to different tasks and situations. When Cole was two, his motor planning was so poor that every task that required him to use two hands in coordination had to be taught separately. Even when he finally learned how to pull his pants up, he was utterly lost when putting his socks on, although it was basically the same process, because like other dyspraxic kids, he had trouble generalizing skills and applying them to other situations.

There are no benchmarks for dyspraxia specifically: "puts legs into pants correctly," for instance, would actually be considered a self-help skill.

Visual-Perceptual Delays

It's no surprise that visual-perceptual delays are common in children with SI dysfunction. Visual-perceptual skill refers to a person's ability to interpret, analyze, and give meaning to what he sees. The Optometric Extension Program Foundation estimates that more than 70 percent of classroom "underachievers" have problems processing visual information, even if they have 20/20 eyesight.

Visual attention lets a child pay attention to what she is doing while blocking out extraneous stimuli. A child who is easily distracted has trouble sustaining visual attention. When reading, a child may feel compelled to look at visual stimuli around him—even visually scanning around all the words on the page rather than just focusing on the words he is currently reading. Some kids have trouble *shifting* their visual attention, getting so absorbed in what they are looking at that they don't notice anything else happening around them. A visually *hypo*responsive child may have problems noticing a visual stimulus or sustaining visual interest, tiring quickly. A child who is not *looking* and visually attending misses out on vital developmental opportunities. However, it should be noted that many children are soaking in information all the time through their other senses, even if they aren't looking (or don't appear to be listening).

Visual discrimination lets your child identify distinct features of objects such as color, shape, size, and orientation, and helps her match and categorize objects. As she grows, she can perceive the difference between a triangle and a circle, or **B** and **b**. The child with visual discrimination problems may have trouble recognizing faces, or noticing the difference between a rectangle and a square.

Visual memory lets your child remember things he has seen, a skill that's essential for imitating new gestures and movements, sequencing writing and spelling tasks, recognizing words and people, and more. With a poor visual memory, he may have excellent memory for life experiences rather than factual information, and may have difficulty relating new visual information to what he already knows.

Figure ground lets your child differentiate between foreground and background, which is essential for attending to important visual stimuli while ignoring distracting surroundings. This skill lets him find his favorite dump truck in a box full of toys and keep his eyes on the teacher in a busy classroom. The child with figure-ground difficulty may have trouble reading because he can't select specific words on a page to read.

Visual closure lets your child use visual clues to recognize objects without seeing the entire image. This skill lets him find his lunchbox if it's partially hidden behind a milk carton and recognize a complete word if he has only seen part of that word (proficient readers do not have to look at every letter).

Form constancy lets your child perceive things as the same regardless of environment, position, size, and other details. When she's younger, she learns that a spoon is a spoon whether it's upside down, turned sideways, a silver tablespoon, or a plastic toy spoon. In school, she learns that the letter **S** is an **S** whether it's handwritten or typed, in print or cursive, or sideways.

Laterality, directionality, and spatial vision: Laterality lets your child differentiate between right and left sides of his own body. Directionality lets him perceive the right and left sides of external objects. Both are essential to spatial vision, which tells him how an object is positioned in space. He learns that his right hand goes into the left sleeve of his jacket when it is facing him. When he is school-age, he learns that the lowercase **b** has a line on the left side, and the **d** has a line on the right side. A child with poor spatial vision may have difficulty playing with toys, learning to climb stairs and catch a ball (both require depth perception), and developing many self-care tasks. He may have persistent letter reversals (beyond age eight), be confused about letter or number sequences, have trouble understanding directional words such as *up, down, in, out, under,* and *over,* and have poor topographical orientation and become easily lost.

Your child also needs to develop her visual-motor integration skills. Her eyes and body must work together to accomplish many developmental tasks, from stringing beads to catching a ball. Also referred to as eye-hand coordination skills, visual-motor integration is the term used for the interaction of motor skills, visual skills, and visual-perceptual skills.

Diagnosing Vision Problems

If your child shows signs of visual problems, such as difficulty reading, headaches and eyestrain, or visual inattention or distractibility, you may be referred to a behavioral optometrist (also called a developmental optometrist). This is different from an optician who works in an eyeglass store or an ophthalmologist who specializes in eye disease. A behavioral optometrist not only checks for eye health and visual acuity, but also how your child is using his eyes to process visual information. If there is an actual vision problem, the behavioral optometrist may recommend vision therapy, special therapeutic activities, or corrective lenses. How often your child may need to visit the optometrist depends on his needs. Some children go regularly for in-office vision therapy, while others are given eye exercises to do at home which are followed up with an office visit every so often.

Consider going to a behavioral optometrist even if no one refers you, because an undiagnosed vision problem is a major obstacle for any child. The American Optometric Association recommends vision exams at six months old, three years, before entering first grade, and then annually. Don't rely on a quick vision screening at school or the pediatrician's. Such a screening often just considers visual acuity from one distance (such as reading from a nearby chart of letters), and doesn't identify the child who, for example, can't read from the blackboard or follow a moving object. Instead, get a full vision evaluation. See Chapter 13: Complementary Therapies and Approaches for more information about optometrists and vision therapy.

Some visual-perceptual benchmarks . . .

By six months:
- follows a moving object with eyes in all directions
- looks at objects several feet away

By around eight or nine months:
- watches surrounding activities more
- follows trajectory of quickly moving objects, such as a ball

By about fifteen months:
- touches pictures while looking at them
- visually guides activity using two hands

By about eighteen months:
- looks at pictures in books
- shows understanding of color and size

By thirty-six months:
- stacks rings in correct order
- watches and imitates other children

During fourth year:
- recognizes own printed name
- knows left and right
- draws and names pictures

Self-Help Skills

Self-help skills include all the activities you do to maintain your body. Children with SI dysfunction often have delays in this area. The previous chapter provides a lot of practical things you can do to help your child with his self-help skills.

Eating. Sequencing and motor planning problems are often quite noticeable when it comes to eating, since this task requires your child to pull a lot of separate tasks together: choosing what to eat, figuring out how to get it to her mouth (with hands or utensils), what mouth movements to use and how (suck, bite, chew, or sip), and how to stop breathing in time to swallow. Of course, eating also requires fine motor skills, such as the ability to finger feed and later to grasp utensils and stabilize a plate with one hand as she aims the fork for the sweet peas (a problem for many of us!). If your child is tactile defensive, she may object to the sensation of a metal spoon in her fingers or inside her mouth.

Dressing. Some children with sensory problems love to be dressed . . . all the time. Some dislike it, fuss during diaper changes, and even experience putting on or taking off clothes as an assault. Some children crave long sleeves and long pants regardless of temperature. Other children would prefer to live naked. Some children with sensory problems quickly learn how to get dressed independently to get those cover-my-body-quick needs met. Other children need help with dressing far more than other kids their age do, because of tactile sensitivity, poor fine motor skills, and, quite often, general difficulty figuring out what goes where and in what order.

Grooming and bathing. Grooming can be a big problem for all children. After all, why comb your hair and brush your teeth when there are so many fun things to do? For children with sensory issues, grooming can be an even bigger problem. For the tactile defensive child, simple tasks like blowing her nose with a tissue or cutting, combing, or brushing hair (not to mention dealing with snarls!) are miserable experiences. The hyposensitive child, on the other hand, may not be aware of grooming needs, and may even be oblivious to the fact that crumbs are clinging to the outside of her mouth or that her scalp is dirty.

On the other hand, some children with sensory issues are fastidious about grooming, preferring a neat, mess-free hairstyle, and the feel of clean hands and face. This can be a welcome blessing for a parent, but can also be a real problem because life is not always so controlled and tidy. There are times for making mudpies, fingerpainting, or jumping into a mucky lake.

Likewise, bathing can be a source of struggle or delight. A child may do anything to avoid getting wet and soapy, and then towel-dried, or she may luxuriate in the bath or shower, splashing water, smelling nice shampoo, and enjoying the safe enclosed space of the bathroom. For these kids, bath time is a sensory wonderland.

Toileting. Some children may dislike the feeling of a soiled diaper so much that they toilet train early on. What lucky parents! Other children have much greater difficulty with toileting skills. These children face a myriad of difficulties: they may dislike having their diaper removed and having their bottoms wiped and powdered or soothed with ointment; they may be unaware of a soiled diaper or even enjoy the mushy, wet sensation; they may object to the feel of the potty or toilet seat, or may have difficulty staying upright on the toilet, especially if their feet don't touch the ground. They may have trouble recognizing the sensation of a full bowel or bladder, need help managing clothing fasteners, or be frightened by the sound of a flushing toilet.

Some self-help benchmarks . . .

By about twelve months:
- finger feeds and holds a spoon
- drinks from a cup held for him
- cooperates with dressing by presenting arms and legs

By about eighteen months:
- holds and drinks from a cup all by herself
- shows discomfort with soiled diaper
- can remove loose socks and hat

By about twenty-four months:
- scoops food with spoon to self-feed
- rubs soapy hands and dries with help
- sits on potty or adapted toilet with help
- can remove shoes with laces undone

By third year:
- uses a fork to stab food
- undresses by himself (except for fasteners) and dresses with supervision
- buttons larger buttons
- uses toilet, needing help with clothing and wiping

By fifth year:
- dresses independently
- grooms hair independently
- brushes teeth independently

Speech-Language Skills

Many children are referred for evaluation because their parents or teachers notice they don't speak as well as others their age. Speech-language delays have many causes, from cognitive disabilities to traumatic brain injury, but we'll focus on delays that are related more directly to sensory processing disorder. First, though, let's consider what speech-language skills actually are.

Speech refers to the sounds that come out of your child's mouth as words. Speaking is a complex process. Your child must decide to communicate something, figure out what combination of sounds to use, and motor plan to produce intelligible speech sounds, including controlling her breath and moving her tongue, lips, and jaw accurately. She must be able to use her hearing to monitor that what she is saying is intelligible, with correct volume, articulation, inflection, and so on.

Receptive language is your child's understanding of what is said to him. *Expressive language* is how he communicates what he means in order to be understood. At first your baby expresses his feelings, wants, and needs through nonverbal language such as facial expressions and gestures. All the while, he is soaking up language. Your child is actively listening for the differences between words, learning and remembering what those words mean, and how they work together in phrases and sentences.

As speech and language develop, so do social skills and imaginary play skills. Imaginary play, from dramatizing with a doll (she can talk! she can hear! she can bake a cherry pie!) to having a make-believe friend, requires language. Singing, too, requires both speech and language skills.

Sensory issues can interfere significantly with the development of speech and language. Your baby's first language milestone is watching your eyes and mouth as you speak, which typically develops by her third month. A child with ocular-motor issues will have trouble making and sustaining eye contact. Auditory processing issues, including hypersensitivity to speech frequencies, may interfere with listening to and combining the sounds of speech. An overaroused or underaroused nervous system makes it hard to pay attention to words and understand their meanings. A child may be so distracted by conflicting sensory input that she is not available for the tasks of listening and speaking. Oral motor planning problems can interfere with the process of putting sounds together in the forms of words (more on this in the next chapter). In Chapter 2, you learned about the connection between movement and hearing. Given this, it makes sense that movement such as running and jumping, which activate your child's inner ear and the rest of her brain and body, often stimulates speech and language production. It's very common to find that a child with speech-language delays also has a poorly functioning vestibular sense. Frequent inner ear infections also contribute to speech-language delays.

If you suspect a problem, get a full evaluation from a speech-language pathologist (SLP) and a comprehensive hearing evaluation by an audiologist who works with auditory processing difficulties. The audiology exam should include:

- The *lowest* decibel level heard. Your child may have hyperacute hearing (hyperacusis), so he should be tested for hearing thresholds *below* "normal."
- Sensitivity to frequency ranges
- Tympanogram to check for fluid in the ears
- Auditory foreground/background discrimination (generally just for children age five and older)

A comprehensive audiogram can reveal some very important things for a child with sensory processing disorder. It's no surprise that a child who hears more sounds than others do, and is also hypersensitive to high frequency sounds of speech, will have trouble filtering out background noise and following what people say. Depending on your child's age and needs, the audiologist—or the SLP or OT—may recommend auditory interventions and strategies to improve your child's auditory attention and listening skills. See Chapter 13: Complementary Therapies and Approaches for more on this.

We'll discuss speech development in greater depth in the next chapter.

Some speech-language benchmarks . . .

By around six months:
- recognizes her own name
- babbles, laughs, vocalizes, and whines purposefully
- cries in response to angry voices
- turns and looks at unfamiliar sounds

By around twelve months:
- understands simple directions
- imitates various sounds, and says one or two words
- identifies two body parts on himself

By around eighteen months:
- recognizes familiar people and objects in pictures
- communicates needs and wants by gesture or vocalization
- may say up to fifteen words

By around second year:
- says his own name

- says two-word phrases often, as well as some three-word phrases
- uses 150–300 words, including nouns, verbs, and adjectives (e.g., *puppy, go, dirty*)

By around third year:
- is understood by strangers most of the time
- follows three-step commands (e.g., get your plate, put it in the sink, and wash your hands)
- imaginary play emerges—plays with dolls, talks to stuffed animals, and uses objects symbolically, such as pretending that a string bean is an airplane

By around fourth year:
- has a complex conversation, asks *who* and *why*
- repeats simple words in order
- shows mastery of simple grammar, but may mispronounce up to half the basic sounds

By about fifth year:
- speaks in detailed sentences
- communicates well with peers and adults
- says most sounds correctly but may have trouble with *l, s, r, v, z, ch, sh,* and *th*

Cognitive Skills

The development of cognitive skills depends on many factors well beyond the scope of this book. For our purposes, we'll just consider how sensory processing challenges affect cognitive development.

A child learns about the world through interactions with people and objects in the environment. If she is not able to pay attention due to an overreactive or underreactive nervous system, if sensations such as movement or touch are frightening, overstimulating, or not even noticed, these problems can contribute to cognitive delays. However, and this is very important to note, most children with sensory processing problems, especially those *without* diagnoses such as low-functioning autism or mental retardation, are of average or even above average intelligence.

You may have a bright or even gifted child who seems, well . . . not so capable, at least not when it comes to certain things. Most cognitive tasks rely on good integration of sensory input, and require some age-level mastery of skills in areas such as motor planning, visual perception, and speech-language. So if your child is found to have a cognitive delay, you must address the underlying sensory and developmental skill foundations. A child with sensory problems *and* cognitive delays will benefit most from a teacher who is familiar with sensory processing disorder and who works cooperatively with an occupational therapist.

Some cognitive benchmarks . . .

By six months:
- uses hands and mouth to explore objects
- finds a partially hidden object

By nine months:
- plays two to three minutes with one toy (examining, rotating, touching, poking)
- imitates a familiar gesture
- finds a completely hidden object
- deliberately touches an adult's hand or toy to start an activity

By twelve months:
- retrieves an object to resume play
- guides a toy with hands
- throws objects to see what happens

By two years:
- rotates an upside-down picture
- uses tools to solve problems such as climbing on a chair to get a toy on a table
- matches sounds to appropriate animal picture
- engages in symbolic play (e.g., uses a stick to brush a doll's hair)

By three years:
- talks to himself to expand on play theme or to an imaginary friend
- understands the concept of *two* (e.g., can pick out two toys when directed)
- discriminates between sizes (points to the Oreo instead of the M&M when asked which is larger)

Social and Emotional Skills

As your child grows, he develops a healthy sense of self and becomes increasingly less dependent on you. He expresses his thoughts and feelings, learns about rules, and develops friendships. He learns how to cope with changes and problems, and starts developing his own solutions, asking for help from others when he needs it and learning how to handle his feelings when solutions are hard or not possible. Developing resilience in the face of life's ups and downs is a challenge for all of us. Sensory problems present a whole second layer of stuff to learn to deal with. Not only does your child with sensory processing disorder have to face the first day of kindergarten—and later on, a first date—he also has to deal with his feelings about his sensory issues. It's hard enough to meet your new teacher without the shirt you are wearing strangling you. Or to find your new locker if you always lose your sense of direction when it's too noisy.

The developmental delays we've been discussing can be very frustrating. The child who has difficulty communicating what he wants, who can't complete a puzzle, or who can't write legibly, usually gets "mad, sad, or bad." A child who can't complete a task may throw things, hit, bite, or scream. Sometimes a child will simply give up if he isn't successful, saying he's not interested or bored. Or, he may decide he's just stupid. So a major goal for you and therapists should be to help your child not only be more age appropriate in what he can do, but also to develop the social, emotional, and coping skills needed to handle all the sticky situations and hard tasks that come up.

Group situations. Many children with sensory issues have a particularly hard time with social situations such as playdates and parties. Charise, a three-year-old, loves playing with her six-year-old brother. But when approached by a child of her own age in the playground or on a playdate, she falls apart, running away and crying. Because her brother is older and familiar, Charise pretty much knows what he will do and how he will act. She knows the ground rules of their relationship and that a parent is nearby to protect her. Younger children, especially "outsiders," don't seem so safe because they're less predictable, and alarm signals go off.

Some children without sensory issues are timid by nature, and take longer to warm up to social situations. But if you have a child who is hypersensitive, you can easily understand how uncomfortable he can become in challenging situations and why he withdraws. As you now know, a child who is *hypo*responsive often seeks *more* input. In many group situations, he may become overexcited, and possibly out of control. However your child responds to sensory input, keep in mind that he is likely to become overstimulated and unhappy in group situations.

Tantrums and outbursts. It's probably an understatement to say that one of the greatest trials you face as a parent is how to handle tantrums. We'll discuss some techniques in Chapter 14: Handling Discipline, Transitions, and Behavioral Issues, but you should know that frustration tantrums are a normal part of development, frequently appearing between twelve to eighteen months, and peaking in the first half of the second year. Occasional tantrums are also common in preschoolers and older children. Tantrums often result when a child who is developing a sense of autonomy and independence realizes that no, he's not actually in control, and they occur most often when the child is tired, hungry, or overstimulated. This is true for children with and without sensory issues.

Dr. Stanley Turecki, author of *The Difficult Child,* distinguishes between two types of tantrums: the familiar, manipulative tantrum (for example, your child rants and raves to get the ice cream cone she wants *before* dinner) and the temperamental tantrum (for example, something happens that violates your child's nature). For the child with sensory problems, the temper tantrum or outburst can be in response to an unbearable sensory offense or to a generalized sensory overload. Of course, your child may also have manipulative tantrums on top of this. How can you tell the difference between manipulative and temperamental tantrums? Dr. Turecki says the manipulative tantrum is less intense and is a direct, clear response to the child not getting something she wants. He says that the temperamental tantrum is associated with an underlying issue (such as a sensory sensitivity), and when you put aside your own emotional reaction, you feel sorry for your child and sense that she can't help herself.

In his book *The Explosive Child,* psychologist Ross Greene says the ability to be flexible and tolerate frustration can be severely compromised by struggles with SI dysfunction (as well as other biologically based problems such as ADHD). "The meltdowns of inflexible-explosive children often look very much like those of two-year-olds," he says, "But the parents of inflexible-explosive children do not describe meltdowns with good humor. They've been enduring them for a long time, and the meltdowns have become much more frequent, intense and uncontrollable."[2] He goes on to say that once these kids reach the meltdown stage of a tantrum, they are not able to reason, listen, or return to a coherent and calm state, even with the coaxing of their parents, for a long time. Greene describes inflexible-explosive children as kids who have very limited abilities to handle change and transitions, have a low tolerance for frustration, get stuck in rigid thinking, and don't respond well to rewards or punishments. Their tantrums can be out of the blue, or be related to something that seems minor to us (like sensations), and they can become more cranky than other children.

Tantrums are even more common in children with speech-language delays who are unable to communicate their needs and feelings. A child who struggles with word retrieval or who can't formulate words because of verbal dyspraxia may become extremely frustrated. As a child learns to express himself verbally, he feels more empowered, his frustration decreases, and typically, so do his tantrums.

Some social-emotional benchmarks . . .

By about twelve months:
- enjoys exploring the environment, but makes sure parent is looking
- shows preferences for certain people, places, and things
- tests parents' reactions (such as throwing food or refusing to go to sleep)

By about eighteen months:
- has frequent temper tantrums, typically no more than six a day, for fewer than ten minutes per episode, with reasonably short recovery time
- may develop fears and show new insecurities that do not significantly interfere with function (for example, she may become afraid of animals or the dishwasher, but not to the point of "freaking out")

By about twenty-four months:
- shows a variety of emotions—affection, happiness, jealousy, fear, anger
- recognizes self in photographs and refers to self by name
- defends possessions

By about third year:
- separates easily from parent in familiar surroundings
- insists on doing things independently, and takes pride in achievements
- parallel plays (alongside, but not interactively) with other children

By about fourth year:
- follows directions and obeys authority figures, such as teachers
- plays cooperatively with other children, needing occasional adult help
- asks lots of questions, frequently starting with *why*

By about fifth year:
- plays games with rules
- accepts disappointment and failure without excessive behavioral outbursts

By about sixth year:
- has a best friend
- likes to finish what he has started
- works in a small group of children for twenty minutes or more

Hand flapping, head banging, and other scary behavior. When a child is oversensitive or undersensitive to sensory stimuli—or a combination of both—his internal sensory "volume controls" are out of whack. Sound may be too loud or too quiet. Visual input may be too startling or too indistinct. Movement may feel too fast and out of control, or difficult and weighted down like lead. There can also be constant mental white noise like static on a TV set, so both the picture and the audio are fuzzy and difficult to stay tuned in to. In an attempt to normalize his nervous system, your child may shut down and withdraw, hyperfocus on something to the exclusion of all else, or engage in some kind of repetitive behavior such as hand flapping or head banging. While these behaviors are typically associated with autism, they do occur in nonautistic children with sensory problems as well.

Dr. Stephen M. Edelson provides several reasons why a child might engage in stereotypical behaviors such as hand flapping. These behaviors can give a hyposensitive child sensory stimulation he craves to wake up his nervous system, while it can calm a hypersensitive child by helping him block out the external environment. These behaviors also release beta-endorphins in the body, which provide pleasure.

While you might find it upsetting and socially unacceptable, there's no practical reason why hand flapping must be prevented unless it interferes with participating in activities such as academics and play. A child with sensory issues may hand flap every so often because it's absorbing, relaxing, and provides a lot of visual input (try it yourself). A child with speech-language delays who hand flaps to communicate when he's excited or frustrated may stop doing so when he develops the words for what he wants to say. Some parents report that hand flapping increases when seasonal allergies kick in, or decreases when their children take certain nutritional supplements (such as essential fatty acids).

Repetitive rocking and spinning are forms of self-therapy, providing intense vestibular stimulation. Yes, they may be very disturbing to watch, but, again, they're not really dangerous. Head banging, which provides intense movement plus dramatic deep pressure, is potentially far more serious. Yet, according to the American Academy of Pediatrics Web site, these behaviors can be part of normal development, peaking between eighteen and twenty-four months, and may just be some children's way of mastering movement. If rocking or head banging worries you, consult your pediatrician.

See pages 175–76 for practical solutions to head banging and hand flapping.

Getting Therapy for Developmental Delays

If your child is found to have developmental delays, you can get help from the same channels we discussed earlier, such as your state's early intervention program, your school district, or through private therapy. Remember, your child may catch up rather quickly if his delays are mild. More severe delays will obviously require more intensive intervention. Yes, it's scary to learn that your child isn't developing exactly as expected, but there is help available and a lot you as a parent can do for your magnificent, delayed child.

Nancy's Story

Viewed separately, Cole's developmental delays might seem minor, but together, at age three, they made up quite a list: a year delay in fine motor and gross motor skills, auditory processing problems, verbal dyspraxia, and motor planning problems. Lucky for George and me, Cole was basically easy going (especially once he got past the so-called terrible twos and threes).

When Cole first began his multiple therapies, it felt like there were just too many things we had to remember and follow through on: don't just give him a toy, hold it above his head so that his weak trunk muscles have to work to reach it; don't just pull his pants up after he uses the potty, show him how to place both hands on the waistband, grasp, keep grasping, and pull them up. We'd start to develop the habit of working on a particular skill, and then his OT or speech therapist or physical therapist would ask us to work on something else as well. Suddenly, we'd have to fit scissors practice or licorice biting into our daily routine. Every time he finally mastered a skill there would be yet another developmental challenge for us to work on. It used to upset us, but then we came to accept that that's just the nature of sensory issues and related delays. All the therapies work together, and the new skills Cole acquires help him develop other skills too. But it definitely took a while for me to not feel my heart sink whenever I learned there was yet another problem we had to address. For the most part, Cole makes it easy to meet his sensory needs because he'll announce it's time for a pillow fight, and he's so active that it's effortless to get him to do a physical activity that will increase his balance and coordination. Just as life presents many teachable moments, it presents many opportunities to work on skills he has yet to master. A colorful Hawaiian shirt that matches Daddy's inspires him to try buttoning, a conversation about what he did at the playground lets me help him express concepts that involve sequence and relationships. Cole's needs have made me more creative: I now find so many everyday opportunities for working on his delays that I wouldn't have thought of when he was first diagnosed.

When it comes to some of his developmental delays, however, we often have to suggest therapeutic activities. He is not a child who will naturally pick up a crayon and start coloring. To get him to work on fine motor skills, we might tell him it's time to color in a coloring book featuring his favorite character, Bob the Builder. Another day we'll have him use scissors to cut paper, or use plastic tongs to eat Cheerios. We also encourage him by helping him with a difficult task, like cutting on a line, then praising his efforts and getting him to try again, offering a suggestion to make the task easier so he can do it better the next time.

Keeping in touch with his therapists who make helpful and simple suggestions prevents us from feeling overwhelmed and thinking, "We must be forgetting something" and "We're not making any progress." Frankly, sometimes it's exhausting and frustrating. And it seems that whenever I decide that I can't take one more day of, say, demonstrating the art of sucking through a straw or blowing a bubble, the guilt creeps up on me: *Bad Mommy!* Being in an online support group, logging every milestone no matter how small and celebrating it, and looking back at old home movies and photos remind me of how far we have come and how well Cole is doing—and that life won't end if we forget to work on every single one of his delays before bedtime.

Yes, I wish my son didn't have any developmental delays, but month after month, I see that he can do more and more—and his innate joyfulness seems to increase each and every day. Really, what's not to love here?

Recommended Reading

Bellis, Teri James, Ph.D. *When the Brain Can't Hear: Unraveling the Mystery of Auditory Processing Disorder.* New York: Simon & Schuster, 2003. A guide to auditory processing, how it works or doesn't work, and the various types of auditory processing disorders.

Greene, Ross, Ph.D. *The Explosive Child.* New York: HarperCollins, 1998, 2001.

Greenspan, Stanley. *The Growth of the Mind.* Cambridge, MA: Perseus Books, 1997.

Greenspan, Stanley, and Serena Weider. *The Child with Special Needs: Encouraging Intellectual and Emotional Growth.* Cambridge, MA: Perseus Books, 1998.

Hamaguchi, Patricia McAleer. *Childhood Speech, Language and Listening Problems: What Every Parent Should Know,* revised edition. New York: John Wiley & Sons, 2001. An explanation of the various types of speech and language problems children can have, and how they are treated.

LeComer, Laurie. *A Parent's Guide to Developmental Delays.* New York: Perigee, 2006.

Schulman, Nancy, and Ellen Birnbaum. *Practical Wisdom for Parents: Demystifying the Preschool Years.* New York: Alfred A. Knopf, 2007. Excellent insights and advice for guiding your child through the preschool years.

Turecki, Stanley, M.D. *The Difficult Child,* second edition. New York: Bantam Books, 2000. Written by a child psychologist, this book provides insight and advice on understanding and working with your child's temperament, dealing with problem behaviors such as tantrums.

CHAPTER 9

Sensory Issues and the Child with an

Autism Spectrum Disorder

Anyone who loves, helps, or simply knows a child with an autism spectrum disorder can tell you that once you've met one person with autism, you've met *one* person with autism. Just like everyone else on the planet, each person with autism is unique. Some are brilliant, while others are not so smart. Some are aloof, while others are affectionate and emotional. Some are nonverbal, while others are chatty. Some have expertise in one or two topics (sometimes of little interest to peers), while others are interested in many subjects.

As we discussed in Chapter 4: Where Did the Wires Cross?, autism spectrum disorders (ASD) can range from mild to severe, and include autism (ranging from profoundly disabled to highly functional individuals), Asperger's syndrome, and pervasive developmental disorder not otherwise specified (PDD-NOS). Autism affects one in 150 children and is four times more common in boys than girls, according to the Centers for Disease Control and Prevention.

ASD casts a wide net, encompassing those quirky kids you may recall from grade school who grow up to be slightly odd or eccentric but often very successful adults (perhaps working as engineers or computer programmers) as well as children and adults who have significant difficulties with learning and independent function. It's a big diagnostic umbrella that covers people with varying degrees of impaired social interaction and communication skills as well as unusual behaviors and interests.

What people "on the spectrum" *do* have in common is that they almost always have significant sensory problems. A survey of children and adults with autism conducted at the Geneva Centre for Autism in Toronto found that over eight out of ten were hypersensitive to touch and sound and had vision problems, and nearly one-third had taste or smell sensitivities.[1] In a study of 200 children with ASD,[2] child psychiatrist Stanley Greenspan, M.D., and psychologist Serena Wieder, Ph.D., found that of the 94 percent who had sensory issues:

- 39 percent were underreactive (28 percent did not respond to sensory stimuli while 11 percent engaged in sensory seeking behavior)
- 19 percent were oversensitive
- 36 percent were both over- *and* undersensitive
- 100 percent had auditory processing dysfunction
- 100 percent had motor planning dysfunction (48 percent with severe motor planning problems and 17 percent with low muscle tone and related problems)

Scientific studies of people with autism document the very real and often striking differences in how their nervous systems respond to sensory input. Sarah A. Schoen, Lucy Jane Miller, and their colleagues have conducted studies measuring the arousal levels and sensory reactivity in children with autism and Asperger's syndrome, finding distinct patterns of either overreacting to sensory input or underreacting to these experiences.[3]

Significant Sensory Differences

People with high functioning autism such as Temple Grandin, who wrote the foreword for this book, have written quite eloquently about their sensory issues, providing us with a window into what young children on (and off) the spectrum may be feeling and thinking. Grandin wears old soft shirts under all of her clothes, and turns her underwear inside out because she can't tolerate the seams. Certain sounds like a fire alarm aren't just annoying, they feel like you are *"inside* the speakers at a rock 'n' roll concert" or "like a dentist drill going down your ear."[4]

One of the key dilemmas of parenting, teaching, or treating any child, and especially a child with autism, is figuring out when to protect your child and when to push him forward. While your initial reaction may be to urge your child to buck up and simply learn to tolerate noxious sensory input, it may simply be too much to ask in some circumstances. Thomas McKean, who has autism, wrote in his memoir, *Soon Will Come the Light*, "There is a constant, low-intensity pain going through me at all times. Sometimes it is not so low-intensity. And there are many things that I want to do, so many things that I know I *should* be doing, and sometimes I cannot do these things because I have to put the energy into dealing with this pain."[5]

Some people on the autism spectrum have severe problems with visual processing, even though they can pass an eye exam. Some act as though they are blind when they're in a strange place, and others have problems with visual whiteouts, which Grandin describes as like seeing snow on a television channel with no signal. Fluorescent lighting may be intolerable because many autistic people can see and hear the rapid flicker. Particular colors can be so distressing that the person with autism has to look away.

Some people on the autism spectrum rely on their peripheral vision because doing so reduces visual distortions that appear in the central part of their vision. This means that a child might actually see you better if he looks at your shoulder! Or it may be that he needs to turn off one sensory channel (his vision) in order to tune in better to another (his hearing). By looking at something less stimulating than your eyes, which provide a lot of sensory input since they move and reflect light,* he may actually be better able to understand what you're saying.

At age 13, Luke Jackson, who has autism, wrote in his memoir, *Freaks, Geeks & Asperger Syndrome: A User Guide to Adolescence,* "Sometimes it is too hard to concentrate on listening and looking at the same time. People are hard enough to understand as their words are often so very cryptic, but when their faces are moving around, their eyebrows rising and falling and their eyes getting wider then squinting, I cannot fathom all that out in one go, so to be honest I don't even try. . . . I have found a compromise to this problem . . . I look at people's mouths."[6]

When a therapist or teacher constantly insists, "Look me in the eye," it can be a big problem for a child with autism. Getting eye contact during communication is a great goal, and an important component of social communication. However, while insisting on eye contact may work well to establish connection with some kids with autism, it may cause other children to go into sensory overload. It's better to save the goal of making eye contact for a time when there's less demand for auditory processing. And be sure to get the child's vision checked by a behavioral optometrist or other qualified vision care provider in case there is an underlying visual problem.

Because children with autism are often "monochannel" in their sensory processing, needing to tune out information from one of their

---

* Movement of the eyes and eye muscles makes a major contribution to non-verbal communication, which people with autism typically have a very difficult time processing.

senses to concentrate on the information from another, some parents say it seems as if their child acts deaf at times. Tuning out what's being said can also be due to hyperfocusing. If your daughter is totally engrossed in watching a Barney* video, she may truly not hear you calling her name. You may need to gently but firmly place a hand on her to gain her attention and help her shift focus. Or, your child may be having a problem with auditory processing, because her attention and energy are centered on making sense out of the stream of sounds and words. (For more on auditory processing disorder, see Chapter 10.)

In one of her memoirs, *Somebody Somewhere,* Donna Williams writes about her experiences, saying that, "Unlike people deaf to sound, I couldn't say, 'Oh sorry, didn't hear you.' I could obviously hear sound perfectly. I couldn't say, 'Sorry, didn't understand,' when I was obviously clever. By the time I got around to it they were usually half a dozen sentences further on anyway. Years of people saying, 'Don't listen to her, she's just waffling,' or 'Listen. Are you deaf or something?' had knocked a lot of the trying out of me. For a long time I gave up waiting to understand or to be understood."[7]

Self-Stimulatory Behaviors

Faced with intense, uncomfortable sensory experiences, or just overloaded by the cumulative effects of sensory and information processing throughout the course of the day, the autistic child, teen, or adult is likely to resort to a limited repertoire of coping mechanisms. All of us have coping mechanisms we use to handle tension and stress. Some of the most well known are:

- *Rationalization*, that is, creating a logical justification for an action, belief, decision, or occurrence that's problematic, such as spending a lot of money on a new outfit when you're broke because you insist it will help you find a high-paying job.

---

*We wish we could tell you why so many kids and even adults with autism get "stuck" on Barney the purple dinosaur, but we can only speculate. Barney's face lacks details such as eyebrows, eyelashes, nostrils, and individual teeth. While you may find this creepy, it may be a pleasant relief for a child who loses the big picture because of too many distracting details. Barney speaks in a predictable midrange singsong, not too high and not too low. His shows cover topics such as how to recognize feelings in others or how to sequence an everyday activity, providing explanations and visuals that reinforce basic concepts many people with autism are either just learning or enjoy reviewing.

- *Idealization*, which involves overestimating the positive qualities of something or someone while underestimating the negatives. An example would be paying attention to how beautiful, smart, and funny your new friend is while ignoring the fact that she always forgets her wallet when she meets you for lunch.
- *Sublimation*, or channeling unwanted impulses into something harmless or even constructive. Cleaning your house when you're furious at your spouse is a form of sublimation.

These and other coping mechanisms are worth learning about should you want to deepen your self-understanding as an individual and as a parent. In general, we accept that everyone reverts to coping mechanisms at times, and we don't usually stigmatize these techniques for managing stress. However, for the child on the autism spectrum with significant sensory issues, coping mechanisms usually take three key forms, which do tend to be considered unacceptable. They are:

- *Tuning out*, that is, withdrawing one's attention or even physically withdrawing from a situation. We expect people to respond to us, particularly children. The child with autism may appear to be ignoring you or may seem lost in his own world. He may actually want to hear what you have to say, but when his sensory issues are intense, he may feel he has to block out external input by shutting down and becoming completely self-absorbed.
- *Acting out*, which involves becoming loud or aggressive. This can range from a child throwing blocks at a wall to shouting or even injuring himself or others. A child may intentionally intimidate others to get them to stop acting in ways he finds threatening, or he may simply be in a panic mode, not thinking about the consequences of screaming an obscenity or biting another child.
- *Engaging in self-stimulatory ("stimming") behaviors*, from hand flapping to humming. Far from "non-purposeful," these behaviors, commonly known as stims and sometimes as "stereotypies," serve very practical purposes. First, they can help a child block out the world and its overwhelming demands. Too much sound? Too many visuals? Like a Zen master, the child with autism may learn to detach and self-calm by flapping his hand in front of his face. Then, once the stim is in place, it may become the child's method of getting attention and telling you that he is frustrated, tired, hungry, and so on, especially if he is nonverbal and has no other means of communication. Second, stims can regulate a poorly functioning

central nervous system. Much as you might wiggle your ankle, pump your leg up and down while sitting, drum your fingers on a table-top, or chew gum, a stim can be a way of using a repetitive physical movement to keep your arousal level in check. Some behaviors, like lining up toy trains, may give the child a sense of organization and control in what he experiences as a chaotic world. Finally, just as you feel a kind of euphoria after a good workout at the gym, there's a natural high that occurs with stims as they trigger the body's natural painkillers, "endogenous opioids," which include endorphins and enkephalins.

Common stim behaviors include:

* *Visual:* flicking fingers, hand flapping, staring at lights, spinning wheels on a toy car, watching doors open and close, lining up toys
* *Vestibular:* rocking, spinning, hanging upside down, jumping, pacing, running in circles
* *Auditory:* unusual vocalizations, humming, singing, tapping/banging objects or ears, playing a recorded song or sound repeatedly
* *Tactile:* touching/rubbing/scratching objects, others, or own body with hands or putting body parts or objects in mouth
* *Proprioceptive:* body slamming, crashing, pounding, throwing, biting, chewing, tooth grinding
* *Taste and Smell:* licking or smelling objects, others, and own body parts

To understand your child's stimming behavior, ask yourself the following questions:

* *In what situations and under what circumstances does my child stim?* Is it when he is tired? Hungry? Anxious? Are there too many unexpected changes in our routine or plans? Is he dealing with an abrupt transition? Overwhelmed by the demands of the environment? Is the behavior worse in a particular place like the supermarket or playground?
* *What does my child get out of this behavior?* Is he using it to get attention he actually needs? What is he trying to tell me? To back off? To get him out of the situation? Is he distressed? Is it a way to block out unpleasant sensations? Does it help him to calm down? Does it help him to rev up for the next activity? Does it help release pent-up energy?

- *What sensory system is most involved? Is it a visual stim? Vestibular? Auditory? Tactile?* If you don't know the answer, perform the stim yourself and see how it feels. You may find that your child who slowly rocks is self-soothing the same way you used to soothe him as an infant. If you start humming while watching the nightly news, you may find that instead of hearing the latest awful news, the newscaster now sounds as if he's just saying "blah blah blah," which may be a relief if you've had a rough day.
- *Is there an underlying medical issue?* This is especially important to consider if the behavior is new. For example, if your child suddenly starts swiping at his ears, it may be that he has allergies or an ear infection, which can be itchy, rather than painful. Head banging can also be a sign of ear infection, headache, migraine, or other condition. Occasionally, visual stims can be a way to self-treat eyes that are strained due to undiagnosed visual acuity or convergence problems.
- *What would help?* Based on what you know about your child and her sensory issues, do you need to reduce the sensory demands of the situation in a particular way (for example, to dim the lights)? Does she need a break from the overstimulating environment (for example, do you need to take her outside of the restaurant for a few minutes)? Does she have low blood sugar and need to eat? Does she need to nap or just rest? Would providing a distraction work? Does she need to engage in one of her sensory diet activities?

When observing a child stimming, it's only natural that your first impulse will be to say or at least think *Stop it!* But as you may already know, what usually happens when you prevent a child from engaging in a stim or repetitive behavior is that he will either do it when you're not looking, or simply replace it with a new one. Stop the hand flapping and he starts finger flicking. Stop the humming and the tapping starts. Take away the Thomas the Tank Engine trains he loves to line up and he starts lining up toy cars or shoes or books.

That's why it's essential to analyze what triggers the behavior, understand what purpose the behavior serves (is it sensory or behavioral or both?), and then develop a plan to meet those needs in a more acceptable way. Your approaches to dealing with stims that are due to sensory issues might include:

Replacement. You may be able to redirect the behavior by distracting your child with an interesting toy or snack. Or you could try making the stim a more functional activity. For example, if your child keeps jumping, allow him to jump on a bouncy board or mini-trampoline. If he's finger flicking, try giving him a hand fidget like a Koosh ball.

Engagement. If the child is in his own world, consider ways you can join him there and forge a connection. For example, if your child is rocking back and forth, sit back to back with him and rock together as a cooperative activity. Or let him rock in a rocking chair or glider facing you, and stop the rocking every so often to engage him in some way, by making a funny face or having him request more rocking, and so on.

Give sensory input. When stims are driven by sensory issues, they frequently decrease or even disappear when the child engages the organizing sensory input his nervous system needs. As much as you would like your child to not spin in circles, if his body craves that vestibular input, it's fine to help him get the movement he needs with a Sit 'n' Spin, Dizzy Disc Jr., office chair, carousel—all more acceptable than spinning around in a supermarket, for example.

Reward. Stims can be incredibly relaxing and soothing. Rather than attempting to completely eliminate stims altogether, you might use them as a reward. For example, after a grueling day at school, it might be just fine for your child to spend half an hour dribbling sand through her fingers or lining up his trucks. Set a time limit, though, so he doesn't get lost in the stim.

Jesse was a kindergartener diagnosed with PDD-NOS that Lindsey worked with at home who had great difficulty participating in structured tasks he was actually interested in, such as coloring a picture or doing a puzzle. He preferred to run in circles around his room while flicking his fingers, or to jump on his bed. Jesse had a strong need to move and he, like many children with ASD, craved predictability. His behavior was compounded by not knowing what would happen next, so Lindsey implemented "The List." This is a simple adaptation of the kindergarten circle time in which the class reviews the day's schedule using a chart. At the beginning of each session, Lindsey would write Jesse's name at the top of The List, and working with him, she created a numbered list of activities, both writing and drawing the entries (grateful that Jesse, like most children, accepted her scribbles as illustrations). Now Jesse knew what would happen for the next sixty minutes. If he wandered away, Lindsey could bring him back to The List and get him back on track. He would cross off each activity as he completed it. Sometimes, by design or chance, it would be impossible to actually engage in the activity, and this became an opportunity to practice soothing self-talk and problem-solving skills (such as learning to say "it's okay, we can do *x* next time"). The first item on the list was almost always an activity that incorporated intense movement, such as jumping on his new mini-trampoline. Some days he so needed to move in order to focus at all that they developed The List for that session as he was jumping. Jesse also used an inflatable seat cushion that let him wiggle while doing tabletop work. The List method was used by the entire treatment team and his parents. Now Jesse was better able to focus and work on his motor skills, social skills, language and speech skills, and cognitive skills, and was soon able to remain seated for the duration of meals most of the time.

Keep It Practical and Concrete

One of the hallmarks of autism is concrete thinking. While everyone who works with kids on the autism spectrum knows this, it's easy to slip up and use idioms or express abstract ideas that the child can't grasp. Lindsey recalls a day when she took a nine-year-old client with autism to the art supply store to pick out some new colored pencils. After selecting a few, the child turned to her and said, "I have to take a poop." Lindsey inquired whether she could wait until they got home, and when the child said she couldn't, Lindsey assured her that she could "go right here." The child was appalled. "No!" she shouted. "In the bathroom!" This was the same child who, on another occasion when asked what she saw in a store window replied, "Glass."

While it's important to teach idioms, when dealing with difficulties such as sensory problems, keep any analogies as concrete as possible and provide a visual if you can. Instead of having a child try to figure out if something is bothering her "just a little bit" or "a whole lot," you may want to teach her a rating scale that assigns numbers to experiences, with number 1 being a minor annoyance she can handle all the way up to a number 5 annoyance which is unbearably uncomfortable. Then, if you notice that the child is showing signs of an impending meltdown, she can self-advocate by giving you a number (verbally, with the fingers of one hand, or by handing you a physical number card or plastic number) and you can act accordingly. A "1" annoyance may only require that you hold her hand or speak in a soothing tone of voice, while a higher number may call for something more proactive like engaging in a calming sensory diet activity, taking a break, or leaving the environment altogether. Kari Dunn Buron and Mitzi Curtis developed this simple, but clever system to help children with autism understand and control their emotional reactions to everyday events, but you can easily use it to create a rating system for sensory problems. (For more on five-point scales, see their books, including *The Incredible Five-Point Scale.*)

The Alert Program, also known as How Does Your Engine Run?, uses the example of a car engine to monitor self-regulation, teaching a child that his body is like an engine and that sometimes it runs on high, sometimes on low, and sometimes it runs just right. Again, the analogy is concrete and something to which the child can relate.

Collaboration Between Educators and Therapists

A wide array of teaching programs are used to educate students on the autism spectrum. Typically, these programs are either relationship based or behavioral. It is well beyond the scope of this book to counsel parents on particular educational interventions aside from stating that you need to find the best educational approach for your child since each program has its own strengths and weaknesses. What must be said, however, is that sensory issues should *never* be ignored, regardless of whether the child is receiving traditional or modified Applied Behavior Analysis (ABA), DIR/Floortime, TEACCH, or another method, and whether your child is in a special ed, general ed, or inclusion class. If your child is uncomfortable or in pain, or if she isn't getting the sensory input she needs for things to "click," or if she is having trouble processing all of the sensory input simultaneously, she simply can't reap the full benefit of any teaching program.

Just as one size never fits all, using just one approach seldom meets all of a child's needs. A child in the midst of an explosive meltdown needs more than having a privilege removed or help closing a "circle of communication." There has been longstanding animosity between "sensory people" and "behaviorists," with each grandstanding about the unique strengths of their methodology. Happily, more and more educators, psychologists, and therapists are putting their heads together, and recognizing that approaches must be *integrated* when it comes to helping children with sensory issues.

Dr. Linda Bambara, Professor of Special Education at Lehigh University, specializes in working with children and adults with problem behaviors. She uses and has written extensively about the positive be-havior support (PBS) framework, which has its roots in ABA but uses a more whole-child approach to behavior analysis and can incorporate other intervention techniques including sensory-based approaches. "Old-school ABA practitioners mapped interventions purely on what they observed, but today's PBS and many ABA practitioners are now looking at underlying causes," says Dr. Bambara. People engage in a be-havior because it helps them to acquire some form of reinforcement, ei-ther by obtaining something desirable or pleasurable or by avoiding something unpleasant or undesirable. "So if a fire alarm goes off and a child runs down the hallway screaming and then sits in the corner and rocks, the first thing to do is not to treat the observed behavior, but to analyze underlying triggers through a functional behavior assessment which looks at factors in the environment and internal factors within the child," says Dr. Bambara. By assessing what causes and maintains the behavior, you can develop positive behavior supports. An occupational therapist who understands sensory issues plays a pivotal role in this team analysis. Dr. Bambara explains that if the team hypothesizes that the child's behavior is due to sensory problems, then the child running down the hall screaming and then stimming during a fire drill will ben-efit from an intervention plan that modifies the environment (such as to dampen the sound or switch to a visual alarm rather than auditory alarm); modifies the child's sensitivity (such as to use earplugs and/or progressive desensitization); and teaches coping strategies and new skills that replace the problem behaviors (such as teaching the child to ask for help if frightened or coaching the child through the experience step-by-step). For more information, see the Association for Positive Behavior Support Web site at www.apbs.org and check the recom-mended reading at the end of this chapter.

Chapter 11: Helping Your Child Learn and Get Organized and Chapter 15: Advocating for Your Child at School are loaded with ways to make the learning environment more friendly to a student with sensory issues. A teacher may find that she is much more successful at teaching new skills to a child if she first reduces noxious environmen-tal stimuli. For example, if a child finds fluorescent lighting painful, she won't be mentally available for new learning. Turn off that over-head light and use a floor lamp or table lamp and lo and behold, the same child may be ready to look at what the teacher is presenting. Or it may be that the teacher will have much greater success if he incor-porates a few of the child's sensory diet activities before or during the teaching session, such as having a child wear a compression or weighted vest on a wearing schedule as recommended by the occupational therapist on the treatment team.

Cindi Alfano, special education teacher and licensed mental health counselor, says that for a child with sensory issues, it's not just a matter of making it "go away" prior to teaching, but of integrating sensory input as needed all the time. She recommends that teachers "don't just sit with a child at a table doing ABA drills, but instead pair the drilling with environmental teaching." She suggests "moving away from the table and into the child's natural world to meet sensory needs, open up opportunities for real social engagement, and to promote generalization of new learning." She also recommends that parents create opportunities for the professionals on the child's team, from the OT to the teacher to the behavioral therapist, to talk to each other. The teacher can share strategies to manage behaviors while the OT may recognize that a behavior the teacher is struggling with is due to a sensory issue.

Parenting the Child Who Has Autism and Sensory Issues

As with any child who has sensory issues, a child with autism will experience increased levels of anxiety and discomfort, and have more difficulty focusing, handling transitions, and managing everyday life than he would otherwise. The child with autism's challenges with social communication can be exacerbated by her difficulty blocking out background noise to focus on a conversation, and children may poke fun at her or call her "weird" because she chews on her shirt sleeves or doesn't understand a joke. The emotional anxiety that will cause an autistic teenager to break down in tears at school when he realizes he forgot his homework folder may be increased by his discomfort with all the movement around him as he stands at his locker, worried about being jostled by the loud, fast-moving students around him. Role playing and using social stories, as well as breaking down new, scary tasks and practicing them step-by-step with your child can help her better navigate the waters of social interaction.

By addressing the sensory piece, parents, grandparents, teachers, and therapists can make it easier for the child to learn, socialize, eat, attend group functions, and participate in therapies. As a parent living with your autistic child every day, you've probably developed strategies that are now automatic. It can be difficult to send your son or daughter into an environment where even the most well-meaning adults or children might be baffled by his behaviors and misjudge your child. Wendy, the parent of fourteen-year-old Savannah, who has high functioning autism, says that over the years, she has usually found that the school team has been open to the idea that Savannah's sensory issues affect her behavior. They've allowed Wendy to bring a beanbag chair to school and establish a place where Savannah can go to regroup if her anxiety is getting the better of her, and let her carry a fidget to prevent her from constantly tapping her head. However, Wendy says, "I'm the one who studied and went to seminars and I figure out the sensory piece for them. They understand the concept but they don't look for how her sensory issues might be at the root of things. I'll immediately think that way, but their first thought is 'It's emotional disturbance and defiance.'" Wendy's had to overcome her own defensiveness and develop patience because very often, the focus is on Savannah as "a problem" as opposed to a young woman doing her best and needing more support. "Recently," says Wendy, "we had a meeting at school to touch base and exchange information, and the case manager asked me, 'So, what is your comfort level here? How do you feel about your support network at the school?' That was the first time anyone had ever asked me that and I almost cried." Wendy feels strongly that getting together every month with her daughter's school team to exchange observations and ideas is very helpful because any issues that crop up can be addressed before they start affecting Savannah's schoolwork, socialization, or self-esteem. But as Wendy has found, advocating for a child with autism can be very challenging. It requires courage, patience, good communication skills, and often, a thick skin.

Physical Activity and a Sensory Diet

Many parents find that regular exercise can be very beneficial for their child, helping him to stay regulated and even boosting self-esteem. Savannah is on the local soccer team, and Wendy reports that Savannah's self-image has soared because her teammates have accepted and encouraged her, and as a result, Savannah's skills have greatly improved. Mary P., mother of Sam, who was diagnosed with Asperger's syndrome four years ago at the age of seven, used to encourage him to jump on a mini-trampoline, which Sam said helped him "feel more like myself." Now Sam swims four to five days a week on a swim team, which gives him excellent calming and focusing input as well as a sense of pride and the opportunity to be part of a team and make friends. Joyce, whose son Michael is four and has Asperger's syndrome, says, "I make sure he exercises every day, either at a park, mall play place, to an exercise DVD or in our basement: we have a trampoline, jump rope, and Sit 'n' Spin down there. It is difficult since it's like pulling teeth to get him to do anything physical!"

Then, too, adjusting your family's lifestyle to include opportunities for regular exercise for everyone not only will benefit your autistic child but the entire family, because regular exercise has been shown to be an extraordinarily effective stress buster. It may take some trial and error to discover what activities work best for your family (you can find some ideas in Chapter 6: The Sensory Diet of Daily Activities) given that your child's sensory issues must be accommodated, but given the payoff, it's worth the effort to establish a more active lifestyle.

Independence and Growing Up

Helping your child to become more independent will boost her self-esteem as well as allow her more options. Your "momma bear" instinct to protect your child from having her feelings hurt has to be balanced with her need to stretch her wings. Says Mary P., "Sam is learning as he matures to read social cues better but at times will just march to his own drum. As his mother, I find this painful to watch. At times, he will not negotiate and may just walk away rather than do something he feels is boring or he is unable to do. The other challenge most recently is his understanding of how his body is maturing and what to make of the feelings he's experiencing. He does not necessarily want to discuss this with me, his mother, yet clearly he is not comfortable discussing it with his father either." Wendy is proud that after much practice and encouragement, Savannah recently walked to the video store on her own, rented a movie, and came home without any mishaps or emotional angst. "I have a daughter who is neurotypical and she has triumphs as well but when you have a child who has special needs, the triumphs are more emotional because you know how hard it was for them and how brave they are to get to that point. They just don't give up. Savannah really does want to learn. Our goal is to have her be the most high functioning, contributing human being she can be, living up to her greatest potential. I think that's what most parents want for their kids."

Each child with autism has his own unique set of wonderful qualities, and it's important to remember not to let all the therapy appointments, meltdowns, social problems, and challenges distract you from how terrific your child is. Mary P. says, "While Sam is not your typical child, he is really a gift. I say this after many tears and feelings of despair. He feels things deeper, sees things more clearly than others do and expresses himself so spontaneously that to know him is to love him. As I struggle with my own medical illness and what lies in front of me, Sam has been my greatest source of strength. When I told him that I was going to undergo chemo and would lose my hair, he very quietly said that it was sad but that I could get a wig and might look better than I do now. This was so refreshing for me that I laughed so hard. It was meant from the heart and meant more to me than other people saying 'all the right words.' "

Parenting a child with sensory issues is a challenge, and even more so when that child also has social, language, and behavioral issues. Raising a sensory smart child, especially one on the autism spectrum, demands persistence, creativity, and a team of people who are dedicated to developing their own sensory smarts and working together. There will be days when you find yourself exhausted by the effort. We strongly encourage you to set up a reliable support system of people who can help you in practical ways as well as those who can offer you sympathy and encouragement. In your quest to do the best by your child, be certain that you take care of yourself as well. Just as the flight attendant instructs you to put on your own oxygen mask before putting on your child's, you must attend to your own needs in order to be a good parent and advocate for your child.

Recommended Reading

Autism Asperger's Digest Magazine, Arlington, TX: Future Horizons.

Bambara, Linda, and Tim Knoster. *Designing Positive Behavior Support Plans*, rev. ed. Washington, D.C.: AAIDD, 2008. Basic philosophy of PBS for professionals.

Grandin, Temple. *On Visual Thinking, Sensory, Careers and Medications.* DVD. Arlington, TX: Future Horizons, 2003.

Grandin, Temple. *The Way I See It: A Personal Look at Autism and Asperger's.* Arlington, TX: Future Horizons, 2008.

Grandin, Temple. *Thinking in Pictures.* New York: Vintage Books, rev. ed., 2006.

Greenspan, Stanley, and Serena Wieder. *Engaging Autism: Using the Floortime Approach to Help Children Relate, Communicate and Think.* Cambridge, MA: DaCapo Lifelong Books, 2006.

Hieneman, Meme, Karen Childs, and Jane Sergay. *Parenting With Positive Behavior Support: A Practical Guide to Resolving Your Child's Difficult*

Behavior. Baltimore: Brookes Publishing, 2006. A parent's guide to functional assessment and PBS.

Jackson, Luke. *Freaks, Geeks & Asperger Syndrome: A User Guide to Adolescence.* London: Jessica Kingsley Publishers, 2002.

Koegel, Lynn Kern, and Claire LaZebnick. Growing Up on the Spectrum: A Guide to Life, Love, and Learning for Teens and Young Adults. New York: Viking, 2009.

Lemer, Patricia, ed. *Envisioning a Bright Future: Interventions that Work for Children and Adults with Autism Spectrum Disorders.* Santa Ana, CA: Optometric Extension Program Foundation, 2008.

McKean, Thomas. *Soon Will Come the Light.* Arlington, TX: Future Horizons, 2001.

Notbohm, Ellen. *Ten Things Every Child with Autism Wishes You Knew.* Arlington, TX: Future Horizons, 2005.

Prince-Hughes, Dawn. *Songs of the Gorilla Nation: My Journey through Autism.* New York: Harmony Books, 2004.

Tammet, Daniel. *Born on a Blue Day: Inside the Extraordinary Mind of an Autistic Savant.* New York: Free Press, 2006.

Williams, Donna. *Somebody Somewhere: Breaking Free from the World of Autism.* New York: Three Rivers Press, 1994.

Wrobel, Mary. *Taking Care of Myself: A Healthy Hygiene, Puberty, and Personal Curriculum for Young People with Autism.* Arlington, TX: Future Horizons, 2003.

CHAPTER 10

Improving Speech Skills and
Picky Eating

Think back to a time when you had dental work done and left the dentist's with a mouth still numb with novocaine. You probably avoided speaking because your tongue felt like lead and your words came out slowly and laboriously. If you drank some water, some of it may have dribbled out. Maybe your mouth felt larger on one side, even though you knew that wasn't the case. And for hours afterward, you had to focus hard to chew only on one side of your mouth.

For a child whose sensory issues affect his mouth, eating and speaking may require a great deal of effort. As you've learned, poor sensory integration can result in abnormal muscle tone (the degree of tension when the muscle is at rest) and tactile processing problems. A child may have low oral muscle tone, resulting in a weak jaw, cheeks, tongue, and lips. Because he is unable to manage his "floppy" mouth, his mouth may hang open when not in use, he may drool frequently, and have difficulty pronouncing certain sounds. To compensate when eating and drinking, the child may clamp down on straws and utensils for extra stability, or use his neck and head muscles to pull back when biting off a piece of food.

The problem is compounded if your child has tactile issues. If she doesn't feel saliva or food, she won't have the tactile cues she needs to know things like when to search around with her tongue, when to swallow, and whether she has food on her lips.

A child with high oral muscle tone will also have difficulties. In this case, he lacks the flexibility he needs, and can't use his jaws, cheeks, tongue, and lips effectively. Tactile hypersensitivity in the mouth can interfere with moving mouth parts against each other, such as placing his teeth on his lower lip to pronounce a *v*, and cause him to avoid certain foods, having his teeth brushed, and so on. What's more, a child with oral-motor dysfunction may know just

what he wants to say, but somewhere between the thought and its ex-
ecution, something gets mixed up and his tongue, lips, and mouth
just don't work quite right. In short, a child with oral-motor problems
will generally have both speech problems and eating issues, however
mild.

SPEECH PROBLEMS

If your child has a speech-language delay, your speech-language pathologist (SLP) will examine your child's mouth and ask a lot of questions
about subjects like drooling, tongue-thrusting, your child's history of
vocalizing, whether she uses a pacifier or bottle or sucks her thumb,
and whether she has any eating issues. Your answers will help determine whether your child has underlying oral-motor issues that affect
speech.

"The Rain in Spain Stays Mainly on the Plain": Articulation

When your child first learns to speak, her mispronunciations can be
downright adorable. As time wears on, if poor articulation continues,
she will become frustrated at not being understood and you will
probably start wondering, why isn't she "getting" this?

In babyhood, children's brains create neural connections when
they hear their native language spoken. This helps them recognize
and reproduce speech sounds when they are developmentally ready to
do so. Typically a baby starts pronouncing vowel sounds, followed by
b, d, and *m.* He develops the ability to make more difficult sounds
later, sometimes not for several years. SLPs consider it appropriate to
mispronounce *s* as *th,* or *r* as *w,* until around age eight. Similarly, it's
common for toddlers to stutter because their mouths can't quite keep
up with their thoughts.

Some articulation problems are not age appropriate, however, and
are caused by something other than immaturity. A child might be unable to create certain sounds (or eat effectively) because of poor muscle tone, tactile hypersensitivity, motor planning problems, or limited
tongue movement. A child may also be tongue-tied, meaning his
frenulum—the skin that stretches from behind the bottom front teeth
to the underside of the tongue—extends too close to the tip of the
tongue. The frenulum may stretch and elongate over time, or it may

need to be surgically clipped in severe cases. If your child has a short frenulum, be sure to mention it to your speech-language pathologist (SLP) so she can determine whether it is affecting your child's speech or eating.

"You Say Potato and I Say Topahhhhhuuuuduh": Problems with Motor Planning

As you've already learned, motor planning can be a challenge for many children with sensory integration dysfunction. And since speaking requires coordinating the breath, the tongue, the lips, the jaws, and the muscles of the mouth, a child with motor planning problems can get tripped up when trying to speak. Her receptive language skills may be excellent, and her mind may well know that she wants to produce the *c*, *a*, and *t* sounds with her mouth, but when she tries to say the word *cat*, there's a breakdown. Some of the signs of verbal dyspraxia are:

- difficulty imitating sounds or oral-motor actions;
- slow, singsong, or robotic speech;
- difficulty producing words or answering questions on demand (words may pop out only when the pressure to speak is off);
- difficulty maintaining words already said (for instance, you may hear her speak a full sentence, but never hear any of those individual words again, or she'll say *water* several times in a row and then not again for months despite much coaxing);
- inconsistency in pronunciation (for example, she says *wuh* for water one day, *wahher* a few days later, and *wooo* the day after that);
- trouble with sequencing sounds (such as *bee bah bee*) or, in an older child, narrating events in sequence.

In addition to isolating movements, working with music or rhythm, and other techniques SLPs commonly use, some specially trained SLPs physically cue the dyspraxic child to create the proper sound, using Deborah Hayden's PROMPT method or similar methods such as Touch Cue and Adapted Cueing. For example, if your child uses the *g* sound for *k*, the SLP would have him make the *g* sound as she pushes her index finger up against the skin under his chin just behind the jawbone to prompt the tongue into the correct position. Of course, if the child is extremely sensitive to touch around the mouth and face, and won't tolerate such cueing, the SLP must start by desensitizing the area in and around the mouth. If you suspect your child has oral-motor planning problems, talk to an SLP who specializes in verbally dyspraxic children. (Note that "apraxia" rather than "dyspraxia" is the term used by many SLPs to refer to developmental apraxia rather than motor planning problems caused by physical trauma.)

BABY SIGN LANGUAGE

A baby typically waves bye-bye before she can say it, and points to the juice in the refrigerator long before she asks for it. Your SLP may teach your baby (and you) some sign language so your child can quickly improve her ability to communicate her needs and desires and reduce frustration. The child who can sign *give me* or *more* instead of whining or throwing a tantrum feels more understood and in control because she can tell you what she wants, at least some of the time. Sign language may also be used to help older children with speech-language delays to reduce frustration and increase communication. Signs should be accompanied by words to enhance speech and language skills.

Other Causes of Speech Difficulty

Auditory sensitivities, a history of ear infections, and auditory processing issues can all have a profound impact on the development of speech.

Kids who have had multiple ear infections often have speech-language delays because they've spent a lot of time with impaired hearing. In her book *Childhood Speech, Language, and Listening Problems: What Every Parent Should Know*, speech therapist Patricia McAleer Hamaguchi says that if your child has had three or more ear infections in her first three years, you should carefully monitor her speech and language.[1] "Additionally," she says, "difficulty with remembering information (auditory memory) and understanding spoken information (auditory processing) may persist long after the hearing ability returns to normal." She urges any parent whose child has had frequent ear infections to have a tympanogram performed by an audiologist to make sure the infections are completely cleared up. This is especially important before age three because you don't want a lingering infection to hamper your child's hearing for weeks or even months. Then, too, babies who have difficulty sucking are more prone to ear infections because sucking helps clear their tiny eustachian tubes so bacteria can't build up.

If your child isn't properly hearing and processing the sounds of speech, he will have trouble reproducing them. An audiological exam can rule out actual hearing problems and, if the child is at least five years old, may be able to rule out auditory processing problems. While you probably think of an audiologist as someone you would go to for a hearing aid, audiologists also assess and treat people who have auditory sensory and processing issues. In addition to administering a tympanogram for eardrum function, and the sensory sensitivity testing discussed on pages 209–10, the audiologist's highly specialized testing also plays the defining role in diagnosing an auditory processing disorder. Make sure to work with an audiologist who spends a good deal of her practice on pediatrics, and who knows how to make testing more fun for kids. See Chapter 13: Complementary Therapies and Approaches for information on auditory interventions and how to find a qualified audiologist.

Making Your Child's Mouth Happy

Once it's determined that your child could indeed benefit from speech-language therapy, the SLP should assess whether he is oversensitive or undersensitive to sensations in his jaw, cheeks, lips, palate, and tongue. Depending on your child's particular needs, your SLP may ask you to follow through on interventions that either calm down or wake up various parts of his mouth area.

You might be asked to do things such as use a Nuk massager, Infa-Dent, or spongy tooth swabs like Dentips or Toothettes (available from www.amazon.com, the *Sammons Preston* catalog, and other therapy catalogs; see photo of Infa-Dent on page 398, or a damp washcloth to stimulate around and inside; give your child a vibrating toothbrush or other oral vibration to parts of the face; provide ice pops; and give crunchy foods to provide deep pressure input.

The Fine Art of Blowing Out Birthday Candles

Once the mouth area has been desensitized, or sensitized if needed, the SLP can begin working with your child to strengthen his face and mouth muscles and improve his ability to coordinate them to make precise movements. For instance, at first a child may be completely unable to blow out the flame of a candle, but after working on various blowing skills, he may be able to extinguish it with a little *pfffft* from the right distance. After that, however, the SLP will help him refine that blowing action, to take in more air, to round his lips and keep them rounded as he performs the action.

Here are some of the oral-motor activities SLPs have children engage in:

Blowing. The child might blow out birthday candles, blow through a straw into a dish of bubbles or at feathers on a table, and blow a bubble off its perch on a bubble wand and then work toward creating the bubble by blowing through the wand. SLPs also use many kinds of whistles, each of which helps the child refine a different movement of the tongue and lips.

Sucking. The child might work first on sucking through a juice-box straw (squeezing the box for a little extra help) and later work on sucking a thick milkshake through a straw. The SLP will work with him to prevent him from biting the straw for stabilization.

Chewing. The child might use chewy candies such as gummy bears or Starburst candies to build up his chewing stamina. He might also be encouraged to bite off pieces of food without using his neck and head muscles.

If your child receives occupational therapy, your OT may also work on feeding issues because so often they involve sensory issues, low or high muscle tone, and fine motor skill development. Because food is involved in many therapy activities, be open with all of your child's therapists about your child's diet. Candy is frequently used either as a challenging food or as a reinforcer, because children are often more likely to try an activity they find difficult or unpleasant if there's a sweet treat involved. If your child has strong reactions to artificial colors and dyes, or becomes hyperactive after eating a small amount of sugar, or you're just trying to avoid having your child eat junk food, talk to your therapist about substitute treats. She may be able to work with pretzels, vegetable sticks, dried fruit, or sugarless chewing gum.

Oral Comforts

Many children with sensory processing disorder continue thumb sucking or using a bottle or pacifier much longer than other kids do. These oral comforts ease anxiety and promote self-calming and self-regulation, so think twice before taking them away from your little one. We promise he won't go to college with it in his mouth. As long as your child discontinues using objects such as a thumb or pacifier to self-soothe before age seven or so, any shifting of baby teeth is likely to reverse on its own, and not affect your child's permanent teeth. However, after age seven or eight, it can influence how permanent teeth grow in. Your OT or SLP can teach you techniques to discourage thumb sucking and pacifier use, and if these don't work, an orthodontist can create an appliance for your child's mouth that eliminates the pleasurable sensation of thumb sucking.

Meanwhile, if your young child is stuck on using a bottle, thumb, or pacifier, try to limit its use—perhaps only at bedtime and naptime—and provide alternative means of comfort. For example, spending ten minutes lying next to your child in bed might make her forget about her pacifier. If you let your child fall asleep with a bottle or use it throughout the day, *never* fill it with juice or milk, because teeth begin to decay when they spend so much time being bathed in sugary liquids. This is known as bottle rot, and even breastfeeding babies are not immune to it, because like cow's milk, human milk is high in sugars. If your child won't take water in the bottle, water down the juice or milk a little more each day until the bottle is filled entirely with water. Nancy says that Cole used to hold up his bottle to the light, squinting to make sure it was cloudy because he thought that meant it was milk, even if it really was just water with two drops of milk. She bought opaque bottles and filled them with water, and he couldn't tell the difference by that point.

If you do allow your child a bottle or pacifier during the day, or a sippy cup for that matter, insist that she take it out of her mouth to speak, even if you can understand her anyway. And save the sippy cup for a special treat of juice that you don't want spilled on the carpet or in the car; it's better for oral-motor development if children drink from regular cups whenever possible, and water really is the best beverage.

As an adult, you may chew gum, drink water or coffee, or consciously breathe deeply to regulate your own arousal level. Your child can use her mouth as a self-calming tool too. A pacifier "pacifies" an infant or toddler. Giving your son a juice box with a straw for sucking while you're in a crowd may give him the sensory input he needs to avoid overload. Licking a lollipop may be a big incentive for a child to stay focused and attentive. Experiment to find the oral tools that make your child calm and comfortable. Here are some more ideas for promoting oral motor skills and sensory comfort:

- Provide a variety of foods, including *crunchy* (pretzels and carrot sticks), *chewy* (bagels and small bits of meat), *creamy* (yogurt and cream cheese), *salty* (popcorn and chips), *sweet* (fruit and candy), *sour* (sour pickles and lemon drops), and *spicy* (cinnamon candy and barbecue chips).
- Encourage a range of mouth actions, including chewing and crunching the foods above, as well as sucking, licking, biting and pulling (such as chomping down on a licorice string to yank off a piece), and blowing (such as to cool down hot soup).
- Make funny noises (clicks, noisy kisses, blowing raspberries) and make silly faces together (facing each other or in front of a mirror).

Your Gorgeous, Drooling Child

Most children stop drooling by about fifteen months of age unless teething or eating certain foods. By two years old, drooling stops altogether. However, many children with sensory problems continue to drool when they eat, concentrate on a challenging fine motor task, do resistive strength work like squeezing clay, or when relaxing with an open mouth position. In addition to following through with your SLP's or OT's instructions on improving oral-motor strength and encouraging more frequent swallowing, you may need to help your child increase her awareness of a drooling mouth with simple cues such as, "Oh, your lips are wet. Let's wipe them." At first you may need to do the wiping, until your child takes over. Wiping lips with a tissue or cloth (wipe lower lip upward and upper lip downward) also gives needed sensory input, encouraging lip awareness and lip closure.

PICKY EATING AND OTHER FOOD ISSUES

Now that you've seen how trouble coordinating mouth movements and handling mouth sensations can lead to expressive speech problems, you can see why such difficulties can lead to picky eating as well.

Picky eating, and insisting on the same foods over and over again, is developmentally appropriate behavior for toddlers, and some children will be fussy about food all their lives without any significant impact on their nutrition. However, having sensory processing challenges makes it even more difficult for a child to try unfamiliar foods, or to eat foods that have a texture, smell, or taste that offends their senses. Even the color and shape of the food may affect their ability to tolerate it. Most of us don't pay close attention to textures, but kids with sensory issues do! For instance, when you put a piece of cut banana in your mouth, the wet interior of the fruit touches your tongue first, but if you eat a banana the regular way, the peel pulled down, your tongue touches the dry exterior and the stringy fibers. Old-fashioned peanut butter is harder to chew than the sugary, popular brands, and you may have to mix the two gradually to get your child to eat the healthier version. Nancy remembers that Cole loved peanut butter cereal and would lick peanut butter when it was on crackers but would never eat it. When she tried a different brand of peanut butter that was smoother and easier to chew, Cole's resistance melted and peanut butter quickly became a staple of his diet.

Some kids will only eat crunchy foods, or mushy foods (although they may eat crunchy cereal that quickly turns mushy in milk). Aversion to a certain texture might be a tactile issue, but it could also be due to low tone in the mouth or a motor planning problem. Some children will actually gag while eating—and avoid foods they fear will make them gag—because their oral-motor coordination is not what it should be.

We take for granted how easy it is to bite, chew, and swallow, but for the child with sensory issues, things don't always go so smoothly. For instance, it takes twenty-six muscles to swallow; you can imagine how a child with motor planning problems would have trouble coordinating all of those at the same time. A child with oral-motor problems might insist on biting and chewing only with his front teeth, or only on one side. She may have trouble using her tongue and mouth muscles to keep the food together in one lump (called a bolus), causing the food to pool in pockets of the mouth. If she can't form a bolus well, she may just take tiny, tiny bites. She might not be able to judge how much saliva and food should be moved to the back of her throat for swallowing at one time. She might overstuff her mouth because she genuinely can't feel how much food she has in it, then gag when she tries to swallow such a large, dry mass. A child who tilts her head while eating might be compensating for poor tongue coordination by using gravity, not her tongue, to move food from one side of her mouth to the other. Also, children with low tone in the mouth tend to have food and saliva collect between the gum and lips, resulting in mouth breathing and dental cavities, and even causing teeth to grow in crookedly.

If you suspect that your child has oral-motor issues that are affecting his ability to bite, chew, and swallow, consult a feeding specialist (these are generally SLPs or OTs) or a feeding clinic.

INAPPROPRIATE CHEWING, BITING, AND LICKING

Parents expect a baby to mouth, chew, and bite things. If your older child still chews, bites, or licks things or people he shouldn't, recognize that these are sensory-seeking behaviors. Give him acceptable items to chew, bite, or lick, such as Chewy Tubes (plastic hammer-shaped chew toys), Ark's Grabbers (plastic tubes with handles), and Chewlery (coiled, chewable jewelry)—all available from therapy catalogs listed in the back of this book. Crunchy snacks such as pretzels and carrot and celery sticks are also appropriate substitutes. Do not let your child chew on cuffs with buttons or the ends of pens or pencils for safety reasons (a ChewEase Pencil Topper from the *Integrations* catalog placed on the end of a writing utensil is a safer alternative). If your child is biting other children due to frustration or anger, see pages 325–26 in Chapter 14: Handling Discipline, Transitions, and Behavioral Issues.

When Do You Need Help?

"He'll eat when he's hungry." "You're just spoiling her." "In my day, we ate what we were served, period." If your child is a picky eater, you may have heard these comments many times, and come to question why it's so difficult for your child to try new foods. It's always hard to tell how much of your child's resistance is due to actual sensory issues and how much to his need to control his world and his eating. Even your pediatrician may tell you not to worry and that your child will simply grow out of it. But is this really true?

Regarding letting kids go hungry if they won't eat what is served, Kelly Dorfman, M.S., L.N., a nutritionist who works extensively with children who have sensory issues, says, "This adage may work if children have a normal sense of hunger and satiety, but children with sensory issues do not. Starving them out is very dangerous." She adds: "A common diet I see in a child who has a sensory problem is dry cereal and juice for breakfast, crackers and grapes for lunch, and a peanut butter sandwich for dinner. Or, the milk version: cereal and milk for breakfast, bagel and cream cheese for lunch, and mac and cheese for dinner, washed down with some juice. Diets like this cannot support optimal brain development and yet, if the child is growing, the doctor usually advises the parents not to worry."

Just as you'd go to a medical specialist for expert advice on a specific medical condition, you may need to consult someone who specializes in feeding and nutrition issues. If you are concerned that your child isn't getting proper nutrition, it's worth talking to a nutrition specialist, ideally one who has experience working with kids who have sensory integration dysfunction. After all, when nutritional issues are addressed, you make it easier for your child's body to handle the sensory issues. For more specific information on nutrition and sensory processing, see Chapter 12: Nutrition, Sleep, and Stress.

Kelly Dorfman suggests you seek extra help with your child's picky eating if he:

- is not gaining weight properly;
- can't join the family in regular activities unless special plans are made to accommodate the eating problems;
- looks pale, pasty, and/or unhealthy;
- frequently disrupts dinnertime if food isn't "just right";
- is frequently sick or has a chronic runny nose or cough;
- refuses to eat anything unless a specific food is presented;
- is chronically moody or has severe temper tantrums about food;
- mostly eats pasta, cereal, or crackers for dinner;
- has frequent gastrointestinal problems, such as constipation or diarrhea;
- gags on food regularly;
- leads you to dread dinnertime or give up on "the eating thing."

Children with sensory processing disorder can remain picky eaters beyond the toddler years because they take comfort in the predictability of foods they know they like. You'll need patience, understanding, and sensory smarts to introduce new foods. You can start with some of the basic "picky eating" tips that follow.

Expanding Food Choices

- Don't give up on introducing new foods! Continue to serve foods even if they're rejected. You may have to serve a food dozens of times before your child will actually try it. Try introducing one new food at a time to increase your child's familiarity with it. Even if he turns up his nose at that small serving of whole grain pasta three nights a week, or that banana slice on his breakfast plate every morning, after a while, his curiosity may well get the better of him.

- Allow your child to take just one bite and let her spit it out into a napkin if she decides it's utterly disgusting. You may have to start with praising and even rewarding her for simply *licking* a food. You can start the familiarization process by showing the child photographs of the offending food, then working your way up to having her eat at the table with the food in plain sight (and close enough to smell), then tolerating it on her plate (don't let the food touch other food on the plate if mixing the textures is repulsive to her), touching it, then touching it to her mouth, then her tongue, etc.

- Consider allowing your child to choose a few specific "repulsive" foods to be on his forbidden list, and promise that you won't force him to eat these. Stick to your promise!

- If your child avoids mixed textures, separate the food using a partitioned plate or several small plates, even allowing him to use separate forks for separate foods. You can also gradually add texture. He might be able to tolerate only a very light coating of tomato sauce on his pasta but over time become more accepting of sauce and, eventually, sauce with tomato chunks and bits of meat mixed in.

- Offering sauces and dips will entice some children to eat but may seem repulsive to a child who hates mixed textures. You might do better encouraging her to eat simple foods such as cheese sticks, apples or apple slices (brush them with lemon to keep them from turning brown if you're taking them on the go), bananas (try slicing them so that the moist inside is exposed), or peeled and deseeded cucumbers (use a spear-like apple corer to easily remove the seeds). Then, when you do serve low nutrition foods like candy, cake, ice cream, or cookies as treats, use those opportunities to encourage your child to try mixed textures. If she'll tolerate sprinkles on her ice cream today, tomorrow she may tolerate Parmesan cheese sprinkled on a healthy food.

- Give your child an incentive by awarding her points, redeemable for a small toy or extra TV time, for trying a new food or eating a small portion of a food that's not a favorite.

- Introduce similarly textured foods for best results with a child who has texture issues. If she'll eat peas, push corn kernels and lima beans. If she won't eat mushy, mixed-texture applesauce, she's probably not going to eat mushy, mixed-texture refried beans. Try to vary the texture, shape, and size of her favorite foods occasionally to stretch her tolerance but be prepared with the familiar version if she refuses this variation. For instance, she may refuse to eat carrot sticks cut with a knife if she's only used to the rounded precut ones (especially since the precut ones often are sweeter). Introduce variations on the foods she typically will eat—break graham crackers into four pieces instead of two, mix a different brand of yogurt or peanut butter into the one she usually eats—and see whether she'll tolerate the change. Often, the sensory challenge isn't the issue so much as anxiety over something that's unfamiliar. Working on getting your child to tolerate variations on her favorite foods will help her broaden her food choices overall, so keep trying.

- If your child does become burned out on a food, take it out of his diet, then reintroduce it in a few weeks as if it were a new food. He may take a very long time to accept it again.

- Vary the temperature of foods. Extracold food might provide sensory input that wakes up your child's mouth and makes him more willing to eat it. If he prefers his food lukewarm, let him eat it that way.

- Use your creativity and presentation skills to coax younger kids to eat. Use cookie cutters to cut foods into fun shapes, or arrange foods on a plate to create animals and faces (such as ants on a log, or a smiley face salad). Put a toy dinosaur on his plate and explain that the meatballs and broccoli are "rocks and trees." Children's cookbooks often have suggestions for cute presentations.

- Avoid serving your child food in the container it came in. Manufacturers frequently change packaging and your child might be convinced that the new package contains a different product and refuse to eat that food again.

- Drinking juice and milk throughout the day or eating snacks or drinking soda will reduce your child's appetite for meals. Limit or dilute juice and try giving plain water or seltzer.

- Don't make the mistake of butting heads with your child by, for example, insisting that he not leave the table until he has eaten his brussels sprouts. When your child does get hungry, offer protein, fruit, and vegetables before allowing your child to fill up on carbohydrates.

- Some kids will go all day nibbling like birds and want to eat the majority of their calories at bedtime, begging for yet another bowl of cereal even as you're pleading with them to go to sleep. Keep in mind that prescription medications can worsen this famine-to-feast behavior. Try to schedule regular mealtimes and snack times.

- Avoid having low-nutrition foods available in your home. This is especially important if your child continually rejects healthier foods. Work with your school lunch program to offer healthier options, such as whole wheat crust pizza or turkey hot dogs, or send in a bag lunch. Insist that your child bring home all the resealable bags or containers. That way you can wash them out (recycling the bags) and see what he is or isn't eating. You might be amazed at how much food children simply throw away. Have a nonjudgmental conversation with him about why he didn't eat the food he packed. It may be that he was famished but the lunchroom atmosphere was so intolerable that he couldn't bring himself to eat there.

- At home and when you're traveling, keep on hand nutritious snacks and easy-to-eat foods such as grapes, vegetable sticks and dip, dried fruit, cheese, yogurt, cherry tomatoes, and whole grain crackers with peanut butter. Encourage your older child or teen to carry along healthy foods that pack easily so that he doesn't have to resort to a quick trip to the candy store to resolve his munchies after school.

- Offer healthy choices so that your child feels some control over her diet—"Corn or peas?" Teach older children to read food labels and learn nutrition basics, such as that a cereal is naturally low in fat, so Super Sugar Munchies' claim to be low in fat doesn't mean much when it contains 16 grams of refined sugar per serving and its ingredients include artificial flavors and colors. Learn about nutrition yourself and encourage your child to educate you and to choose better foods for himself.

- Check your local health food store, or the health food section of your grocery store, for healthier foods with "kid friendly" shapes and packaging. However, keep in mind that even if it's made from all-organic ingredients, a cookie should still be a treat, not a dietary staple.

- Make whole grain pancakes or waffles with your usual pancake mix but substitute steamed acorn or butternut squash or canned pumpkin for the milk. Puree vegetables and slip them into pizza sauce, soup, etc.

- Learn to cook, and have your children learn with you. Convenience foods are high in sodium (salt) and often have fewer vitamins and minerals than fresher versions of the same food. Don't feel you have to be a Food Network chef and whip up three fancy dishes for each meal. Start simply by focusing on easy recipes using whole grains and extremely fresh produce.

- Grow a garden and have your children help with the planning, planting, and tending. It's always more fun to eat foods you helped produce.

- To help your family eat more nutritiously and make food preparation and planning more fun, take the family to a farmer's market and ask the farmers how to prepare the vegetables they're selling. Try the purple potatoes, the yellow tomatoes, and the hybrid of broccoli and cauliflower. Consider joining a food co-op in which you put in a certain amount of money and have in-season vegetables delivered to your home. (You don't know what you'll get until it arrives; of course, have some reliable favorites on hand if you aren't sure your picky eater will try the kohlrabi.)

- When you find a recipe everyone in the family pretty much agrees on—perhaps you sauté the garlic and onions separately and serve them only on the adults' entrees—make it regularly and have the whole family involved in husking corn, snapping beans, and setting the table. Make mealtime a fun, social time.

- Spy and gossip! Kids will often try a new food at a relative's or neighbor's house because of the social pressure to not draw attention to themselves and to be polite. Let your most understanding, nonjudgmental friends and family members know you're trying to expand your child's diet, and tell them what foods they can count on your child eating. (We're big believers in making sure your child will eat at least some of the simple foods most people have on hand, such as apples and bananas, but it's also important to teach your child that at a friend's house, he should eat what's served or say "No, thank you" rather than insisting on a different food.) Ask your friend or family member to let you know whether your child actually did eat tofu dogs or yogurt, so that you know what foods you might be able to introduce into his diet.

Changing the Eating Experience

- Serve small portions that aren't overwhelming. If your child has trouble biting or swallowing, tends to gag, or overstuffs his mouth with food, cut the food into very small pieces.
- Try different utensils. A too-big or too-small fork, or a spoon whose edge feels rough, can cause problems for a child with sensory issues.
- With younger kids, try using kid-friendly utensils, plates, and cups featuring animals, licensed characters, or bright colors. Make mealtime more interesting by having a picnic night on a sheet in the family room, or try a fun cooking project like fondue.
- Consider serving meals in another area of your home. Kitchens can be too bright (you might also change the lighting) and the sounds and smells of meal preparation can be too intense for some kids.
- Have your toddler bring a doll or stuffed animal to the table to "try" foods before she does.
- Always keep mealtimes pleasant. Power struggles, scolding, and threats will actually make your child *less* likely to eat or try new foods. Positive and even playful attitudes toward eating go a long way to reassuring the picky eater who is anxious about certain foods. Praise your child whenever she tries a new food or one she rarely eats.

Restaurants

- If your child resists foods with mixed textures, bring simple vegetables or fruits, preprepared, to a restaurant or family gathering so that she doesn't have to subsist on crackers, bread, or plain white pasta or rice.
- Family restaurants will often provide crayons and paper for coloring, but pack your own along with small toys and other distractions. However, recognize that the sensory environment of a restaurant may be too intense for your child to be able to sit still and focus on coloring. He may actually need to leave the environment for a few minutes and get some calming, focusing input.
- Always be aware of the sensory environment at mealtime. Strong smells, eating and serving noises (a table near the kitchen in a restaurant, people chatting and rattling menus, etc.), and intolerable lighting (dim restaurant lighting or bright sunlight streaming through a window) at home or away may be so challenging for a child that he can't focus on eating. Loud, stimulating kid-oriented

restaurants may make him utterly miserable or giddy and uncontrollably hyper.

- If your child is having difficulty tolerating the restaurant environment, a trip to the car, an empty back dining room, or an empty bathroom for quiet can help (beware of loudly flushing toilets and noisy water hitting porcelain sinks, however). If your child is hyper, try going outside and letting her do calming, focusing activities like push-ups against a wall, jumping off a low retaining wall while holding your hand, or marching. Also do these types of calming, focusing activities before entering the restaurant.

- In a restaurant, offer your child earplugs if the background noise is really hard for him to handle. Some kids with sensory issues have poor body awareness or a high need for movement, and sitting on a smooth or bumpy inflatable cushion will do wonders for keeping them in their seat, so consider bringing one with you.

- Don't be afraid to order off the menu. If your child wants a soda pop, ask if they can mix seltzer and juice for him instead. Read the menu and see what vegetables they have in the kitchen that could be ordered separately: a burger joint will usually be willing to serve you a plate of tomato slices, for instance.

- Remember that everyone in a restaurant is paying to have a pleasant meal. If your child is screeching in an attempt to overcome his auditory sensitivities, throwing food, whining in discomfort, or dashing out of his seat to run in circles (which is a safety hazard as well as distracting), just say no to restaurants. Get takeout and have a picnic or serve the food at home. Toddlers and preschoolers with sensory issues have a particularly hard time with restaurants. Their tolerance will improve over time, but strongly consider your alternatives rather than put them, you, and everyone else through a stressful restaurant experience.

Picky Eating Can Be a Huge Challenge

Okay, so you've tried and tried to expand your child's food repertoire, but nothing seems to be working. Kelly Dorfman adds this advice:

- You can take bad things out of the diet, but it is hard to get the good things in. Work with the nutritious foods they will eat. It's better for them to have chicken nuggets every day for dinner (while you are doing oral sensitivity work at other times and trying to expand the diet) than to allow them to have crackers and sugary juice. Or, if a child only eats one fruit, hot dogs, and peanut butter sandwiches, have him eat a (nitrate-free) hot dog for breakfast, and fruit with peanut butter sandwiches for lunch and dinner.

- *Do not withhold meals.* Hunger does not work as an incentive. When children are very hungry, they tend to be cranky and *less* likely to try new things. Better to let them know in advance what new food will be introduced and when. They can certainly help pick the food if they have any inclination to do so. You could also use snack time for introducing a new food if this is a more relaxed time of day, and he is not stressed out and tired (as he is likely to be at dinnertime, after a long school day). Use other consequences for not eating. For example, your child's "job" this week might be to eat *one* bite of carrot with dinner (start small!). If he refuses, let him eat the rest of what he normally eats (avoiding dessert foods and sugary foods), and do not move on to other activities until his job is done. Do not threaten or punish him. In a calm, clear voice tell him that you would love to turn on the TV, play a game—whatever you might do with him after dinner—but you are not ready yet because his job is not done. If he cooperates, give him attention; if he doesn't, be unavailable. Do not have long conversations and engage him in a power struggle that reinforces his negative behavior. If he throws a fit, leave the room (if he is safe from choking or falling out of a chair) and say in a calm, clear voice, "I will return when you calm down."
- Do not forget that children with sensory issues often escalate their behavior in order to control their environment. If escalation works (for example, your child throws up and you stop presenting him with an offending food item), he will keep doing it. If he throws up, calmly clean it up and tell your child he can try again tomorrow. This way, he will learn that throwing up, or throwing a plate, or whatever negative behavior he is using to try to control the situation, is not useful. However, some children with smell and taste sensitivities *are* truly nauseated by particular foods. If your sensory smarts tell you this is the case for your child, do not continue to present the offending food. Some parents let their children pick out a small number of foods they will never, ever be forced to eat.

Nancy's Story

Cole had been a bad latch as a newborn, and I remember thinking at the time that despite all the great advice and support I was getting from the lactation consultant, three sisters-in-law, and my La Leche

League breastfeeding book, the problem wasn't me, it was him. Somehow, he wasn't "getting" how to latch and suck properly. When he was two and a half, he was diagnosed with verbal dyspraxia by an SLP, who finally gave me an answer to why Cole had taken so long to learn how to nurse: the motor planning had been too difficult for him. His speech-language pathologist began to work on his dyspraxia using the PROMPT method of verbal cueing; he began to catch up, and by age four he was very articulate and understandable.

However, his picky eating concerned me, so I took him to a nutritionist as well as to an SLP who is a feeding specialist. I discovered that while he had learned to compensate for poor coordination in his mouth so that he could speak clearly, he was still struggling with the basics of biting and chewing, sensing how much food should be in his mouth, and keeping that food together in a lump for swallowing. Chewy foods were the biggest challenge, and he was avoiding them. First, they required lots of motor planning to eat and lots of stamina in his jaw, where he had somewhat poor tone (he was a *very* drooly baby—luckily, he had overcome that). Cole was happy to chew soft bubblegum, but if it was hard bubblegum or a caramel, he'd suck it for a while and spit it out. He balked at every meat except one: hot Italian turkey sausage.

I learned from the nutritionist that picky eaters, particularly those who don't eat meat, often have certain deficiencies, such as magnesium and zinc. Luckily, Cole was eating enough whole grains to give him his magnesium. The zinc in his multivitamin, however, was not enough to compensate for his low-zinc diet. When I gave him a taste of a supplement called Zinc Tally, which tastes like chalk or rotten eggs if you're not zinc deficient and water if you are, he thought it was water. Zinc deficiency, I learned, can dull the taste buds, which might explain why the cayenne in his sausage suited Cole just fine.

Working with the nutritionist to look closely at exactly what Cole was eating, we discovered where all the holes in his diet were. We decided to continue using his favorite "gummy bear" vitamins (after all, that was good chewing practice!) and to add a custom vitamin solution to his diluted juice every day so that he could get full nutrition. In the meantime, I continued working on his oral-motor issues with his OT and SLP and encouraging him to try chewy treats and play oral-motor games so that eventually he would be less resistant to meat and other chewy foods.

Recommended Reading

Acredolo, L., S. Goodwyn, and D. Abrams. *Baby Signs: How to Talk with Your Baby Before Your Baby Can Talk.* New York: McGraw-Hill, 2002.

Agin, Marilyn C., Lisa F. Geng, and Malcolm Nicholl. *The Late Talker: What to Do If Your Child Isn't Talking Yet.* New York: St. Martin's Press, 2003. Excellent advice on dealing with late talking due to verbal dyspraxia, but take their dire warnings about untreated dyspraxia with a grain of salt.

Ernsperger, Lori, and Tania Stegen-Hanson. *Just Take a Bite: Easy, Effective Answers to Food Aversions and Eating Challenges.* Arlington, TX: Future Horizons, 2004.

Hamaguchi, Patricia M. *Childhood Speech, Language, and Listening Problems: What Every Parent Should Know.* New York: John Wiley & Sons, 2001.

Lapine, Missy. *The Sneaky Chef: Simple Strategies for Hiding Healthy Food in Kids' Favorite Meals.* Philadelphia: Running Press, 2007. Good tricks for making tasty, wholesome meals many kids enjoy. Remember, though, that a child with sensory issues may be exquisitely attuned to changes in taste and texture.

Sears, William, M.D., and Martha Sears, R.N. *Feeding the Picky Eater.* Boston: Little Brown and Co., 2001.

CHAPTER 11

Helping Your Child Learn and Get Organized

Jake is extremely bright. At age five, he can read *Captain Underpants*, and write his mommy a love letter. He knows the names of all the planets and can point out several constellations in the night sky. But his parents and teachers are concerned that he never sits still in school and refuses to join circle time or participate in art projects. They are considering assigning a "shadow"—a one-to-one special teacher—to help him stay engaged and on task at school.

Shaniqua is smart too. She can tell you how a flamingo gets so pink by eating brine shrimp and that it is the male seahorse that gives birth. At age nine, she can draw virtually any critter and tell you its habitat, favorite foods, and natural predators. Yet at the end of each grading period, teachers complain about her sloppy handwriting and terrible math skills, and that she always loses her books and forgets her homework.

Joshua is brilliant with his hands. When he was sixteen, he got a job working in an auto repair shop after school. He can fix nearly anything: his sister's dollhouse, his friend's bicycle, even his own laptop computer. His dad once dreamed Joshua would become a surgeon like him, but there's just no way his son could handle medical school. He's just squeaking by in high school, passing exams only with thousands of dollars' worth of tutoring.

All of these kids are intelligent and motivated to learn—at least about things that interest them. And all of these kids have teachers and parents who do their best to help. So what's the problem?

By now you know that sensory problems affect every aspect of life. School provides precisely the kind of high-stimulation environment that can exacerbate sensory issues. In fact, maybe you didn't notice that your child was having difficulty until she started school and then . . .

wham! You were called in for extra parent-teacher meetings, spent hours pleading with your child to work harder, and maybe even thought about alternate schooling options.

Some kids love school from day one. They adore getting called on in class, meeting friends in the lunchroom, burning off their excess energy during recess, keeping their school supplies neat and organized, and they take enormous pride in doing their assignments. Other kids have school difficulties for various reasons, from low IQ to emotional and physical conditions to learning disabilities. And some have trouble purely due to sensory processing problems. For children who have help managing sensory issues and cooperative school staff and proactive parents, learning can be a boundless source of delight. Unmanaged, school can transform into a monster. Luckily, there are many ways to tame the dragon, as we shall see.

OVERLOAD AT SCHOOL

Some kids, despite being overwhelmed, manage to hold it together in school and find ingenious ways to minimize their stress—at least until they get home and either collapse, exhausted, in front of their favorite TV programs or morph into their grumpiest selves. Other kids find the "school thing" so difficult that they act out or shut down to cope. While a teacher may prefer quiet Ginny who spaces out and day-dreams to Richard who regularly jumps out of his seat and punches the kid next to him, both of these children may be cut off from learning because they're unable to cope with sensory overload.

For a child with sensory issues, the stress of the day begins the moment he wakes up. Because school starts much earlier today than it did fifty years ago and families stay up later, kids often have to get up before they've gotten enough sleep. Of course, a child with self-regulation problems may have had trouble getting to sleep the night before or sleeping soundly, so he may be fuzzy brained upon waking and in a bad mood. If he has gotten less sleep than he needs, his school performance won't be his best. A noisy, chaotic school-bus ride doesn't help either.

The school environment itself may not be kid friendly. Most schools do not use sound-absorbent carpeting or curtains to cut down on noise and glare from outside. Cheap and effective, the fluorescent lights used in most schools actually increase indoor glare, and some children can actually see and hear the flickering of these lights. Studies by Dr. John Ott and school principal William Titoff and others show that fluorescent bulbs directly contribute to physical stress, anxiety, depression, hyperactivity, poor attention, and other factors that lead to learning difficulty.[1]

Staying Focused

In most schools, children are asked to be quiet, look, and listen—that is, to be auditory and visual learners. They are expected to easily tune out extraneous sights, sounds, and other sensations and to be passive sponges for information. And they are required to sit still for increasingly long periods as they mature. Younger children must sit on the floor at circle time, either on a bare surface or on a low-pile, noncushioned rug, without squirming around, while older children must sit on hard chairs at hard desks for long periods of time without slumping over. Because most school chairs and desks are not height adjustable, some children's feet can't touch the floor—but they're admonished to not swing their feet. Sitting still in badly designed chairs or on the floor is especially difficult for children with low muscle tone or poor strength, endurance, or body awareness, or who physiologically *need* to move in order to stay alert and on task.

In the classroom, a child may also have a hard time sustaining auditory focus on the teacher, and may have difficulty discriminating between the teacher's voice and sounds from within the classroom and outside. Auditory and language processing issues, fine motor problems, anxiety, and other factors may interfere with staying on task when taking lecture notes, writing down assignments, participating in group projects, and so on.

Any undiagnosed, untreated visual problem makes it extremely difficult to concentrate for a long time, resulting in short attention span, fidgeting, restlessness, careless errors, and poor organization. Children may have difficulty with visual acuity, or they may have problems refocusing back and forth from the board or teacher to their notebooks. Or, they may be bothered by indoor glare. As children begin to read and write, visual problems, such as convergence insufficiency or excess, become more significant. Such children have trouble coordinating their eyes for close-up work like reading and writing. The eyes may tend to move outward (convergence insufficiency) or overly inward (convergence excess). These kids use a huge portion of their visual energy to keep the print clear and single on the page. This can result in eyestrain, headache, fatigue, and inattention.*

Lunchtime scheduled very early or late in the day to accommodate all the students can interfere with focus if a child has to wait too long for lunch or didn't have an appetite for lunch because it was too soon after eating breakfast. A picky eater often sticks out in the lunchroom, embarrassed because she is stuck eating the few foods she can tolerate instead of what everyone else is having. Lunchrooms are often extremely noisy and chaotic, which can be excruciating for a child with auditory sensitivities and processing difficulties. Strong lunchroom smells can also be disturbing.

On the Move

Many middle schools and high schools have a high-pitched bell or buzzer to signal when it's time to change classes. Kids are expected to quickly gather their belongings, to navigate chaotic hallways to race to their next class, and then sit still and attend for yet another long period of time. Kids who have difficulty with transitions, dealing with noisy crowds, or climbing stairs, and who are oversensitive to being jostled, have a very difficult time during classroom changes.

Most gym classes have highly structured and often competitive activities such as organized team sports in which a child must follow directions rapidly and compete with other children, many of whom may be very athletic. A child with motor planning and coordination problems will have a miserable time when it comes to gym and recess, fumbling with sneaker laces, stumbling when running, missing "easy shots," and facing ridicule from unkind classmates. Then they have to listen to the gym teacher who typically speaks loudly and blows a high-pitched whistle. Add to that the echo-filled gym and locker rooms, having to change and shower in front of other kids, the cold floor and water that's hard to adjust to the right temperature, and oh, those scratchy towels! Gym can be a nightmare for *any* self-conscious child, and significantly more so for a child with sensory issues.

----

* Studies conducted by Dr. David B. Granet, director of Pediatric Ophthalmology at the University of California at San Diego, show that children with convergence insufficiency are three times more likely to be diagnosed with ADHD than those without it.

Keeping It Together

Many of the same problems with learning and organization at school occur at home too. A child may have trouble carrying out household chores such as keeping his room clean. He may find it impossible to keep school supplies and other possessions organized. Studying and doing homework, even if he remembers to bring home his books and assignments, may take far longer than it should. The student who has been working hard to tolerate the stressors in school may be too mentally and physically fatigued to tackle homework. Even when teachers and parents try to be supportive, imploring him to work harder and get organized, nagging him to get his work done, he may find learning and keeping organized a seemingly insurmountable task.

MAKING SCHOOL DAYS EASIER

You can bet that given the opportunity, most school staff would create ideal learning environments that provide the right mix of physical comfort to maximize learning. There are plenty of innovative schools and teachers (especially those with backgrounds in special education) who work wonders to create warm, comfortable learning environments—from carpeted hallways to individual study carrels. And there are many schools that come up with creative solutions, reengineering their classrooms with quiet spaces, beanbag chairs, rugs, curtains, and improved lighting. If you're lucky, you can choose a school for your child that has a sensory-friendly environment. If not, you may find your school is willing to use items donated by parents, or paid for with funds raised by parent associations. Items such as rugs and vacuum cleaners with HEPA filters, floor and seat cushions, and lamps with incandescent or full-spectrum bulbs can make a huge difference in children's comfort in school.

Some of the problems in school can be resolved by accommodations listed in an IEP or 504 plan, which we'll look at in Chapter 15: Advocating for Your Child at School. You might be able to schedule your child's lunch for a time that is more reasonable for him and get the school to provide a less-chaotic eating area. If you speak to other parents of children at the school, you might find that even the children without sensory issues are uncomfortable with the rowdy bus experience and the headache-inducing school cafeteria. Other parents may be eager to work with you to change matters, and might be thrilled that someone has raised the issue.

You can help your child to help himself. Here are some other ideas for making school more conducive to learning for your child:

- Talk to your child's gym teacher about how the class and activities can be modified. Can students run a few laps to blow off excess energy before sitting down for directions for today's gym class? Can he be last in line for shooting hoops so there aren't twenty other kids waiting behind him? Also, consider having your child wear earplugs to dull the harsh sounds of echoes, whistles, and squeaky sneakers.

- Today's students carry far more than the maximum backpack load of 15 percent of body weight recommended by the American Occupational Therapy Association. Lugging around a huge backpack is very hard on the back, shoulders, and neck. If your child has too many books to carry, try to get a second set of books for home, or lobby the school to invest in more lockers. Teach your child to carry some books in the backpack and others by hand. Try a rolling backpack that comes with wheels and a collapsible handle. When packing a backpack, teach your child to put the heaviest items nearest his back, and arrange materials so nothing slides around. Tell him to always use both shoulder straps (look for ones with thick padding) and fasten the waist strap, if there is one, to better distribute the weight.

- If you can't get the school to change your child's lunch hour to a more reasonable one, provide your child with healthy protein snacks (such as string cheese or peanut butter crackers) to carry her through until lunchtime.

- See if your child's school is willing to provide an alternate lunchroom for students who need more quiet. At one school, students organized a lunch club. They ate in a quiet room as one student read aloud from a book they all agreed upon.

- If your child has problems carrying a lunch tray, make a game of it at home, having him help set the table using a tray to transport items from kitchen to table. Teach him to place heaviest items in the center and practice carrying it across a room. You may want to give him no-skid matting (a placemat or drawer liner) to place on the tray so items don't slide around. If it helps, have him bring some to school (use something inexpensive and disposable since he may leave it on the tray after eating). If necessary, speak with the lunchroom aide about having someone else carry the tray.

- If your child has difficulty tuning out extraneous noise and listening to the teacher, consider *where* he is sitting. Sitting up front may be counterproductive; he may end up turning around often to see who's making noise behind him. Have him sit away from vents, windows, and the door.
- Ask the teacher to provide copies of notes instead of just talking. Request written instructions for exams and assignments.
- If your child has a convergence problem, he must be allowed to take visual breaks: looking out the window or at other children, going to the water fountain, sharpening a pencil, or just "defocusing" (visually tuning out).
- Ask the school to consider installing Cozy Shades (available from the *Integrations* catalog), which fit over standard flourescent fixtures and which will soften harsh lighting in the classroom or cafeteria.

See Chapter 15: Advocating for Your Child at School for more ideas on helping your child at school.

LEARNING DIFFICULTIES

Your child may be quite bright—even gifted—but if his sensory problems get in the way, he may be disorganized, have poor study and work habits, and suffer from low academic achievement. Some 10 to 20 percent of school-age children have a degree of academic difficulty, writes Dr. Larry Silver, author of *The Misunderstood Child*.[2] Certainly not all children with SPD have learning disabilities, but about 70 percent of learning disabled kids have sensory processing issues.[3] A learning disability is diagnosed when there is a significant discrepancy between a child's intellectual ability and academic performance that can't be attributed to factors such as low intelligence, mental illness, emotional trauma, or a major sensory impairment such as hearing loss or blindness. A learning disability interferes with learning at school, at work, and in everyday life situations with friends, family, and in the community.

Fortunately, children with learning disabilities can get excellent help from resource rooms, tutors, integrated or special classrooms, and, if need be, schools specifically for the learning disabled. There are now colleges for students with ADHD and learning disabilities such as Landmark College in Vermont. Through customized teaching, modifications, and accommodations, millions of children with learning disabilities can—and do—excel.

The National Center for Learning Disabilities defines learning disabilities as a group of neurological disorders that affect the brain's ability to store, process, and communicate information. Children with learning disabilities may have problems with:

- reading, handwriting, and spelling;
- letter and numeral reversals;
- directionality, such as top, bottom, right, left;
- sequencing thoughts, events, and activities;
- generating and organizing ideas for composition;
- math concepts, numbers, and symbols;
- impaired fine and gross motor skills.

If you are concerned about a potential learning disability, speak with your child's school about a psychoeducational evaluation. At the same time, keep in mind that children with uncorrected vision problems, auditory processing disorders, sensory processing disorder, and ADHD exhibit many of the same symptoms as the child with a learning disability, and a child may have any combination of these impairments. So while you must get educational testing and help, you should also consult specialists to identify any other issues. You may end up getting several evaluations, such as from an OT, behavioral optometrist, audiologist, and neuropsychologist. While it may be stressful—and expensive—to see so many specialists, it's essential to get an accurate diagnosis in order to get your child the help he really needs.

Whether your child has a true learning disability, or simply uses too much of his inner resources dealing with sensory issues, he may find that the demands of school—and the increasing demands to be organized and responsible at home—are overwhelming him.

Learning and Organizational Ideas for School and Home

If your child needs extra help learning and staying organized, you should certainly seek professional assistance. Meanwhile, here are some ideas you can use right now. You may find that many of the ideas in this section are so effective that they should be incorporated as official strategies that *must* be used at school. You'll learn about individualized education plans (IEPs) and accommodations in Chapter 15: Advocating for Your Child at School.

Managing and organizing time. Some kids—and some adults too—have no sense of time. They may have trouble starting tasks, not only because they don't want to do the work, but often because they have no sense of time limitations or deadlines. Many children and grown-ups have no idea of how long things take. A child may think: *Oh, I just have to do four math problems; that should only take a few minutes.* But he doesn't consider that it takes time to pull out the work, sit down, sharpen a pencil, complete the calculations, double-check the work, and put his assignment in his math folder and his math book into his backpack. A common pitfall is to forget to factor in travel time. Sure, dropping a library book into the book slot only takes a few minutes, but it may take an extra thirty minutes to get to the library and back.

- Use timers appropriate to the task: an egg timer for brushing teeth, an alarm clock or stopwatch set for a specific time or duration, a visual timer such as the Time Timer with a movable colored disk that visually shows time as it elapses (available from *Integrations* and Southpaw Enterprises; see photo on page 397). If a child has thirty minutes to complete a task, let her know when she's used up half of her time, and when she has five minutes left.
- Break up large tasks into small parts. Send a child to her trashed bedroom to clean it, and she'll be overwhelmed and feel as if it will take forever (and it probably will). Try playing "beat the clock." For example, she has seven minutes to find all her dirty clothes and get them into the hamper. You might even encourage her to play some fast-paced music in the background to make it more fun. Then she has three minutes to put her books back on the bookshelf. Give her plenty of praise for doing so much in just ten minutes. Then keep going until the room is clean. The same holds true for schoolwork. Say your child has to write a three-page essay on Australian animals. Her first task is just to list all the animals she will write about. Then she must organize this information into an outline, developing and prioritizing categories such as marsupials and reptiles. Now she can begin the actual writing. Going step-by-step turns a big scary job into a lot of little, manageable tasks.
- Create a daily schedule, with your child's help, using a computer spreadsheet or simply writing it out. This will help him understand and prioritize what he needs to accomplish each day. Help him to identify free gaps in the day to motivate him to work harder to keep those gaps open for fun! This will also help *you* to identify any unreasonable expectations you have for your child. For example, given such a busy schedule, does your child really have time to keep his

room neat? Have you given him so many chores that they eat up his entire weekend? Have you overscheduled school days? Does he have enough time with friends? Enough time for physical activity? Enough downtime (which all kids need)? Have you truly given him enough time to do homework without rushing? Is he so tired by the time he starts his homework that it takes even longer to do it?

Remembering and completing assignments and chores. Kids are expected to have good work habits, but most often, they are not *taught* any of those habits. Many children forget to bring home assignments or forget due dates and other details about the assignments.

- Help your child select *one* place to file assignments, worksheets, and other handouts, such as a special folder aptly labeled *homework*. He could select an especially appealing one—with racing cars or superheroes on the cover—so it really sticks out from the rest of his school stuff. If school requires him to write assignments in separate notebooks for each class, he can use a master homework list to note which notebooks have homework in them, so at the end of the day he can bring home just those notebooks and leave the rest in his locker.
- Help your child pick out and learn to use a daily planner (such as a Day Runner, Filofax, or DayMinder). He can note due dates, block out hours/days for longer assignments, mark special occasions like birthdays, and so on. A younger child can select a cute wall calendar to help learn the concept of days, weeks, months, and years, and to note birthdays, parties, playdates, etc.
- If your child uses a computer every day, use an electronic calendar with built-in to-do lists set to run automatically when the computer starts up or she logs on. New PCs ship with Outlook built in, and new Macs ship with iCal built in. You can also buy electronic calendar software or download it from the Internet. You might also look into Stickies software, which works like computerized Post-it notes. All of these calendar programs can generate automated reminders for assignment due dates, appointments, birthdays, and more.
- Consider an assistive device such as the WatchMinder, a wristwatch with preprogrammed messages you can set for your child. You could, for example, have the watch vibrate every ten minutes and display the message "Pay attention" to help your child stay on task. It could remind your child to copy down his homework, do his chores,

and other important tasks. Check out the WatchMinder at www
.watchminder.com or call 800-961-0023.

- Use real (as opposed to online) sticky notes as easy no-nag reminders. You can use different colors for different categories; for
instance, yellow for school reminders, blue for chores, green for afterschool events, and pink for morale boosters (e.g., I love you!).

- Prepare for each day the night before. Have your child select and
set out what she will wear tomorrow. If you send in lunch, agree on
the menu and prepare it the night before (leave a note on your
child's backpack reminding her to grab it from the fridge). Be sure
she packs her backpack with her completed homework and all necessary school supplies each night. Don't expect her to organize her
stuff in the morning when she is still half-asleep.

- Create to-do lists that your child can check off as he completes
tasks. (This is a great strategy for busy parents too!) The checklist
could include diverse tasks that need to be accomplished or identify
steps in a particular activity. For example, if you often battle about
getting ready for school, create a chart together listing what he must
do before he's out the door. This may include self-care tasks (brush
teeth, wash face, etc.), particular clothing items to put on, taking his
backpack, and so on. For a younger child, try a picture to-do list.
Using photographs or simple line drawings, hand drawn or down-
loaded from a source like www.do2learn.com, make a list of the day's
agenda. For example: Breakfast (drawing of a cereal bowl), vitamins
(drawing of vitamin bottle), brush teeth (drawing of toothbrush),
get dressed (drawing of clothes), brush hair (drawing of hairbrush),
wash and dry hands (drawing of hands under faucet), put on backpack (drawing of backpack), go to preschool (drawing of bus). If
you are going to spend the day doing chores, or are going to visit relatives for the weekend, draw up a new to-do list to bring with activities such as "go to Grandma's house" and "eat dinner with cousins
at Grandma's house."

- You may need to develop a school assignment checklist as well. You
may need just one general checklist or customized checklists for individual subjects. For example, if your child always forgets to end a
sentence with a period, add a checkbox for this purpose. Checklists
can be used at home, at school, wherever your child needs extra
prompts to do her best work.

A sample checklist for a fourth grader:

AMY'S LIST

WRITTEN WORK: ENGLISH, HISTORY, ETC.	MATHEMATICS
❏ Wrote my name and date?	❏ Wrote my name and date?
❏ Included a title if an essay?	❏ Are numbers of equal size?
❏ Is the grammar correct?	❏ Are numbers lined up?
❏ Are letters the same size?	❏ Did I use the correct symbols?
❏ Do words sit nicely on lines?	(+, −, ×, ÷, etc.)
❏ Are words spelled correctly?	❏ Did I do all the problems?
❏ Did I skip any words?	❏ Did I double-check my math?
❏ Did I double-check my work?	❏ Is this really my best try?
❏ Is this really my best try?	

You can find more of these types of checklists under "bookmarks" and "desktop helpers" on www.reallygoodstuff.com.

Kids who forget or lose things

*   If your child tends to lose things, have replacements handy. If your child frequently misplaces pencils, for example, make sure he has a dozen of them.
*   If your child frequently forgets to bring things back and forth to school, or loses them on the way, get a second set that stays at home.
*   If your child loses things often, don't add to the guilt by giving her really expensive versions. If your child needs to take an umbrella to school, don't lend her the favorite wood-handled one you splurged on at a pricey department store. Make sure she never carries more cash than she requires.
*   If your child's teacher is cooperative, get assignments ahead of time— but still hold your child responsible for bringing home worksheets and assignments. This way you have a backup so you don't have to call the teacher or another student, but you'll be instilling responsibility in your child.
*   Set up a simple reward system with clear expectations and consequences. For example, if your child takes out the garbage every night for seven days, he could earn a new DVD.

EDDIE'S WEEKLY CHART

	MON	TUES	WED	THURS	FRI	SAT	SUN
Fed the dog after school	✓	✓	✓		✓		
Did homework without reminders		✓					
Stayed at dinner table	✓		✓		✓		
Did not hit brother	✓	✓	✓		✓	✓	✓
Packed backpack by himself	✓	✓					

You can give your child a star or smiley face for each day he accomplishes a task without a major ordeal. Eventually, he should get a reward only if he does his tasks every day. At first, though, you may need intermediate rewards, such as if he does it for three out of seven days.

Sample rewards:
- Rent a movie.
- Go biking with Mom or Dad.
- Get a toy for under ten dollars (or for a larger sum if he does it all month).
- Get a new CD.
- Get to pick what's for dinner.

General attention and learning boosters. As a sensory smart parent, you already know that your child is at his best when he is calm and alert. When he is too laid-back, he can't seem to tune in to anything but the TV. When he is too revved up, he's like a frenetic little grasshopper. A child who has trouble reaching and sustaining the focus he needs throughout the school day will need extra help from understanding teachers and perhaps school-based therapists. Your goal is that as he grows up, he will become sensory smart and self-aware enough to recognize his own neurological state and to self-regulate, that is, to give himself the sensory input he needs to keep on track.

You can teach your child techniques, such as deep breathing to calm down or splashing his face with water in the bathroom to wake up, without involving the teacher. Chapter 6: The Sensory Diet of Daily Activities lists lots of ways to help your child maintain that calm, alert state that promotes learning. Other techniques may require permission from the teacher as well as special equipment. We'll discuss these in Chapter 15: Advocating for Your Child at School. Here are some other factors to consider:

- The morning sets the tone for the entire day. Rushing, disorganization, and harsh words are terribly hard to overcome once your child gets to school (and you start your own day). Even if the morning is horrible, always try to sincerely tell your child that you love him (even if you're furious) and that you hope he has a good day (even if you doubt it), and that you look forward to seeing him later (even if you're delighted to have a break).

- Human beings do not function well when they are hungry or tired. Make sure your child has a protein-rich snack to boost brainpower before tackling schoolwork. If her energy tends to dip during the school day, make sure she has a snack in her backpack. If she's pooped when she comes home, let her rest a bit before starting her homework. Also make sure she is getting adequate sleep each night. See Chapter 12: Nutrition, Sleep, and Stress for more about sleep.

- Students who have trouble staying on task need extra help to filter out distractions and attend to what's important. First, structure how time is to be used. It's not a case of "well, before you go to bed you'll want to watch TV, eat dinner, do your homework, chat on the phone, and so on." There must be a clear-cut time that's set aside for work and only work. Don't expect your distractible child to focus if she's working on a cluttered kitchen table with her favorite TV show on in the next room. Set up an efficient work area, preferably a desk in a quiet room equipped with all needed work supplies such as pencils, erasers, a stapler, notepaper, and a dictionary. Don't expect your child to stay focused if she needs to get up and find things required to complete an assignment. Do not allow interruptions during homework time. Turn off the phone ringer if there's a phone in that room or nearby, disable instant online messaging and chat boards if your child uses the computer, and do not allow siblings— or yourself—to walk in and out of your child's work area.

- Some children need extra help to visually attend to important features in their schoolwork. Teach your child to use a highlighter to emphasize key words and concepts. If your child gets confused by instructions for math equations, have her highlight plus signs, minus signs, and so on. Teach your child to highlight a key word or phrase in homework instructions or on tests. For example, consider this instruction on a multiple-choice question: *Which of the following answers is not true?* If a child misses the word *not*, she will give the wrong answer even if she knows the material inside out. At home, she can read directions out loud, word for word, to make sure she gets the full communication. Highlighting key phrases and concepts when studying texts adds a kinesthetic dimension (touch and movement) to reading, and makes it easier to locate and review important information in books for exams and papers. The Web site www.reallygoodstuff.com has terrific tools for highlighting and masking (selectively covering up) printed materials to help your child in school.

- Have your child read written work out loud before submitting it. This can help him find errors he misses when reading silently.
- Provide your child with a name stamp if she frequently forgets to write her name on homework and tests.
- A child with visual issues can be easily overwhelmed by a lot of information on a page. She can use a ruler or bookmark to ensure she's reading just one line or text section at a time. She may also be overwhelmed by seeing a lot of work on one page, having trouble answering item number one because she's distracted by and worried about numbers ten and eleven. She can cover other problems on the page, so that all she sees is one or two at a time. You can also let her take a break every time she completes a set number of problems.
- Use graph paper for math homework to help align numbers in columns.
- Worksheets can be visually inviting, or, more often than not, difficult or unpleasant to read. Copies of old copies and the like can result in faint, blurry graphics and stray marks. Work with your child's teacher to make sure handouts are of good graphic quality.
- If it's okay with the school, consider letting your child do homework on a computer. He can then easily check grammar and spelling, and focus on expressing concepts rather than struggling with individual letter formation and page organization (which he will also need to improve).
- Make sure the lighting is good. Use a lamp at eye level rather than overhead lighting to reduce glare.
- Use a familiar melody, special phrase, or mnemonic to help remember information, sequences, and multiplication tables.

Melody

To learn days of the week, sing this to the tune of "My Darling Clementine" (Oh my darlin', oh my darlin', oh my darlin' Clementine . . .): There are seven days, there are seven days, there are seven days in a week—Sunday, Monday, Tuesday, Wednesday, Thursday, Friday, Saturday.

Phrase

For example, "I before E except after C."

Mnemonic

The planets from closest to farthest from the sun are Mercury, Venus, Earth, Mars, Jupiter, Saturn, Uranus, Neptune, Pluto. Teach your child: **M**y **V**ery **E**arnest **M**other **J**ust **S**erved **U**s **N**ine **P**ickles.

You can find more mnemonic devices on the Internet by searching for "mnemonic devices."

Taking tests and writing essays. Children take a huge number of tests but are rarely taught *how* to take them. You can help by teaching them some simple strategies:

- Cross out wrong answers on multiple-choice tests before circling the correct one.
- Circle, highlight, or underline key instructions or phrases on assignments and tests.
- On long tests, complete the questions she's confident about and return to the difficult ones later. This way, she won't use valuable time and get nervous grappling with question two when she could skip it and move on to answer ten other questions. Two warnings: She should be sure to circle skipped questions so she can easily find them later. Also, on an answer sheet with bubbles she must fill in, she should be sure to skip the corresponding bubble if she skips a question.
- Encourage your child not to feel self-conscious about asking a question if he is unclear about directions. Chances are, other children have the same question but are too shy to ask.
- Sketch out a basic outline before writing an essay, even on a test. This will help develop a roadmap of what needs to be accomplished, and help define the beginning, middle, and end.
- Have your child create his own flash cards using index cards to review vocabulary or simple ideas on the school bus, while waiting on the lunch line, or wherever.

Organizing Your Family with Its Sensory Kids

Children (and adults) with sensory issues often have organizational challenges when it comes to time (tasks to be done) and space (organizing possessions, homework, rooms), and if you have more than one disorganized person in the house, it can get pretty chaotic and frustrating for everyone. If you're the parent of a child or children with sensory issues and you're disorganized yourself, be patient and positive as you all learn how to get organized. Choose the most frustrating area of the house, put on some fun music while you're setting up a system, and spend at least a week working on maintaining it before tackling the next organizing project so as to build everyone's confidence about being able to stay organized.

Remember, if you all work together on figuring out how to create a mudroom type area for shoes, boots, coats, caps, and backpacks, you'll all be more likely to use the system than if one person does it and tries to explain why hats go on hooks and not the floor (and your child will point out that she can't reach the hook, which is why that cap keeps ending up next to her shoes!).

- Have designated places for *everything* so you're not distracted by having to make decisions about where something might go. You may need to label these areas with words or pictures. If you have something transitional (flyers from school and mail that has to be read, for instance), find a place for that, too, even if it means the dining room table is the one spot where everything that's on its way in or out of the house ends up. Designate a spot for outdoor gear, seasonal storage, and items that have to go out of the house (returned to the library or a friend, mailed, brought to Goodwill, etc.).
- Set aside a specific time, such as Sunday afternoon, to put away any items that ended up where they don't belong, with everyone pitching in and noticing what items never seem to gravitate back to their spot. Talk about why the action figures always end up sitting in the bathtub or why clothing is draped in several places. Only by recognizing why the owner didn't put the item where it belongs can you discover the flaws in your organizational systems.
- Design your systems around how everyone actually operates. If your son's action figures end up in the bath every other day, maybe they should be stored in the bathroom instead of his room down the hall. If your daughter's shoes come off in her room when she

sits down at her homework desk, maybe that's where she should keep whatever pair she's wearing most often.

- Put like items together and store them with items you're likely to use at the same time, and keep extras of items you use often so that you have them nearby whenever you need them. Keep a toiletries bag fully packed so that when you go on vacation, you don't have to buy miscellaneous items and pack them (keep a master packing list on your computer and print it out to use as a checklist when you go on trips). In the summertime, keep a bottle of mosquito repellent on the porch, in the car, and in the backyard so you can spray your child as soon as the bugs begin biting rather than running back and forth, searching for the lone bottle.

- When cleaning up, focus on one type of item at a time. A child can focus on putting all his vehicles away in the vehicle bin first, then on gathering all his books and returning them to his bookshelf. In a kitchen, have everyone work as a team putting the food away after a meal before tackling the dirty dishes. Attending to one type of item at a time helps you to stay focused on the larger task and feel a sense of accomplishment. If you find items that belong elsewhere, pile them up before leaving the room or you'll tire yourself out running back and forth.

- Demonstrate to your children how you decide what to clean up first—for example, getting the toys off of the floor so that you can easily walk through the room as you begin actually putting items away. Explain why you empty the dishwasher or dish drainer of clean dishes before washing a new load. In doing so, you're actually teaching your child the basic skills of organizing any task from packing his backpack before heading home from school to writing a college application essay.

- If you or your child are always running late, get a stopwatch and actually time how much time particular tasks require, from doing a "quick load of laundry" to getting dressed in the morning. Many people perpetually run late because they honestly don't know how long everyday tasks take. You don't have to schedule yourself by fifteen-minute increments necessarily, but knowing that it takes thirty-five minutes to dry that load of laundry and fifteen to fold it and put it away will prevent you from trying to squeeze it in before you have to drop your child off for her violin lesson. Also, knowing that your child can only tolerate having her hair washed, dried, and brushed if she has a good hour to do so and isn't rushed will allow you to plan for the time needed and stop feeling frustrated by how long it takes.

- Work from a to-do list you consult religiously. If you keep it on a computer, you can easily cut and paste items on your list to rearrange your priorities. Consider using strikethrough mode when crossing items off until your list looks illegible—it can be motivating to see your progress instead of having your completed tasks simply deleted from your list. If you write down next to each task how long it will take to complete, then, when you have a spare fifteen minutes, you can scan your list to see what you can complete in that period of time. Children often have a much easier time staying focused and getting their chores, homework, and morning routine done if they have a to-do list. Even preverbal children often work well from a photo or picture to-do list. (You can download images from www.do2learn.com to make one.)
- Don't feel you have to master a particular technology to stay organized. If a low-tech system works best for you, stick with that, and don't allow anyone in the family to make any dates unless they're immediately written on a big wall calendar kept in the kitchen or hallway. If using computer software to organize yourself works better for you—whether it's spreadsheets, Quicken, online bill paying, or iCal—then use that.
- Organize your time according to your priorities. Schedule time for yourself, for exercise, or for just playing with your children. Learn to say "No," or at least, "I think I have something going that day. Let me check my calendar and get back to you" when pressured to commit to an activity you don't feel you have time for.
- Organize your space to allow for the least amount of decision making and the greatest convenience for you. For example, you might create one file folder for your child's IEP and report cards and another for schoolwork rather than putting everything in one overstuffed file labeled "School."
- Be flexible about how others in the household operate. Your partner may need a toothbrush and dental floss out on the sink in order to remember to use it, while you prefer a clutterless countertop. If a pile of visual clutter bothers you, close the door or drape a curtain over it (for example, staple a curtain over the front of a bookshelf full of mismatched items).

General organization tips for home and school. Organization expert Julie Morgenstern and her teenage daughter, Jessi Morgenstern-Colón, offer great ideas for getting organized in *Organizing from the Inside Out for Teens.* They note that reward systems can be used at first to encourage kids to get and stay organized, but ultimately the system must work for them and they have to want to stay organized for their own reasons—not wanting to waste valuable time searching for possessions, wanting to feel the serenity that comes from seeing their possessions in order, wanting to feel in control of time, etc. They suggest you accentuate the positive aspects of getting organized rather than the negative consequences of being disorganized. They recommend that you:

- Use the "kindergarten model" of organizing space, grouping all the items pertaining to one activity in the spot where that activity takes place. So, for example, everything your daughter might use for grooming in the morning should be in the same place near a mirror and sink rather than having her hairbrush in her bedroom, makeup in her backpack, toothbrush by the sink, etc.
- Help your child organize his locker and backpack by zones as well. For instance, keep a basket for personal items on one shelf in the locker to separate them from school items.
- Avoid setting up overly complex systems that take too much energy and effort. Putting items back where they belong should be a no-brainer, or your child will probably avoid it.

Figuring out the right strategies and systems to help your child learn and stay organized does take a lot of work in the beginning. Fortunately, the payoffs can be huge because once you have them in place, they are self-propagating and will help your child focus on and tackle the work she needs to accomplish rather than just worrying about how on earth she's going to get herself together enough to even start the process.

HELP FOR HORRIBLE HANDWRITING

Handwriting, also called graphomotor skill, is a very challenging and complex task. It requires good muscle tone, strength, and endurance in the hands and upper body; proprioceptive skill to hold the writing instrument correctly and control tiny movements of the fingers; visual-perceptual skills to remember and reproduce letters; the ability to refocus when copying; and the ability to concentrate

(continued)

and focus for increasingly long durations—all of which must be bolstered by attention, motivation, and persistence. Many children with sensory problems have trouble with handwriting.

Sloppy writing (graphomotor delay) is one of the most common reasons why students are referred to an OT in school. Following are some of the things OTs do with kids who have handwriting problems. Talk to your child's OT about whether these activities are appropriate for your son or daughter and ask your OT for other specific suggestions.

- Make sure your child is seated properly and that lighting is effective for the task.
- To improve writing tool grasp, try a molded pencil grip such as The Pencil Grip, Grotto Grip, Stetro, or Start Right (see photo on page 399).
- Improve wrist position by writing on an inclined or vertical surface: on a slantboard, easel, chalkboard, or on paper tacked to the wall.
- Strengthen hands with clay and hand exercisers from sporting goods stores.
- Play pickup games with tweezers and tongs.
- Look into multisensory handwriting programs such as Handwriting Without Tears by occupational therapist Jan Olsen.
- Have your child write in different ways: use a vibrating pen or a squirt gun, write in the air using big arm movements or on the wall using a flashlight, squeeze white glue onto paper and sprinkle with glitter or birdseed, and so on. Write with a finger in pudding, shaving cream, sand, or on a carpet square.
- Write letters on your child's back and have her write them on your back; try to guess what they are.
- Form letters and words out of clay "snakes" and Wikki Stix (wax-covered yarn, available in stores and therapy catalogs).
- Have your child work on precision by doing mazes and dot-to-dots, and tracing over line drawings as a break from working on letters and numbers (see www.activitypad.com for free, downloadable activities).

DIFFERENCES IN LEARNING STYLES: MAKING THE MOST OF YOUR CHILD'S GIFTS

If your child is having learning, focus, and organizational problems, it's easy to fall into the trap of thinking: *Oh, he's just not very smart. Or He's lazy. Or Because he has sensory issues, he can't be expected to keep up.* Yes, it seems like every other child is doing fine in school and comes home smiling with a swell fingerpainting or an A on his latest essay. Yes, some kids thrive in any given learning environment. Other kids struggle but make it through okay. And some need special classrooms or schools and customized teaching strategies.

We don't all learn the same way, although we are generally all taught the same way. Remember that kids learn through their senses, gathering, synthesizing, and responding to information about the world through their eyes, ears, noses, mouths, and limbs. That's why a multisensory approach that taps into more than one or two senses works best. This applies to *all* children, and especially to a child with sensory issues who has a strongly preferred mode of learning. For example, a child with auditory issues will have trouble learning by just listening to a lecture. A child with vision issues will have a hard time learning from textbooks. Others tune out certain sensory channels to maximize just one or two. Temple Grandin, for whom "hearing is like having a sound amplifier set on maximum loudness," writes that she is forced to choose between turning her ears on and getting deluged with sound or shutting her ears off.[4] Rather than pulling information from the world through language, she is a visual thinker. She explains that "thinking in language and words is alien to me. I think totally in pictures" and that "for me there is no language-based information in my memory. To access spoken information, I replay a video. . . ."

Now that more educators are recognizing the value of multisensory learning, many early math classes no longer consist of endless addition and subtraction worksheets and memorization of times tables. Now kids use "manipulatives," small objects that they can feel and see and use to make learning come alive. Kids understand geography when they watch films about people living in different places, and hear foreign languages. Kids will never forget the metamorphosis from chrysalis to butterfly if they hold a chrysalis in their hands and watch the process occur in their own classroom. A child with tactile defensiveness who may despise touching clay in art class may gain a profound, lifelong appreciation of sculpture by visiting a museum. We all learn best through memorable personal experience.

Once people believed there was just one kind of intelligence: book smarts. Now it's widely recognized that there are several types of intelligence. Most people have one or two dominant types, and it's often a matter of finding materials and strategies that best speak to that intelligence. Howard Gardner, author of *Frames of Mind: The Theory of Multiple Intelligences,* explores six basic categories of intelligence.

Linguistic Intelligence

Such children have a great capacity for words, both written and spoken. They love telling and writing stories, jokes, and riddles, reading books, playing word games, and so on.

Harnessing the strength. To help her learn math concepts, she may do best with word problems or a story in which she must count, multiply, and divide items. She may retain historical facts better if she reads historical novels. She may become more interested in dry facts if they are set in a context. For example, she'll be more motivated to study anatomy and physiology by learning about how body parts work together rather than just memorizing the names of bones, muscles, and other structures. She may recall rules of behavior when hearing anecdotal stories about how children ought to act in specific situations.

Adult outlook. Writers, editors, avid readers, and teachers all have high linguistic intelligence.

Musical Intelligence

Such children have a great capacity for pitch, tone, melody, and rhythm. They love to listen to music, play instruments, sing, dance, and create their own songs.

Harnessing the strength. Some children can sing but have difficulty speaking, as is often the case with children who stutter or have speech delays. An ear for rhythm and tone can be leveraged to learn the musicality of speech. To learn math, he can count beats in his early years, and analyze musical compositions later on. He can use songs to memorize facts and sequence activities.

Adult outlook. Musicians, composers, and serious music lovers all have high musical intelligence.

Logical-Mathematical Intelligence

Such children have a great capacity to reason logically, comparing and contrasting objects and ideas to establish hierarchies and order. They may enjoy working with numbers, asking questions, and doing activities that require precision and measurement such as cooking from recipes and construction projects.

Harnessing the strength. It takes a bit of creativity to inspire a logical math mind to explore other subjects. To appreciate art, she may like learning about techniques and color theory. Music theory may inspire her to play an instrument. Outlining ideas in numerical form can help her organize her writing, and research done by computer may help expand her interest to a wider range of subjects. Card games, two-person computer games, and science projects may help her interact socially.

Adult outlook. Scientists, mathematicians, computer programmers, and many musicians all show strong logical-mathematical intelligence.

Spatial Intelligence

Such children have well-developed visual perceptual skills and look for patterns and relationships between objects and within systems. They enjoy drawing and painting, looking at pictures and photos, doing puzzles, building things, and so on.

Harnessing the strength. A child may grasp new concepts more readily if given a picture or diagram rather than just a verbal explanation. He may become more motivated to learn in science class if he is allowed to draw pictures of his observations to illustrate his essays. Geometry and pattern recognition may increase his interest in math concepts. Graphic outlines drawn by hand or with software such as Inspiration can help organize his written work.

Adult outlook. Artists, architects, carpenters, surgeons, and again, computer programmers, all have particularly strong spatial intelligence.

Bodily-Kinesthetic Intelligence

Such children use their bodies to learn through touch and movement. They enjoy all types of physical activity, sports, dancing, acting, manipulating objects with their hands, and using body language to help them communicate with others.

Harnessing the strength. It's important for such children to take a hands-on, learn-by-doing approach. To learn to write the alphabet, for example, it may help to make letters out of clay, write in shaving cream, or use a finger to trace over textured letters. She may learn math concepts best by measuring how far she can jump, and so on. She may become more interested in science by conducting actual experiments than through gathering factual information from books or lectures.

Adult outlook. Dancers, athletes, actors, and sculptors all have particularly strong bodily-kinesthetic intelligence. Children with hyperactivity often have strength in this area, but may require help to channel their need to move, touch, and do in positive ways.

THE MOVEMENT-LEARNING CONNECTION

Movement is essential to all learning from the womb onward. The infant learns as she moves her eyes, explores her feet and hands by moving them and mouthing them, and learns increasingly more as she rolls over, sits up, crawls, walks, and runs. The tie between movement and learning continues throughout life. Studies show that movement fires up the brain, strengthening neural linkages for learning. In *Smart Moves: Why Learning Is Not All in Your Head,* Carla Hannaford cites plenty of research, including a Canadian study in which children who spent an extra hour a day in gym class had significantly higher test scores than other children. Needless to say, a child with vestibular overreactivity, low tone, poor motor planning, or low endurance may avoid the very movement activities that would help jazz up her body for learning.

Personal Intelligence

A child with *inter*personal intelligence tends to have lots of friends, enjoy group games and discussions, and take on a leadership role.

The child with *intra*personal intelligence is in touch with and uses her feelings, emotions, and reactions to understand herself and others. Rather than being a big talker, she may be a quiet listener and observer, and prefer to work and learn alone. A child may have greater interpersonal or intrapersonal intelligence or both types.

Harnessing the strength. Such children may benefit from study groups, group projects, and opportunities to talk and listen to people who are interested in a wide variety of subjects. Less appealing topics will come alive for this child when related to human experience. For example, a child may be more motivated to work on math skills if asked to help teach math to another less skilled child or if she needs to manage a budget for her own party. Math may be more interesting if the child is shown how it can help people function in real-life situations. She may take better notes if she shares them with a classmate, and may improve her writing skills by composing letters and sharing stories with other people.

Adult outlook. Teachers, therapists, most doctors, and many politicians generally have excellent personal intelligence.

One of the hallmarks of autism is a profound difficulty in personal intelligence, resulting in poor social skills, such as limited ability to read others' emotions and pick up on cues embedded in social language. As an example of how one intelligence can be used to compensate for another, a person with impaired people skills can memorize the spatial orientation of facial features that compose a smiling or sad face or how people use certain gestures to communicate specific things, and "download" these images to better read and interact with others.

How It Works in Real Life

Consider seven-year-old Krista, who absolutely, positively has given up on ever being able to draw a good square. They always come out like lumpy ovals. Part of the problem is that she is constantly moving around and touching things. She'd rather chat about her new cat and how her best friend Maggie came to school wearing one pink and one purple sock. Tapping in to her bodily-kinesthetic intelligence, Krista helps insert pushpins into four marked points on a piece of Styrofoam. As she strings yarn from pushpin to pushpin, she feels the four straight lines and four corners, and how she must change direction four times. Voila: a square. With repetition, her movements create a mental map.

She then draws a 2-D representation of the four pushpins and yarn. A square. Tapping in to her personal intelligence, she teaches her pal Maggie how to make a square with pushpins and yarn. Maggie shows her how to draw a hopscotch board using squares, and they play for hours.

Recommended Reading

Armstrong, Thomas. *ADD/ADHD Alternatives in the Classroom.* Alexandria, VA: Association for Supervision and Curriculum Development, 1999.

Ayres, Jean A. *Sensory Integration and Learning Disorders.* Los Angeles: Western Psychological Services, 1972.

Davis, Ronald. *The Gift of Learning: Proven New Methods for Correcting ADD, Math & Handwriting Problems.* New York: Perigee, 2003.

Eide, Brock, and Fernette Eide. *The Mislabeled Child: How Understanding Your Child's Unique Learning Style Can Open the Door to Success.* New York: Hyperion, 2006. This book explains the inaccurate diagnoses sometimes given to students with learning problems, and provides specific suggestions to help children learn at school and home.

Levine, Mel. *A Mind at a Time.* New York: Simon & Schuster, 2002. Levine explores how all minds do not learn alike, individual learning patterns, and how to maximize learning potential.

Levine, Mel. *The Myth of Laziness.* New York: Simon & Schuster, 2003. Levine explains the nuances of various learning disabilities.

Morgenstern, Julie, and Jessi Morgenstern-Colón. *Organizing from the Inside Out for Teens: The Foolproof System for Organizing Your Room, Your Time, and Your Life.* New York: Owl Books, 2002. Detailed advice for the organizationally challenged teenager who needs help managing time, possessions, social life, and schoolwork.

Rief, Sandra F. *The ADHD Book of Lists: A Practical Guide for Helping Children and Teens with Attention Deficit Disorder.* San Francisco: Jossey-Bass, 2003. Creative ideas for kids having difficulty with focus, organization, transitions, and auditory processing.

Rossner, Jerome. *Helping Children Overcome Learning Difficulties,* third edition. New York: Walker and Company, 1993.

"Vision and Learning." Children's Vision Information Network, sponsored by the Kansas Vision Development Center, Web site: www.childrensvision.com/learning.htm.

www.yourhomework.com. This site helps teachers, parents, and students keep track of assignments and test dates.

CHAPTER 12

Nutrition, Sleep, and Stress

By now, you've got enough sensory smarts to know you have to cut your child some slack on a few things. For instance, demanding that your child instantly comply with your requests without any time for transition is a big, unnecessary scoop plopped onto an already-weakened paper plate loaded with life stress. Family gatherings and special events are not something you want to, or should, avoid just because your child doesn't handle them well, but you can take steps to make such situations less taxing for your child. Sometimes the stressors in life are ones you simply can't avoid: parents are called away to military duty, grandparents suddenly move into your home and upset the established household dynamic, friends move away, and beloved pets die. Your child may find it very difficult to handle all these changes on top of the everyday challenge of living with SI dysfunction. Fortunately, some of the biggest stress monsters are ones you *can* do something about, and yet they are so easily overlooked: inadequate nutrition and lack of sleep.

EATING RIGHT

Essential nutrients are those the body absolutely requires for functioning, and missing just *one* can significantly affect your child's well-being. Part of a healthy diet, these nutrients provide necessary fuel for physical development, brain function, behavior, attention, mood, sensory and motor skills, the immune system, and more.

Proteins support the brain and muscles, enhancing attention and alertness, muscle tone, building and repairing body tissues, producing and balancing neurotransmitters/hormones, and much more. Good sources of protein include lean meat, poultry, seafood, eggs, nuts, beans and legumes, milk and milk products such as cheese and yogurt (unless your child is lactose or casein intolerant, in which case she should not consume milk products; see Chapter 13: Complementary Therapies and Approaches for more on food intolerances).

Carbohydrates provide fast energy to the brain and body tissues, and should be combined with proteins to maintain a steady energy rate. Good sources of healthy "carbs" include fruit, vegetables, and whole grains. Other sources, which are not as nutritious, include refined flour products (such as white bread and white pasta), candy, and junk food. These highly processed "simple carb" foods deluge the body with energy that is quickly burned off—and can burn out a child too.

Vitamins regulate metabolism, the chemical process of breaking down and using nutrients. The body can't produce most vitamins, so they must be obtained through food or supplements. Some vitamins, such as B and C, are water soluble and are not stored by the body so they need to be consumed regularly. When foods are cooked, many water-soluble vitamins may dissolve into the water or be damaged by heat.

Minerals are naturally occurring inorganic elements the body needs to regulate its metabolism. Calcium is the most abundant mineral in the body. A few other essential minerals are iron, sodium, potassium, magnesium, copper, and zinc, all of which must be in balance.

Water, accounting for about 60 percent of the body, is the single most important nutrient. Water supports all biochemical reactions in the body: breaking down nutrients, transporting chemicals in and out of cells and throughout the body, regulating temperature, eliminating toxins and waste material, and more. Signs of dehydration include poor memory, impaired attention, hunger, and "spaciness."

Lipids (fats) support the nervous system, coat nerves, cushion internal organs, provide body insulation, help regulate body temperature, build cell membranes and normal growth, maintain healthy skin, and more. While fats are essential, overall fat intake should be limited to reduce the risk of certain types of cancer, heart disease, and excessive weight gain. Good sources of fat include deep water fish such as wild salmon, mackerel, and halibut, as well as olive oil. And you guessed it: the cookies, cupcakes, fries, and chips your child loves contain the worst types of fat.

Essential Fatty Acids

There are certain fats that are a crucial part of a healthy diet, affecting both the nervous system and the skin. These are called essential fatty acids: omega-3 and omega-6. EFAs can be naturally found in foods including deep water fish such as wild salmon, tuna, mackerel, and halibut (particularly near the skin of the fish, where, unfortunately, environmental toxins accumulate as well), flaxseed and flaxseed oil, buffalo meat, venison, dark green leafy vegetables such as spinach and kale, soybeans and tofu, nuts such as walnuts and almonds, seeds such as pumpkin and sunflower, canola oil, wheat germ, and omega-3 fortified eggs and breads.

Several studies show that children with dyspraxia, dyslexia, autism, and ADHD are often deficient in essential fatty acids (EFAs), and that symptoms improve with EFA supplementation.[1] Given that EFAs are needed to help the nervous system run smoothly, and that many children with SI dysfunction don't get enough EFAs in their diet, you might want to consider making sure that they do. Moreover, when a child eats transfats—also known as hydrogenated and partially hydrogenated oils—it makes it very difficult for his body to metabolize EFAs. Thus, even if he eats plenty of fish, if he's consuming a lot of crackers, cookies, and margarine, he's probably not benefiting from those wonderful EFAs.

Many parents report that sensory issues improve when their kids consume more EFAs, in either food or supplement form. Nutritionist Jacqueline Stordy's book, *The LCP Solution,* is a wonderful primer on how EFAs work and the various EFA supplements available. Given all the warnings about toxins in albacore (white) tuna and other deep water fish, EFA supplements may well be worth looking into.

Nutrition 101

A healthy diet for someone without food allergies or intolerances consists of whole grains (not refined white flour), vegetables and fruit in their natural form (that is, with fiber and not processed), and protein (such as meat, cheese, milk, nuts, etc.). How can you help your child make healthier food choices?

- Instead of white bread, rice, and pasta, use foods like wheat bread, basmati or brown rice, and whole wheat pasta. Experiment with brands to find products your child likes.

- Instead of fruit roll-ups, serve real fruit. Instead of jelly, serve all-fruit spread. Instead of juice, serve water, or at the very least, watered-down juice. The American Academy of Pediatrics recommends that children ages one to six drink no more than four to six ounces of fruit juice a day, and that children ages seven to eighteen drink no more than eight to twelve ounces a day. The AAP also says that excessive consumption of juice is associated with malnutrition, diarrhea, stomach problems, and tooth decay.

- It's often a challenge to get kids to eat vegetables, but make them fun or different, or disguise them, and you might have some luck. Some kids enjoy munching on frozen vegetables (which provides lots of sensory information, between the cold and the crunch). You can also puree vegetables and slip them into pancakes, pizza, or spaghetti sauce.

- Animal fats contribute to heart disease, obesity, diabetes, and cancer. If you serve meats, make sure they are lean and do not make them the focal point of the meal. Instead of high-fat hot dogs, serve tofu dogs or turkey sausage. Instead of piling high-fat bologna and salami on sandwiches, use a few slices of lower-fat turkey or chicken. Serve beans and rice or use tofu as a protein source instead of meat.

- Avoid fatty dairy products. The American Academy of Pediatrics states that children older than age two do not need the extra fat in whole milk, so feel free to use skim or 1 percent milk. By the time your child is five, only 30 percent of her total calories should come from fats. Also, too much milk can dampen your child's appetite as well as cause anemia. Use low-fat dairy products or use less of the full-fat products. Sauté in olive oil or broth instead of butter. Grate cheese over food rather than using chunky slices.

- Avoid too much sugar. Instead of soda pop (which many children with sensory issues love because of the bubbles), serve flavored or unflavored seltzer without sugar, or just water mixed with a squeeze of lemon, lime, or orange, or with a very small amount of juice. Don't buy sugary cereals for your child. Use molasses, brown sugar, or honey (if your child is over age two) instead of refined white sugar. Avoid high fructose corn syrup.

- Watch portion sizes, which have bloated in recent years. A generation or two ago, a standard size soda pop bottle from a vending machine was ten ounces; now it is typically twice the size and contains more sugar than two candy bars. Occasional treats are fine, but movie theater-size chocolate bars or humongous muffins or cookies at the mall provide far more fat, sugar, and empty calories than even the most active teenagers need.

- Avoid fried foods. Grilling, using high quality produce and meats, and flavoring with herbs and spices will add taste without adding fat. Instead of buying French fries, bake your own in an oven, using considerably less fat. Instead of frying chicken in its fatty skin, marinate and grill skinless chicken breasts. Instead of serving deep-fried chicken nuggets, buy the baked versions.

Children as well as adults need a good breakfast containing protein to give them stamina, focus, and energy for the day after many hours of not eating. They also need to eat protein-rich snacks regularly throughout the day to maintain mental focus and energy. When a child doesn't eat for hours on end, his blood sugar drops very low. Going for long stretches between meals and then wolfing down sugar or refined carbohydrates, such as sugary breakfast cereals, white bread, and white potatoes, which quickly convert to sugar in the body, is not a good idea. The effect is like slamming on the gas and then slamming on the brakes when driving a car—you put tremendous stress on your engine.

Diets that are high in simple carbohydrates and low in protein may contribute to chronic low blood sugar, a condition called hypoglycemia. In a hypoglycemic state, the pancreas oversecretes insulin, making the level of glucose (sugar) in the blood drop too low, depriving the brain of the fuel it needs. Symptoms of hypoglycemia include confusion, decreased memory and learning, dizziness, mood swings, being inattentive and spacey, hyperactivity, and craving more sugary food (which only feeds the cycle).

Extremely low appetite may be due to many factors, including depression and anxiety, ear infection, allergies, or anemia. Be sure to consult your pediatrician and possibly a nutritionist if you notice a decrease in your child's appetite.

The Nutritionist's Role

If you read the headlines about nutrition, you can become very confused about the pros and cons of all sorts of foods and special diets. That's because the media seizes on individual studies whose results grab our attention, but they don't necessarily give you an overview of how that study fits into what is known about nutrition.

Nutritionists keep up on the latest research and may know of supplements and dietary intervention that can be especially helpful for your child. When doing your own research, it's vitally important to note that there are nuances to analyzing information. For instance, there are subtle differences between natural enzymes and ones you get in supplement form. Not all EFAs are alike: the amount of omega-3 fatty acid consumed needs to be in proportion to the omega-6 fatty acid. If you get too much of one micromineral or vitamin, you create an imbalance. Some forms of vitamins are easier to metabolize than others, and the absorption of vitamins is often affected by what else you consume with them; for instance, magnesium enhances calcium absorption. And while you may read glowing testimonials from parents who claim they "cured" their child's hyperactivity or tactile sensitivity using nutritional interventions, keep in mind that no two children are alike, so what works wonders for one child might not work at all for yours. Worse, treating a nutritional problem that your child doesn't actually have may actually cause other problems by creating imbalances.

Our advice is to be open to enhancing your child's treatment with better nutrition and, possibly, supplementation—but always, always, work with a professional nutritionist, preferably one who is familiar with, and has worked with, children with sensory issues. Ask your pediatrician, OT, or other therapist if he or she can recommend an appropriate nutritionist. If not, you'll need to do some footwork yourself. Try entering the word *nutritionist* and the name of your city in an Internet search engine or look in the yellow pages under nutrition, alternative medicine, and wellness centers.

Of course, getting a supplement into a child who has sensory issues isn't always easy. Few children happily swallow big capsules of fish oil or enjoy unfamiliar powders and strong-tasting oils sprinkled onto food. Vitamin manufacturers have caught on to this and you can now get children's multivitamins in many forms, from gumballs to gummy bears, and fish oil that looks and tastes like orange pudding (Coromega brand), has a strawberry flavor (Nordic Natural), or looks like a Starburst candy (GNC). Dr. David Perlmutter (www.perlhealth.com) offers an excellent chocolate-flavored "brain formula" vitamin powder containing essential fatty acids that you blend with milk.

You can also check into VitaMist Spray Vitamins online at www.myvitamist.com, or call 800-582-5273 for vitamins that you spray on the inside of your child's cheeks. Also see pages 155–56 in Chapter 7 for advice on how to get your child to swallow vitamin capsules or tablets.

SWEET DREAMS

Sleep is a huge topic, and there are many theories and excellent books on fostering healthy sleep in children. One thing is clear: children need adequate amounts of consistent, *high-quality* sleep to properly rest and develop their minds and bodies. Well-rested children are more attentive, have a more positive mood, and learn more quickly. Most experts agree that children between ages three and five need ten–twelve hours of sleep while kids between ages seven and twelve need nine–ten hours. Even if a child gets an adequate quantity of sleep overall, if he's disturbed by sleep apnea or frequent waking, he won't get enough deep, restful REM (rapid eye movement) sleep. Keep in mind, too, that certain medications, such as antihistamines, stimulants, and mood stabilizers, may interfere with quality of sleep. Consult your pediatrician if your child is taking medicine and his sleeping habits have changed.

Persistent sleep disturbances result in higher levels of stress hormones, irregular biorhythms, decreased attention and cognitive skills, and heightened arousal level (as the body compensates to combat sleepiness). The chronically tired child (and the overtired adults who live with him) is stressed out, irritable, spacey, and prone to illness. What's more, once a child is in a negative sleep-wake cycle, he may be unable to lower his level of alertness, making it difficult to fall asleep and stay asleep. A child who has had an overstimulating day might end up lying awake in bed, tossing and turning for hours, unable to wind down despite being in a dark, quiet room.

Children with sensory issues often lack adequate sleep and have some pretty good reasons why. A child may have trouble filtering out sounds inside and outside the house, whether it's traffic or crickets outside or even the sound of her sister breathing in the next bed. She may find it difficult to cope with the sensation of sleepwear, sheets, pillows, blankets and the mattress itself—a real-life princess and the pea. She may be unable to lower her arousal level enough to reach the state of calm needed to drift off to sleep, or she may have difficulty waking from daytime naps, causing her to oversleep and then be unable to fall asleep again until very late at night. Emotional factors such as anxiety can also interfere with getting a good night's sleep.

Kids with special needs, especially autism, can have significant difficulty with sleep because they are more likely to have insomnia, teeth grinding, sleep apnea and heavy breathing, and melatonin insufficiency. Melatonin, a naturally occurring hormone, helps your body to regulate sleep-wake cycles. Certain prescription medications commonly taken by kids with special needs interfere with melatonin levels, causing the side effect of poor sleep.

If your child isn't sleeping well, consult your pediatrician, OT, or a sleep specialist to address biological issues like sleep apnea and tooth grinding and to look again at the medications your child takes. Usually some fairly simple changes will make a big difference.

Strategies for Improving Sleep

- Make sure your child goes to sleep and wakes up at the same time each day. It's tempting to let kids stay up late and sleep late on weekends, but this confuses the body's natural internal clock and can cause insomnia and difficulty falling asleep.

- Avoid caffeine, found in colas, chocolate, and even some light-colored soda pops (such as Mountain Dew), as well as in less obvious sources such as some desserts and candies, and nonprescription drugs such as Midol Extra Strength and Excedrin Migraine. Even a small dose of caffeine can result in headaches, irritability, tremors, and nervousness.

- Try not to let your child drink or eat heavily before bed. Drinking fluids just before retiring can cause a child to wake up to urinate just as she should be falling into the deepest, most restorative sleep cycle.

- If possible, don't let your child do homework while lying in bed. Associating the bed with "thinking work" can interfere with sleep.

- Don't allow your child to sleep with the television on because it can interfere with the quality of sleep.

- Encourage your child to exercise regularly, which can help regulate the sleep cycle. Exercise may need to be done earlier in the day, since late-night activity can make it hard to wind down and fall asleep.

- If your child is not sleepy by bedtime, help induce drowsiness by having her listen to calming music, sit in a dark or dim room, or take a bath. Scented lotion can encourage sleep, as can listening to a white noise machine, a radio set to static, an aquarium, a bubbling fountain, or a fan (you may need to make sure it doesn't blow directly on your child).

- Avoid late naps. If your toddler is at that stage where he's outgrowing the need for naps, try to limit nap length. If he's starting to doze off and it's late in the afternoon, try to keep him awake until an early bedtime.

- Make sure his sleeping environment has low light and is quiet and comfortable for him. A small nightlight might comfort one child, while light creeping in through the curtains might prevent another from falling asleep.

- A warm bath before bed is an old standby for helping a child to sleep. A bath can be very relaxing, and essential oils added to the bath will create an aromatherapy experience that he may find further calming and relaxing. Epsom salt baths, which add magnesium to the body by soaking into the skin's pores, can be very effective for relaxing a child (or yourself). Start small, with a half cup of Epsom salts. If your child becomes more agitated, try again the next night with half that amount. Only try this if you are certain that your child will not drink the bath water because Epsom salts, ingested, cause loose bowels (in fact, never let your child drink bath water from a porcelain tub because of the risk of lead poisoning).

- Vibration can help some kids sleep better. Try a vibrating pillow, vibrating mattress (Sealy's Tender Vibes), Vibramat (a vibrating mat you can place beneath the mattress or use elsewhere), or vibrating toy (*Integrations* has an excellent selection). Place it in your child's bed or attach to crib bars.

- For some kids, a shower or even a bath is actually *over*stimulating just before bedtime. If this is the case, move bath time to the afternoon or earlier in the evening.

- A light protein and complex carbohydrate snack can calm down some children. Sugary cereals, fruit leather/fruit roll-ups, or undiluted juice before bed makes some children too wired to fall asleep. And yes, there is evidence that warm milk before bed can help a child fall asleep. However, if this will cause your child to interrupt his sleep to urinate, you might not want to try this.

- Melatonin, a supplement available in health food stores, has been shown to help regulate sleep. Consult a doctor or nutritionist if you'd like to try this.

- Routine, routine, routine. For some kids, a calming and reassuring bedtime routine means not just pajamas, toothbrushing, story, and lights out, but having each of those activities take place in exactly that order every night at the same time: with the same toothbrush, the same story, etc. A picture to-do list (see page 266 in Chapter 11: Helping Your Child Learn and Get Organized), transition warnings, and consistent bedtime can all help a child who resists bedtime.

- Try spending a few minutes lying or sitting down next to your child, discussing the day, and what will happen tomorrow. Often, children resist going to sleep because they don't want to miss out on exciting activities. Reassurance that first thing tomorrow they can play with their favorite toy may help them get over their reluctance to call it a day.

- A weighted blanket may help a child who needs sensory input to fall asleep and stay asleep. Speak with your OT about whether a weighted blanket is appropriate for your child. You can make one or buy one from one of the therapy catalogs listed in Part Five: Recommended Products and Resources. Please see pages 113–115 for safety precautions for using a weighted blanket, including never leaving a small child unattended and never covering his face with the blanket.

- Try giving your child a backrub or massage, or squeeze his feet, legs, hands, and arms tightly before he falls asleep.

- TV or music before bed is far too stimulating for some kids, but the right music or video might be soothing. Moms have reported that their babies with sensory issues fall asleep more easily when they watch the Baby Bach DVD, a particular infomercial on TV, and even heavy metal music!

- For deep pressure input, let your child roll and burrow in a couch or bed. Wrap her tightly in a quilt and hug her, or press pillows against her.

- Try extrasnug pjs, or extraloose ones. Respect your child's sense of temperature: let him determine whether he needs layers of clothing and blankets to be warm enough, or just a T-shirt on a winter's night. Try warming his pajamas in the dryer before bed.

- If your child insists on having a bottle to go to sleep, give him a bottle filled only with water, never juice or milk to avoid teeth problems (see Oral Comforts on pages 241–243). For older children who get up multiple times during the night asking for water, put a glass of water on the night table so they can get the drink they need without fully waking.

- Encourage your child to sleep with a comfort object such as a favorite blanket (hint: keep an identical one on hand in case you need to wash it!), doll, or stuffed animal.

- If your child has trouble staying asleep, you may want to avoid having him fall asleep in one place (e.g., the couch or your bed) and moving him to another place while he's asleep (e.g., his own bed). Small children can be disquieted by the realization that they're suddenly in unfamiliar surroundings, making it difficult for them to relax and fall back to sleep.

- Sleep expert Dr. Marc Weissbluth strongly advises against waiting for your young child to become so exhausted that he crashes into sleep. He recommends you get your child right to bed when you see drowsy signs such as slower movements, droopy eyelids, yawning, and being quieter and less interested in surroundings. Act fast, because the window between drowsy sleepiness and being overtired is short: before you know it, your child is fussy, irritable, cranky, and struggling against going to sleep. Also, often an overly tired child is quite clumsy and can hurt herself far more easily than when she is rested.

- Finally, a sense of serenity and calm works like a charm to help your child fall asleep and stay asleep. Try to resolve any conflicts well before bedtime, and provide plenty of reassurance that tomorrow is a brand-new day full of wonderful possibilities.

THE STRESS FACTOR

Stress is such an everyday term that most of us have forgotten what it really means, and how physically and emotionally damaging it can be. Stress refers to a constellation of physiological and emotional changes that occur in response to a perceived challenge or threat. Not all stressors are bad. Even happy events like getting married, having a baby, making a new friend, and getting a job promotion are changes you must adapt to.

How the Body Responds to Stress

Hans Selye, the father of stress research, was the first to describe the body's reaction to stress and how we adapt to it:

Alarm phase. During an acutely stressful event, the body reacts with a fight or flight response, a series of biochemical changes in the body that prepare you to deal with real or imagined threats. The brain sends out an alarm signal that sharpens all your senses and puts your entire system on high alert. Hormones such as adrenaline kick in to increase heart and breathing rates, blood pressure, muscle tone, perspiration, and metabolism. Glands release beta-endorphins, which elevate mood and decrease pain perception, as well as cortisol and cortisone, which increase blood sugar for instant energy. You're totally alert and prepared to battle with a mastodon or the tax auditor, or to run like crazy. Children who are hypersensitive to sensory input may be in a constant state of alarm, always on "high trigger" and ready to fight or flee.

Adaptation phase. Here, the body begins to recover from heightened physiological arousal. People with a lot of stress in their lives, and those who tend to perceive everyday events as threats, have a hard time returning to normal. What's more, an overaroused child with an immature or poorly functioning parasympathetic nervous system may be unable to calm himself.

Exhaustion phase. The neurophysiological changes that occur in the alarm phase are very demanding on the body, requiring an enormous amount of energy. So long as the mind perceives things as alarming, the body stays overaroused and hypervigilant. Continuous bombardment with stressors, or a physiological inability to return to a normal resting baseline, lead to a chronic stress state of exhaustion and depletion of the body's resources.

Virtually every system in your body is susceptible to the ravages of stress. Many studies have linked stress with heart disease, persistent headaches, back pain and other musculoskeletal problems, gastrointestinal and respiratory disorders, depression, impaired concentration and learning, and low immunity against colds, flus, and other diseases.

When stress and poor nutrition cause various glands in the body to be sluggish, the adrenal glands kick in as relief workers, working overtime to make up for the other glands' inefficiency. At the same time, the adrenal glands still have to perform their usual job, releasing essential hormones that energize the body and handle stress. Over time, the adrenals can become so stressed themselves that they too begin to work inefficiently, and this leads to a metabolic slowdown and that tired-wired feeling: too tired to think straight, too wired to sleep. Teens are especially prone to overstressing their bodies and then trying to make up for that sleepy feeling with caffeine or sweets, which only worsens the stress on the adrenal glands. It's a vicious cycle.

Multiple Sources of Stress

Your child may experience stress from some obvious and some not-so-obvious sources:

External physical stressors. The everyday environment is filled with stressors, such as traffic, noise, air pollution, poor ventilation and lighting, and overcrowding. For a child with sensory sensitivities, the list of environmental stressors can be massive, with sock seams and chalk grating against the blackboard rating right up there with breaking a leg and listening to jackhammers.

Physiological stressors. Our own bodies can be a big source of stress. Growth spurts, hormonal changes, allergies, feeling ill, not getting enough exercise, poor nutrition, and inadequate sleep all take a toll on the body. Magnify that many times over for the child who has trouble processing sensations from within her body, for whom just getting washed and dressed in the morning is physically and emotionally taxing.

Social stressors. Dealing with people and social demands are familiar stress sources. Managing homework, deadlines, worries about school, and disagreements with a parent, friend, or sibling can make life tough for any child, but sensory issues often amplify social stress. For example, starting a new school year is hard for most children, but especially so for a child with sensory problems who may become extremely stressed out by all the unknowns: a new teacher, new classmates, new learning requirements, and a new route to the bathroom and cafeteria.

Thought-based stressors. Your brain perceives and interprets experience as potentially threatening or not—triggering a biochemical avalanche or not. The key here is perception. Some people are more resilient. They see changes as positive and exciting, feel in control of themselves and their environment, and can ride the waves well most of the time. Other people perceive change as a threat and feel out of control and lost, overresponding again and again. They are even more likely to suffer from stress.

What You Can Do About It

Obviously, there are no simple solutions to dealing with stress. Before you can really deal with your child's stress level, however, you need to get a handle on your own. If you're exhausted, irritable, frustrated, and overwhelmed, start pinpointing what's really eating at you. Prioritize your responsibilities and let go of stressors wherever you can: hire someone to help you clean the house if you can swing it financially, re-sign from that volunteer group that's become an unpleasant chore. Get a friend to help you reorganize your living space if it drives you crazy.

The bigger stressors may not be so easy to cope with. Call on your inner and outer resources for help. Start exercising: join a gym, take an exercise class, or practice yoga using a DVD at home. Walk to the corner store instead of driving, or take the stairs instead of the elevator, to help clear your head and invigorate your body. Rethink what you eat, and look into books on nutritional health or consult a nutritionist or dietician if you need to. Listen to music that soothes you. Set aside a few minutes each and every day that belong to *you*.

Use outer resources too. Friends, family, support groups, and online chat boards can be important allies in managing stress. A counselor or therapist can help you sort things out, set goals, and take concrete actions toward tackling life stressors. Other methods for relieving stress that you might look into include:

- deep breathing
- meditation
- therapeutic massage and other types of bodywork
- progressive relaxation
- visualization techniques

A great place to start is with a self-help book such as *The Relaxation & Stress Reduction Workbook* (see Recommended Reading).

Helping your child deal with stress. Talk to your child about the stressors in his life. You can do this with your child at any age if you use language and examples she can understand. For a toddler, you can help make the connection between it being hard to attach two pop beads and getting angry. An older child will obviously be more able to tell you about the stress he experiences. It may take a bit of work, though: teenagers often think their parents are the last people on earth who could possibly understand their woes. And yet, a sensory smart parent is in the best position in the world to understand! Carve out time to engage in a mutually enjoyable activity with your older child, and you may well find he opens up more easily than when he feels interrogated by you while sitting at the kitchen table.

Stressors naturally increase as your child gets older because of the responsibilities that go along with greater independence. Fortunately, your older child is also more capable of articulating what's bugging him and taking positive actions toward stress management. Again, help your child identify and prioritize stressors. As a sensory smart parent, you will be equipped to recognize, manage, and even eliminate many stressors (like providing compensations: earplugs for noise sensitivity and setting up work spaces to reduce distractions).

Here are some more stress-busting ideas:

- Get your child engaged in an activity—playing a ball game, making a collage, painting, baking cookies, making mudpies—whatever is meaningful and pleasurable to him. Try to get your child so absorbed in the activity that all sense of time disappears, as well as preoccupation with problems. Deep absorption in activity creates biochemical changes that promote a sense of well-being.[2]

- Enroll your child in yoga, swimming, dance, or other type of exercise class (individual and small-group classes are usually best). Movement releases natural opiates in the body called endorphins and enkephalins that decrease pain and improve mood. If a class or team situation only causes more stress, figure out a good movement activity he can enjoy alone, with friends, or with you. Go for a run, bike ride, or swim together. You'll both feel and function better.

- Deep pressure and "heavy work" are extremely calming. Big bear hugs; being squished between pillows or sofa cushions; wheelbarrow walking; and lifting, pushing, or pulling weighted objects can help soothe a stressed-out child.

- Look into books and CDs on stress management techniques for children. Many preschool and middle school children with sensory problems love the *Ready . . . Set . . . Release!* CD, which contains stress-reducing exercises that use music, breathing, muscle relaxation, and active imagination to soothe and release tension.

- Encourage your child to listen to music she finds soothing. Remember that while you may find Bach, the Beatles, or Sarah McLachlan calming, your child may relax best to the Wiggles, Radiohead, or Nine Inch Nails. Some children find they can actually think and focus better on work if they have music playing quietly in the background as white noise.

- Remember simple things that help modulate arousal level such as soaking in a warm bath, chewing gum, sucking on a pacifier or hard candy, taking deep breaths, inhaling essential oils, and other "state changers" that appeal to your child.

We know that thinking about how to reduce stress can be, well, stressful. How could you possibly get your child—or yourself, for that matter—to the gym? How are you supposed to take some time for yourself when you already lack a free second? It's a matter of rethinking priorities and scheduling it in, just like everything else—and perhaps trimming a few minutes off one task to get to the stress-busting task. Once you and your child begin to take action, though, the payoff can be enormous.

Recommended Reading

Baker, S. M., M.D. *The Circadian Prescription.* New York: G. P. Putnam's Sons, 2000. Techniques for enhancing the sleep-wake cycle, stress reduction, and healthy eating.

Davis, K. F., R.N., M.S.N., C.P.N.P.; K. P. Parker, Ph.D., R.N., F.A.A.N.; and G. L. Montgomery, M.D. "Sleep in Infants and Young Children: Part One: Normal Sleep." *Journal of Pediatric Health Care* 18:2 (2004): 65–71. Available online at http://www.medscape.com/viewarticle/471909.

Davis, M., E. R. Eshelman, and M. McKay. *The Relaxation & Stress Reduction Workbook,* fifth edition. Oakland, CA: New Harbinger Publications, 2000.

Galland, Leo. *Superimmunity for Kids: What to Feed Your Children to Keep Them Healthy Now—and Prevent Disease in the Future.* New York: Dell, 1989.

Stordy, Jacqueline B. *The LCP Solution: The Remarkable Nutritional Treatment for ADHD, Dyslexia & Dyspraxia.* New York: Ballantine Books, 2000.

Swinney, Bridget. *Healthy Foods for Healthy Kids: A Practical and Tasty Guide to Your Child's Nutrition.* Deephaven, MN: Meadowbrook Press, 1999.

Weissbluth, Marc, M.D. *Healthy Sleep Habits, Happy Child.* New York: Ballantine Books, 1999.

CHAPTER 13

Complementary Therapies and Approaches

While OT is the standard treatment for sensory processing disorder, you may hear about various special therapies and approaches that people claim have helped their children with sensory issues. An OT may suggest that your child participate in a therapeutic listening program or an audiologist might recommend Auditory Integration Training. Someone might suggest that you look into food intolerances. Or you may read something on the Internet that promotes a particular nutritional supplement or type of bodywork as *the* solution for your child's sensory problems.

As a sensory smart parent, you'll want to keep your eyes, ears, and mind open to techniques that might help your child, but make sure you get all the information before you act. You may, indeed, find a complementary approach that helps your child a little or even a lot. You may find that something reduces your child's actual symptoms, or something that helps him feel more capable of handling his daily life challenges. But beware of any "miracle cures," and don't feel pressured into trying an expensive, inconvenient therapy just because it did wonders for someone else's child.

There is anecdotal evidence to support the approaches described in this chapter, and scientific efficacy studies for some of these treatments, but keep in mind that just because something has not been proven in double-blind scientific studies doesn't mean it's ineffective or worthless. It simply hasn't been proven. And it's no surprise that there aren't more scientific studies of what works for kids with sensory problems, since they are all so varied and unique, and it's quite difficult to pull together a statistically valid sample of this population in order to rigorously test interventions. There is, however, a good deal of research underway, and you can expect to read more scientifically validated information in the years ahead.

What's more, each child's biochemistry is different. Even if a parent swears that, say, the gluten- and casein-free diet made a world of difference in her daughter's sensory issues, if your child digests these substances with no problem, you could spend a lot of time, effort, and money trying this dietary regimen. Then again, an alternative treatment like giving your child an Epsom salt bath requires so little of an investment that it's hard to see any reason not to try it.

We neither endorse nor disapprove of any of these treatments. We have labeled this chapter Complementary Therapies and Approaches rather than Alternative Therapies because we believe these methods should be considered *in addition to* rather than *instead of* therapy that directly treats sensory processing issues. A definitive exploration of complementary approaches is well beyond the scope of this book, but we have included some of the most common ones. Before embarking on any complementary therapies and approaches, be sure to consult with your child's doctors and therapists, and check into the provider's professional certification and track record of helping children with sensory problems.

Medication

There is currently no medication that cures sensory processing disorder itself. However, as discussed in Chapter 4: Where Did the Wires Cross? many children with SPD also have overlapping conditions such as ADHD, depression, and anxiety, and medication may be of benefit in treating these coexisting conditions. After consulting with a sensory smart pediatrician (or a developmental pediatrician), your first plan of attack, before you even begin to consider medication, is to get your child the therapies he needs that directly address the *underlying* sensory problems—and at the same time, to make environmental modifications and changes that will help him function more effectively and happily. You may well find that medications such as stimulants and antidepressants end up being unnecessary.

What's most important is to get at the root cause, and to eliminate the symptoms for the long haul. Should you decide to opt for medication, please proceed with extreme caution regarding side effects, contraindications, and long-term health effects, especially for a younger child.

Vision Therapy

Most vision problems can easily be corrected with eyeglasses or contact lenses, especially those we are most familiar with such as near- or farsightedness and astigmatism. However, not all vision problems can be treated with eyeglasses alone; some require vision therapy.

Vision therapy, also referred to as optometric vision training, eye training, or orthoptics, is a subspecialty within the field of optometry. Vision therapy is a nonsurgical, therapeutic regimen that addresses a variety of visual conditions including accommodative disorders (eye focusing), binocular vision disorders (eye teaming and alignment) such as convergence insufficiency and strabismus, ocular-motor dysfunction (eye movements and tracking), and visual-perceptual disorders.

After an in-depth evaluation of visual acuity and visual skills, the behavioral optometrist designs a treatment program that is tailored to your child's needs. Depending on the type and severity of the visual problem, the behavioral optometrist may prescribe eyeglasses with special lenses, or wearing an eyepatch over the "good eye" to stimulate a so-called lazy eye, or he may recommend eye exercises for you (and perhaps your OT) to do with your child. He may recommend that you bring your child into the office regularly for vision therapy using special optical instruments, infrared sensing devices, or specialized computer programs.

There is a wealth of research detailing the effectiveness of vision therapy for various vision disorders. Please note that vision therapy is not a direct treatment for dyslexia, learning disabilities, sensory processing disorder, or ADHD. However, because these disorders have a well-established connection with vision and visual processing skills, vision therapy, if called for, can be invaluable.

To find a qualified behavioral optometrist, ask your OT or call the College of Optometrists in Vision Development at 888-268-3770 or check out www.COVD.org. You can also contact the OEP Foundation at 949-250-8070 or check out www.oepf.org. If you can't find a COVD optometrist in your area, ask the optometrist you do find whether he or she assesses visual processing skills such as convergence, saccades, pursuits, and visual memory.

Irlen Therapy

As discussed on pages 45–46 in Chapter 2: The *Seven* Senses, some people with sensory issues, particularly those with autism, may have scotopic sensitivity syndrome, also called Irlen syndrome. The Irlen Institute and its clinics offer specialized vision screenings, and may prescribe colored filters or overlays, which some people have found extremely helpful. However, you should know that some studies show that 90 percent of people identified as Irlen candidates actually have significant, uncorrected vision problems.[1] Therefore, it makes sense to first get a comprehensive evaluation from a behavioral optometrist to see whether the visual problem can be corrected by more traditional optometric methods before exploring the Irlen program.

For more information, see the Irlen Institute's Web site at www.irlen.com/index.php or call the Irlen Institute International Headquarters at 1-800-55-IRLEN.

Auditory Interventions

There are many auditory interventions available, and what will work for your child depends on her needs. If your child has oversensitive hearing, you will certainly want to protect her from distressing noises as much as possible, using earmuffs or earplugs in high-noise situations like watching a fireworks display or taking a subway. Meanwhile, you will want to enhance her ability to tolerate a wide variety of sounds. If the oversensitivity is mild and your child is quite young, it *is* possible that she will grow out of it. However, this is often not the case. Your audiologist, OT, or another professional may recommend that your child participate in a "listening program." Some OTs (and some speech-language pathologists, special education teachers, and other professionals) have obtained special training in programs such as Therapeutic Listening and The Listening Program, which are generally used with children older than two years of age. Based on the work of auditory intervention pioneers Dr. Alfred Tomatis, Dr. Guy Berard, and others, these listening therapies use electronically engineered CDs, headphones with detailed acoustic specifications, and portable CD players to exercise specific muscles in the middle ear. The listening volume should always be set at an extremely low, safe level between 45–55 decibels. Programs such as The Listening Program have a set, defined progression of what your child will listen to. Other programs, such as Therapeutic Listening, rely on the therapist's clinical skills and understanding of your child: the OT will select the CDs and develop a personalized listening schedule for your child.

Your child will begin the listening program under direct supervision of a therapist, who may then have you continue the program with your child at home or possibly at school. While listening, your child can do other activities such as arts and crafts or puzzles, or better yet, sensory diet activities such as swinging and bouncing to enhance integration of auditory input with other types of sensory input.

Children with more severe auditory integration problems, as is often seen with autism spectrum disorders, may benefit from more intensive (and more time-consuming) interventions such as Dr. Berard's Auditory Integration Training or the Tomatis Method. These programs may be conducted in freestanding, dedicated centers or within full service therapy practices. Always check that you are working with a certified consultant.

Efficacy studies have been conducted on many of these listening programs, yet they remain somewhat controversial. Bear in mind that many parents, therapists, and teachers report excellent results from these programs.

If your child is having difficulty following along in class, the audiologist, SLP, or OT may recommend an FM transmitter and receiver unit for school. With this device, the teacher speaks into the transmitter and the receiver sits on the student's desk or is installed nearby, or the child may wear headphones. The FM unit helps bring the teacher's voice to the foreground so the child can't miss what she is saying.

The audiologist, SLP, or another professional may recommend auditory exercises as well as computer programs to improve your child's auditory processing skills. The Earobics computer program aims to help children with phonological awareness, auditory processing, and phonics training. The FastForWord computer program addresses critical thinking, listening, and reading skills.

Ask your OT, SLP, or audiologist whether an auditory intervention is right for your child, and which type of program would be most appropriate.

To find a qualified audiologist, ask your OT, SLP or another professional. Be sure to find one who is quite experienced with auditory processing and sensory issues. You can also try the American Speech-Language-Hearing Foundation's (ASHA) online referral service at www.asha.org/proserv/ or call 800-638-8255. Another place to check is www.ldinfo.org/professionals/audiologists.html. Your local university or hospital may also have good providers. The official Tomatis Web site is www.tomatis-group.com, and you can find certified Tomatis consultants at www.iarctc.com. Also see the Society for Auditory Integration Training at www.sait.org, which has more information about auditory integration training.

Nutritional/Biochemical Approaches

If you have any suspicion that a food is exacerbating or contributing to your child's sensory problems, start keeping a journal of the foods your child eats and her behavior afterward to look for any patterns. If you suspect one food or type of food is the culprit, remove it from the diet completely for several days to see if there is an improvement in symptoms.

If your child is truly allergic to a food instead of just intolerant of it, he will have a powerful reaction whether he has a tiny portion or a large one. His body will manufacture histamines and antibodies, and the reaction will be dramatic. For example, some children are so overly sensitive to nuts that one or two peanut M&Ms will set off hyperactive behavior. You can also have an allergist do a blood test on your child to comprehensively test for allergies. If your child has a food intolerance, on the other hand, he may be able to eat small amounts of that food with little or no effect, but have trouble when he eats a lot of it.

The most well-known sign of a food allergy or intolerance is a rash, but there are other signs as well, such as headaches, dark undereye circles, hyperactivity, stomachaches, itching, scratchy throat or difficulty swallowing, diarrhea, runny nose or congestion, and light-headedness.

Among all children, foods such as strawberries, shellfish, peanuts, fruits, tomatoes, food additives, and milk are common culprits. Among children with sensory issues, especially those who also have autism, Asperger's syndrome, or PDD, allergies or intolerances to gluten (in wheat and some other grains), casein (in milk), corn products, phenols (in many fruits), and artificial colors and flavors are quite common.

Some nutritionists say that if the child self-limits his food to breads and dairy it may be because even though his digestive system has great difficulty breaking them down, they are calming to the child. A child who severely self-limits his foods—perhaps existing only on Goldfish crackers and plain pasta—may well have an undetected digestive problem that causes him constant pain or nausea.

Enzymes. Instead of following extremely restricted diets, some parents give their children enzyme supplements that are purported to improve digestion. This allows the child who has food intolerances (not allergies) to eat small amounts of the food with no ill effects. The theory is that if you can help the body break down these foods more easily, the child's system will be less stressed overall, and his sensory issues will bother him less. There is much talk in the autistic community about the use of enzymes, because so many people with autism are intolerant of gluten and casein in particular. Some parents say enzymes allow their children to eat a wider variety of foods while reducing sensory issues. Others say that their gluten- and casein-intolerant child got better on enzymes but does best on a strict gluten- and casein-free diet.

Gluten- and casein-free diet. Some parents of kids with sensory processing disorder, and particularly parents of children with autism, have discovered that their child's sensory issues improve dramatically when they remove gluten (found in wheat, rye, oats, and soy products) and casein (found in dairy products) from the diet (or when their children take enzymes to help them digest these substances).

Gluten and casein break down into peptides that interact with opiate receptors in the brain, which produce calming, pain-reducing feelings. Some children (especially many children with autism) incompletely break down and excessively absorb these peptides which "may cause disruption in biochemical and neuroregulatory processes in the brain, affecting brain functions," according to the Autism Society of America. In other words, it is probably not that gluten and casein *cause* sensory issues but if a particular child is sensitive to them and you remove these substances from his diet, his system will be better able to handle sensory issues. The Web site www.gfcfdiet.com is a great site for learning more about this diet.

The Feingold diet. The Feingold diet is based on the idea that some children's hyperactive or poor behavior is due to sensitivity to certain food additives. The Feingold diet eliminates artificial colors and flavors, preservatives (BHA, BHT, TBHQ), and, for the first four to six weeks of the diet, aspirin and foods containing salicylates (certain natural colorings and flavorings, many fruits, some spices, vinegar, some vegetables, etc.). To truly follow the Feingold diet, you have to buy their safe foods lists that tell you what brands of foods are acceptable (they have contacted the manufacturers to identify the exact ingredients). See the Web site www.feingold.org for more information on this diet.

Epsom salt baths. A low-cost and easy way to help lessen a child's sensory issues that has worked for many is Epsom salt baths. Epsom salts, sold in bulk in drug stores and sometimes grocery stores, are magnesium and sulfate crystals, and traditionally have been used in baths to ease sore muscles and detoxify the system. Through the skin, one can absorb magnesium, a trace mineral associated with a healthy nervous system, as well as sulfate. In lieu of Epsom salt baths, you can also mix Epsom salts into lotion to rub on your child's skin (a premixed Epsom salt lotion is available from www.kirkmanlabs.com). Epsom salts should not be used on a child with high blood pressure or kidney or heart problems. For more information, see the Web site www.enzymestuff .com/epsomsalts.htm.

Chelation therapy for heavy metal toxicity. In the autism community, there are parents and doctors who believe that many children developed their sensory issues as a result of mercury toxicity caused by vaccines, mercury amalgam fillings that leached mercury into the mother's bloodstream when she was pregnant, and/or other sources. To remove this mercury lead or other heavy metals from the system, they may have the child undergo chelation therapy, which involves administering a drug—a chelating agent—by suppository, topically, orally, or intravenously. This chelating agent binds to heavy metals, which are then eliminated by the body, while a physician monitors the process. Some parents have claimed their children's sensory issues have been "cured" by chelation. However, removing metals from the body while maintaining a proper, healthy balance of metals and minerals is an extremely fine art. Given that the traditional method of chelation is potentially dangerous and very expensive, we do not recommend it for the treatment of sensory processing issues. However, we do recommend that if you're interested, look into alternate means of chelation that are safer and more affordable, such as homeopathic and naturopathic methods—and then work on removing heavy metals under the supervision of a qualified naturopath, homeopath, nutritionist, or doctor.

Bodywork

There are many different types of hands-on bodywork, including massage therapy, craniosacral therapy, myofascial release, traditional chiropractic, Network Chiropractic, and Reiki to name just a few. All are designed to enhance a person's well-being by manipulating the body's soft tissues, although each "school" is based on a different theory and uses specific techniques. For example, craniosacral therapy incorporates very gentle, light touch to subtly and slowly enhance the craniosacral system (which includes the spinal column, cranial bones, and cerebral spinal fluid), whereas deep tissue massage is applied with strong, deep pressure to release chronic, deep muscular tension.

Generally speaking, bodywork aims to relieve pain and discomfort by promoting neuromuscular relaxation, increasing blood flow and lymphatic circulation, improving posture and alignment, and, ultimately, rebalancing the nervous system to help the person feel relaxed and self-regulated. You will need to do your homework to learn about the many kinds of manual therapies to find the one that's appropriate for your child's needs and sensory preferences (particularly regarding light touch and deep pressure) and to find the bodyworker who has both excellent technical skills and a personality your child can click with. Note that some OTs and PTs have obtained additional training in bodywork, particularly craniosacral therapy and myofascial release. Ask your OT or PT if she does bodywork or can recommend a provider. You can also check into www.craniosacraltherapy.org and www.myofascialrelease.com, which both list local providers. Ask your OT or PT if she can teach you how to massage your child or infant. You can find an infant massage class at many community centers, or contact the International Loving Touch Foundation at 503-253-8482, www.lovingtouch.com.

Aquatic Therapy

Being surrounded by water instead of air provides a very special sensory experience. Water has a distinctive feel on the skin, and the even, hydrostatic pressure enveloping the body can be soothing and calming. Generally, warm water relaxes the body, while cooler water invigorates and activates it. Buoyancy creates a sense of weightless and freer motion, while moving against the resistance of water provides wonderful sensory input. Best of all, water-based activity can be a fun, motivating way to improve sensory comfort, sensorimotor skills, and overall physical fitness.

Aquatic therapy involves swimming and therapeutic activities and games that take advantage of this special sensory environment. Some PTs and OTs use the water as a therapeutic medium to help children with sensory problems, but you should be aware that an aquatic therapy instructor isn't necessarily an OT or PT, or someone who will be at all knowledgeable or compassionate about sensory issues. Many children with SPD adore water-based therapy, while others have difficulty tolerating the smell of chlorine and the echoes of indoor pools.

An outdoor pool may emit a less offensive odor, but children must be able to tolerate sun and glare, and, potentially, greater differences in temperature and other sensory irritants (cold water and hot air, wind, etc.). For more information, ask your PT or OT. Or try Aquatic Resources Network at www.aquaticnet.com, 715-248-7258, or the International Council for Aquatic Therapy and Rehabilitation Industry Certification at www.icatric.org, 509-747-2542.

Hippotherapy

Hippotherapy, also called therapeutic riding, couples horseback riding with therapeutic activities such as horse grooming. No hippos involved! Being around horses is a wonderful multisensory activity: from the tactile input of petting and brushing a horse to the powerful movement input of actually riding one. Hippotherapy can incorporate frequent starts and stops, several postures (such as straddling and lying prone), and different gait patterns (walking versus galloping) to activate your child's sensory receptors, particularly the tactile, vestibular, and proprioceptive ones. Benefits are reported to include improved balance, muscle tone, posture, coordination, and strength, not to mention enhanced physical confidence and emotional well-being.

For more information on hippotherapy in your area, ask your OT or PT, or contact the American Hippotherapy Association at www.americanhippotherapyassociation.org or 888-851-4592, or North American Riding for the Handicapped Association at www.narha.org or 800-369-Ride (7433).

MAKING THE RIGHT TREATMENT CHOICES

So how do you select the right approach, or combination of approaches, to help your child? Of course, your OT, developmental pediatrician, or other professional can recommend the ones she thinks will most likely benefit your child. Even so, there's some element of trial and error. In your well-intentioned quest to find help for your child, avoid piling on treatments, because you'll have difficulty telling which approach (or combination) is working. Yet, you'll probably find that you can't try just one at a time (the only sure way to test efficacy); for example, don't stop OT sessions to see whether removing a suspect food really makes a difference (is it the food or the OT?). Just take it slowly, keep track of any differences you see in your child, and make your changes one at a time.

To make it all more confusing, many of the very different approaches we've discussed address precisely the same symptoms. Patricia Lemer, cofounder and executive director of Developmental Delay Resources, notes that the classic ADHD behaviors are virtually identical to the symptoms of sensory processing difficulties, learning-related visual problems, and food intolerances. While the actual symptoms may be the same, the label is different, depending on whom you consult. An OT will instantly recognize sensory problems. A behavioral optometrist will recognize vision-related learning problems. And a pediatrician or pediatric neuropsychologist will recognize ADHD. So whom should you consult, and whose advice should you follow?

Although it entails a lot of consultations with several specialists, it makes sense to look at all of these options and frames of reference. Your child's difficulties may be a combination of them: she may have sensory problems *plus* food intolerances *and* undetected vision problems *and* ADHD.

Start with the least invasive, standard approach for sensory issues: occupational therapy. Make the modifications she needs at school and at home. Then, be sure to have her vision checked, and get the vision therapy or eyeglasses she may need. If you have concerns about her hearing or auditory processing, consult an audiologist, your OT, and perhaps an SLP as well. Look into nutrition and food intolerances, and make any changes that are necessary. Weigh the cost of any particular complementary therapy; whether there is evidence that it will work for your child given her unique set of issues; and the inconvenience and effort involved for you, your child, and your family. Work only with professionals whose credentials you trust. If problems such as anxiety, depression, anger, impulsivity, or inability to focus still persist, and profoundly interfere with her life, then you may want to consider medication.

Recommended Reading

Block, Mary Ann. *No More Ritalin: Treating ADHD Without Drugs.* New York: Kensington Publishing, 1996.

Bock, Kenneth. *Healing the New Childhood Epidemics: Autism, ADHD, Asthma, and Allergies.* New York: Ballantine Books, 2007.

DeFelice, Karen L. *Enzymes for Autism and Other Neurological Conditions.* Philadelphia: Thundersnow Interactive, 2002.

Feingold, Ben. *Feingold Cookbook for Hyperactive Children.* New York: Random House, 1979.

————. *Why Your Child Is Hyperactive.* New York: Random House, 1985.

Kaplan, Melvin. *Seeing Through New Eyes: Changing the Lives of Children with Autism, Asperger Syndrome and other Developmental Disabilities through Vision Therapy.* London: Jessica Kingsley Publishers, 2005.

Lewis, Lisa. *Special Diets for Special Kids.* Arlington, TX: Future Horizons, 1998. How to follow a gluten- and casein-free diet, including recipes.

McCandless, Jaquelyn. *Children with Starving Brains: A Medical Treatment Guide for Autism Spectrum Disorder.* North Bergen, NJ: Bramble Co., 2003.

Rapp, Doris. *Is This Your Child? Discovering and Treating Unrecognized Allergies in Children and Adults.* New York: William Morrow, 1992.

Rapp, Doris. *Is This Your Child's World? How You Can Fix the Schools and Homes That Are Making Your Children Sick.* New York: Bantam, 1997.

PART FOUR

Parenting with Sensory Smarts

CHAPTER 14

Handling Discipline, Transitions, and Behavioral Issues

When your typically developing three-year-old easily dresses herself in the morning, while your five-year-old needs two transition warnings, lots of coaxing, and help pulling his pajamas off and putting his shirt on, and he absolutely insists on wearing beat-up, too-tight sneakers and the same ratty sweatpants he's been wearing for the past three days, you may find yourself getting angry and frustrated, sad, or even overwhelmed. Or, if yours is an only child, you might feel just a little jealous of parents whose low-maintenance kid dashes joyously onto the playground while yours needs you right by her side, patiently encouraging her to join the others lining up to go down the slide or across the monkey bars.

One day you may well find yourself doing therapeutic brushing and joint compressions, pondering how to make time for a trip to the grocery store to pick up more grapes because that's the only green food he's eating these days, trying to figure out when you're going to squeeze in his straw and bubble-blowing exercises this afternoon when you've got to take your other son to the pediatrician, and feeling downright resentful. After all, as parent to a child with sensory issues, you've got to plan more, organize your time even better, and have extra patience. Marisa, mother of a little girl with sensory processing disorder adopted from overseas, says, "We need to be extremely creative to answer all of our kid's sensory needs, especially since what works one day may not work the next. But some days you're exhausted and just can't do it. Try not to beat yourself up so much for not being 100 percent supportive and creative in meeting your child's needs each minute of the day, day after day. We're just humans, after all. You can make up for it the next day by being extra creative."

Sometimes it's difficult to keep things in perspective, to take the sensory issues in stride and focus on what is amazing about your child. He might be the kindest boy in the neighborhood, happily taking the hand of the child no one else reaches out to, and ready to bear-hug anyone at anytime. She may be a talented singer with a ready laugh and a terrific attitude. Whatever it is that makes your child uniquely wonderful, don't let yourself lose sight of it on those days when her issues seem to dominate your life.

The "Just Right" Parenting Challenge

It may be hard to believe on your worst days, but when you give your child a "just right" challenge by nudging her to the next level of sensory tolerance while accommodating her sensory needs, her behavior and attitude will improve. Over time, your child will learn to better regulate her nervous system, handle discomfort, and identify her sensory needs and find acceptable ways to meet them on her own. One day she may surprise you with her self-reliance, self-insight, and ability to persevere in the face of challenge.

How can you and your child achieve this? It starts with accepting your child as he is. Maybe he will never be the athlete you imagined, but he might enjoy watching sports with the family, or participating in a nonathletic activity with passion and learning the lessons of teamwork. Maybe she will never be a genteel little girl hosting teddy bear tea parties, but instead will grow up to be a smart, self-assured introvert whose scientific research benefits mankind. Open your mind to your child's possibilities and her challenges will feel less overwhelming.

This is easier said than done when you first learn that your child has SPD. Don't get caught up in thinking that because your child needs extra accommodations, he has to be protected from every difficulty. Be confident that your child will develop more acceptable behavior, and recognize that building skills is a process that involves a lot of repetition over time. If you feel that your child is not making enough progress, and should be able to, say, handle getting on the school bus without a tantrum by now, start looking at reducing other stressors and lower the bar a little. Maybe you need to ride to school with him on Monday mornings for a while and slowly ease off: you leave him in the classroom one day, you leave him at the front door with the aides the next time, you put him on the bus and step off it the next.

Sometimes you'll push your child, sometimes you'll let things go. In any given situation, your understanding and acceptance of your child is the best guide to how to balance the demands placed on her.

However, it will help you tremendously to be creative and willing to ask yourself why it's important for your child to do this right now. Why do you hold the behavioral standards you hold? Are you feeling pressured to show that your child is just like everyone else's and can sit nicely at the Thanksgiving table? What's really important and what just isn't? What's the goal behind your rule, and is there another way to achieve that goal? Does your child *have* to wear snowpants and snow boots like all the other kids, or can she wear wind pants over two pairs of leggings and brush the snow off her gym shoes, and head inside a little earlier than the other children do because she won't tolerate warmer, waterproof clothes? *Pick your battles.*

During stressful times, you will need to be even more discerning about which behaviors you want to address and which you can accept. Chaotic family gatherings, the beginning of a new school year, and Monday mornings are harried and high-pressured enough for kids without adding unnecessary demands. Maybe the time for working on independent dressing skills with your preschooler is Saturday and Sunday mornings, when neither of you feel rushed. Let go of unnecessary pressures, make it easier for your child to cooperate, and you'll face fewer power struggles.

DISCIPLINE: TEACHING CHILDREN TO BEHAVE WELL

We all know children need discipline, but you may not realize that the word *discipline* comes from the Latin word for *to teach.* Punishment may be involved—although perhaps it's more accurate to call sensible, measured punishments "logical consequences"—but at its core, discipline is designed to teach a child crucial social skills, such as self-control, so he can function in the world with other people.

Of course, if your child has sensory processing issues, it will be more challenging for him to learn these lessons. His body's signals are not predictable and are often quite intense, and yet he will still have to learn how to meet his needs in an acceptable way. At two years old, he can get away with not wearing a bathing suit while running through the sprinklers at the playground, but he's got to tolerate a bathing suit when he gets older or he'll miss out on the fun (assuming he enjoys sprinklers, that is; some kids with sensory issues hate them!). As the years pass, the demands on him will increase, and you want his ability to handle those demands to increase as well.

Teaching Kids to Ask for What They Need

Even very small children with sensory processing challenges can begin to learn to identify their needs and get them met in acceptable
ways. One mom, Delia, says that a few months after beginning OT,
her one-year-old, Ivy, began to communicate to her mother her desire
to be bounced on a large ball or swung in a blanket because these
activities were deeply calming to her system. As you use your sensory
smarts and find ways to help your child get the input he needs
throughout the day, point out solutions that you, or he, have discovered: "It's nice and calming to play boats in the bath, isn't it?" "It
seems like you have an easier time getting started on your homework
when you shoot baskets for a few minutes first."

Kids with sensory issues often have a knack for seeking out the
sensations they need when they need them. While you might be annoyed that your toddler keeps opening and shutting the sliding glass
door at your in-laws' house, recognize that she may be trying to get
calming sensory input. If sliding the door endlessly is not acceptable
to you (or your in-laws), do wheelbarrows with her or let her toss
stones into the creek with you.

Kids also need to learn to identify sensations that are bothering
them so they can either find a way to cope or get help from an understanding adult. One mom, Erika, learned how important it was to teach
her son to ask for the tools he needed to handle sensory annoyances.
While Erika knew that a baseball cap would make him more comfortable outdoors on a sunny day, her son Ritchie's grandmother wasn't
aware of this, so she didn't know what to do when the boy complained
that he didn't want to go outside to play because the sun hurt his eyes.
Erika taught Ritchie to ask for what he needed—in this case, his baseball cap—so that when his mom wasn't around, other people would be
able to help him out.

Reinforce Positive, Not Negative, Behavior

Kids want attention, and if they feel they have to act up to get it, they
will. Give them the attention *before* they have to resort to acting out or
whining and you will teach them that good behavior gets them what
they want. It's easy to notice negative behaviors because they stir up
strong reactions, but it's important not to give your child a lot of attention for acting out.

It's also crucial to reinforce positive behavior. Catch your child behaving well. Tell him you're proud he's been so patient waiting for you to get through an extralong checkout line instead of taking it for granted. Remember, too, that compliments that work best at reinforcing positive behavior are specific: "good job" and "good girl" are nice, but they don't make as much of an impression on your child as "I see you put your dishes in the sink without my having to ask you. Thanks, honey." Don't buy into the idea that if you praise your child too much, he'll become a "praise junkie." It's more likely that he'll take a cue from you, and you'll hear "thank you" and "nice job fixing my bike, Dad" from his lips more often.

However, don't feel you have to constantly lavish your child with praise for everyday behaviors, or he will wonder what you're up to. Kids know when they've put forth a little extra effort and when they're being showered with insincere, undeserved compliments.

Applaud your child's efforts, not just her achievements. Tell her you're proud of her, and ask, "Aren't you proud of yourself?" Celebrate the milestones you and your child know are no small matter. For a kid with sensory problems, the first time he puts on a scratchy suit and tie for a formal occasion and keeps it on all day *is* a big deal. Call Grandma to brag, burst into applause, bake a cake—whatever feels appropriate.

Establishing Routines and Guiding Kids Through Transitions

If you wrote a list detailing everything your child has to do on any one given day, you might be quite surprised at how many times she has to stop what she's doing in order to do something else (often a task she dislikes). This can be really stressful on both of you. Even a young child at school constantly finds he must change what he's doing; just when he's finally got that Duplo spaceship ready for takeoff, it's time to put away the toys, find his jacket, and line up for recess. Then, just when he's getting the hang of soccer baseball, it's time to line up again and go to music class.

It's a fact that small children—and often, older children, especially those with sensory processing disorder—thrive on routine. Some kids need a very rigid schedule to quell their anxiety, with activities in the same order and at the same time every day. Others just need to know that after breakfast comes floor playtime, then snack, then playground time, etc. Knowing the sequence of activities, and approximately how long they take, can be very organizing and reassuring to a child with sensory issues. At the beginning of an OT session, Lindsey often helps a child decide which toys they will play with and in what order. As each activity finishes, she has the child help her clean up before taking out the next toy. This actually helps train very young children to recognize that activities have a beginning, middle, and end, and reduces anxiety about the unknown. Remember, to a child whose world is very unpredictable due to sensory issues, having a grasp on what's next is very calming, so whenever possible, let him know ahead of time when he has to switch activities or locales, or that his environment is about to change.

Many parents find that their kids have the most focus first thing in the morning, right after breakfast, and need movement activities by midmorning to stay focused. Some kids do well with watching television or playing computer games immediately after school, while others become overly aroused by these activities and have trouble settling down to do their homework. In general, if you are going to work with your child on tasks he finds difficult, choose his most alert time of the day or at least do it after he's had some calming input. For example, if you are going to work on fine motor skills, consider having the child wake up his muscles by squeezing a fidget toy, hard clay, or a guitar finger-exerciser (available in music stores that sell guitar accessories); have him wake up his mouth before doing oral-motor exercises by drinking fizzy seltzer, or eating Pop Rocks or sour candy.

"You've got ten minutes!" In addition to using the techniques for teaching children time awareness and management described in Chapter 11: Helping Your Child Learn and Get Organized, telling your child that he's going to have to switch gears in a certain amount of time will help him prepare himself mentally for the switch. Giving a child a few minutes before he has to set the table is fair warning, but for a child who has a poor sense of time and time management, you may have to be more specific: "It's 6:20. I want the table set by 6:30." If you want to give a child "five more minutes" of engaging in her present task before switching gears, set an egg timer (with sand) or a kitchen timer (with a bell, but remember that the ticking and the ringing might be too irritating to an auditory defensive child).

To be fair, however, when you tell your child that you'll be off the phone and ready to help her with her diorama in five minutes, don't let that five minutes stretch out to ten or twenty!

Express time in terms of sequence. Statements such as "*First* you need to take a shower. *Then* you can play your new game," or "*After* you finish washing the dishes, you can call your friend back" make your expectations clear. Children with motor planning and learning problems may have an especially hard time grasping sequence, and benefit from having sequences pointed out to them again and again. And some kids will even comfort themselves with self-talk about sequence: "Today is Friday, tomorrow is Saturday. No school tomorrow!" or "First I have to make the track and *then* I can put Thomas on it." Every morning, discuss what day of the week it is, what the day's agenda is, the weather, etc., to help a young child develop a sense of sequence and time.

Have a backup alarm clock. If your child has trouble waking up, or needs a few reminders to get ready for something, use *two* alarm clocks. Set the first one within arm's reach for a time that leaves a little wiggle room, and the second one across the room for the absolute do-it-or-else deadline. And make sure the second clock doesn't have a snooze button!

Work with written to-do lists and picture to-do lists. Kids with sensory processing disorder need to know what is coming up—whether they're reading it on a written to-do list or on a calendar, or "reading" it from a visual to-do list using pictures. This gives them a sense of focus and control over their world and their time, and makes it easier to transition to new activities. In a central area, post a large calendar, with all the family obligations written on it, and/or tape up a to-do list for him. Go over his schedule with him at least once a day so he doesn't forget it's there. For a child who can't read yet, try a picture to-do list (see page 266 in Chapter 11).

While you can't predict everything—the car won't start, the dog gets ill and needs to go to the vet—you can help your child understand that the day is not open-ended and unlimited, and help him learn to predict and plan for transitions.

Stick to your agenda. With some kids, it's crucial not to change the order of tasks and activities that you've agreed upon. Says Erika of her son Ritchie, who has sensory processing disorder as well as ADHD, "We learned early on that he couldn't tolerate any change in plans. If we said we were going to the grocery store, then lunch, then to Target, we had to make sure we actually went to those places in that order. He would get himself psyched up for the grocery store being bright and cold in places, but if we decided to go into a noisy restaurant first it would throw him off and he just couldn't cope with it. We learned to make sure that if we change plans, we have to prepare him for it."

Always transition to new house rules. Sometimes you've got to rethink your house rules or schedule, and get tough about anything from afterschool television to too much junk food. While kids can grudgingly accept that you're establishing a new rule, be sure to spring the bad news on them ahead of time so they can prepare themselves for it. Pick a time when you know your child is focused and able to listen, and really hear, that you mean business about this new rule. Don't announce it just as she's plopping down in front of her favorite show with a bag of chips.

Try to give multiple warnings, while leaving some extra room for yourself. Warnings such as "You can have two more tries at getting to the next level on that game and then we have to leave" help define time for kids. Very young children might need several warnings before ending an activity they enjoy and beginning one they don't care for. Be sure to leave enough flexibility in the schedule to allow you to stay calm if your child still resists the transition. If you can avoid getting angry and acknowledge that the transition is difficult but crucial at this point, it will help in the long run, even if he struggles in the moment.

Bribe them with something they were going to be able to do or get anyway. It's not really a bribe when you entice a child into leaving his favored activity by promising him something you would have allowed anyway, for instance, "Okay, we have to go home and play with those new monster trucks you got for your birthday" or "It's one o'clock now. Time to get a slice of pizza for lunch and go home." A kid who is hyperfocused on an activity he enjoys may simply need reminding that there are other fun activities to be undertaken today.

Be generous with your praise when your child pulls it together and handles a transition smoothly, and don't be afraid to reward him with an extra treat, whether it's an ice cream cone or an extra half hour watching videos.

Use calming and alerting activities when your child needs them. A child who is lounging like a blob on the couch may need a pillow fight, to play catch-the-monster (you), or some upbeat music to get into gear. Deep pressure like a bear hug or being squished between pillows usually quickly calms a rambunctious child (see Chapter 6: The Sensory Diet of Daily Activities for more ways to give deep pressure input). One mom, Delia, placed a tightly fitting cap on her crying one-year-old's head, and her daughter instantly calmed down. You can also try lowering the lights, turning off the radio and television, closing the windows to outside noise, speaking in a softer voice, and playing soothing music to help bring your child's energy level down.

Have a laugh. Humor can be a magical tool for transforming a cranky child into a laughing one. A silly comment ("You don't want to get in the car? How about we let your baby sister drive? Think she'd get us to Grandma's house faster?"), a histrionic burst of phony wailing, a playful voice as you flip the child upside down or tickle her ("Maybe the tickle monster has to put your coat on for you?") might be enough to switch her mood to a more cooperative one. For other children, attempts at humor may be perceived as teasing and they will just get further agitated. Try being playful with your child and see if it works, but if it doesn't, don't fight her temperament. Find another way to help her transition.

Spin the transition positively. Nancy's husband, George, always referred to a break in routine that required Cole to go out of the apartment as "an adventure." The "adventure" might be a trip to the grocery store and the hardware store, or a trip to the video store and the pizzeria. This positive spin on a break in routine helped Cole get over his reluctance to put on his shoes and coat and leave the apartment, which he had trouble doing, even though once he got outside he always enjoyed himself. If your child grumbles about the sudden change in weather when autumn comes around, engage her in activities of the season so that she's reminded that there are fun things you can only do during this time of year.

Provide comfort objects. A child might feel more secure with transitions—whether it's a change in activity or locale—if he can take his favorite blanket or stuffed animal with him, keep one of his toy cars or dinosaurs in his pocket, or even bring along a smooth stone from his backyard.

Be honest—and detailed—about what lies ahead. Prepare your child for doctor visits and other potentially unpleasant situations rather than hoping for the best and springing it on him last minute. His fears might actually be worse than the reality. A child who screams in protest at going to the dentist may be imagining getting a shot like he does sometimes at the pediatrician's. When you can, use books to familiarize a younger child with the situation, such as going on an airplane or going to the dentist (also, see Chapter 7: Practical Solutions for Everyday Sensory Problems). With older children, be honest about what's going to happen so they can mentally prepare themselves. Some kids will want to know all the details of who will be at the family reunion, where exactly they will sleep, whether they can bring their favorite pillow: details you might find unimportant but that they need to know about to ease their worries.

SENSORY SEEKING, RISKY BEHAVIOR

Darting into traffic or across a parking lot or in front of children on the swings is a relatively common impulsive behavior for kids seeking sensory input. Excited and overstimulated, they are attuned to their body's need for movement and aren't thinking about safety. The best way to deal with these behaviors is, obviously, to avoid dangerous areas such as streets and parking lots when your child is wound up. Also, encourage him to get grounding sensory input, such as by stomping on the sidewalk like a giant or doing standing push-ups against the wall.

Before bedtime is prime time for sensory seeking roughhousing accidents, because you're tired, he's tired, and you're probably not spotting him as well as you would if you were more alert. Be especially cautious with your sensory seeker at this time and provide safe opportunities for him to get movement and deep pressure input.

Tantrums

"There's nothing wrong with that kid that a good spanking wouldn't cure." "Send him over to my house. I'll straighten him out in no time!"

Is there a parent of a child with sensory issues who hasn't heard one of these ridiculous pronouncements (or perceived that everyone is thinking this)? Chances are, you know well the feeling of struggling with a child having a tantrum while wishing you could just turn around and breathe fire onto the "expert" bystander doling out such helpful advice.

Of course, all small children have tantrums. It's part of the process—and it *is* a process—of learning impulse control and frustration tolerance. Unfortunately, kids with SPD may have to control more impulses and tolerate more frustrations than most other kids do, so their meltdowns are usually more intense and more frequent, and they have them for a longer stretch of childhood. Or, their tantrums can take less obvious but still frustrating forms: they might crawl under a table or behind a bush and refuse to emerge, or lower themselves to the ground wherever they are and simply lie there, unwilling to get up. What do you do if your child hasn't yet learned to stop himself from going into overload?

Stop the meltdown as it is beginning. Psychologist Dr. Ross Greene says that inflexible-explosive children, who have low frustration tolerance, experience meltdowns in three stages. At stage one, they are in "vapor lock": they get stuck in their intense emotions and need help pulling themselves back. At stage two, the crossroads, the parent can still intervene if he or she can avoid getting angry and escalating the situation. In stage three, the meltdown, the child can no longer think rationally or learn anything. Attempts to reason with him at this point will get you nowhere.

How do you avoid the meltdown? You might quickly divert your child's attention to a more acceptable activity, or give him deep pressure input to calm him.[1]

Using your sensory smarts, you can head off many cases of stress overload before they begin. Knowing your child's rhythms, you can anticipate and plan for changes that might otherwise deeply upset him. By now, you know that dragging along your child while trying to squeeze in a few extra chores at the end of a long day can lead to a meltdown. Even as your child passes out of the tantrum phase—or if his way of dealing with overload is to quietly withdraw—you still need to use your sensory smarts to protect him from high-stress situations whenever you can. Of course, you can't anticipate everything in life, but very often you can predict enough about events to prevent your child from being totally stressed out by the unexpected.

Model calmness. It's very difficult not to give into anxiety and anger when your child is behaving badly, but she really does need you to be calm, not to escalate the intensity with your own frustration and fury. If you can, take a few deep, slow breaths before reacting.

Conserve words. A child who is melting down is not able to listen to a lecture. Says Marisa, "When my daughter, Nina, shows sensory behaviors like being unable to control herself because she is totally overaroused, I remove her from the situation. Later on, when she's calm, we talk about what happened and how much better she felt and acted when she felt calm. You *can't* discipline the sensory behavior when she's in the middle of it, but you can talk it all through after she's finished the cycle, and remind her of what happened the last time if it begins to happen again. At age five, she now has more language and logic to work within situations. When she was two, I'd simply avoid high-risk situations or leave early, before she'd get overaroused. Now she's beginning to tell *me* when it's too much and asks for what she needs, such as a break or to leave. For classic kid misbehaviors that I know aren't sensory, like rudeness, I give her short time-outs with a timer that gives her auditory signals, and end with a discussion about what went wrong."

Be willing to remove your child from the situation no matter how inconvenient it is. This requires flexibility and planning. For example, in a restaurant you might decide not to check your coat, knowing you might have to take your child outside at some point. There may be times when you have to physically pick up your small child and place him in his car seat or stroller, or carry him up the stairs. It's no fun to carry a screaming, thrashing two- or three-year-old, but do your best to remain calm and in control.

Recognize when your child needs connection. There are times when you need to just stop and give your child some sensory input and a few words of support. Says Marisa, "From time to time, I can keep my daughter from going into overload if I can get her to look me in the eyes so she reconnects and can really hear me."

Remember that sharing is highly overrated. Most children have a very hard time sharing: whether it's toys, food, art supplies, or even space. Just as you probably wouldn't be comfortable lending a casual acquaintance your car or letting a coworker wear your favorite, really expensive bracelet for a while, it's not always reasonable to expect your child to share her precious treasures with others just because you say so. Respect that your child may need to hold on to her Elmo just now, or to know that the wonderful bounty of cookies on her plate is hers and hers alone. The same holds true for physical space. If you think about how you feel when someone you're not crazy about stands too close or keeps touching you, it's easier to understand why your child doesn't want another child encroaching on his personal space either.

This is not to say that you should never require your child to share. Sharing is something we all need to learn if we hope to get along with others. Work on teaching your child to share when she's feeling comfortable and confident, and be sure to use items that she doesn't need for self-calming, security, or a sense of well-being. Start by having her share with people she likes best. Try to have enough of everything so your child doesn't feel deprived. If there are only three cookies, serve your two children one and a half each. Help your kids have more personal space whenever possible. If there isn't enough room in the backseat to avoid having the kids crammed in with their winter coats, heat up the car and take the coats off. When waiting in line with your child, find a spot with plenty of room (usually the end or beginning of the line). And when your child is very young, model turn taking: roll a ball to your child and say, "Now it's your turn; roll it to me," to help her learn the give-and-take of sharing toys.

Hitting and Biting

Hitting and biting are common behaviors among many kids with SI dysfunction. Not only does smacking up against or biting his brother let a child with sensory problems express his irritation, it gives him plenty of deep pressure and proprioceptive input that he can control, and it may be very calming to his system. To stop your child from hitting and biting, you need to teach him impulse control and frustration tolerance, and give him lots of input that will prevent him from feeling the need to hit or bite in the first place.

Indeed, some children with sensory processing problems hit or bite even when they aren't angry. They may be unsettled because a child is sitting too close to them, or upset by the amount of noise in the room, or they just may need some sensory input, and they respond by striking or biting another child.

If your child needs to hit, give him plenty of toys and objects he can hit throughout the day: musical instruments such as drums and keyboards, a therapy ball, punching bag, sofa cushion, beanbag chair, etc. If he needs to bite, give him safe items to chew on, such as Chewy Tubes, teething toys, or crunchy or chewy foods that don't turn mushy in the mouth such as fruit roll-ups or bubblegum (in fact, if your young child is biting, it may be a sign that he's hungry). If your child injures another child, give the attention to the other child before dealing with your own so as not to reinforce the negative behavior. Then give your child a time-out if age appropriate, and redirect him toward something he is allowed to hit or bite.

COMMON DISCIPLINE TECHNIQUES AND KIDS WITH SPD

Parents of children with sensory processing disorder report that many of the forms of discipline parents use on other children just don't work for their kids. Or, they find that some forms of discipline work well for them if they make key modifications. Finding discipline techniques that work for your child requires knowing his unique temperament and respecting it.

Please Don't Spank!

There is a multitude of evidence that spanking is an ineffective form of discipline for all children. William and Martha Sears, authors of *The Discipline Book,* say, "One of the goals of disciplinary action is to stop the misbehavior immediately, and spanking may do that. But it is more important to create the conviction within the child that he doesn't want to repeat the misbehavior (that is, to promote internal rather than external control). One of the reasons for the ineffectiveness of spanking in creating internal controls is that during and immediately after the spanking the child is so preoccupied with the humiliation of the physical punishment (and the degree of it he's getting) that he 'forgets' the reason for which he was spanked. Sitting down with him and talking after the spanking to be sure he's aware of what he did can be done much better without the spanking part."[2]

For children with sensory processing disorder, spanking is a particularly problematic form of discipline, even if it is used sparingly and without anger. An altered sense of pain and touch makes a swat on the behind far less of a "wake-up" than you intend, or its intensity may terrify the oversensitive child. Then too, hitting a child who has difficulty moderating how hard she touches people and objects is asking for trouble. If one moment you tell your child not to hit others, and to use a moderate touch when getting a friend's attention or playfully roughhousing, and the next moment you're hitting her to "send her a message," you're going to have an exceptionally hard time getting her to stop hitting others.

I Said *No Yelling!!!*

When you yell at your kids, it's stressful for you and them. You teach them that it's okay to yell and scream if you don't get your way, which doesn't work very well in the real world.

If your child doesn't listen to you when you speak in a firm, insistent, nonangry, respectful tone of voice, consider that his behavior may not be deliberate. He might be unable to listen because he's shut off his ears to the distraction of all sounds so that he can focus on what he's doing. If he has auditory processing problems, he might have enormous difficulty discerning your voice from background noise or taking in the information you're giving him.

When you need to get his attention, try calling his name once or twice first; you might be surprised at how often you issue orders to a kid without having his undivided attention! If that doesn't get his attention, come down to his level physically if you must (kneel or even sit on the floor) and place a firm hand on his shoulder while saying his name (you might not want to insist on eye contact if that is a problem for him). Use simple, clear language to express yourself, and ask him to repeat back what you said so that you're sure he understood you.

If your child gets into the habit of saying yes to you without following through, then it's time to consider what the logical consequences for his behavior should be.

1-2-3 "Magic"

One popular book on discipline touts counting aloud to three when children start to misbehave (*one* and *two* are warnings; when you get to *three* punishment occurs). The idea is that giving the child a countdown will let him know in no uncertain terms that he'd better pull back, exercise impulse control, and behave—or else.

It makes sense that any child, but particularly a child with SI dysfunction, would benefit from a warning that her behavior has to be checked, giving her a second chance instead of springing on her instantaneous punishment for an impulsive act. Many moms of kids with sensory challenges have found this counting approach works well for their child. However, counting at a child with impulsivity problems, no matter how minor, increases pressure on her and may backfire. A child feeling that she has to pull herself together by the count of three may get so overwhelmed that she ends up having a tantrum.

Also, a child may feel that being counted at is disrespectful, or a challenge to lock into a power struggle with the parent—and it can be tempting for you to try to prove that you're in charge. Children, just like everyone else, would naturally prefer to be the masters of their universe. Starting with the intention of showing your child that you can defeat him in a battle of wills isn't a particularly productive approach to this fact of life.

Of course, every kid crosses the line sometimes, and it's irritating to be defied and disobeyed, but there are alternatives to threatening, aggressive pronouncements. Why not acknowledge that the child has overstepped and deserves a chance to regroup, correct himself, and make amends? For example, saying, "*Excuse me?* I think you want to reword that" or "Rewind. Is that how you approach your brother about borrowing his skateboard?" offers the child a chance to think again and change his behavior without putting him in an adversarial position and tempting him to argue with you to win the power struggle. After your child corrects his behavior, you can remind him that while it's okay for him to get angry or frustrated, it's not okay for him to act as he just did. By validating his feelings, and giving him a chance to regroup, you make it easier for him to feel ready to apologize.

Sticker Charts and Other Reward Systems

Many parents find that sticker charts and other reward systems work well for their children: a sticker for each time you poop in the potty and after five stickers you can get a new doll, a star every time you get off to school on time without any complaints and after three stars you can have an hour on the computer, etc. These systems work best when there are clear and consistent guidelines for earning rewards; for instance, earning a sticker for "being good" is too abstract whereas earning a sticker for "good listening at the dinner table," especially when a child has trouble listening to and following directions, really means something to him. Watching the line of stickers or stars increase can help motivate some children, although if you are using this method for more than one child it can be fodder for sibling competition, particularly if the sticker charts are kept in a public area of the home where everyone can see that Jeremy lags behind Tiffany in star earning.

Another problem with sticker charts and earning rewards is that if the child's behavior is due to difficulty controlling impulses, or to something beyond his control (such as bedwetting or being unable to get dressed without assistance), the pressure to earn a sticker might be too much, causing him to give up. Keep in mind that you want that "just right" challenge: don't make that gold star tantalizing but always elusive.

Then too, some kids never make the mental leap from earning stickers and little toys or treats to doing things without being rewarded. If they don't get a Matchbox car after a week of not grabbing toys away from their siblings, why should they bother? Then, too, kids can become jaded by all the stickers and little toys they receive. Be judicious when choosing rewards intended to motivate your child.

Logical Consequences

The way to teach the underlying *why* of good behavior is to use logical consequences for breaking house rules. For example, let's say you want your child to grasp the real reason she should do her chores: not to avoid punishment but because she's part of the family team. If she doesn't do her chores, then you, as another member of the family team, will have to do them for her, which means you won't have time to drive her to her friend's house after all.

Logical consequences for behavior aren't always obvious in the moment when you've discovered your child's behavior, so it's good to think ahead to how you might handle the typical misbehaviors kids engage in and to allow yourself time to consider what the most sensible consequences will be. Or, give yourself a little time to think of an appropriate response to the behavior. Yes, logical consequences are a form of punishment, but they're a form that makes a lot of sense: the toy the preschoolers are bickering over goes into time-out, the sweater that got borrowed without asking must be replaced by the teenager if she ruins it.

"Because Those Are the Rules"

Some children with sensory issues can be rigid, black-and-white thinkers. They might respond beautifully when you tell them that they can't do something, or must do something, because "those are the rules." Knowing that wearing a bicycle helmet whenever he's on a bike is the rule may be enough to keep him consistently using the helmet. However, kids whose minds work this way might take rules so literally that they cannot tolerate deviation from the rules they've learned. If *you* break the rules, your child may be very offended by this seeming inconsistency (for instance, if, out of politeness, you were to sample the chocolates someone brought as a holiday gift even though dinner's about to be served and treats are for after meals).

Time-outs and Holding

Most parenting books insist that when used properly, a time-out should not be perceived or treated as a punishment but a chance to regroup. In practice, the line between the two can get rather fuzzy. Of course, your first reaction to seeing your child throw a metal toy truck across the room is not to say, "You need a time-out" in a calm and gentle tone of voice. "*Go to your room—now!*" is probably closer to what really comes out of your mouth. But if you follow the rules of trying to prevent stress overload and head off those bad behaviors at the pass, and if you childproof your home as appropriate for your children's age, it really will be easier to stay levelheaded when these events happen.

Time away from the scene works wonders for some kids, to the point where they'll seek out their own time-out. Cole went through a stage where he would put himself in time-out in Nancy and George's dark, quiet bedroom several times a day when he felt himself getting very frustrated and about to blow. Delia's son Trevor would, as a toddler, immediately crawl under a table in a restaurant to get away from the stress of the noise. Think about creating a safe space or quiet spot (see page 121) that your child can use as an acceptable getaway to relieve stress before he gets to the point of whining, crying, or acting out. Your child may need the security of having you sit with him in time-out.

Some children might need to be held tightly to be calmed, while others need a different kind of touch. Says Marisa, "At first I thought my adopted daughter Nina's behaviors—her impulsiveness, her distractibility, her intensity—were something I could discipline her out of if I said 'sit still' and 'don't do that' enough times. Then I realized that it had nothing to do with being stubborn, willful, or independent. She was physically incapable of acting otherwise, and *I* had to change. She would fall on the floor and rock wildly from side to side, with her two fists tight up against her chest when upset. I learned to reach her through gentle, loving touch, like placing one hand on her chest and one on her cheek. I gave her lots of nonrestraining cuddles and massages, and lots of movement to release all that energy."

Children like Nina actually become more intense if you try to restrain them when they are upset or hyperactive. If your child reacts this way, respect that reaction. If it doesn't sit right with you to hold her, or it agitates her further, don't.

On your worst days, remember, it will get easier as you and your child develop sensory smarts. In the next chapter, we'll look at the special challenges of helping your child, and his teachers, use sensory smarts at school.

Recommended Reading

Baker, Jed. *No More Meltdowns: Positive Strategies for Managing and Preventing Out-of-Control Behavior.* Arlington, TX: Future Horizons, 2008.

DeGangi, Georgia, and Anne Kendall. *Effective Parenting for the Hard-to-Manage Child.* New York: Routledge, 2008.

Greene, Ross W., Ph.D. *The Explosive Child: A New Approach for Understanding and Parenting Easily Frustrated, "Chronically Inflexible" Children.* New York: HarperCollins, 1998. Greene also has a useful Web site: www .explosivechild.com.

Kurcinka, Mary Sheedy. *Kids, Parents and Power Struggles.* New York: Quill, 2001. An exceptionally positive guidebook to handling intense, sensitive, and spirited children.

Sears, William, and Martha Sears. *The Discipline Book.* Boston: Little, Brown & Company, 1995.

Taffel, Ron, with Melinda Blau. *Nurturing Good Children Now: 10 Basic Skills to Protect and Strengthen Your Child's Core Self.* New York: St. Martin's Press, 1999.

Turecki, Stanley. *The Difficult Child,* second edition. New York: Bantam Books, 2000. Help for parenting a temperamentally hard-to-raise child.

Weinhaus, Evonne, and Karen Friedman. *Stop Struggling with Your Child: Quick-tip Parenting Solutions That Will Work for You—And Your Kids, Ages 4 to 12.* New York: HarperPerennial, 1991. Excellent advice on communicating with older kids and following through with logical consequences.

CHAPTER 15

Advocating for Your Child at School

Nancy's Story

Before I had Cole, I thought that enrolling him in school would be as simple as walking up the street to my neighborhood school a few months before he would start kindergarten, giving the principal my son's name, address, and birth date, and waiting for a letter telling me which classroom he should report to in September. Then again, I'm from an era when there was no such thing as "mainstreaming," "resource room," or "inclusion programs," and I had never expected to enter the complex and ever-changing world of special education. And what a world it is, complete with its own glossary of fun abbreviations, like FAPE and LRE and IEP, meetings and procedures with a zillion forms to be photocopied and signed, evaluators and therapists. I dreaded my first IEP meeting, as it was all so new to me and I felt like I'd never figure out what all the jargon meant, but I soon found out that getting a handle on the basics was a lot easier than it looked on the surface.

Special Needs, Special Education

To be sure, not all children with sensory issues need to enter the special education system in its various forms. Many kids who have mild sensory issues and no other coexisting conditions that significantly interfere with accessing the educational curriculum do just fine with a bit of understanding, extra support, a sensory diet, and a few simple accommodations. You may be able to work all this out informally with your child's school. Quite often, though, a child with sensory challenges needs more than this to do well in school.

If you have a child with special needs like sensory integration dysfunction you should know about IDEA, the Individuals with Disabilities Education Act. It is the federal law regarding special education services to be provided by public schools for children who have disabilities. At the core of IDEA, which was enacted in 1975, is the mandate that children with disabilities are entitled to a "free and appropriate public education" (FAPE) and should be educated in the "least restrictive environment" (LRE). This means that whenever possible, children are to be educated in regular classrooms rather than special ed classes, and given whatever accommodations they need to be "mainstreamed" into the general school population. It also means that schools are only required to give your child an "appropriate" education, not the very best one they can provide. Procuring the *best* education, services, and situation for a child is up to the parent.

If a child needs special help, such as therapy or assistance with reading or handwriting, she may get assistance within the classroom or may be pulled out of her classroom to work on these challenges in a separate room, often dubbed the resource room. Children who qualify for school-based OT for sensory processing disorder may get these services in the OT room, the school gym, or in another facility (in this case, transportation between the school and that facility must be provided).

Deciding which type of classroom is best for your child can be confusing. Your child may need a smaller than usual class size so that he can get extra help and attention and not be overwhelmed by large numbers of children. Perhaps your child needs even more assistance, such as an aide (or "shadow") to help him. There are also special education classes, or learning disabled classes in some schools, which may or may not be right for your child. Or maybe he really needs to be in a small class with a mix of learning disabled and non-learning-disabled children, which may be called an "integrated" or "inclusion" class. This way, your child gets the individualized teaching he needs, but also has access to the general education curriculum. Keep in mind that if the class is filled with children with very different disabilities than your child, or who are not nearly as far along in play, social, and other skills, it might actually be more difficult for your child to learn in this environment.

You'll want to get input from your child's teachers and therapists—including, perhaps, private therapists you've hired—before discussing with school administrators what type of classroom will be right for your child.

The Pros and Cons of Labels

Most parents resist the idea of labeling their child with sensory problems. Labels seem to pigeonhole fabulous, multidimensional kids into neat little categories that have nothing to do with who they are. But having a label, or a diagnosis, can open up doors for getting the services your child needs. And a label helps everyone to remember that your child has special needs and isn't just being difficult. Finally, having a label can really help the child who wonders why he's different. Mel Levine writes in *A Mind at a Time*, "When people, adults and children, learn about their own gaps, they frequently show, or actually report, a sense of relief, because for the first time in their lives they are able to understand exactly why they've been struggling to meet certain demands and how they can go about conquering or bypassing these challenges. They can forgive themselves and set about becoming stronger people."[1] So rather than feeling like an oddball or a freak, your sensory smart child gets to say, "Oh, this is one of my sensory issues popping up, and I know what to do about it."

The IEP

The IEP, or individualized education plan, is the document that spells out your child's unique needs and how the school is going to meet these needs. It includes long-term goals for the year. If your child needs assistive technology such as a laptop computer to take class notes, or test accommodations such as being tested in a small room with minimal distractions, it must be spelled out in the IEP. If your child needs therapy such as OT, PT, or speech, the IEP must list therapeutic goals, frequency (e.g., twice a week), duration (e.g., thirty minutes per session), location (e.g., in class, in the resource room), and whether these are individual or group sessions.

The IEP should also include specifics about discipline and health needs. For example, it might state that your child will not be punished by having recess taken away (which is usually counterproductive for a child with sensory issues) and that your child has the right to eat frequent snacks if he has hypoglycemia.

Push In, Pull Out, After School, or Private?

In school, services such as occupational or physical therapy are called "related services," and all goals and treatments must directly address your child's function *at school*. This is not as limited as it sounds; in addition to the academic curriculum, related service providers can address any school-related task: getting on and off the bus, taking off a coat, tying shoelaces, carrying books, sitting in a chair, note taking, behaving appropriately, communicating with others, eating lunch, playing during recess, and so on. School-based therapy can be "push in" (the therapist works with your child in the classroom) or "pull out" (the child leaves the classroom for therapy). In the best scenario, the therapist could tailor sessions to meet your child's changing needs. For example, she would work with your child in the classroom on classroom issues; in a separate room for low-distraction, one-on-one work; and in other locations such as the gym, playground, library, and cafeteria, as needed.

In some school districts, OT may be provided on a consultation basis rather than direct, one-on-one service. It is also possible to arrange for therapy through the school system with therapists who have special contracts with your school district. In this case, therapy can be scheduled before or after school hours at the school, at your home, or in a therapy clinic. Finally, you can always obtain therapy on a self-pay basis with the provider of your choice. Private therapy is not limited to school-related goals; you may develop goals with a private therapist that relate to your child in settings other than school: washing his hair, organizing his bedroom, and avoiding meltdowns in the supermarket.

There are several benefits and drawbacks to each type of therapy arrangement:

	PUSH IN	PULL OUT	BEFORE/ AFTER SCHOOL (provided through the school system)	PRIVATE
P R O S	Therapist can observe and address issues in class as they occur. Facilitates therapist-teacher collaboration. Free.	Therapist works with your child without distractions. Child can use special supplies and equipment such as swings and therapy balls. May give child a needed break from classroom. Free.	Greater privacy— classmates are unaware child receives therapy. Child has access to special supplies and equipment. Child does not lose any class time. Free.	Completely confidential. It's up to you whether the school knows your child gets therapy. Goals can focus on home, community, and social life as well as school. You can choose your own therapist. Therapy session length and frequency are up to you and the therapist.
C O N S	Child may feel singled out by special attention. May be distracted by other children. May be limited to interventions that do not disturb classmates. Must accept therapist who works in that school.	Child may feel embarrassed to leave room. Child misses class time. Therapy time may be wasted picking up and dropping off child. Must accept therapist who works in that school.	Requires additional paperwork with school board. Limited choice of providers (must have contract with the school). You must facilitate communication between the school and therapist. Occurs outside school hours when your child may be tired or want to be with friends.	Self-pay (often partially reimbursed by private insurance). You must facilitate communication between the school and therapist. Occurs outside school hours when your child may be tired or want to be with friends.

IEP Basics

By law, you are an equal partner in creating your child's IEP. In an ideal world, you and the school system will be completely in agreement at all times. Of course, the reality is that sometimes parents disagree with the recommendations.

The IEP meeting should be attended by the parents, the child's teacher (not just "a" teacher), the child if she is old enough to participate, any specialists such as an OT or a psychologist, the school's special ed administrator, and anyone else you or the school thinks should attend. If your child receives special education, both her special ed teacher *and* a general education teacher must be present. You are entitled to invite anyone you wish to, including private therapists, a lawyer, spouse, and even a nanny, if appropriate. Do not assume that your child's school-based therapists will be invited. Be sure that *you* arrange for therapists to attend, especially if you are asking for changes in service (reductions or increases), new therapy goals, or any classroom accommodations. If you don't know what someone's role at the meeting is, ask. For instance, a "parent coordinator" is different from a "parent advocate" so don't assume this person is there to speak up on your behalf.

If the school wants to invite someone who you feel has no reason to be there, such as a psychologist who has never even met your child, you have a right to object and ask them to show cause why that person should attend (do this in writing). You can also request that certain papers be removed from your child's school records, say, a note from a school counselor unfamiliar with sensory processing disorder that interprets your child's sensory seeking as willful misbehavior caused by poor parental discipline. Finally, the district must provide an interpreter if English is not your first language or if you are hearing impaired.

Here are some key points about IEPs to keep in mind:

- Under IDEA, *disabilities* include mental retardation; orthopedic impairments; brain injury; hearing, speech-language, or visual impairment; learning disabilities; ADHD; emotional disturbance; autism; and "other health impairments." In many school systems, sensory processing disorder falls under the last category. Some school districts inaccurately classify SPD as autism.
- Currently, the IEP is reviewed annually. However, if you or the school need to revise it midyear, the district is required to set up a new IEP meeting (the old IEP stays in place until everyone agrees on the provisions in the new one). Thus, you can call for a new IEP meeting if you think one is needed: for instance, if your child is not

doing well in school and you believe he needs some extra services, such as OT or assistive technology (see pages 351–53).

- The IEP is a legal document. The school *must* provide the services agreed to in the IEP. Budget cuts, limited resources, and staff or equipment shortages do not change the school's legal obligations as spelled out in the IEP.

- An IEP is supposed to be in place before the school year starts, so the annual meeting to determine what changes if any should be made usually happens in the spring. That way, if you and the school district don't agree, you can work it out over the summer so that everyone is in agreement by the time school starts in the fall.

- The school district must provide you with written materials regarding evaluations and recommendations well before the meeting so that you have time to review them and formulate questions.

- The initial determination of eligibility for an IEP might be combined with the first actual IEP meeting, or the meetings can be held separately.

- Any classroom accommodations (such as seating the child near the teacher, using special devices like a computer or adapted chair) as well as any transportation issues (such as requiring an adult to ride in the bus with the child) should be spelled out in the IEP.

- If you have any doubts whatsoever about what is in the IEP, don't feel pressured to sign it at the end of the meeting; go home and start checking further into your other options and your legal rights. If the school recommends a particular program, such as an inclusion class, ask to visit the program before agreeing to put your child in it (they may not let you do this). Remember that you can always change your mind and refuse services or ask for a change in the IEP.

- Keep a paper trail. Save anything your district sends you regarding the IEP meeting or the IEP itself, any notes from the teacher, notes you've made from in-person or phone conversations with teachers or therapists, health assessments from medical professionals, copies of independent assessments (such as an evaluation from a private OT or SLP), report cards, and copies of letters requesting evaluations and IEP meetings. You should also keep your own copies of your child's school records.

- Your child may be eligible for free summer-session classes and therapy. Generally, this happens when there's concern that the child's skills will deteriorate over the summer.

- Find out if your child qualifies for an adaptive physical education (APE) program if regular gym class is too difficult for your child.

An IEP meeting should not be intimidating or adversarial. Know your legal rights, don't be scared, and don't walk in with a defensive, aggressive attitude because you've heard horror stories from other people.

A wonderful book for helping you further understand the IEP process and all your rights, deal effectively with the school, and resolve disputes is *The Complete IEP Guide: How to Advocate for Your Special Ed Child* by Lawrence M. Siegel. It provides sample letters for all sorts of snafus you might run into.

Whatever your child's disability, if it "adversely affects education" he has a right to special education services. IDEA clearly states that problems with educational performance include not only physical problems, but social problems, a gap between ability and performance, cognitive problems, and a lack of progress. If your child is reading three grade levels ahead but is not progressing, or can't make friends because he has a nonverbal learning disability and his social skills are interfering with his ability to read social cues, he is eligible for special services. This is especially important if your school district doesn't recognize sensory processing disorder as a legitimate disability under IDEA. Watch for any legislative changes that may affect your child (check out the Web site www.wrightslaw.com for legislative updates).

504 Plans

A 504 plan is a legal document spelling out the school's obligations to accommodate a child with special needs. It's different from the IEP in that it is not governed by IDEA but by the Rehabilitation Act of 1973. Section 504, intended to protect the rights of those who have mental or physical impairments, protects students who don't qualify for special education but still need assistance in school because of their disability.

A 504 plan might include accommodations such as special seating, protocol for administering medication, adjustments to the classroom or school environment such as allowing a child to eat lunch somewhere other than the noisy cafeteria, adjustments to assignments such as more time allotted for completing tests, etc. If your child is receiving therapies, or is in a special education classroom, or has an aide, he should have an IEP, not just a 504 plan.

As with the IEP, a 504 plan is a legal document and you have a right to participate in its construction. You can call a meeting to set up or change the 504, and refuse to sign the document until you're happy with it.

The Small Stuff

In addition to any accommodations you might want written into your child's IEP or 504 plan, it's a good idea to communicate with the teacher, any aides or coaches, or other adults your child will be interacting with about your child's sensory quirks and unusual needs. A friendly chat at the beginning of the school year is a good place to start, and a great opening line to this particular discussion is, "I have a few things I want to tell you about my child that will help make things easier for you this year." In addition to the ever-effective "I want to make your job easier" approach, the "I'm hoping you can help me" approach is a good one to master—especially if you're trying to gather information from a reluctant source, or have a rule bent. Yes, it's annoying to have to ask the teacher not to make an issue out of your child's need to wear his winter jacket during class when everyone else is more comfortable with theirs off. It's irritating to have to defend the fact that your daughter needs to break eye contact in order to process a teacher's question and formulate an answer. However, some people are so used to doing things the way they've always done them that they need a gentle nudge to get them to consider changing rules that aren't necessary and might even be downright ridiculous. Be flexible and open to compromise. For example, Lindsey spoke to a kindergarten teacher who agreed to many accommodations for a child with sensory issues but drew the line at letting the girl chew gum for proprioceptive input as she didn't want to break school rules and get in trouble with the principal. However, she was perfectly willing to let the girl use a chewable necklace and to chew gum on the sly during tests.

You might be surprised by how cooperative your school is. Lindsey often recommends the Disc'O'Sit inflatable cushion for children who have trouble sitting still on the floor or on a chair. *Every* teacher she has suggested this to has been willing to try it, and each has been pleased with the difference it made. A public school child's parent generously provided eight cushions so other children could use them. A private school purchased six as an experiment and plans to buy more for other classrooms.

Of course, not all teachers and schools are so open to new ideas, especially if they are inconvenient and take some extra work. To be fair, teachers already struggle with limited time and resources without your asking for a special accommodation for your child, such as providing written assignments instead of just dictating homework. If you run up against a teacher who is downright frosty and defensive, claiming that he doesn't believe in "newfangled labels" or "making exceptions," take a deep breath and a different approach. Get specific about your own child's behavior. Instead of trying to explain that proprioceptive input is calming and organizing for children with sensory issues, say, "Last year we discovered that when Tyrell is allowed to do push-ups in his chair or against the wall, it really helps focus him so that he listens much better." Focus on the behavior and offer solutions, and remind yourself that soon you'll be able to say, "I'm so glad that Tyrell is doing better listening in your class. The chair push-ups really helped, didn't they?" And after this teacher validates your solution, you can smile sweetly and say, "Yes, deep pressure input truly does focus him."

While it's true that at some point you probably will have to face down a naysayer or a know-it-all, when you speak to the people at your child's school—or, for that matter, an athletic coach who runs the soccer team at the Y, or any other adult who will be working with your child—start with the assumption that they genuinely have your child's best interests at heart. You might be surprised at how open to suggestions they are, or how much they already know about accommodating kids who are a little "different," even if they know nothing about sensory problems.

What If the Local School Can't Provide a Free, Appropriate Public Education for Your Child?

In some school districts, services such as OT, PT, and speech-language therapy might be provided at a different school from the one your child attends, or perhaps their inclusion program or special ed class is in a school far from your home. You may be able to get the school district to pay for private school placement. If you think your child would be best served by attending a private school, discuss this with the school district as part of the IEP if you want to be reimbursed. You can't simply enroll your child in private school and then ask for reimbursement for tuition. If your child qualifies for special education services, the district must provide them, even if you choose to send your child to private school. However, there are restrictions on how much money the district has to spend when providing special services to children who are not enrolled in public schools, so know what the situation is before you enroll your child in private school. And while there are rules to prevent religious schools from receiving public money, IDEA clearly states that your child can receive special services even if she is attending a religious private school.

Increasingly, parents of kids with special needs are considering the possibility of homeschooling. At home, you have more control over your child's environment and can design a curriculum that works well with your child's learning style and sensory needs. Some parents have decided that the amount of effort it takes to try to get the school to meet their child's needs would be better spent homeschooling, at least until such time as he's able to handle a school environment.

If you're homeschooling, you can make liberal use of all the sensory diet techniques and tips for accommodation listed in this book. For instance, one mother we know lets her son recite his multiplication tables while jumping on a mini-trampoline and his spelling words while walking in a circle, options he wouldn't have in a typical classroom. You're also not limited by the school's rules about chewing gum or wearing socially acceptable clothing (maybe your child focuses best when he's in his pajamas or other very loose clothing). You can also design the space to have lighting your child can tolerate and a comfortable chair (perhaps a therapy ball in a holder or a spinning office chair).

Take advantage of the freedom to work with your child's learning style. Allow a kinesthetic learner to act out the answer to his reading comprehension problem before turning it into words on a page. Allow your visual-spatial/associative learner to digress into a discussion of the role of the Hoover Dam in the Transformers movie before pulling his attention back to his worksheet on dams and waterways. Of course, you don't have to be a homeschooler to use these techniques. Apply them to homework sessions, and consider doing your own "homeschooling" during summer, winter, and spring breaks. Even very short but regular homeschooling sessions at these times can help your child ease back into school more easily, retain what he's learned, and have a comfortably predictable routine.

You may find that teaching your child is just too frustrating for you because of clashing temperaments, or because you're not comfortable teaching. If you find that you and your child are miserable working together, homeschooling may not be for you. It might be best to hire tutors to work with your child outside of the regular school day (this is true also if you find yourself engaging in homework battles).

If you do decide to homeschool, discuss with your local public school your options for taking advantage of their music, art, and other programs. You're paying for them through property taxes, even if you're a renter, so you have a right to use these services although it will take some coordination with your local school to make it happen.

Look into local recreation department activities and camps as well as camps or classes for kids available through museums, aquariums, cultural centers, universities, and ecology centers to supplement your child's home-based learning.

Your child's OT, speech therapist, teacher, psychologist, or another professional may be able to hook you up with a social skills group so that your child can learn and practice his social skills in a small, controlled environment. If an appropriate one is not available, consider setting up a play group yourself, teaming up with other parents. Keep it small, make sure kids are of compatible ages and abilities, and set up clear expectations about how it will run and what to do if there's a behavior problem.

If you're thinking about homeschooling, you'll need to research the laws in your state as well as the laws about special education because IDEA is a little fuzzy on this issue. Some states (such as New York and Indiana) assert that homeschooled children have the right to special education services through the public schools. In Arkansas, you must be a certified special education teacher to homeschool your special needs child. The Web site www.nhen.org links you to some basic information about homeschooling laws in your state and suggests key questions you should find the answers to, such as what authority regulates homeschooling (state or district department of education). There is such a patchwork of laws and interpretations of those laws that you will have to do a lot of research.

Keep in mind, too, that homeschooling does not have to be a permanent, all-or-nothing option. You might homeschool your child for just a couple of years, or work with the local school to have your child participate in some school activities.

Many people have strong opinions about homeschooling versus public or private schooling and may try to influence your decision. Consider the source, and consider your child's unique needs. Maybe you feel your daughter just isn't ready for state-mandated, all-day kindergarten right now and you prefer to homeschool her for a year. Maybe you had your heart set on homeschooling, but you realize that the school district can offer your preschooler the chance to attend a special ed preschool where he can benefit from peer modeling and a curriculum tailored to the needs of kids with developmental delays and sensory issues. Maybe you will end up homeschooling one of your children and not the others. Then, too, some homeschooling organizations, even those that specifically address parents of kids with special needs, promote a particular set of political or religious beliefs so strongly that it might make you uncomfortable. Whatever the case, gather as much information as you can before deciding, and remember that if things don't work out you can consider other schooling options.

Changing Schools

Sometimes, a school just isn't the right fit for your child. If you're fortunate, you have other options right in your area. If you're considering moving to a new area or new school district, you might want to rent before buying a home just in case the school turns out to be a problem.

Before moving to another area, do your research into both the schools and nonschool resources, such as afterschool programs, developmental pediatricians, private therapists, and so on. Post queries on online support groups, call local professionals listed in places such as www.spdfoundation.net, and, if appropriate, check in with the local autism support group. Other parents of special needs kids may have helpful insider information that can guide you in making a decision about the best schools for your child with special needs, the best sensory gyms, and so on. Keep in mind that a school may be highly touted but not good for your child. It may focus on the needs of neurotypical or gifted children, not children who have learning disabilities or sensory issues. Private school, if you can afford the tuition on top of private therapy, may be another option. Although you *may* be able to get the local public school district to provide your child's therapy or even pay for private school tuition, don't count on it—often parents have to fight long and hard to get this accommodation, and then only after the public school administrators have realized that they can't provide a free and appropriate education for a particular child.

Don't be afraid to call the director of instruction or the director of special education in the school district you're considering moving to, and ask:

- What services are available?
- Are the therapists, or even the teachers, familiar with sensory integration issues/sensory processing disorder, and how to work with children with sensory issues?
- What are some examples of accommodations they've used for children in the past? If the director doesn't know, ask if you can speak with an occupational therapist who works with kids in the schools.
- Is there one occupational therapist for the entire district who travels from school to school?

- Is there a long waiting list for related services such as OT, PT, and speech?
- Is there more than one school in the district you're moving to, and is there the possibility of changing schools within the district should the school your child is assigned to not working out?
- How long will the school honor your child's IEP from her previous school before scheduling a meeting to consider changing it? Will they insist on new testing right away?

Keep notes of your conversation and repeat back what the person said before hanging up; they may have misspoken or you may have misunderstood.

NANCY'S STORY

Before moving back to my hometown, I had a conversation with the director of instruction as well as an old high school friend who was now working with children with cognitive delays in one of the public elementary schools. I asked a lot of questions, and then compared them to the answers I received to those provided by the director of special education in the neighboring district. In the other district, I learned, I would have no control over which school Cole would be assigned to, and in all likelihood he would be bused several miles away, which was completely unacceptable to me. I felt it was important to have him in a neighborhood school where George and I could drop him off and pick him up and get to know the parents and children on the playground, through the local recreation department programs, and through activities in the neighborhood.

I also paid out of pocket for updated evaluations from a speech language pathologist as well as an audiologist. I wanted to bring with me evaluations from therapists who had seen Cole previously and might have better insight than a new evaluator. Besides, I wanted to know where he was with his language processing, since it had been a couple of years since he'd been formally evaluated.

Because I was familiar with the school itself, I didn't feel the need to visit it before committing to the move, but I would have if that hadn't been the case. Even so, I was very pleasantly surprised to discover just how *quiet* it is compared to our old school (and neighborhood) in New York City, and I believe that was a factor in Cole's being able to handle the school environment very well. What's more, they have a terrific playground, with grass, trees, and plenty of climbing and sliding equipment, which gives him opportunities to get the movement he needs at recess and lunch, before school, and after school. I also discovered on the school's Web site information about our local recreation department which has some great, affordable programs for kids, from swimming to Cole's new favorite sport, bowling.

Cole's first teacher readily agreed to let him come and check out the classroom before school began so that it wouldn't feel completely unfamiliar. And since we had moved in the middle of summer, we made sure to get him into some recreation department programs and set up some playdates with other children before school started. Also, because I visited the area and our new home shortly before the actual move, I came home with photographs and videos of his new bedroom, school, and neighborhood to prepare him for the big transition. I'm happy to say that he adjusted beautifully and loves his new school!

Making School Life Easier for Kids with SPD

So what kind of accommodations for your child, in addition to any therapies she receives, will help her to thrive in the classroom environment? Remember, the *I* in *IEP* stands for *individualized,* and that's just what your child's educational plan should be. If you haven't already read the suggestions for modifying your child's school environment in Chapter 6: The Sensory Diet of Daily Activities, be sure to go back and look at them. Many times, teachers will be happy to make low-cost, low-hassle modifications to the classroom; sometimes they will need some persuading; other times, you might actually need to spell out these modifications.

Depending on your child's needs, you might want to consider some of the following accommodations. Many teachers are more than willing to arrange for many of these accommodations informally. For example, most teachers will be happy to let your child avoid eye contact while answering a question if she understands that this helps your child to think more clearly. However, many accommodations (such as having your child take tests in a quiet, separate room) will need to be formalized in the IEP.

Avoiding overload—some accommodations to consider

- A classroom aide will accompany your child on five-minute walks down the hall approximately once every hour and a half.
- Your child is allowed to listen to calming music through headphones during "quiet time."

- If your child is to be punished, recess and outdoor time at lunch will not be taken away.
- Your child is allowed to eat lunch in a quiet, low-stimulation environment instead of in the lunchroom.
- When the teacher needs to get your child's attention, he should not use a light touch; instead, he should use a firm hand on the shoulder or tap on the child's desk.
- Your child is allowed to avoid making eye contact when answering a question that requires his concentration if he needs to "block off" his visual sense to focus.
- When lining up with the other children, your child should always be at the front or end of the line so she isn't disturbed by the other children bumping into her. (You might ask the teacher to appoint her "line monitor" so that this doesn't seem like a punishment.) Also, she is allowed to sit at the end of a table or at a separate desk so other children at the table don't get too close to her physically.
- During circle time, your child is allowed to sit on a bumpy cushion like a Disc'O'Sit, have a weighted blanket in his lap, wrap himself in a stretchy piece of Lycra-like material, or wear a weighted or compression vest to help him stay calm, organized, and focused.
- When your child attends circle time, he must be allowed to sit on a square of rug that defines the boundaries of his space and gives him something to touch other than the child sitting next to him— and if he can't keep his hands to himself, he is to sit next to the teacher, who can use firm touch to help him refocus.
- Your child will be seated preferentially according to determined needs. (This varies from child to child and you, the teacher, and an OT may need to brainstorm to figure out the best seat location. Children with sensory issues often do best in the front of the classroom close to the teacher, where there is less conflicting visual stimulation, away from distractions, and out of direct sunlight which makes it hard for the child to concentrate. A child may also need to be seated where she can't see out the door, or need to sit next to a wall for security.)
- The student is to be warned in advance about fire drills.

Managing transitions

Transitions are a time when a child who may have struggled to get focused on an activity must suddenly shift focus, process new instructions, and motor plan the movements he needs to change activities like going from "free choice" play time to getting coats and lining up to go outside. Such a transition can be particularly hard for a child with sensory issues, who may become overwhelmed by the hustle, bustle, and noise of children moving around or those who use this time for sensory seeking like crashing into other children or banging into furniture. Here are a few tips:

- Review the schedule of activities verbally and visually, using a picture schedule so kids know what to expect and can anticipate the sequence of activities.
- During cleanup, assign a concrete two-step task using simple directions, such as, "Take all of the glue containers and put them in this bin." Allow a sensitive child to do a task on the sidelines, such as placing books on a cart on the edge of the activity.
- If children need to form a line, remember that a child with special needs may not know exactly what you mean. Consider putting a long piece of colored electrical tape on the carpet and asking children to go stand on that tape. A child who cannot tolerate casual touch should have a special place of honor ("line guard") at the end of the line.
- Transitions are a great time to incorporate movement activities. Have kids stand up to reach for the sky and bend down for the earth, do "Head, Shoulders, Knees and Toes," etc. Give calming input by having kids wheelbarrow walk if there are enough adults around, take alternating giant steps and baby steps, or alternate noisy monster steps and quiet mouse steps. Anything that involves using big muscles is great—carrying a pile of books, pushing a table, pulling on something, etc.
- For a child who seems to be ignoring you, get yourself within the child's field of vision, and place a hand firmly on his shoulder to give the child a tactile cue that it is time to shift attention.
- Some children struggle to process visual and verbal information simultaneously. Reconsider the requirement for a child to make eye contact while you are speaking to him.

Tests, classroom assignments, organization

- Your child is allowed to take tests in a separate room (to reduce distractions), have extended time (if she has slow processing), and record her answers in any manner (if writing is a problem, for instance, her answers may be typed or dictated to a scribe).

- Each day, the teacher will check the communications notebook provided by the parent and keep the parent posted of problems *as they occur* (instead of waiting until the next scheduled parent-teacher conference).
- The student is to be provided a checklist for classwork to be completed during the school day, with assignments due by lunchtime listed separately from assignments due by the end of the day.
- All instructions are to be given not just verbally but visually as well: either written on the board or provided in writing to the student.
- A written (or picture) list of what will be done in the classroom today will be provided to your child each day.
- Your child will be given extra time to provide an answer to a question from the teacher.
- The teacher or aide will help the student check her backpack at the end of the day to be sure that no items have been left behind or misfiled in the wrong section of the backpack.
- Your child will be allowed to have a second set of books, kept at home.
- Unfinished worksheets and classwork are to be sent home to be completed.
- The child is allowed to have a bag on the back of her chair or an extra storage space under her chair or desk so that she doesn't have to put all her items inside her desk and can be more organized. (You can make your own or try the Desk Buddy or Aussie Pouch available from *Pocket Full of Therapy*.)
- Your child is allowed to sit at a desk by himself instead of a table when working on multistep, complex assignments, for better concentration.
- Your child is allowed to wear any prescribed eyewear, including colored lenses and sunglasses, that has been determined necessary for her to function in the classroom.
- Your child is allowed to doodle during lectures if this helps him concentrate.
- Your child is allowed to chew gum to help him focus. (Chewing gum gives some children the oral stimulation and movement their bodies need to concentrate on schoolwork or another quiet activity. Most schools do not allow gum chewing because of the potential mess—gum under tables and chairs, on the floor, and so on. Your child's school, however, may be open to "studying" the effect of letting kids chew gum during certain activities such as handwriting.)

Reducing anxiety in school

- Find out what your child's music, art, and gym teachers will be teaching. If you can't observe a class, at least meet them in their classrooms and give them some suggestions for problematic behaviors that might come up, such as regression or withdrawing as a result of auditory sensitivities. Latex or vinyl gloves may make paint and clay textures more tolerable. Earplugs can make the squeaking and echoing sounds in the gym less noxious. In the music room, your child may be able to sit in a part of the room where the acoustics don't bother him as much.

- Find out whether your child can eat lunch somewhere other than the loud cafeteria. Consider helping your school improve the lunchroom acoustics by slicing an X into tennis balls and squeezing them onto the bottom of table and bench legs.

- Learn the teacher's bathroom policy as soon as you can. Some may automatically limit every child's trips to the bathroom and your child may actually need to go more often. Or, your child may ask for extra bathroom visits because he needs a break from the classroom routine in order to remain focused. If so, discuss it with the teacher to prevent automatic limiting of bathroom breaks and to discuss other acceptable ways for your child to get away and regroup.

- Make a small scrapbook of your preschooler's favorite people and possessions at home that he can look at in school for comfort.

- Rather than relying on the old question "How was school today?" ask specific questions, such as, "What did you do in art class today?" "What vegetable did they serve for lunch?" Ask your child if he enjoyed the activity and whether he ate the green beans. You might be surprised by what you learn, because children will often push themselves out of their sensory comfort zone in school in order to fit in. You may also learn about a sensory challenge he didn't know how to handle well that he would not have mentioned otherwise. If he says, "I hate gym!" ask him what part of class he doesn't like: the sounds? How difficult it is for him to perform the skills? Was he uncomfortable with how the other children behaved?

- If you can't get to the bottom of what's causing your child anxiety in school, ask to sit in on her classes so that you can closely observe her.

- Read the entire school handbook at the beginning of the year and pay attention to the section on discipline and rule breaking. Discuss the rules and consequences with your child. If your child does receive a detention or is punished, keep an open mind as you get the story from your child, whoever assigned the punishment (the teacher, the playground supervisor, etc.), and whoever oversaw its implementation (for example, the school guidance counselor or assistant principal). If after getting the details, you feel the punishment was unfair given your child's issues, focus first on how to help him follow the rules next time. Then approach those who instituted the punishment to discuss how to prevent the problem in the future. Make sure your child feels he's been heard and respected and understands the seriousness of the infraction. For example, if your child threw snowballs because he forgot the rule and needed to do something calming and focusing before reentering the classroom, talk with him about ways he can get proprioceptive input without throwing snowballs which could injure someone. If your daughter lashed out physically when she was provoked by a classmate teasing her, work with the school psychologist or guidance counselor to help your child handle her frustration better and know what to do in this situation. Find out what your school's anti-bullying program is, learn more, and consider getting involved in improving it if you feel it isn't what it should be.

Assistive Technology

IDEA also requires schools to consider assistive technology (AT) for all children in special education, and to provide any devices and services a child requires in order to obtain a free and appropriate education. Both the Tech Act and IDEA define an AT *device* as "any item, piece of equipment, or product system (whether acquired commercially or off the shelf, modified or customized) that is used to increase, maintain, or improve the functional capabilities of a child with a disability." AT *services* are defined as "any service that directly assists a child with a disability in the selection, acquisition, or use of an assistive technology device." There is a huge variety of devices, equipment, modifications, and strategies that satisfy IDEA's definition of AT and are therefore eligible for funding through the schools.

Assistive technology can range from no tech to low tech to high tech. Take handwriting. No-tech solutions include environmental modifications and special teaching strategies. Low-tech devices include raised-line or other modified paper, tape recorders for taping lectures, electronic dictionaries and spellers (children with poor handwriting usually have even greater difficulty with spelling if they have to hand-write the words), slant boards to improve hand positioning, and pencil grips to improve grasp (there are several types of pencil grips, each de-signed to correct a different awkward grasp; see photo on page 399). High-tech devices include laptop and desktop computers, adapted key-boards, and specialized software including word prediction (such as Co:Writer), auditory feedback (such as Write:OutLoud), and graphic organizers (such as Kidspiration, Inspiration, or Draft:Builder). See Part Five's Sources for Useful Toys, Equipment, and Products for assis-tive technology resources.

Auditory issues also nicely illustrate the hierarchy of no-, low-, and high-tech solutions. A no-tech solution for a child easily distracted by auditory stimuli would be to seat the child away from auditory dis-tractions. A low-tech solution would be to have the child wear earplugs on the playground or in gym. A high-tech solution would be an FM unit (see page 303).

Ask your school district office for an assistive technology evalua-tion to determine whether AT would help your child at school. Most AT evaluators are OTs with advanced training on the wide variety of devices, equipments, and strategies out there, but some PTs and spe-cial ed teachers are also quite knowledgeable about AT. If your child has speech-language impairments, an SLP may recommend an aug-mentative communication device or system, often working with an OT who helps with access issues such as fine motor skills needed to operate the device. Ideally, you would simply request an AT evalua-tion, the school would purchase recommended devices and equip-ment, and these would be implemented at school, with someone training your child and anyone working with him on how to use the AT. However, some AT is quite expensive, and a school may have a tight AT budget and limited support staff. If you have difficulty get-ting the assistive technology and services recommended for your child, you can fight your school district for it, but also consider op-tions such as purchasing recommended devices yourself (especially inexpensive items like pencil grips); raising funds through the parent association or community organizations such as Rotary, Kiwanis, or Lions clubs; buying items on eBay or through classified ads in com-munity newspapers; or contacting foundations such as Easter Seals, the Masons, and the Starlight Children's Foundation for help.

Once your child receives her AT, make sure it is actually being used in school, and that your child and any adults working with her know how to use it. And make sure that assistive technology is included on your child's IEP. AT devices and needs change so make sure to keep IEP statements general. In other words, rather than having an IEP goal along the lines of: "Using her iBook computer and Kidspiration, Jenny will . . . ," make sure the school uses a more general AT statement such as, "Using assistive technology, Jenny will. . . ." This way, the IEP stays current even if the AT changes.

Marvin's Marvelous School Day

Marvin is a fifth grader who attends a general education class in a public school. In the morning, he hits the snooze button on his first alarm clock without thinking, but actually gets out of bed when the second alarm clock across the room goes off. He does his morning routine automatically by now, but still glances at his get-ready checklist to be sure. He gobbles down breakfast and puts on his backpack, which he double-checked last night to make sure he had everything he needs for the day. He loves riding his Razor Scooter to school, or even marching to school if it's snowy, because it really wakes him up.

At school, he pulls out his AlphaSmart, the portable word processor he uses for note taking, spelling tests, and writing essays. He's proud of his keyboarding skills, and his grades have improved now that he doesn't have to worry about keeping his notebooks organized or reading his own handwriting. Using his AlphaSmart's infrared system he can beam his plain text files into any computer program or print his work out by simply pressing a button. His teacher lets him distribute the worksheets, and if he needs to, he can take a short break in the hall to do some jumping jacks.

Lunchtime is pretty good this year. He belongs to the lunch club, a small group of fifth graders who eat together. While waiting to get his lunch, he rolls from his heels to his toes and back. He uses his special lunch mat so his dishes don't slide off the table. He likes drinking his thick yogurt drink through a straw, sucking hard. The kids eat quickly, because they want to get to the art class, where they help the kindergarteners with their art projects. It can get so noisy in there! Marvin always has his foam earplugs handy in case the roar gets to be too much. He wears his earplugs in gym class too. Good thing Mom found those seamless tube socks so they don't bother him when he runs. Last year, he was in APE (adapted physical education) because he kept getting overloaded. But now, between the soft clothes he can wear and the earplugs, he's doing okay in regular gym. The coach lets him take a break whenever he needs it—and even persuaded his mom to get him those totally cool fingerless gloves so he can grip the uneven bars without sliding or feeling that nasty surface.

When it's time to go home, Marvin checks the assignment file on his AlphaSmart. He has his science and math homework worksheets in his homework folder, and he just needs to grab his lab manual. He leaves the rest in his desk, which is still, amazingly, neat. He'll get his homework done without any help tonight, and earn his fifth star for the week. Just one more and he gets to play miniature golf this weekend!

Recommended Reading

Siegel, Lawrence. *The Complete IEP Guide: How to Advocate for Your Special Ed Child,* sixth edition. Berkeley, CA: Nolo Press, 2009. An invaluable resource that includes the entire text of IDEA, explains the law simply, and provides guidance on everything from how to write a letter requesting an IEP meeting to what to do when your child is denied services.

Wright, Peter W. D., and Pamela Darr Wright. *Wrightslaw: Special Education Law,* second edition. Hartfield, VA: Harbor House Law Press, 2007. This book provides an overview of special education law, including the latest U.S. Supreme Court decisions and practical information and tips.

CHAPTER 16

The Special Challenges for Teenagers

Even though theories about Sensory Processing Disorder in children have been around for more than thirty years, many professionals and parents simply were unaware of it until recently. No wonder many kids have reached adolescence without having sensory problems diagnosed. Many teens are referred to occupational therapy by teachers in the upper grades because their handwriting is still so bad that they can't turn in legible assignments, only to have the OT spot a long-standing, undiagnosed problem with sensory processing. Or perhaps the child has been in school for years and then happens to come across a savvy teacher or school psychologist who suspects that sensory issues underlie his apathetic or defiant behavior. Or perhaps you, as a parent, only recently learned about SPD and realized that it's something your child has always struggled with.

By now you know that people who receive help with their sensory issues can make great strides regardless of how old they are. However, teenagers with sensory problems, and their parents, face several special challenges.

The "Cool" Factor

A teen who has been struggling with sensory issues for years, without knowing why he is different from his peers or what is going on in his body, is likely to feel insecure. He doesn't want to seem weird or uncool in any way. As Michael, an adult with SPD, put it, "I saw my uniqueness as a terrible, unfair burden, something that made me feel as if I were some sort of freak. It was something I kept secret and hidden from everyone I knew. As a teenager, you're naturally trying to define yourself and trying to fit in. As I've gotten older, I have become very determined to fit into the world as comfortably as I can without worrying what other people think of me."

Of course, as a parent, you want to help your child overcome his sensory processing problems; but he probably gets prickly and defensive anytime you tell him what he needs to do, whether it's "You'd better start in on that English paper" or "You'd better do your therapeutic listening program because the OT said it would help you tolerate noise." If you've just discovered that your teenager has sensory processing disorder, you probably realize that you won't be able to simply set up OT sessions and sit back as your child eagerly dives in to this new regimen, taking responsibility for following through on whatever the OT asks him to do because it's good for him. But while it may be difficult at first to get your teenager to recognize the value of OT and sensory diet activities, and get past his self-consciousness about admitting that he needs help for some very real problems, at least he is much more adept at identifying how his body feels and articulating it than a very young child is. Still, you and his OT will need to be sensitive to his need to be in control of how he deals with his sensory issues.

Sensory Diet Activities Your Teen Will Consent To

It's very hard for most of us to admit that we're struggling and need help, but it's especially difficult for a vulnerable teenager trying to figure out who she is and how she fits in to the world. If your child has sensory issues that haven't been addressed before now, we can pretty much guarantee that while she may not have a term or explanation for them, she's fully aware of them. Your job is to work with an OT to explain to your child what is going on with her sensory system, and how she can help herself.

If your child sees an OT at a sensory gym, try to schedule your teenager for a time when younger kids aren't around to avoid making her feel embarrassed about doing activities that preschoolers or grade schoolers do. While at the sensory gym, the teen may notice lots of equipment that's way too small for her to use. Make sure your OT is sensitive to this, and brings larger teen-size equipment like trampolines into the forefront.

Steven Kane, an occupational therapist who works with high school students, engages teens in Brain Gym, a program that uses movement to help the body reorganize itself neurologically and doesn't require any special equipment. Brain Gym activities include things like drawing Lazy 8's in the air (figure eights drawn sideways like the infinity symbol), Cross-Crawl (an activity that coordinates both sides of the body), muscle lengthening exercises, and other movements most kids really enjoy. To motivate the teenagers to try it, he starts with something that personally excites them. If football interests a student, he'll relate everything to football, saying, "We're going work on your eye movements now because you need to see the whole field when you throw the ball." Afterward, he'll say, "Let's see if that activity has helped you throw the ball."

Sometimes OTs can even make "uncool" activities seem cool just because of their own confidence. OT Claudia Meyer plays focusing music for the high schoolers she works with during their sessions, but because the music (from the Alert Program) is intended for preschoolers, she jokingly refers to it as "Mrs. Meyer's Goofy Music." Rolling their eyes, the teens laugh and go along with it, as well as with her admittedly goofy suggestions like sitting on a therapy ball or T-stool while talking to her, only to discover that there's something in her ideas that help them focus and feel more at ease in their bodies.

When working with your teenager to address his sensory issues, make it a partnership. As Meyer explains, "I say to the teens I work with, 'You need to tell me if you think this is helping. Let's see how this feels, but you tell me how you think you're doing.' " Jerry Lindquist, Ph.D., OTR, says, "I think it's really essential to use a psychosocial model to educate kids about the problem so they can make their own choices about what to do. An adolescent may want to wear some fashionable piece of clothing but may find it too difficult and then feel bad, isolated, and rejected. Really understanding the reasons for why something is so hard helps them accept the situation and consider some new strategies."

Many teenagers have already figured out that certain activities help them feel less bothered by their surroundings, or less restless. Try to help them identify these activities and why they work so well, and figure out ways to incorporate them into daily life. For instance, if a teenager can't walk or ride a bike or scooter to school, brainstorm with him about other ways that he can get that movement and deep pressure before class starts. During the school day, teenagers can brush themselves in a bathroom stall as part of their tactile desensitization program, or listen to calming music on headphones (you may have to check with the school about the policy on headphones). After school, your teenager may find martial arts, gymnastics, dance, or swimming provides the input she needs to be more coordinated and comfortable in her body.

By this point in their lives, many teenagers are acutely aware of what they are not good at and will find all sorts of ways to get out of any embarrassing situations. Don't mistake this for an outright rejection of doing something peers are doing. Your "clumsy" teenager might yearn to play tennis or take ballet, but may require private lessons rather than group lessons to avoid public humiliation. Helping a teenager discover what is going on with his body and what to do about it isn't always easy. Occupational therapist Paula McCreedy, of New York City–based SPOTS (Special Programs in Occupational Therapy Services), notes that adolescents usually don't want to pay attention to their sensory problems. "Teens always feel like they have an audience anyway, and then you're asking them to become vigilant about watching themselves," says McCreedy. "It can be very embarrassing. So be sure you and your OT help motivate your child to do those sensory diet activities and make sure they aren't too intrusive and damaging to his self-esteem."

A lot of teenagers are open to doing therapeutic listening programs for auditory processing problems because it's socially acceptable to walk around wearing headphones at this age, as occupational therapist Lindsay Koss points out. "Another one is swimming," she says. "A lot of kids will get into swimming because they get proprioceptive and tactile input through their skin. Girls especially love gymnastics because there's a lot of jumping, bouncing, tumbling, and flipping."

Teens with sensory issues may find it fulfilling to work with animals, whether it's helping out at a horse stable, tending to farm animals, or caring for family pets. This is probably due to the nonjudgmental, unconditional love and often irresistible sensory delights animals offer.

Martial arts are another good option. Says Michael, an adult with SPD, "I joined a Tae Kwon Do school, and spent the next several years doing it. It was a huge struggle, as I was a klutz and had a difficult time memorizing all the moves. It made me really aware of my own body in relation to objects, to do controlled movements and choosing to actually connect or not with something or somebody. While I didn't become a Jackie Chan, I made huge strides in my body awareness, and found that the highly structured classes worked liked therapy to help me avoid sensory overload." Other teenagers may enjoy working out with free weights or on exercise equipment, biking, or bowling, all of which involve proprioceptive input. Hobbies such as cooking and doing arts and crafts, scrapbooking, woodworking, or quilting can give great sensory input while helping a teen express herself creatively. Mastery of any skill—from playing drums to making handicrafts to building a great Web site—boosts self-esteem.

Socialization

Delia, who has never had OT for her sensory issues, says that even as an adult she still doesn't like to be touched unless she initiates it, and is sensitive to light and noise. As a teen, she spent a lot of time reading and working in a library rather than socializing. In school, "The hallways and changing classes were awful. People were always bumping into me. I used to try to sit in the seat closest to the door so as soon as the bell rang I could dash out and run to the next class . . . or I'd be late for class because I would weave in and out of the crowd, trying not to be touched." Chandra, a college student, had a similar experience, and adds, "I'm *incredibly* sound sensitive, which makes most social situations really overwhelming. I can't do concerts or parties because between the sounds and the lights I'm shut down within half an hour. Anywhere crowded isn't an option because of the whole don't-touch-me-without-warning-me thing, too. My coping skill in school is to find a *quiet* group of friends. We don't do loud parties. We sit around in people's basements or outside and talk, or run around and play Ultimate Frisbee or whatever. I love the exercise when we do that. Walks are good too. I just had to get dreams of hanging with the popular crowd out of my head."

If your teenager has trouble with overloading around large groups of kids, consider getting him involved in activities where he won't be constantly pressured to be a part of a group or, worse, part of a group of kids competing against one another. Many teens do well with scouting, for instance, which incorporates activities involving the whole troop, smaller groups, or just the individual. A local clinic or community center may offer a social skills group for teens with Asperger's, autism, or nonverbal learning disorder.

Another reason teens with sensory processing issues can have trouble socializing is because they may be immature. Remember, we learn through our senses, so even if a child doesn't have noticeable developmental delays that set off alarms for parents, he may very well have subtle emotional and behavioral delays. Teens with sensory processing disorder may have gotten by for years cleverly avoiding the very activities that would help them develop certain skills, including emotional ones. It's common for kids with SPD who are less mature than their peers to "own it" by acting as if they don't care that anyone thinks they're strange, which is a useful coping method if you can't control the behaviors that cause the other kids to judge you.

One challenge, common to all parents of teenagers, is that their teens are still in between child-like thinking processes and adult ones, so they may not fully grasp the consequences of their risky behaviors. But for a child who is insecure emotionally, uncomfortable in his body, and seeking sensations that will help him feel better, drugs and alcohol, piercing and tattoos, and driving quickly or doing dangerous stunts with bikes and skateboards can be especially appealing. Helping your teenager find positive ways of getting the sensory input he needs, and coping with distressing sensory input, will go a long way toward preventing negative behaviors.

WHO AM I?

At twenty-one, Chandra, who has sensory processing disorder and Asperger's syndrome, offers this advice to teenagers with SPD: "*Be who you are.* I know, it's a pain in the neck, because everyone else can handle this input or get by without that input and you can't, but you are who you are. Find a way to use it as a strength, if at all possible. Be creative. Remember, you are perfect just the way you are . . . and if you decide to work on one issue, and it helps, you are still perfect, as long as you don't let the core of *you* change. I know self-esteem is a big thing when you feel different, but don't change for anyone but yourself. I've been there, and it really isn't worth it."

Changing Bodies

If typical teenagers have trouble adjusting to their changing bodies, adolescents with sensory issues have an exceptionally challenging time. In addition to hormonal changes causing stress, teenagers with sensory issues have to deal with slimy topical creams to treat pimples, gloppy shaving cream, wet and sticky deodorants, and uncomfortably bulky and scratchy sanitary pads that can drive them nutty. A teenage girl might struggle between the social pressure to put a layer of makeup on her face and her own physical comfort. Wearing the extratight or extrabaggy clothes popular among peers might be too much hassle for a teenager who would rather suffer ridicule than tolerate the latest style. An understanding parent or OT can help teenagers find creative solutions, from perfume-free cosmetics to spray-on deodorant, tampons, Lycra bicycle shorts worn under baggy clothing (for boys or girls), to all-cotton sports bras or tagless underwear (see Chapter 7: Practical Solutions for Everyday Sensory Problems for some teen-saving ideas).

Driving

America is a car culture, and many teenagers can't wait for the day when they can get behind the wheel. For a kid with sensory issues, however, even if he craves the independence associated with it, the thought of driving can be terrifying. Visual and auditory processing problems can make it extremely difficult to concentrate, particularly if there is any noise coming from the passengers, radio, engine, or outside the windows. Vestibular issues can disorient teenage drivers too: it's hard enough to remember which direction you're facing when you have to change classes at school, but it's far more nerve-wracking to make sense of where you are in relation to traffic and lanes when you're in a fast-moving car.

If your teenager resists driving, encourage him to start slow, and don't pressure him to get that license. Have him begin with just a drive around the corner or in an empty parking lot. With helpful sensory input from the wind, movement, and proprioceptive input of pushing the pedals, bike riding, particularly in low-traffic areas, could help your teenager get accustomed to handling traffic and lane changes *before* he does it in a car. Other teens may require extra lessons and practice time to get comfortable behind a car wheel. For some teens with auditory processing problems, booming music can help block out background noise and increase focus better—but make sure it's not distracting him or too loud for him to hear what's happening on the road.

See Chapter 7: Practical Solutions for Everyday Sensory Problems for driving tips.

Eating

As we discussed in Chapter 10: Improving Speech Skills and Picky Eating, eating is a very sensory activity. Picky eating among young children is grudgingly accepted in our culture as pretty much normal, even if some people pressure their kids to "eat what's on your plate or starve." By the time your child is a teenager, she will face even more social disapproval if her eating habits are different. Your teenager may become so anxious about having to eat popular foods in front of her peers or judgmental adults that she avoids social engagements that would require her to do so. She may feel really uncomfortable trying to sit up straight at the table because of low tone, or have difficulty with the motor planning involved in breathing, chewing, swallowing, and carrying on a conversation, and be ashamed about it. Or she may know that she still ends up with food on her face, tends to spill her beverage, or awkwardly handles eating utensils, but she's defensive about working on these challenges. If this is the case, occupational therapist Prudence Heisler from SPOTS advises you to remember, "There's no quick solution. You have to make compromises—does it really matter if they eat with their fork? Make a list of priorities. If you want to work on improving table manners, concentrate on breakfast rather than meals at night when your kid is tired and has homework. Don't make a big deal about it and try serving a simpler meal to make things easier."

College and Career Plans

Looking ahead, both you and your teenager probably feel an equal mix of excitement and trepidation about the day high school ends and the next phase begins. This is an unsettling time for every parent and child, and probably more so for you and your child with SI dysfunction. By the time you send your child out of the nest to begin his adult life, he will, hopefully, have the tools and sensory smarts he needs to tackle any remaining sensory issues.

Every parent wishes she could protect her baby forever, and the best way you can do that is to have faith in your child's ability to master his own destiny—and equip him with whatever he needs to do this while providing love and support wherever he goes!

If your child has been receiving services in school, by law, he should have had transition services from age fourteen on. His IEP should include strategies for helping him to assess his interests and to get information about potential jobs, higher education, living independently, functioning as a member of a community, etc. If your child does not receive any services at school, an OT knowledgeable about transition planning can be a big help. In any case, you may need to help your child make some decisions about his future—ones that accommodate his sensory issues as well as his dreams. By now, you and your child probably have a pretty good handle on what sensory issues may get in the way in which particular situations—and what role they make take in planning for the future.

CHAPTER 17

Empowering Your Child in the World

As your child grows up, she will have to develop her own sensory smarts and take responsibility for meeting her needs. She will also have to learn how to handle herself in situations where other people treat her differences with disrespect and even meanness. As a parent, you want to protect your child from ever being hurt, but we all know that's not realistic. What you can do, however, is show her through your words and actions that she is a lovable person worthy of respect, and explain to her that there are people who, because of problems of their own, may not treat her kindly—*and it has nothing to do with her.*

So how can you reinforce your child's sense of self-esteem? First, you can help her to understand and accept herself as she is, reminding her in a variety of ways that being different can be a wonderful gift. Second, you can respect her growing independence. Finally, of course, you'll need to teach her what she can do when others don't respect her.

TALKING TO YOUR CHILD ABOUT SENSORY PROCESSING DISORDER

Figuring out how to talk to your child about SPD and the therapy he receives depends on his maturity level, how aware he is about his difficulties, and the nature of his sensory issues. A toddler or preschooler will likely be satisfied with being told that he is going to play with a new friend (the OT) who has special toys. A child in an early intervention or special ed preschool will probably see that his classmates are at many different stages of development, and with so many children working with therapists, being pulled out of class, and getting special accommodations he may assume this is the norm.

As your child gets older, however, he may begin to notice things are harder for him than for his siblings or other children at school. He may notice that his younger brother, for example, can easily ride a tricycle or put on his coat. At preschool or school, he may notice that other children do not seem to be bothered by a lot of noise or need to be constantly told to sit still during story time.

Some children are extremely aware of differences. Once a child begins to compare herself with other children, she may begin to wonder whether something is wrong with her. Why does Sara get to have playdates after school, but I have to go to the sensory gym? By giving her simple, direct information, you can prevent her from concluding that she is weird, stupid, lazy, or bad. How you do that depends on her level of sophistication.

A child who is aware of her differentness may already have a vocabulary about her sensory experiences that you can work with: she might say that she feels tired, or wired, and that certain activities make her feel more "together." You can explain that working her joints and muscles is what makes her feel more "together" after riding her bike, and that you'd like to help her find more ways she can get that feeling throughout the day.

Whatever your child's age, be honest with him. Children have built-in dishonesty detectors, so don't tell your child, "You play with Lana [the OT] because she likes to play with certain kids." Tell him, "Lana's job is to help you get strong [or less bothered by noise, etc.]." If you can agree with your child on what tasks he finds difficult, he will be more motivated and cooperative during therapy and any therapeutic homework. For example, if your child understands that he is tactile defensive around his mouth, he will be more able to tolerate desensitizing touch input on his jaws and lips knowing it will help him become better able to blow bubbles from that teddy bear bubble toy. He will be more willing to do hand strengthening exercises that he dislikes if he knows it will help him use scissors better. If you talk to your child honestly, your child will feel understood.

Remember that a child may not realize that she feels things differently from any other kid. Or if she does realize it, she may be extremely relieved to know that someone understands and knows a lot of other kids who have the same kind of experiences. Once sensory processing disorder is explained to her, instead of telling herself, "I can't do such-and-such because I'm dumb," a child can tell herself, "My body is very sensitive and picks up too many sights and sounds and this gets in my way. I am teaching my body to ignore the sights and sounds that bug me." If you're uncomfortable raising the subject of sensory issues because your child is touchy, try bringing it up while doing a fun, low-pressure activity, whether it's going on a walk in the woods, kicking a ball around, or preparing a meal together.

Says Chandra, a college student with SPD, "I wish that I had known that I had SPD back when I was in kindergarten, because that was when it was really obvious to me that what was easy for the other kids—coloring, cutting, learning to write, skipping, etc.—was hard for me, and what was hard for the other kids—reading, memorizing facts—was easy for me. My parents didn't know either, though. I wish they could have sat me down and said, 'Chandra, we know you are very smart and have noticed that the other kids in your class can't read like you can, but they can color and cut much more easily. They have an easier time making friends, but you have an easier time learning. You don't get dizzy, but they don't suddenly fall out of their chairs (I had mixed tone so I tended to fall out of my chair). Some sounds and touches are too much for you, but the other kids don't mind. That's because you have something called sensory integration dysfunction and autism. That means that your brain works differently. It isn't better or worse, it is just different. And there are ways to make the world more comfortable for you. Would you like to try them?'"

Beth's sensory seeking six-year-old has low muscle tone which affects his entire body. Since he is underresponsive to tactile, proprioceptive, and vestibular input, he constantly seeks out sensory input so he can feel things more accurately. Her son is quite interested in how things like his body work: "Basically," Beth explains, "I told Mike his brain was like a big computer, sending out messages all over his body. These messages make him sit up, run, speak, hold things, throw, catch. The problem is the messages aren't loud enough, aren't strong enough to be received and understood. So while the computer [pointing to his head] works very well and the machine [pointing to his body] works well, somewhere in between the connection gets lost.

"He asked me if he had a disease. I told him no, it's more like a condition, like me having trouble seeing without glasses. And just like I have glasses to help me see, he can have help as well. I explained therapy would go over the connections again and again to make them stronger. That we would reprogram the computer to make it work more quickly and efficiently. He really liked the idea of reprogramming his brain himself."

If your child is a sensory seeker, you might tell him, "Your body has a lot of energy, and you like to do a lot of things. It's like a really fast racing car. A race car driver needs to take his foot off the gas and hit the brakes sometimes so he can slow down. I'm going to help you slow down your body when you need to." Analogies can be really helpful, especially at a young age. You might ask your young child whether he feels like high-energy Tigger or low-energy Eeyore to give him words to express his alertness level. Other children are old enough to understand the basics of sensory processing disorder, and even terms like *vestibular* and *proprioceptive*. In fact, one mom said that her six-year-old son asked his aunt if he could crush some boxes she was throwing away and, as he gleefully stomped on them, announced, "This is great proprioceptive input!"

Getting Your Child to "Buy In"

When Lindsey talks to a child about his sensory issues and developmental delays, she always starts off by detailing his strengths. For example, she might say, "You are a very nice, smart, wonderful boy, and you're really good at drawing, building things, being nice to your cat, and telling funny jokes. Your hearing is very good—too good! Your ears hear more than mine. Do sounds bother you sometimes? We're going to help your ears feel more comfortable." When discussing weaknesses, she keeps it very specific: "It's hard for you to get your eyes and hands to work together to catch a ball," or, "It seems like you're uncomfortable when there's a lot of noise and kids running around, like in gym class."

It's important to tell older children what an OT or other therapist (such as an SLP) does. Your school-age child may associate the term *occupational therapist* with the person at school who helps Jackie in the wheelchair. For preschoolers, Lindsey often explains that while she is called an occupational therapist, she is more like a teacher, who can make a child better at hopping, or teach kids to have fun taking a bath. An older child or teenager may associate the term *therapist* with the psychotherapist her "nutty" Uncle Ned sees and think that if she sees a therapist it means she's "nutty" too. Lindsey finds that older children and teenagers are amenable to a brief definition of occupational therapy and then referring to her as an "OT" (never "therapist") or even a sensory teacher. An easy definition you can give an older child is that an OT is really good at helping kids with hard things such as handling noisy places, or dealing with clothing that bothers you, or sitting still in class for a long time, or handwriting (give your child an example of something he personally finds difficult).

It's essential for a preteen or teenager to "buy in" to the concept of getting help. When they meet, Lindsey might have a child do something difficult, like walking heel-to-toe a few feet or writing a few sentences, and then ask how he feels about how he did it, and whether he'd like to do it even better. Then she explains that she knows a lot of tricks that have helped other kids his age. Kids seem to really respond to the term *tricks*—it's not that something's impossible to do, it's just that you need to know some special tricks to be more successful. Instead of saying, for example, that a child isn't strong, she'll say, "Well, you're pretty strong, but I know some ways to help you be even stronger." She may even confess to being unable to do certain things herself (such as hitting a baseball with a bat or stopping when she's ice-skating without crashing into a wall or another person) to show she's got some weaknesses too—and share her genuine wish that someone had taught *her* some tricks. The child may then be able to show *her* a few tricks, which empowers him and makes him more open to finding out about *her* tricks.

As a parent, you can share some of your own weaknesses with your child to help reduce his feelings of isolation and embarrassment about needing some help. If you're willing, you could model how to face and overcome your inabilities—such as finally learning how to repair a broken faucet or how to swim—to show your child that it can be done and that you refuse to let your embarrassment stop you. And, of course, if you learn new things together it will really seal the deal.

Me and My Shadow

As a parent, perhaps you have sensory issues of your own, which makes you more understanding of your child's sensory issues. You might also find yourself wishing you could "fix" your child, remembering how hard it was to be different when you were growing up. Michelle laughs when she recalls that when her son's OT asked if tags bothered him, "I said I didn't know because I automatically cut them out! I just assumed that everyone is tortured by them." And yet, she admits, "His sensitivities are different from mine: he has trouble with movement and noise, while I'm tactile defensive."

If you have sensory issues yourself, keep in mind that sensory problems manifest differently in every person, and they can even differ from day to day. Maybe your child really is ready to be pushed to the next level of tolerance and try those lima beans Grandpa put on his plate even if *you* think they're so slimy no human should be encouraged to eat them. Maybe he's never going to enjoy playing basketball like the rest of the kids in the neighborhood, but maybe, unlike you, he's not going to care because he'll be too busy becoming the local chess champion, cheered on by his understanding and accepting parents. And most important, keep in mind that unlike you, your child is going to learn about his sensory issues when he's still young, and he's going to get OT and any other therapies he needs.

EXPLAINING SENSORY PROCESSING DISORDER TO FAMILY AND FRIENDS

People who spend a lot of time around your child, including your spouse, your child's siblings, close family members, teachers, and caretakers, need to be educated about SPD. Some will be open to reading an entire book, or at least parts of a book that you photocopy, highlight, or bookmark. You might even want to jot your own comments on the material, such as, "This is why Marisol often licks objects or puts them in her mouth," or, "This activity works especially well to perk up Bradley when he seems sluggish." Other people will respond better to reading smaller amounts of material: a Web site that details one aspect of sensory processing disorder, along with the simple explanation that SPD has a neurological basis and manifests in many ways, might be all they can digest. Still others are best approached with simple, verbal explanations.

Yet another way to help people better understand your child's sensory behavior is for them to spend more time around him. If they and you observe your child engaging in an adaptive behavior—like putting in earplugs or pressing against the wall for deep pressure in a noisy restaurant vestibule—point it out to them when your child is not within earshot: "Seth is so hypersensitive to sound that background noise can make him feel very anxious and upset, so we always keep earplugs handy."

Your Spouse or Partner

There are increasing numbers of fathers who provide a great deal of the parenting—or even *all* of the parenting as a single dad or a member of a same-sex couple. It may well be the dad who searches for answers to the child's difficulties. However, for the sake of simplicity, let's assume that it's the mom who is the primary caregiver for the child with sensory problems. Many moms report that they have an easier time than their husbands do accepting the sensory processing disorder diagnosis and the need for a sensory diet and accommodations because, as the primary caregivers, they are more in tune with the child's sensory issues. The same likely holds true for a parent of either gender who is the primary caregiver. Often, it's attending OT sessions and discussing sensory challenges with the OT that helps a dad to accept that there's something "wrong" with his child—something that he can help address. Generally speaking, dads love to engage and challenge their kids more physically than moms do. A father who observes that certain types of play actually help calm and focus his child learns firsthand that a sensory diet contributes to a child's ability to regulate his nervous system. Encourage Dad to spot his child on the mini-trampoline. Have him bathe your two-year-old with you as you point out, "I've noticed that Samantha really responds best to having her hair washed if I press down on her head a few times before scrubbing, and I dump a big cup of water over her head to wet her hair," and then have your husband do it on his own the next time.

Be willing to accept that he may do things his own way instead of your tried-and-proven method. Be sure to avoid excluding him from the process of learning what helps the child, even if he bumbles and fumbles and totally blows it several times. Certainly, share what you find works, but avoid making him feel incompetent and unable to develop his own, special bond with the child. Dr. Kyle Pruett, author of *Fatherneed,* explains that mothers and fathers parent differently. They naturally do different things with their children, and children respond differently to each one. So your husband may well come up with a certain technique that works just for him. You may ask yourself, "Why will Jacob brush his teeth without a big fuss when Dad does it with him?" Perhaps Dad uses a deeper, lower tone of voice to clearly and firmly talk him through the steps. In all, one of the jobs of the primary caregiver is to help the secondary caregiver develop a healthy, happy relationship with the child.

Get your spouse or partner involved. One dad who was handy around the house installed dimmer switches in every room so that his son could avoid overly bright light. If your significant other resists talking about your child's challenges, then mention your child's improvements and what is working for her. If he resists the SPD label, then don't use it unnecessarily. Remind him that your child is wired differently and that when she gets certain types of input, her nervous system is better able to tolerate sensations and she's better able to stop inappropriate seeking or avoiding behaviors.

Siblings

Kids with sensory processing disorder need a lot of attention. You may have to take them to therapy sessions and spend extra time with them working on their developmental delays. You will definitely have to give them extra attention, comfort, and time during transitions, and do sensory diet activities with them. It's only natural for your other children to feel resentful that you're not giving them as much time and attention.

Since many sensory diet activities lend themselves to involving more than one child, you might be able to get them all to participate. Encourage all the kids to play in the big ball pit you've set up in the basement. Have your older children design a fun, challenging obstacle course that they, along with your younger child with motor planning problems, can climb, run, and crawl through. Garden, cook, or splash around in a pool together as a family. Just be sure that you give your other children the one-on-one attention they need as well, or you'll end up spending extra time resolving sibling squabbles anyway. *Siblings Without Rivalry* by Adele Faber and Elaine Mazlish is an excellent book for advice on how to keep the peace among brothers and sisters.

Handling Insensitive Comments from Family and Friends

Family members may or may not be willing to open their minds to the idea that your child's behavior stems from sensory challenges and/or related delays. You can try to educate them, but in the end, you may have to accept that some people just won't get it and you will have to do what you can to protect your child from their comments. Lisa, who had her son evaluated for developmental delays because of his frequent, intense tantrums, says, "I got so much criticism in the beginning. People mostly would rather believe my son's behavior is due to bad parenting than accept that something is wrong with him. I tried to educate those around me and when that didn't work, I became angry with them. That made most of them back off, or at least think before speaking. I think most of our family came around because he kept getting older and wasn't outgrowing his behavior."

What if you've already done your best to explain that your child has sensory issues, but stubborn Uncle Steve says to your son, "You're five years old and you can't tie your own shoes? What's the matter with you?" You could say something like, "He's working on it, and we're always so proud of him for doing his best!" Or, tell your child, "Don't pay any attention to Uncle Steve, he doesn't know much about children." When your son is not present you can explain to Uncle Steve why his comment was inappropriate and unappreciated.

Handling Insensitive Comments from Strangers

While all parents have to put up with unsolicited advice from other people at some time, the general lack of awareness about SPD and how it manifests often results in your getting an extra dose of "you shoulds" from well-meaning—and not-so-well-meaning—folks. Your child may also get scoldings and angry looks from people who just don't get it. Some people will not understand or accept the hidden problem of sensory integration dysfunction, and might even scoff at the very concept because it's unfamiliar, saying, "I don't buy all these new labels and syndromes."

Unfortunately, too many people don't give credence to neurobiological reasons for behavior, so they automatically assume a child is behaving inappropriately because he's had bad parenting, or worse, because he is "a bad kid." Even if your child has a related condition that has been in the news more often, such as ADHD or autism, you may find that some people have preconceived notions about these conditions and their inclination is to lecture you on why your child is behaving the way she is and what to do about it.

These situations can be extremely frustrating. Our advice is, when your child acts inappropriately in public, deal with his immediate needs, discipline him if necessary, apologize if he harms someone, clean up the store display he knocked over, and don't feel you have to take the time to explain or defend yourself or your child to strangers. You might be tempted to retort, "At least my child is getting help for his underlying neurological problems, are you getting help for your rudeness?" or handing them a preprinted card (such as the ones sold through autism Web sites) that explains your child's diagnosis. But maybe you don't want to teach your son or daughter that people on the street who are rude and judgmental deserve a response at all. Ignoring them might actually feel more empowering. On the other hand, if you feel this is a great opportunity for teaching your child how to advocate for himself, you might say something along the lines of "Lauren has sensory issues that make it hard for her to tolerate certain difficult situations and unpleasant people."

The clerk at the shoe store needs to hear nothing more than "Sorry about the screaming—he has an extremely difficult time tolerating shoes," but the Sunday school nursery director, the karate instructor, and your relatives are a different story. To them, you might simply say something like "Madison has something called sensory integration dysfunction, which means that her nervous system is wired a little differently so you might see her exhibit behaviors that seem a little unusual. If she gets very wound up, just remind her that she should shuffle her feet or jump in place." As your child gets better able to seek out the input she needs appropriately, or to ask for it from the people who are in authority ("Could I please go to a quiet area to regroup? I'm a little overwhelmed by all the noise and movement right now."), you won't have to monitor her or explain her behavior as often.

Teasing and Bullying

Teasing may seem like kid's play to the perpetrators, and even to some adults, but it can become serious business. Any child who is different in any way is a potential target: Nancy remembers a girl in her grade school who was tormented for having the initials B.M., and another girl who was cruelly teased just because she had red hair. Children without friends are also more likely to be teased or bullied. Of course, as a parent, your heart drops into your stomach at the thought of someone being mean to your child. It may happen at some point, but by talking honestly with your child and helping her to feel good about herself, you can help her to see the bullies for the insecure kids they are, and to dismiss their comments.

Standing up and answering tormenters with a retort as simple as "Yeah, so what?" or "Tell it to the hand 'cause the face ain't listening" can often defuse teasing. A sense of humor can be an effective tool for silencing teasers, and an appointed older child who acts as a "buddy" can often convince bullies to back off just by his presence. But sometimes the behavior goes beyond ugly words and escalates to threats—in person and on Web sites and in e-mails—and even physical intimidation and violence. You may have to get assertive with the school to make sure they follow through on their policy of no tolerance toward bullying with practical, proven-effective steps to stop it. Ultimately, bullying is a community problem, not an individual one.

Nancy's—and George's—Story

As in many families, in ours school meetings and doctors' appointments are Mom's department. But early on my husband, George, and I realized that he could play a very important role in Cole's therapeutic goals by taking on playground duty and overseeing playdates. We fell into these roles because it made sense for who we are: I'm good at communicating and coordinating, and exchanging and researching information online. George is a very physical, extroverted person who enjoys biking to the park with Cole in tow, engaging with whoever is at the playground that day, and challenging Cole to walk on a retaining wall or make it all the way across the monkey bars.

George first truly grasped the importance of his role when Cole was three and his teacher telephoned to say that she'd seen enormous improvements in Cole's ability to focus and self-regulate his energy level—just what were we doing at home? The answer was that George, who runs a home business and has very flexible hours, had begun regularly taking Cole to the park, deliberately riding over a bumpy cobblestone surface (which Cole begged him to do), and spending hours dashing through sprinklers, jumping and running in circles, climbing and hanging, sliding, and digging in the sandbox. All of this provided an enormous amount of tactile, vestibular, and proprioceptive input.

While George was at the park, he and Cole also began to meet other kids and parents, and George started to set up playdates. During play times that George supervised, he helped Cole learn and practice important skills like playing cooperatively and imaginatively, and sharing. He taught Cole what to do when another child bops him over the head and takes his toy away, and how to start a game of tag with a child you've never met before (Cole's instinct was to slap the child hard on the back and flash a smile).

George and I are comfortable in our different roles, and we are flexible about them; there are times when I take Cole to a birthday party or George takes him to the doctor. To keep each other up on what's happening, we've developed the habit of exchanging information over breakfast after Cole goes to school. We both feel confident that our contribution is important, and we are grateful that we've got a partner who can take over the duties that we're less comfortable with.

This may sound idyllic, but the reality is that raising Cole takes a lot of time and energy. George and I both tend to forget to nurture ourselves and we have to work at remembering how important it is for both of us to get a break. I love to go to movies alone, or go out for dinner with a girlfriend, or play guitar, while George loves to go see a live band perform, or retreat to his art and music studio to create. And, of course, we need couple's time too. These breaks are important for the mental health of our whole family.

The more stressed out or resentful either parent gets, the harder it is on everyone. And while we'd love to have a well-organized, spiffy clean apartment at all times, and get photo reprints off to Grandma promptly, we know that chores eat up energy we'd rather use to deal with Cole's needs and our own, so we often let these types of things slide. As time goes on and Cole makes progress, maturing and becoming more independent and responsible for meeting his own needs while helping out around the house, it really does get easier. Meanwhile, we choose to let certain tasks linger at the bottom of the to-do list indefinitely and, when necessary, we hire a college student who helps us straighten up our apartment, or we ask favors of whoever else can help us out with certain tasks that never seem to get done.

Addressing Social Difficulties

Some kids with SPD have problems socially due to their sensory issues or related conditions. A child with auditory processing problems might think he needs to put his face right up to another child's and speak very loudly because he is having so much difficulty blocking out the background noise on the playground or in the schoolroom that he doesn't realize the other kid can hear him perfectly well if he keeps his distance and speaks in a normal tone of voice. A child may not understand why "Do you know how many species of beetles there are?" is usually not a great conversation starter.

How do you help kids to understand what is appropriate social behavior? One way is to tell them a "social" story: a little tale you make up about another child in the same situation, that illustrates social cues, typical responses, and solutions to problems. Carol Gray, a consultant to families with children on the autism spectrum, has written several books and created a video on how to use this method.

Other kids might find it easier to talk about their social problems, and identify what's not working for them, if they see their situation played out in a fictional way. In his book *Playful Parenting,* child psychologist Lawrence J. Cohen describes how parents can use play scenarios to reconnect with their kids and help them work through their social anxieties. Also, you can do cinematherapy and bibliotherapy with your child by watching movies together and reading books that help children access, identify, and work through their difficult feelings in a safe way. Ask your child how she thinks Dumbo feels when he's ridiculed for his big ears, or talk about how Stellaluna feels about being the only creature in the nest who wants to hang upside down. Read to them and discuss books such as *We Eat Dinner in the Bathtub* by Angela Shelf Medearis or *It's Okay to be Different* by Todd Parr.

CONNECTING WITH A SUPPORTIVE COMMUNITY

You might be surprised at the people who will be supportive and accepting of you and your child: the parents we interviewed told us about wonderful schoolteachers, martial arts instructors, music teachers, and even clothing salespeople who readily accepted their child's sensory differences and were eager to accommodate them. You might be surprised at the second cousin who, upon hearing you say that your child is in a special ed preschool at age two, gives you kudos for being a wonderful parent—and says she wishes she'd gotten help for her learning disability years ago.

But on a day-to-day basis, for all that good friends and loving family members can be supportive, it can also be very helpful to communicate with other parents of children with sensory issues.

Support Groups

Support groups are a forum for exchanging information as well as offering and receiving advice and tips. They're a place where people can talk about difficult feelings with other parents who really do understand what you're going through.

If you can find or start a local support group, you will benefit from being able to do all these things in person and you might even end up socializing with other members outside of the group (and we'll bet you won't be taking all your kids to Chuck E. Cheese or the chlorinated indoor pool on a busy Saturday!). You might be able to locate a local support group through SPD Parent Connections, e-mail: SPDNational@KIDFoundation.org or www.SPDnetwork.org/parentconnection/. You can start your own support group by putting up a flyer in your child's special ed preschool, or asking your child's OT to let other parents know you're interested in starting a support group for kids with sensory challenges, or asking the speech-language pathologist to let others know you're starting a support group for parents of late talkers.

In addition, you can consider joining an online support group. These groups let you connect with parents all over the world who are also dealing with kids who have sensory issues, while remaining anonymous. Says Delia, "I started looking on Yahoo groups (www .yahoogroups.com) and the SID (Sensory Integration Dysfunction) list was the first list I ever joined. It was so amazing because I sat there for the first two days and read all the posts thinking, this is unbelievable! This is everything I've been going through! The SID list has been the biggest eye-opener to me, and the biggest help, because from there I found links and information. Now, I don't think I could live without my e-mail loops because that's where a lot of my support comes from."

THE SENSORY SMART CHILD GROWS UP

Every parent of a child with sensory issues wonders what the future holds. Will he always be the victim of his senses? Will she become more comfortable in her body? The truth is, it's impossible for any parent to know what his or her child will be like as an adult. But we can tell you that the sensory smart child of sensory smart parents is a person who is empowered to take responsibility for himself, for his body, and for his behavior. That's an outstanding quality any parent would be proud to see in a child. Many children do outgrow their strong reactions to sensory input, particularly if they've had effective therapy and strong family support.

Others learn to use their sensory issues in a positive way. Says Chandra, a young adult with SPD and Asperger's syndrome, "For work I teach tumbling, which is *heaven* for a vestibular and proprioceptive seeker. I get to *demonstrate*! I also work with autistic kids, since I was one myself. My big thing that I do at the in-home program I work in involves sensory stuff, because *my* sensory issues are such a big part of my life. We have a grand old time, playing on the teeter-totter, or creatively with a ball or a balance beam. I use my disability as a strength, because it's not going to go away."

Regardless of whether your child perceives her sensory issues as a disability or just a part of who she is, you never can tell to what degree they'll factor in to her future, especially once she's become sensory smart. The child who was once a picky eater could end up being a gourmet chef. The child who couldn't follow complex verbal directions could end up being a fabulous writer. The child who constantly sought out movement could become a professional athlete. The one who sprawled on the couch like a wet noodle, daydreaming, could become a successful artist. Your "odd" child with poor social skills could become a brilliant researcher, computer programmer, inventor, or sensory smart parent, like you are. You just never know.

Recommended Reading

Chara, Kathleen A., Paul J. Chara, and Christian Chara. *Sensory Smarts: A Book for Kids with ADHD or Autism Spectrum Disorders Struggling with Sensory Integration Problems*. Philadelphia: Jessica Kingsley Publishers, 2004. Written from the perspective of a twelve-year-old boy with sensory issues, this book provides wonderful insights and practical help for children, families, and caregivers.

Cohen, Lawrence J., Ph.D. *Playful Parenting*. New York: Ballantine Books, 2001. A child psychologist explains the importance of play, and how to use play to help your child work through difficult emotions.

Faber, Adele, and Elaine Mazlish. *Siblings Without Rivalry*. New York: Avon, 1987. An excellent guide to keeping the peace among siblings.

Gray, Carol. *The New Social Story Book,* illustrated edition. Arlington, TX: Future Horizons, 2000. Web site: www.thegraycenter.com.

Medearis, Angela Shelf. Illustrated by Jaqueline Rogers. *We Eat Dinner in the Bathtub*. New York: Scholastic, 1999. A children's book about a boy whose family does things just a little differently.

Mucklow, Nancy. *The Sensory Team Handbook for Pre-Teens*. A hands-on tool for pre-teens to help them manage their sensory issues, filled with cartoons, worksheets, and information. Available for download at www.sensoryteamhandbook.com.

Parr, Todd. *It's Okay to Be Different*. Boston: Little, Brown and Company Books for Young Readers, 2004. Simple, colorful, and charming declarations about being different will reassure and delight kids and parents.

Renna, Diane. *Meghan's World: The Story of One Girl's Triumph over Sensory Processing Disorder*. Speonk, NY: Indigo Impressions, 2007. Written by a parent and illustrated by her daughter, this is a great book to read with children and to help explain sensory problems to others.

Veenendall, Jennifer. *Arnie and His School Tools: Simple Sensory Solutions that Build Success*. Shawnee Mission, KS: Autism Asperger Pub., 2008. A story about using sensory modulation tools and strategies at school for elementary-school-age students.

PART FIVE

Recommended Products and Resources

Sources for Useful Toys, Equipment, and Products

There are some excellent sources for toys and equipment kids with sensory issues, from weighted vests and therapy balls to fidgets, special seat cushions, and pencil grips. We suggest you at least take a look through a couple of therapy catalogs to get some idea of what might be helpful for your child. Remember, too, that some of these items can be found in toy stores, large discount stores, drugstores, dollar stores, closeout stores, thrift shops, or office supply stores, on eBay, or even through individual vendors online. Plus, some items can be fashioned at home, such as weighted blankets, swings, and sand tables.

Your OT can best advise you on what items your child would find most useful, and how to use what you already have in your home. For instance, beds, pillows, cushions, and blankets (especially down comforters) can be used to create a safe roughhousing, tactile space without your having to spend any extra money. Bath toys like funnels, plastic cups, and turkey basters can come right from your own kitchen.

If you are searching for a particular item we've recommended here, be aware that sometimes the names are different in various catalogs. We've gone with names we found in the larger therapy catalogs—particularly *Integrations* and *Achievement Products for Kids*.

If your child is under age three, or if you have children in the house under age three, please be extremely cautious about choking hazards, particularly with used toys and equipment. You can contact the manufacturer to check whether an item has been recalled for safety purposes.

Top Therapy Catalogs

Please note that catalog Web sites show only a small portion of what's available in the print version. So, if you do check them out online, be sure to request that a printed catalog get mailed to you.

Abilitations, 800-850-8602, www.abilitations.com.
Many of Abilitations's products are for kids with physical disabilities, but they also carry plenty of popular items for kids with SI dysfunction.

Achievement Products for Children, 800-373-4699,
www.specialkidszone.com.
Sells a wide variety of adapted utensils and special cups and dishes plus thousands of excellent products including therapy balls, weighted wristbands, massagers, etc.

Flaghouse, 800-793-7900, www.flaghouse.com.
A wide assortment of sensory therapy products and adaptive living tools, including the full Snoezelen product line.

Fun and Function, 800-231-6329, www.funandfunction.com.
A great variety of therapeutic play and educational items, including fun weighted costumes, vibrating toys, fine and gross motor and balance toys, reward charts, and more.

Integrations, 800-850-8602, www.integrationscatalog.com.
Owned by the parent company of Abilitations, Integrations focuses on toys and equipment perfect for children with learning and sensory differences and has lots of guidance on how specific products meet particular sensory needs. Source for scooter boards, visual timers, vibrating hairbrushes, Body Sox, surgical scrub brushes, weighted balls, etc.

Lakeshore, 800-778-4456, www.lakeshorelearning.com.
This is where teachers find some of their most fun school supplies, including sensory tables, puzzles, blocks, stencils, and arts and crafts supplies.

Pocket Full of Therapy, 800-PFOT-124, www.pfot.com.
Sells weighted blankets, Desk Buddy and Aussie Pouch organizational pouches for school chairs and desks, fidgets, Dizzy Disc Jr., accordion

pipes, therapy balls, Zoomballs, chewing toys, BLOpens, lots of class-room tools and adapted school supplies, and much more.

Professional Development Programs/PDP Products, 651-439-8865, www.pdppro.com.
Products include inflatable seat cushions, Nuk massager, Infadent finger cots, whistles, pencil grips, Theraband, surgical scrub brushes, special scissors, fidgets and vibrating toys, and tools for children with visual tracking problems.

Southpaw Enterprises, 800-228-1698, 937-252-7676, www.southpawenterprises.com.
This is a great source for toys and many of the kinds of equipment found in sensory gyms and OT clinics.

Therapro, 800-257-5376, 508-872-9494, www.theraproducts.com.
Sells a large variety of products for kids with sensory issues and develop-mental delays, including pencil grips, weighted gloves, Mozart for Mod-ulation CD, and much more.

The Therapy Shoppe, 800-261-5590, 616-696-7441, www.therapyshoppe.com.
Sells a very large variety of products including slant boards, massagers, therapy balls, weighted vests and blankets, inflatable cushions, surgical scrub brushes, and more.

Other Excellent Sources for Toys and Products

www.amazon.com.
Sells books, CDs, videos, toys, personal care items, and more. Source for Dentips, Sit 'n Spin, Dizzy Disc Jr., For Crying Out Loud CD, etc.

Beyond Play, 877-428-1244, www.beyondplay.com.
Sells weighted and textured utensils, educational toys, tactile brushes, Disc'O'Sit, balance beams, Nuk brushes, toys, and more.

www.colichelp.com.
Sells For Crying Out Loud CD, white noise machines, and swaddling blankets to help colicky babies.

Corwin Press, 800-233-9936, 805-499-9734, www.corwinpress.com.
Sells a variety of teaching and learning books, including many for children with special needs.

Different Roads to Learning, 800-853-1057, 212-604-9637,
www.difflearn.com.
Sells items such as PECS cards, visual timers, auditory games, manipulatives, puzzles, etc.

Discovery Toys, 800-341-8697, www.discoverytoysinc.com.
Sells high-quality educational toys, many of which are exceptionally useful for kids with SPD. Toys are sold via consultants with their e-mail addresses provided.

The First Years, 800-704-8697, www.thefirstyears.com.
Sells products and toys for newborns, infants, and toddlers, many of which are also available in drugstores and children's stores.

Hemi-Sync, 800-541-2488, www.hemi-sync.com.
Source for Hemi-Sync Metamusic CDs for focusing and self-regulation.

IKEA, www.ikea.com.
This furnishings store carries a lot of great storage equipment, seat cushions, and kids' furniture such as a swivel chair with a hood (a great hideout), hanging chairs, and rockers. Toys include trapezes, hanging ladders, and tents.

In Your Pocket Designs, 888-388-3224, 920-882-5994,
www.weightedvest.com.
Sells weighted vests and patterns for making your own.

International Jock, 888-658-5444, www.internationaljock.com.
Source for all-cotton underwear, compression shorts, and soft-cup jockstraps for boys and men.

Learning Gear Plus, 978-597-9056, www.learninggearplus.com.
Sells educational products, with a few especially helpful to kids with sensory issues, such as shoelaces that don't need tying, Theraputty, pencil grips, Wikki Stix, and foam covering for utensil handles.

Nasco Arts & Crafts, 800-558-9595, 920-563-2446, www.enasco.com.
Sells a huge variety of arts and craft supplies appropriate for children
through adults, including fun craft kits.

One Step Ahead, 800-950-5120, www.onestepahead.com.
Sells For Crying Out Loud background noise CD, portable potties for toddlers, foam soap dispenser, earbands for swimming, foam puzzle mats, etc.

OT Ideas, 877-768-4332, www.otideas.com.
A great source of tools for help with fine motor delay, such as easels and
slant boards, special pencils and pencil grips, special scissors, kits and
papers for working on handwriting, etc. No catalog available.

Really Good Stuff, 800-366-1920, 203-261-1920, www.reallygoodstuff.com.
An excellent source of educational materials and school-related products
including homework checklists, Store More pockets for chairs and desks,
masks for homework, and highlighter tape.

Sensory Comfort, 888-436-2622, www.sensorycomfort.com.
Sells seamless, soft cotton underwear and underwear with cotton-covered
waistbands, noise-blocking headphones, white noise machines, odor pu-
rifiers, chewing toys, supersoft pillows and blankets, fidget toys, vibrating
toys, modulating music CDs, yoga-for-children videos, and more.

Sensory Edge, 800-734-8019, www.sensoryedge.com.
Sells children's furniture and toys, such as sand tables and ball pits, in
addition to many types of therapy toys and equipment.

Sportime, 800-283-5700, 770-449-5700, www.sportime.com.
Sells equipment for physical and sporting activities, including tunnels,
mats, and obstacle course items.

Stress Relief, 410-290-7058, www.parentsuccess.com.
Sells the book *Ready, Set, R.E.L.A.X.* by J. S. Allen and R. J. Klein (Water-
town, WI: Inner Coaching, 1997) and the companion CD *Ready . . .
Set . . . Release!*

Therafin, 800-843-7234, 708-479-7300, www.therafin.com.
Source for the Squeeze Machine as well as scooter boards and T-stools.

Sources for Low-Price Toys and Products

www.Bizrate.com and www.shopping.com.
These sites comparison-shop for you, and are especially useful for checking prices on larger, expensive items like a sensory table, trampoline, ball pit, etc.

Ebay, www.ebay.com.
An online auction site where you can buy used and new items. It's a great source for vintage games and toys that lack modern-day sound and light chips, and sometimes are made from sturdier materials (and surprisingly, the older versions are often less expensive than the newer ones). Also, type in *sensory* or *autism* and many therapy-type products will come up. Always check shipping charges and sellers' policies and feedback profile before bidding, as your bid is a legal contract.

Free Downloadable Pages

www.activitypad.com.
Features free downloads of mazes and connect-the-dots pictures that you can use to help your child practice fine motor skills.

www.do2learn.com.
Free downloads of simple line drawings that can be used to create picture to-do lists.

Make Your Own Sensory Diet Materials

Instructions for Making Your Own Weighted Blanket, www.jeena.org/autism/ot.htm#Making%20your%20own%20weighted%20blanket%A0

Make Your Own Bubble Liquid, www.wikihow.com/Make-Bubble-Solution

Make Your Own Playdough, http://www.cooks.com.
Enter "how to make playdough" in the recipe search box. This is a great site because it contains the basic playdough recipe plus some really weird variations like Kool Aid Playdough and peanut butter playdough.

Helpful Books and Web Sites About Play and Toys

Dr. Toy's Smart Play: How to Raise a Child with High P.Q. (PLAY QUOTIENT) by Stevanne Auerbach (San Francisco, CA: Institute for Childhood Resources, 2006). A guide to toys with tremendous play and educational value for babies through children age twelve, with a chapter on special needs, resources, and advice on how to help your child get the most out of them. Check out Dr. Toy online at www.drtoy.com.

National Lekotek Center, 800-366-PLAY, 773-528-5766, www.lekotek.org. Lekotek has toy lending libraries for disabled children all over the country as well as programs such as toy exchanges, computer centers, and parent support groups.

Wonderplay by Freida Reitzes and Beth Teitelman, with Lois Alter Mark (Philadelphia: Running Press Publishers, 1995). Games, crafts, and fun activities for infants, toddlers, and preschoolers from the 92nd St. Y Parenting Center.

Sources of Items for Children with Developmental Delays

Organizational Problems

Assistive Technology Resources, 800-514-0301, www.ada.gov. General information about Americans with Disabilities Act, U.S. Department of Justice.

Attention Control Systems, Inc., 650-494-2002, www.brainaid.com. Sells PEAT software for handheld computers, which helps people with ADHD by reminding them to do particular activities at certain times.

Center for Assistive Technology, 800-628-2281, www.cat.buffalo.edu.

Rehabilitation Engineering and Assistive Technology Service of North America, 703-524-6686, www.resna.org.

WatchMinder, 800-961-0023, www.watchminder.com. Sells a wristwatch that can be programmed with important reminders.

Educational/Learning Software and Devices

AlphaSmart, Inc., 888-274-0680, www.alphasmart.com.
Portable, lightweight, inexpensive word processor.

Attainment Company, Inc., 800-327-4269, www.AttainmentCompany.com.
Sells a variety of software for education, life skills, work skills, as well as
IEP resources and free downloads.

Don Johnston, Inc., 800-999-4660, 847-740-0749, www.donjohnston.com.
A comprehensive source of access devices (adapted keyboards, touch
screens, alternative input devices) and software products for early liter-
acy, reading, writing, and math. Sells Inspiration and Kidspiration software. Offers several free downloads so your child can try out software
before purchasing.

Intellitools, Inc., 800-547-6747, 303-651-2829, www.intellitools.com.
Sells adapted keyboards and input devices and loads of educational software.

Mayer-Johnson, Inc., 800-588-4548, www.mayer-johnson.com.
Sells communication devices, hardware, software, and training aids.

Fine Motor Delay, Visual-Perceptual Skills

Handwriting Without Tears, 301-263-2700, www.hwtears.com.
The Web site has excellent tips and resources, as well as the full product
line for this multisensory program for teaching print and cursive writing.

School Zone, 616-846-5030, www.schoolzone.com.
Carries inexpensive workbooks, including fun hidden picture books,
alphabet and number dot-to-dot books, crossword puzzle books, workbooks and software for learning shapes, colors, and concepts such as
same/different, and more.

Speech-Language Delay and/or Auditory Processing

Cognitive Concepts, 888-242-6747, www.earobics.com.
Makers of Earobics software, which teaches reading and language skills while playfully challenging listening skills.

The Earplug Store, 485-844-5080, www.earplugstore.com.
An excellent selection of premolded and moldable silicone earplugs designed to fit kids' ears. They offer an assortment kit for you to figure out which kind your child will find most comfortable. Also sells a neoprene stretch headband to keep earplugs in place while swimming and playing in water.

Innovative Therapists International, 520-795-1036, www.talktools.net.
Has excellent articles, research, and links. Features the *TalkTools* catalog, which is full of great products and information about oral sensory issues, feeding, oral-motor skills, and more.

Scientific Learning, 888-358-0212, www.scilearn.com.
Makers of Fast ForWord software, used to develop phonemic awareness, reading, and auditory processing skills.

Sources for Grooming Products

www.drugstore.com.
Sells nonfluoridated toothpastes (Tom's of Maine Silly Strawberry, Nature's Gate), nonfoaming toothpaste (Orajel Toddler Training), electric toothbrushes, dental floss (Glide ribbon floss, cinnamon and mint flavored floss), and licensed-character toothbrushes that can inspire sensitive kids to tolerate grooming.

Just4Teeth, www.just4teeth.com.
Carries several types of electric toothbrushes.

SammonsPreston, 800-323-5547, www.sammonspreston.com
(to request a print catalog only). A good source for self-care products such as gum massagers, headbands and visors to keep shampoo out of the eyes, adapted eating utensils, special cups and plates, and so on.

Photos of Toys, Equipment, and Products

These toys, equipment, and products are all described in the text as noted, and most can be found in the larger therapy catalogs listed in Sources for Useful Toys, Equipment, and Products; a few are more likely to be found in retail stores. Please consult with your OT about the most effective and safe ways to use these items with your child, and we hope you will consider taking a look through a few therapy catalogs to see what other helpful products are available.

A bilateral bolster swing, commonly found in sensory gyms. (Photo courtesy Southpaw Enterprises)

The Cuddle Swing gives lots
of deep pressure input as well
as vestibular stimulation.
(Photo courtesy
Southpaw Enterprises)

A platform swing, com-
monly found in sensory
gyms. This one has
removable safety padding
for use with infants.
(Photo courtesy Southpaw
Enterprises)

The Sit 'n Spin is great for motor planning plus vestibular stimulation.

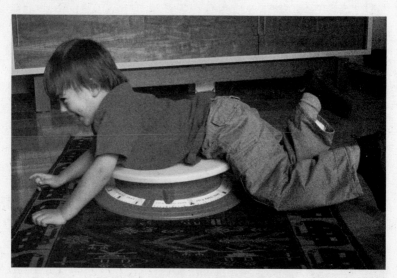

The Dizzy Disc Jr. works like a lazy Susan, providing vestibular stimulation.

Airplane position on a textured therapy cushion. (Photo courtesy Southpaw Enterprises)

A child on a textured therapy ball. When working with any therapy ball, make sure both the child and the ball are stable. (Photo courtesy Southpaw Enterprises)

Body Sox, made of stretchy Lycra material, helps with body awareness. It comes in several sizes.
(Photo courtesy Southpaw Enterprises)

The Steamroller Deluxe, a variation on Temple Grandin's squeeze machine.
(Photo courtesy Southpaw Enterprises)

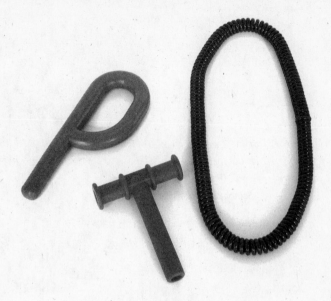

Three types of chew toys:
ARK's Grabber, Chewy Tube, and Chewlery
(left to right).

An inflatable seat cushion like the Disc'O'Sit gives kids opportunities to move while seated.

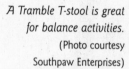

*A Tramble T-stool is great
for balance activities.*
(Photo courtesy
Southpaw Enterprises)

*Zoo Sticks tongs can be
used to pick up small toys
or to eat, enhancing fine
motor skills.*

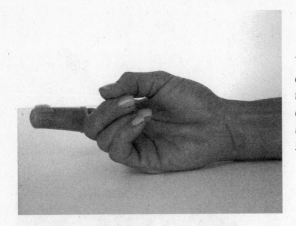

The Infa-Dent cleans teeth and massages gums, and can help reduce oral sensitivity.

The Time Timer increases kids' awareness of how time elapses. (Photo courtesy Southpaw Enterprises)

Three types of pencil grips: Start Right (left), The Pencil Grip (in hand), and Stetro (in front).

Lindsey and Nancy's Fifty
Favorite Toys

We could fill an entire book with specifics about wonderful toys, special equipment, and how to use them all in a variety of ways! Meanwhile, here are fifty of our favorite items that can be really helpful and loads of fun for kids with sensory processing issues, not in any particular order of preference.

1. Squiggle Wiggle Writer and other vibrating toys like the Bumble Ball
2. Stacking rings and cups
3. Mr. Potato Head
4. Radio Flyer Red Wagon
5. Mighty Mind and other visual-perceptual games
6. Bop It electronic toy
7. Lite-Brite
8. Clay, Silly Putty, Slime, Theraputty, Play-Doh, and Play-Doh Fun Factory
9. Sit 'n Spin and Dizzy Disc Jr. (see photos on page 392)
10. Body Sox (see photo on page 394)
11. Resistance tunnel and play tunnels
12. Big therapy balls (see photo on page 393), Hop balls (also called Pon-Pon balls and Hippity Hops)
13. Bubbles with various wands
14. Arts and crafts supplies of all types, including scented markers, Do-A-Dot Markers, paint, and BLOpens
15. Zoo Sticks (see photo on page 396) and other tongs and tweezers to pick up food and small objects
16. Ball pits
17. Zoomball ball-and-rope game (PFOT.com)

18. Kerplunk marble game and Trouble board game
19. Elefun butterfly-catching game
20. Candyland, Cariboo, and other age-appropriate board games
21. Blockhead, Connect Four, Don't Break the Ice, Rush Hour, and other games of strategy
22. A sensory bin filled with dry rice and beans, sand, Styrofoam peanuts, or other interesting materials
23. Trampolines and mini-trampolines
24. Whistles and blow toys, especially those sold in therapy catalogs
25. Velcro-mitt catching set
26. Gertie balls, Nerf balls, medicine balls, Wiggly Giggly ball, Koosh balls, and other odd balls
27. Riding toys: tricycles, bicycles, scooters, and skateboards
28. Shape sorters
29. Books that incorporate the senses: textured books, scratch and sniff, lift-the-flap interactive books, Leapfrog books
30. Age-appropriate puzzles: from peg puzzles to foam floor puzzles to jigsaw puzzles, and foam alphabet mats
31. Push toys
32. Costumes and makeup for dress-ups
33. Construction toys: Duplo, wood blocks, Bristle Blocks, Legos, Lincoln Logs, Tinker Toys, Atollo, K'NEX Capsela
34. Age-appropriate beads from pop beads to pony beads to jewelry-stringing beads
35. Musical instruments
36. Bop bags and punching bags
37. Rocking toys like Rockin' Rody
38. Funny "shoes" like Moonwalkers and Big Foot Striders
39. Wikki Stix
40. Lacing forms and sewing activities
41. Swings, slides, and climbing equipment of all sorts
42. Slinky
43. Etch-A-Sketch and Spirograph
44. Finger and hand puppets
45. Plastic "rapper snapper" pipes that make sounds when you twirl them
46. Funny straws and pinwheels
47. Silly String, colored shaving cream, foamy soap
48. Motor planning challenges such as Astrojax, Hula Hoops, jump rope, Pogo sticks, Bungee Jumpers, and Honeybee Hop Bungee Jumpers

49. Jack-in-the-box and old-fashioned spinning tops with pump mechanisms
50. Any ordinary object you use imaginatively with your child, actively playing together

Turn off your cell phone. Turn off the television. This is your special time together. We hope you have fun playing!

Organizations and Web Sites

WWW.SENSORYSMARTS.COM

The official Web site for *Raising a Sensory Smart Child: The Definitive Guide to Helping Your Child with Sensory Processing Issues*. Includes sensory diet ideas, practical tips, early intervention providers, speaking engagements, recommended toys and books, and more.

If you would like to correspond with us, or have practical solutions and insights you'd like to share with other parents, please e-mail us at mail@sensorysmarts.com.

SENSORY PROCESSING INFORMATION, HELP, AND SUPPORT

www.aota.org. The American Occupational Therapy Association, 800-377-8555. The American Occupational Therapy Association can link you to your state's organization, which you can contact to find an occupational therapist who is trained and experienced in working with children and/or adults with sensory issues.

www.otworks.ca. This Web site helps find an OT in Canada. Click on "OT Finder."

www.childrensdisabilities.info. This site has several articles on SPD as well as links to resources and parent support groups for apraxia, speech delay, auditory processing, and more.

www.ot-innovations.com. This Web site has excellent information and advice on sensory modulation techniques used in mental health with adults, research on weighted blankets, and more.

Sensory Processing Disorder Foundation, 5655 S. Yosemite St., Suite 305, Greenwood Village, CO 80111, 303-794-1182, www. spdfoundation.net. The SPD Foundation (formerly Kid Foundation) Web site has a directory of OTs and other professionals who specialize in sensory issues (click on "Find Services"), connections to parenting support groups, research, and more.

S.I. Focus Magazine, P.O. Box 821404, Dallas, TX 75382, 214-341-9999, www.sifocus.com. A quarterly magazine for parents and professionals interested in sensory processing disorder.

www.yahoogroups.com. Yahoo has free e-mail groups for just about any interest you can imagine, including sensory issues. Type in *sensory integration* to find support groups for individuals with SI dysfunction or parents of children with SI dysfunction.

Western Psychological Services, www.wpspublish.com. This publisher has a list of occupational therapists who are certified to perform the Sensory Integration Praxis Test (SIPT).

DELAYS AND DISABILITIES

Exceptional Parent, www.eparent.com. This is a monthly magazine for parents of children with disabilities.

Early Intervention (Children Under Age Three)

First Signs, Inc., 978-346-4380, www.firstsigns.org.

www.sensorysmarts.com. Includes contact information for early intervention programs in the U.S.

Zero to Three, National Center for Infants, Toddlers and Families, 202-638-1144, www.zerotothree.org.

Learning Disabilities

www.LDonline.org. Articles and information on learning disabilities for parents, teachers, and professionals.

The National Center for Learning Disabilities, 212-545-7510, 888-575-7373, www.ld.org.

www.schwablearning.org. Provides information for parents on learning difficulties to message boards for exchanging information and support.

Auditory Processing

www.getreadytoread.org. This site suggests several fun and simple activities for prereaders who have auditory processing challenges and helps them better discriminate sounds and rhymes.

www.ldinfo.org/professionals/audiologists.html. Source for finding an audiologist who can diagnose and treat auditory processing disorder.

The National Coalition on Auditory Processing Disorders (NCAPD), P.O. Box 494, Rockville Centre, NY 11571, www.ncapd.org.

www.samonas.com, 800-726-6627, e-mail: info@samonas.com. Provides information about the Samonas listening program.

Society for Auditory Intervention Techniques, www.berardait website.com/sait/index.html. Interesting articles on sound sensitivity and auditory processing.

www.tomatis-group.com. Provides general information on the Tomatis Method. Click flag icon for info in English or Spanish.

www.iarctc.com. Lists certified Tomatis consultants.

Speech-Language Delays

American Speech-Language-Hearing Foundation, 800-638-8255, www.asha.org/proserv/. Source for finding a qualified professional who can treat auditory processing disorder.

www.apraxia-kids.org. This Web site is for parents of children who have oral apraxia or dyspraxia.

www.childrensdisabilities.info/speech/. Children's Disabilities Information has some excellent articles on speech and communication, as well as other developmental issues.

www.pammarshalla.com. 425-379-6443. SLP Pam Marshalla has written a series of wonderful small books including *How to Stop Thumbsucking, How to Stop Drooling,* and *Becoming Verbal with Childhood Apraxia.*

www.speechdelay.com. Offers insights and help with speech delays.

Therapeutic Approaches

Brain Gym International, 800-356-2109, 805-658-7942, www.braingym.org. Brain Gym is a program that uses movement to help people improve organizational, reading, writing, concentration, and memory skills.

TherapyWorks, 877-897-3478, www.alertprogram.com. This program helps kids, preschool to age twelve, with regulation problems to identify their alertness level and adjust it when appropriate. The site sells the book *An Introduction to "How Does Your Engine Run?"* and CD.

Vision Issues

Children's Vision Information Network, www.childrensvision.com. Loads of interesting articles on vision and children, current research, and vision therapy efficacy studies.

The College of Optometrists in Vision Development, 330-995-0718, 888-268-3770, www.covd.org. Excellent articles on vision and learning, ADHD and autism, and information on vision therapy, as well as how to find a local optometrist.

Irlen Institute International Headquarters, 800-554-7536, www.irlen.com. Information about Irlen syndrome.

OEP Foundation, 949-250-8070, www.oepf.org. Information on behavioral optometry, books for parents and professionals, and a referral list to find a local doctor.

Optometrists Network, www.optometrists.org. This site has excellent articles on vision, learning, ADHD, and more.

Parents Active for Vision Education, 619-287-0081, 860-728-3988, www.pavevision.org. A nonprofit organization founded by parents and teachers to help children with vision-related learning problems.

RELATED SYNDROMES AND DISORDERS

Anxiety Disorders

www.childhoodanxietynetwork.org. Provides information about conditions such as SPD, depression, ADHD, OCD, panic disorder, separation anxiety, social anxiety, posttraumatic stress disorder, and others.

Attention Deficit Hyperactivity Disorder

ADDitude Magazine, 888-762-8475, www.additudemag.com. Lifestyle magazine for parents of children with ADHD/ADD and adults with ADHD/ADD.

Attention Deficit Disorder Association, 800-939-1019, www.add.org. An online meeting place for adults, teens, and parents of children with ADHD. It includes message boards and articles on a variety of ADHD-related topics.

CHADD (Children and Adults with Attention Deficit Disorder), 800-233-4050, 301-306-7070, www.chadd.org. Offers information and support for children and adults with ADHD. Some of the Web site is available in Spanish.

incrediblehorizons.com/mimic-adhd.htm. A list of fifty conditions that can be mistaken for ADHD.

Autism Spectrum Disorders

Autism Research Institute, 866-366-3361, www.autism.com.
This organization is primarily devoted to research and education on the causes of autism and on methods of preventing, diagnosing, and treating autism and other severe behavioral disorders of childhood.

Autism Society of America, 301-657-0881, 800-3AUTISM, www .autism-society.org. A leading source of information on autism from a group originally begun by parents in 1965, which now has more than twenty thousand members.

www.autistics.org. An organization run by autistic people for the purpose of providing community, support, and information to other autistic people.

www.autismspot.com. Has excellent, free online videos, forums, blogs, news, advice, and support for parents, professionals, and others in the autism community.

Autism Speaks, 888-AUTISM2, http://www.autismspeaks.org. One of the largest foundations dedicated to autism in the world, Autism Speaks is involved in research, policy, fundraising, family services, and more.

MAAP Services for Autism and Asperger Syndrome,
219-662-1311, www.maapservices.org. A source of information on autism, Asperger syndrome, and PDD.

The Nonverbal Learning Disorders Association, 860-658-5522, www.nlda.org.

O.A.S.I.S. (Online Asperger Syndrome Information and Support), www.udel.edu/bkirby/asperger/. A comprehensive Asperger's syndrome Web site with support groups, schools and camps, articles, research, and more.

Adopted Children, Foster Children, Premature Children

Adoptive Families Magazine, 800-372-3300,
www.adoptivefamilies.com.

www.childrensdisabilities.info. Has a variety of interesting articles, with a special focus on the needs of preemies and young adoptees.

www.orphandoctor.com. Some good articles on common developmental and medical issues that affect adopted children.

www.preemie-L.org. Parents of Premature Babies Inc. is a nonprofit foundation providing support to families and caregivers of premature babies.

Fetal Alcohol Syndrome

FAS Community Resource Center, www.come-over.to/FASCRC/. Provides information about research, living with FAS, and legislation on issues related to fetal alcohol syndrome.

National Organization on Fetal Alcohol Syndrome, 202-785-4585, www.nofas.org.

Fragile X Syndrome

The National Fragile X Foundation, 800-688-8765, www.fragilex.org.

Tourette Syndrome

The Tourette Syndrome Association, 718-224-2999, www.tsa-usa.org.

COMPLEMENTARY THERAPIES, NONFOOD

The American Hippotherapy Association, 888-851-4592, www.americanhippotherapyassociation.org, and **North American Riding for the Handicapped Association,** 800-369-7433, www.narha.org. These two sites will help you find local sources for therapeutic riding, with state-by-state directories.

Aquatic Resources Network, 715-248-7258, www.aquaticnet.com. Information on water-based therapies.

Craniosacral Therapy Association of North America, 734-904-0546, www.craniosacraltherapy.org. Basic information and help finding a local practitioner.

Interactive Metronome, www.interactivemetronome.com.
This is a program for increasing focus, reading, language processing, organizational ability, and fine motor skills while decreasing impulsivity. It is a computer-based program that is done in fifteen one-hour sessions over three to five weeks. Using hands and feet, students work to get in sync with a metronome.

The International Council for Aquatic Therapy and Rehabilitation Industry Certification, 509-747-4927, www.icatric.org.

International Loving Touch Foundation, 800-929-7492, 503-253-8482, www.lovingtouch.com.
Baby massage articles, related products, and local practitioners.

Myofascial Release, 800-FASCIAL, 610-644-0136, www.myofascialrelease.com.
Basic information and help finding a local practitioner.

HEAVY METAL POISONING

National Lead Information Center, 800-424-LEAD (5323).
See the EPA's Web site at www.epa.gov/lead/index.html.

www.cdc.gov and **www.fda.gov.**
The Web sites for the Centers for Disease Control and Prevention and the Food and Drug Administration have information about lead and mercury poisoning and toxicity as well as information on vaccine safety studies.

HOMESCHOOLING

National Home Education Network, fax 413-581-1463, www.nhen.org.
Source for information on and support for homeschooling.

NUTRITION, SPECIAL DIETS, SUPPLEMENTS

enzymesandautism@yahoogroups.com. An online support group for parents using digestive enzymes to treat their children's autism and sensory issues.

www.enzymestuff.com. Source for information about digestive enzyme supplementation. It also has a good article on Epsom salt baths and lotions for children with autism.

The Feingold Association of the United States, 800-321-3287 in the U.S., 631-369-9340 outside the U.S., www.feingold.org. Key source for information on the Feingold diet.

www.gfcfdiet.com. Provides information on the gluten-free, casein-free diet.

Houston Neutraceuticals, Inc., 866-757-8627 (U.S. only), 479-549-4536, www.houston-enzymes.com. Source of enzymes for digestive support.

iNutritionals.com. Source for essential fatty acid supplements for kids, in chocolate milk powder form.

www.kellydorfman.com. The Web site of nutritionist Kelly Dorfman. Great articles on nutrition and sensory processing.

Kirkman Labs, 800-245-8282, 503-694-1600, www.kirkmanlabs.com. Sells dietary enzymes, magnesium sulfate (Epsom salt) cream, and essential fatty acid supplements.

Vitamist, 800-582-5273, www.myvitamist.com. Source for vitamins that you spray on the inside of cheeks rather than swallow.

PARENTING AND SOCIALIZATION

The Center for Collaborative Problem Solving, www.explosivechild. com. This center provides clinical services, training, and consultation to professionals and parents for understanding and implementing the

Collaborative Problem Solving approach described in *The Explosive Child* by Dr. Ross Greene. Includes information on support groups and counselors for children.

www.med.umich.edu/1libr/yourchild/specneed.htm. This University of Michigan Web site has several articles on the siblings of special needs children.

www.thegraycenter.org. Web site of Carol Gray, who teaches parents how to use social stories with children who have nonverbal learning disorder, to help them understand the rules of social intercourse.

Sensory Friendly Films, http://www.autism-society.org/site/PageServer ?pagename=sensoryfilms.
AMC Entertainment and the Autism Society of America have teamed up to bring families affected by autism and other disabilities an opportunity to go to the movies in a safe and accepting environment each month with the "Sensory Friendly Films" program.

SPECIAL EDUCATION AND LEGAL ISSUES

The Council of Parent Attorneys and Advocates, 410-372-0208, www.copaa.net. A not-for-profit organization for parents of children with disabilities needing legal assistance. The site has a state-by-state list of links to sites with information on special education law.

www.wrightslaw.com. This Web site is the place to go for the latest information on special education law.

Notes

CHAPTER 1:
Why Is My Child So . . . Unusual?

1. Sensory Integration International estimates that SI dysfunction affects 15 percent of the general population, while a 1997 study published in the *Occupational Therapy Journal of Research* found that 10 percent of American children are affected.
2. Miller, L. J., M. E. Anzalone, S. J. Lane, S. A. Cermak, and E. T. Osten. "Concept Evolution in Sensory Integration: A Proposed Nosology for Diagnosis." *American Journal of Occupational Therapy* 61 (2007): 135–40.

General references:

Ayres, Jean A. *Sensory Integration and the Child.* Los Angeles: Western Psychological Services, 1979.

Bundy, A. C., S. J. Lane, and E. A. Murray. *Sensory Integration Theory and Practice,* 2nd ed. Philadelphia: F. A. Davis Company, 1991.

Eide, Fernette F., M.D. "Sensory Integration: Current Concepts and Practical Implications." *Sensory Integration Special Interest Quarterly* 26:3 (2003), American Occupational Therapy Association.

CHAPTER 2:
The Seven Senses

1. Fisher, A. G., and A. C. Bundy. "Vestibular Stimulation in the Treatment of Postural and Related Disorders." Edited by O. D. Payton, R. P. DiFabio, S. V. Paris, E. J. Protas, and A. F. VanSant. *Manual of Physical Therapy Techniques.* New York: Churchill Livingstone, 1989, 239–58.

2. Frick, S. M., and C. H. Hacker. *Listening with the Whole Body*. Madison, WI: Vital Links, 2000, 3:27–39.

3. Ray, T. C., L. J. King, and T. Grandin. "The Effectiveness of Self-Initiated Vestibular Stimulation in Producing Speech Sounds in an Autistic Child." *Occupational Therapy Journal of Research* 8:3 (1988): 187–91. www. thechildrenscenteraz.org/research_art2.htm.

   Schueli, H., V. Henn, and P. Brugger. "Vestibular Stimulation Affects Dichotic Lexical Decision Performance." *Neuropsychologia,* 37:6 (1999): 653–59.

4. Irlen, H. *Reading by the Colors: Overcoming Dyslexia and Other Reading Disabilities through the Irlen Method*. New York: Perigee, 1991.

   Edelson, Stephen M. *Scotopic Sensitivity Syndrome and the Irlen Lens system*. Online article from the Center for the Study of Autism. www. autism.org/irlen.html.

5. Veitch, J. A., and S. L. McColl. "Modulation of Fluorescent Light: Flicker Rate and Light Source Effects on Visual Performance and Visual Comfort." *Lighting Research and Technology* 27 (1995): 243–56.

General references:

Bear, M. F., B. W. Connors, and M. A. Paradiso. *Neuroscience: Exploring the Brain*. Baltimore: Williams & Wilkins, 1996.

Bundy, A. C., S. J. Lane, and E. A. Murray. *Sensory Integration: Theory and Practice,* 2nd ed. Philadelphia: F. A. Davis Company, 2002.

Ratey, John J., M.D. *A User's Guide to the Brain*. New York: Vintage Books, 2001.

Wynsberghe, D. V., C. R. Noback, and R. Carola. *Human Anatomy & Physiology,* 3rd ed. New York: McGraw-Hill, 1995.

CHAPTER 4:
Where Did the Wires Cross?

1. Ratey, John J., M.D. *A User's Guide to the Brain*. New York: Vintage Books, 2001, 24.

2. McIntosh, H. "Neuroimaging Tools Offer New Ways to Study Autism." *APA Monitor* 29:11 (1998). Available online at www.apa.org/monitor/ nov98/neuro.html.

3. Reeves, G. D. "From Neuron to Behavior: Regulation, Arousal, and Attention as Important Substrates for the Process of Sensory Integration." In *Understanding the Nature of Sensory Integration with Diverse Populations.*

Edited by S. Smith-Roley, E. Imperatore-Blanche, and R. C. Schaaf. San Antonio, TX: Therapy Skill Builders, 2001, 89–108.

4. Grandin, T. "Calming Effects of Deep Touch Pressure in Patients with Autistic Disorder, College Students, and Animals." *Journal of Child and Adolescent Psychopharmacology* 2:1 (1992): 63–72.

5. McIntosh, H. "Neuroimaging Tools Offer New Ways to Study Autism."

6. McIntosh, D. N., L. J. Miller, V. Shya, and R. J. Hagerman. "Sensory-Modulation Disruption, Electrodermal Responses, and Functional Behaviors." *Developmental Medical and Child Neurology* 41 (1999): 608–15.

   Schaaf, R. C., L. J. Miller, D. Seawell, and S. O'Keefe. "Children with Disturbances in Sensory Processing: A Pilot Study Examining the Role of the Parasympathetic Nervous System." *American Journal of Occupational Therapy* 57:4 (2003): 442–49.

   Schoen, S. A., L. J. Miller, B. Brett-Green, and S. L. Hepburn. "Psychophysiology of Children with Autism Spectrum Disorder." *Research in Autism Spectrum Disorders* 2:3 (2007): 417–29.

7. Kessenich, Maureen. "Developmental Outcomes of Premature, Low Birth Weight, and Medically Fragile Infants." *Newborn and Infant Nursing Reviews* 3:3 (2003): 80–87. Available online at www.medscape.com/viewarticle/461571.

8. Federici, R. S. *Raising the Post-Institutionalized Child: Risks, Challenges and Innovative Treatment* (1997). Available online at www.drfederici.com/Raising%20the%20P-I%20Child.htm.

9. Judge, S. L. "Eastern European Adoptions: Current Status and Implications for Intervention." *Topics in Early Childhood Special Education* 19:4, 244–52.

10. According to the CDC, a Food and Drug Administration review concluded that until recently, the use of thimerosal as a vaccine preservative may have resulted in mercury intake during the first six months of life that exceeds the guidelines of the Environmental Protection Agency, but not those of the FDA, the Agency for Toxic Substances and Disease Registry, or the World Health Organization. The National Institutes of Health admits that the number of children in special education in U.S. schools took a dramatic leap in the 1990s, and these are children who would have received excess mercury by EPA standards if their pediatricians followed the standard vaccine schedule.

11. Turecki, Stanley, M.D. "The Behavioral Complaint: Symptom of a Psychiatric Disorder or a Matter of Temperament?" *Contemporary Pediatrics* 20:8 (2003): 111–19. Available online at www.medscape.com, article 460592.

12. Silver, Larry B., M.D. *The Misunderstood Child,* 3rd ed. New York: Three Rivers Press, 1998, 77.
13. Rapoport, J. L., and D. R. Ismond. *DSM-IV Training Guide for Diagnosis of Childhood Disorders.* New York: Brunner-Routledge, 1996, 148.
14. Kuhne, M., et al. "Impact of Comorbid Oppositional or Conduct Problems on Attention-Deficit Hyperactivity Disorder." *Journal of the American Academy of Child & Adolescent Psychiatry* 36:12 (1997): 1715–25. Available online at www.klis.com/chandler/pamphlet/oddcd/ about.htm.
15. Popper, Charles, M.D. "Diagnosing Bipolar vs. ADHD: A Pharmacological Point of View." *The Link* 13 (1996).

General references:

Hamdy, S., J. C. Rothwell, Q. Aziz, K. D. Singh, and D. G. Thompson. "Longterm Reorganization of Human Motor Cortex Driven by Short-Term Sensory Stimulation." *Nature Neuroscience* 1 (1998): 64–68.

Kilgard, M. P., P. K. Pandya, J. Vazquez, A. Gehi, C. E. Schreiner, and M. M. Merzenich. "Sensory Input Directs Spatial and Temporal Plasticity in Primary Auditory Cortex." *Journal of Neurophysiology* 86 (2001): 326–38.

Miller, L. J., and B. Brett-Green. "Current DSI Program Research at the KID Foundation." *Sensory Integration Special Interest Section Quarterly* 27:4 (2004), American Occupational Therapy Association.

Miller, L. J., J. Reisman, D. N. McIntosh, and J. Simon. "An Ecological Model of Sensory Modulation." In *Understanding the Nature of Sensory Integration with Diverse Populations.* Edited by S. Smith-Roley, E. Imperatore-Blanche, and R. C. Schaaf. San Antonio, TX: Therapy Skill Builders, 2001, 57–88.

CHAPTER 5:
Finding and Working with an Occupational Therapist

1. Jung, C. G. *The Development of Personality: Papers on Child Psychology, Education, and Related Subjects.* Princeton, NJ: Princeton University Press, 1954, 140.

CHAPTER 6:
The Sensory Diet of Daily Activities

1. American Occupational Therapy Association Backpack Guidelines, www.aota.org.

2. Grandin, Temple. *Thinking in Pictures: And Other Reports from My Life with Autism.* New York: Vintage Books, 1995, 62.
3. Edelson, S. M., M. G. Edelson, D. C. R. Kerr, and T. Grandin. "Behavioral and Physiological Effects of Deep Pressure on Children with Autism: A Pilot Study Evaluating the Efficacy of Grandin's Hug Machine." *American Journal of Occupational Therapy* 53 (1999): 145–52. The study measured physiological arousal, anxiety, tension, and restlessness-hyperactivity, and found that deep pressure had a behavioral and physiological calming effect with significant reduction in tension and a slight reduction in anxiety for autistic children who received deep pressure twice a week for twenty minutes over six weeks. The study found that deep pressure worked best for children with higher levels of anxiety or arousal.

Grandin, T. "Calming Effects of Deep Touch Pressure in Patients with Autistic Disorder, College Students, and Animals." *Journal of Child and Adolescent Psychopharmacology* 2:1 (1992): 63–70.
4. Marlier, L., M.D., C. Gaugler, M.D., and J. Messer, M.D. "Airway Obstruction in Premature Newborns: A Missing Link." *Pediatrics* 115:1 (2005): 83–8. This study of premature infants in a French neonatal ICU found that pumping vanillin into the incubators of fourteen infants born between twenty-four and twenty-eight weeks of gestation reduced the frequency of apneic (sleep apnea disruptions) events, effectively increasing respiratory rate especially during sleep.

General references:

Champagne, T. *Sensory Modulation and Environment: Essential Elements of Occupation,* 3rd ed. Southampton, MA: Champagne Conferences, 2008.

Edelson, S., M. Edelson, D. Kerr, and T. Grandin. "Behavioral and Physiological Effects of Deep Pressure on Children with Autism: A Pilot Study Evaluating the Efficacy of Grandin's Hug Machine." *American Journal of Occupational Therapy* 53 (1999): 145–52.

Fertel-Daly, D., G. Bedell, and J. Hinjosa. "Effects of a Weighted Vest on Attention to Task and Self-Stimulatory Behaviors in Preschoolers with Pervasive Developmental Disorders." *American Journal of Occupational Therapy* 55:6 (2001): 629–40.

Field, T., D. Lasko, P. Mundy, T. Henteleff, S. Kabat, S. Talpins, and M. Dowling. "Brief Report: Autistic Children's Attentiveness and Responsivity Improve after Touch Therapy." *Journal of Autism and Developmental Disorders* 27 (1997): 333–38.

Field, T. M., S. M. Schanberg, F. Scafidi, C. R. Bauer, N. Vega-Lahr, R. Garcia, J. Nystrom, and C. M. Kuhn. "Tactile/Kinesthetic Stimulation Effects on Preterm Neonates." *Pediatrics* 77:5 (1986): 654–58. This University of Miami Medical Center study found that preterm infants receiving tactile input (stroking) and passive limb movement averaged 47 percent greater daily weight gain, were more alert and active, and showed more mature sensory habituation and orientation, motor skills, and range of state behaviors than nonstimulated preterm neonates.

Foss, A., Y. Smith, J. McGruder, and G. Tomlin. "Sensory Modulation Dysfunction and the Wilbarger Protocol: An Evidence Review." *OT Practice,* July 2003.

Honaker D., and L. M. Rossie. "Proprioception and Participation at School: Are Weighted Vests Effective? Appraising the Evidence." *Sensory Integration Special Interest Section Quarterly* 3, 4: (2005): 1–4.

Mullen, B., T. Champagne, S. Krishnamurty, D. Dickson, and R. Gao. "Exploring the Safety and Therapeutic Effects of Deep Pressure Stimulation Using a Weighted Blanket." *Occupational Therapy in Mental Health* 24:1 (2008): 65–89.

Schilling, D. L., K. Washington, F. F. Billingsley, and J. Deitz. "Classroom Seating for Children with Attention Deficit Hyperactivity Disorder: Therapy Balls versus Chairs." *American Journal of Occupational Therapy* 57 (2003): 534–57.

Stevens, S., and J. Gruzelier. "Electrodermal Activity to Auditory Stimuli in Autistic, Retarded, and Normal Children." *Journal of Autism and Developmental Disorders* 14:3 (1984): 245–60.

Vandenberg, N. L. "The Use of a Weighted Vest to Increase On Task Behavior in Children with Attention Difficulties." *American Journal of Occupational Therapy* 55:6 (2001): 621–28.

Walker, D., and K. McCormack. *The Weighted Blanket: An Essential Nutrient in a Sensory Diet.* Everett, MA: Village Therapy, 2002.

Wilbarger, Patricia, and Julia Wilbarger. "The Wilbarger Approach to Treating Sensory Defensiveness." In *Sensory Integration: Theory and Practice,* 2nd ed. Edited by A. C. Bundy, S. J. Lane, and E. A. Murray. Philadelphia: F. A. Davis Company, 2002, 335.

CHAPTER 7:
Practical Solutions for Everyday Sensory Problems

1. Doidge, Norman, M.D. *The Brain That Changes Itself.* New York: Penguin, 2007.

General reference:

Grandin, Temple, and Kate Duffy. *Developing Talents: Careers for Individuals with Asperger Syndrome and High-Functioning Autism.* Shawnee Mission, KS: Autism Asperger Publishing Co., 2004.

CHAPTER 8:
Dealing with Developmental Delays

1. Dunkle, Margaret, and Louis Vismara, M.D. "A Different Kind of Test." *Education Week,* September 2003. Available online at www.edweek.org/ew/ewstory.cfm?slug=04dunkle.h23&keywords=autism.
2. Greene, Ross W., Ph.D. *The Explosive Child: A New Approach for Understanding and Parenting Easily Frustrated, "Chronically Inflexible" Children.* New York: HarperCollins, 1998, 23.

General references:

American Academy of Pediatrics online Web site: www.aap.org/. National Headquarters: The American Academy of Pediatrics, 141 Northwest Point Boulevard, Elk Grove Village, IL 60007-1098. Phone 847-434-4000, fax 847-434-8000.

Brazelton, T. B. *Neonatal Behavioral Assessment Scale,* 2nd ed. Philadelphia: J. B. Lippincott, 1984.

Brigance, Albert H. *Revised Brigance Diagnostic Inventory of Early Development: Birth to Seven Years.* North Billerica, MA: Curriculum Associates, Inc., 1991.

DeGangi, G. *Pediatric Disorders of Regulation and Affect in Behavior: A Therapist's Guide to Assessment and Treatment.* San Diego: Academic Press, 2000.

Edelson, Stephen M., Center for the Study of Autism, *Stereotypic (Self-Stimulatory) Behavior,* available online at www.autism.org/stim.html.

HELP Strands Curriculum-Based Developmental Assessment: Birth to Three Years. Palo Alto, CA: Vort Corporation, 1994.

HELP for Preschoolers Checklist: Three to Six Years. Palo Alto, CA: Vort Corporation, 1995.

The Rossetti Infant-Toddler Language Scale. East Moline, IL: LinguiSystems, Inc., 1990.

Turecki, Stanley, M.D. *The Difficult Child,* 2nd ed. New York: Bantam Books, 2000.

Williamson, G. G., and M. E. Anzalone. *Sensory Integration and Self-Regulation in Infants and Toddlers: Helping Very Young Children*

Interact with their Environment. Washington, D.C.: Zero to Three, 2001.

CHAPTER 9:
Sensory Issues and the Child with an Autism Spectrum Disorder

1. Walker, N., and M. Whelan. Geneva Symposium on Autism, October 27, 1994, Toronto. Surveyed autistic children and adults reported hypersensitivity to touch (80 percent) and sound (87 percent), problems with vision (86 percent), and sensitivity to taste or smell (30 percent).
2. Greenspan, S. I., and S. Wieder. "Developmental Patterns and Outcomes in Infants and Children with Disorders in Relating and Communicating: A Chart Review of 200 Cases of Children with Autism Spectrum Diagnoses." *The Journal of Developmental and Learning Disorders* 1 (1997): 87–142.
3. Schoen, S. A., L. J. Miller, B. Brett-Green, and S. L. Hepburn. "Psychophysiology of Children with Autism Spectrum Disorder." *Research in Autism Spectrum Disorders* 2:3 (2008): 417–29. Electrodermal activity studies measuring the arousal levels and sensory reactivity in children with high functioning autism and Asperger's syndrome showed distinct patterns of high arousal with slow habituation (overresponsivity), and low arousal with more rapid habituation (underresponsivity).
4. Grandin, T. *On Visual Thinking, Sensory, Careers and Medications.* DVD. Arlington, TX: Future Horizons, 2003.
5. McKean, T. *Soon Will Come the Light,* Arlington, TX: Future Horizons, 2001, 63.
6. Jackson, L. *Freaks, Geeks & Asperger Syndrome: A User Guide to Adolescence.* London: Jessica Kingsley Publishers, 2002, 71.
7. Williams, D. *Somebody Somewhere: Breaking Free from the World of Autism.* New York: Three Rivers Press, 1994, 96.

General references:

Dunn Buron, K., and M. Curtis. *The Incredible 5-Point Scale: Assisting Students with Autism Spectrum Disorders in Understanding Social Interactions and Controlling Their Emotional Responses.* Shawnee Mission, KS: Autism Asperger Publishing, 2004.

Edelson, Stephen M. Center for the Study of Autism. *Stereotypic (Self-Stimulatory) Behavior.* Available online at http://autism.org/stim.html.

Lovaas, I., C. Newsom, and C. Hickman. "Self-Stimulatory Behavior and Perceptual Reinforcement." *Journal of Applied Behavioral Analysis* 20:1 (1987): 45–68.

Miller, L. J., J. Reisman, D. N. McIntosh, and J. Simon. "An Ecological Model of Sensory Modulation." In *The Nature of Sensory Integration with Diverse Populations.* San Antonio, TX: The Psychological Corp., 2001, 57–8.

Williams, M. S., and S. Shellenberger. *Introduction to How Does Your Engine Run? The Alert Program for Self-Regulation.* Albuquerque, NM: TherapyWorks, Inc., 1996.

CHAPTER 10:
Improving Speech Skills and Picky Eating

1. Hamaguchi, Patricia M. *Childhood Speech, Language, and Listening Problems: What Every Parent Should Know.* New York: John Wiley & Sons, 2001, 171.

General references:

Leung, A. K., and W. L. Robson. "The toddler who does not eat." *American Family Physician* 49 (1994): 1770–94, quoted in "Addressing the Complex Needs of Children Who Refuse to Eat," by Susan Bazyk, *OT Practice,* January 17, 2000.

Morris, Suzanne E., and Marsha D. Klein. *Pre-Feeding Skills: A Comprehensive Resource for Mealtime Development,* 2nd ed. San Antonio: Therapy Skill Builders, 2000.

CHAPTER 11:
Helping Your Child Learn and Get Organized

1. Martell, L. D. *Light: An Element in the Ergonomics of Learning,* National Academy of Integrative Learning. Available online at: www.intellearn.org/media/light%20elem%20lrng.pdf.

    Liberman, J. *Light: Medicine of the Future.* Santa Fe, NM: Bear & Co, 1992.

2. Silver, L., M.D. *The Misunderstood Child.* New York: Three Rivers Press, 1998, 17.

3. Carte, E., D. Morrison, J. Sublett, A. Uemura, and W. Setrakian. "Sensory Integration Therapy: A Trial of a Specific Neurodevelopmental Therapy for the Remediation of Learning Disabilities." *Developmental and Behavioral Pediatrics* 5 (1984): 189–94.

4. Grandin, Temple. "My Experiences with Visual Thinking, Sensory Problems, and Communication Difficulties." *Center for the Study of Autism* (June 2000). Available online at www.autism.com/families/therapy/visual.htm.

General references:

Gardner, Howard. *Frames of Mind: The Theory of Multiple Intelligences*, 10th anniversary edition. New York: Basic Books, 1983.

Grandin, Temple. "Teaching Tips for Children and Adults with Autism." *Center for the Study of Autism* (December 2002). Available online at www.autism.org/temple/tips.html.

Hannaford, Carla. *Smart Moves: Why Learning Is Not All in Your Head.* Arlington, VA: Great Ocean Publishers, 1995.

Hoerr, Thomas. *Becoming a Multiple Intelligences School.* Alexandria, VA: Association for Supervision & Curriculum Development, 2000.

Kiesa, Kay, ed. *Uniquely Gifted: Identifying and Meeting the Needs of the Twice-Exceptional Student.* Gilsum, NH: Avocus Publishing, 2000.

Morgenstern, Julie, and Jessi Morgenstern-Colón. *Organizing from the Inside Out for Teens.* New York: Owl Books, 2002.

Silver, Larry, M.D. *The Misunderstood Child,* 3rd ed. New York: Three Rivers Press, 1998.

CHAPTER 12:
Nutrition, Sleep, and Stress

1. Stordy, J., and M. J. Nicholl. *The LCP Solution.* New York: Ballantine Books, 2000.
2. Gutman, Sharon A., and Lindsey Biel. "Promoting the Neurological Substrates of Well-Being Through Occupation." *Occupational Therapy in Mental Health* 17:1 (2001): 1–22.

General references:

Fat Intake Recommendations from the American Academy of Pediatrics available online at www.healthychildcare.org/pdf/nutrition.pdf.

Isaacs, S. *Hormonal Balance: Understanding Hormones, Weight, and Your Metabolism.* Boulder, CO: Bull Publishing, 2002.

Neistadt, M. "Stress Management." In *Willard and Spackman's Occupational Therapy,* 8th ed. Edited by H. L. Hopkins and H. D. Smith. Philadelphia: J. B. Lippincott Company, 1993, 588–96.

Pert, Candace B. *Molecules of Emotion: The Science Behind Mind-Body Medicine.* New York: Simon & Schuster, 1999.

Weissbluth, Mare, M.D. *Healthy Sleep Habits, Happy Child.* New York: Ballantine Books, 1999.

CHAPTER 13:
Complementary Therapies and Approaches

1. Scheiman, M., P. Blaskey, M. Gallaway, E. Ciner, and M. Parisi. "Vision Characteristics of Adult Irlen Filter Candidates: Case Studies." *Journal of Behavioral Optometry* 1:7 (1990): 174–78.

General references:

American Optometric Association report: *The Effectiveness of Vision Therapy in Improving Visual Function.* Available online at http://www .childrensvision.com/Efficacy.htm or call the American Optometric Association at 314-991-4100 for a copy. Contains more than two hundred professional references, including clinical research, scientific studies, and professional articles documenting the effectiveness of vision therapy.

DeFelice, Karen L. *Enzymes for Autism and Other Neurological Conditions.* Philadelphia: Jessica Kingsley Publishers, 2002.

Edelson, Stephen M., and Bernard Rimland. *The Efficacy of Auditory Integration Training.* Available online at www.autism.com/ari/index.html or by contacting the Autism Research Institute at 4182 Adams Avenue, San Diego, California 92116. Summaries and critiques of twenty-eight reports.

Feingold, Ben. *Why Your Child Is Hyperactive.* New York: Random House, 1985.

Lemer, Patricia. *Attention Deficits: A Developmental Approach,* available on the Developmental Delay Resources Web site: www.devdelay .org/adhd.htm.

Lewis, Lisa. *Special Diets for Special Kids.* Arlington, TX: Future Horizons, 1998.

McCandless, Jaquelyn. *Children with Starving Brains: A Medical Treatment Guide for Autism Spectrum Disorder.* North Bergen, NJ: Bramble Co., 2003.

Rapp, Doris. *Is This Your Child? Discovering and Treating Unrecognized Allergies in Children and Adults.* New York: William Morrow, 1992.

Scheiman, M. *Understanding and Managing Vision Deficits: A Guide for Occupational Therapists.* Thorofare, NJ: SLACK Incorporated, 1997.

Tomatis Method efficacy research is available online at www.tomatis .com/English/Articles/research.html.

CHAPTER 14:
Handling Discipline, Transitions, and Behavioral Issues

1. Greene, Ross W., Ph.D. *The Explosive Child: A New Approach for Understanding and Parenting Easily Frustrated, "Chronically Inflexible" Children.* New York: HarperCollins, 1998.
2. Sears, William, and Martha Sears. *The Discipline Book.* Boston: Little, Brown & Company, 1995, 150.

CHAPTER 15:
Advocating for Your Child at School

1. Levine, Mel. *A Mind at a Time.* New York: Simon & Schuster, 2002, 26.

General references:

Bissell, Julie, and Shu-Chin Jessica Peng. "Assistive Technology to Support Sensory Integration, Praxis and Self-Regulation: Needs of Children with Autism." *Sensory Integration Special Interest Section Quarterly* 24 (September 2001): 1–4.

Individuals with Disabilities Education Act (IDEA) *Amendments of 1997,* P.L. 105–17: 300.5, 300.6.

Krantz, G. C., M. A. Christenson, and A. Lindquist. *Assistive Products: An Illustrated Guide to Terminology.* Bethesda, MD: American Occupational Therapy Association, 1998.

Siegel, Lawrence. *The Complete IEP Guide: How to Advocate for Your Special Ed Child,* 3rd ed. Berkeley, CA: Nolo Press, 2004.

The Technology-Related Assistance for Individuals with Disabilities Act of 1988 (The Tech Act), P.L. 100–407.

Wright, Peter W. D., and Pamela Darr Wright. *Wrightslaw: Special Education Law.* Hartfield, VA: Harbor House Law Press, 2004.

CHAPTER 17:
Empowering Your Child in the World

General reference:

Pruett, Kyle D. *Fatherneed: Why Father Care Is as Essential as Mother Care for Your Child.* New York: Broadway Books, 2000.

Index

Page numbers in italics refer to figures and tables.

LINDSEY BIEL, M.A., OTR/L (*at left*) received her training at New York University and is an occupational therapist specializing in pediatrics. Formerly an occupational therapist for the New York City Department of Education, she currently works with children with diagnoses including sensory processing disorder, autism spectrum disorders, physical disabilities, developmental delays, and other special needs through New York State's early intervention program as well as with older school-age children in her private practice.

NANCY PESKE is a freelance writer and editor, and the coauthor of the *Cinematherapy* series. She lives in Shorewood, Wisconsin, with her husband and son, who has sensory processing issues.